The ESSENTIAL ACCOUNTING DICTIONARY

es·sen·tial ADJ. Of the utmost importance.

The
ESSENTIAL
ACCOUNTING
DICTIONARY

es·sen·tial ADJ. Of the utmost importance.

Kate Mooney

SPHINX® PUBLISHING
AN IMPRINT OF SOURCEBOOKS, INC.®
NAPERVILLE, ILLINOIS
www.SphinxLegal.com

First Edition: 2008

Published by: **Sphinx® Publishing, An imprint of Sourcebooks, Inc.®**
Naperville Office
P.O. Box 4410
Naperville, Illinois 60567-4410
(630) 961-3900
Fax: (630) 961-2168
www.sourcebooks.com
www.sphinxlegal.com

This publication is designed to provide accurate and authoritative information in regard to the subject matter covered. It is sold with the understanding that the publisher is not engaged in rendering legal, accounting, or other professional service. If legal advice or other expert assistance is required, the services of a competent professional person should be sought.
From a Declaration of Principles Jointly Adopted by a Committee of the American Bar Association and a Committee of Publishers and Associations

This product is not a substitute for legal advice.
Disclaimer required by Texas statutes.

Library of Congress Cataloging-in-Publication Data
Mooney, Kate.
  Essential accounting dictionary / by Kate Mooney. – 1st ed.
    p. cm.
  ISBN 978-1-57248-651-5 (pbk. : alk. paper) 1. Accounting–Dictionaries. I. Title.
HF5621.M658 2008
657.03–dc22

                                    2008009932

Printed and bound in Canada.
TR 10 9 8 7 6 5 4 3 2 1

CONTENTS

INTRODUCTION

Accounting has always been seen as a necessary task that enables business to occur. Important activities such as investing, regulating, and the gathering, reporting, and analysis of financial data all depend upon the principles and procedures of accounting.

In the past decade, names such as Enron and WorldCom have become everyday news items. As huge, well-respected companies have been failing and restating their earnings, the importance of understanding accounting terms and procedures has taken on a whole new meaning.

I have designed this book for the average person who needs a working knowledge of accounting terms in order to understand financial statements, investment reports, financial news articles, or college courses. It is also a useful reference for business-people who need to communicate with accountants.

Each term is defined in clear, concise, and understandable language. The terms are also placed in context with examples, common synonyms, and cross-references to help the reader truly understand the term rather than just its factual aspects.

I have enjoyed this challenge and hope that you gain from using this dictionary.

—Kate Mooney, PhD, CPA

DEFINITIONS

10-K. N. A form that companies file within ninety days of the year-end to comply with Securities and Exchange Commission (SEC) rules. The 10-K includes the annual report plus some other detailed financial and legal information. The purpose of the 10-K is to provide a comprehensive synopsis of the company's performance over the past year to people outside the company. The SEC maintains a database that allows anyone to view the filings.

10-Q. N. A form filed by public companies that presents unaudited quarterly information similar to the annual report 10-K, only with less detail. The Securities and Exchange Commission requires this filing. Synonymous with *quarterly report*.

1040. N. The Internal Revenue Service form number for an individual tax return. The number may have letters following it to indicate an abbreviated individual tax return, such as 1040EZ, in which "EZ" stands for "easy."

1099-DIV. N. A tax form that indicates the amount of dividends or other distributions a company paid to an individual or other tax-paying entity. The company must provide the recipient with this form and report the amount to the government if it is more than $10. That limit is increased to $600 if the distribution is from a liquidation of the company.

1099-INT. N. A tax form that indicates the amount of interest paid to an individual or other tax-paying entity. The payer must provide the recipient with this form and report the amount to the government if it is more than $600.

1099-R. N. A tax form that indicates the amount of pension, annuity, or lump-sum payments an individual receives from a pension plan or profit-sharing plan. The plan must issue the form to the recipient and report the amount to the government if the amount received is over $10.

12b-1 fees. N. Mutual fund costs that can be passed along to share-holders and can amount to up to 0.75% of the average assets held by the fund. Costs included in these fees are advertising, sales brochures, annual reports, prospectuses, and commissions to the sales force. Different classes of shares in a mutual fund are charged different amounts of 12b-1 fees, depending on the type of costs the class pays to get in or out of the fund. These fees are paid from the fund assets.

401(k). N. An employer-sponsored way for employees to save tax-free until the savings are withdrawn. The employer deducts the dollars from the employee's gross pay, may or may not add some additional dollars, and then invests it in stocks, bonds, or mutual funds. The employer then calculates and withholds income taxes on the remaining salary. The employee does not pay any taxes on the deducted dollars, the employer's contribution, or the earnings on the investment until those dollars are taken out of the plan, usually at retirement. While the regulations limit the amount of dollars involved (to $15,500 in 2007), this type of plan is an excellent way to save because the tax rate at retirement is usually lower than it is during the employee's career. See also *403(b)*. Synonymous with *salary reduction plan*.

403(b). N. An employer-sponsored way for employees to save tax-free until the savings are withdrawn. The employer deducts the dollars from the employee's gross pay, adds some additional dollars, and then invests it in stocks, bonds, or funds. The employer then calculates and withholds income taxes on the remaining salary. The employee does not pay any taxes on the deducted dollars, the employer's contribution, or the earnings on the invest-ment until those dollars are taken out of the plan, usually at retire-ment. While the regulations limit the amount of dollars involved, this type of plan is an excellent way to save because the tax rate at retirement is usually lower than during the employee's career. A

403(b) plan is similar to a 401(k) plan, except 403(b) plans are used when the employer is a not-for-profit entity.

529 plan. N. A state-sponsored mechanism for saving that allows for generous contribution limits, no taxes on growth until withdrawal, and tax-free withdrawals for education expenses. Unlike 530 ESAs or Coverdell Education Savings Accounts, this plan applies to college education expenses. Synonymous with *qualified tuition plans*.

530 ESA. N. See *Coverdell Education Savings Account*.

8-K. N. A form filed by public companies when some major event happens that affects the corporation's financial position. The Securities and Exchange Commission requires this filing within five business days of the happening. Examples of events that trigger this requirement include the changing of auditors, a major lawsuit filed against the company, or the resignation of one of the company's top executives. The filings are available at www.sec.gov/edgar/searchedgar/currentevents.htm.

AAA. ABBRV. American Accounting Association.

AAER. ABBRV. Accounting and Auditing Enforcement Release.

abatement. N. The process of allocating the shortfall of estate assets to the distributions. Distributions from the estate proceed in a particular order starting with specific legacies, demonstrative legacies, general legacies, and finally residuary legacies. If estate assets are not adequate to meet the will's provisions for the legacy category, all legacies in the category are reduced by the same percentage.

ABC. ABBRV. Activity-based costing.

ABM. ABBRV. Activity-based management.

abnormal profits. N. Earnings that produce a rate of return either above or below the cost of capital. Positive abnormal profits produce a rate of return above the cost of capital. Negative abnormal profits produce a rate below the cost of capital. The term is used most frequently by technical analysts and researchers.

abnormal spoilage. N. Spoilage that results from errors, break-downs, accidents, etc., in a manufacturing process. Abnormal spoilage is in excess of normal spoilage and the cost is a separate line item on the income statement. It is not included in the unit cost because it is avoidable.

abnormal yield curve. N. See *inverted yield curve*.

ABO. ABBRV. Accumulated benefit obligation.

absorption costing. N. A system of assigning costs to products that includes all the costs it takes to manufacture the product, both fixed and variable. Absorption costing is the required system for financial reporting purposes. An alternative to absorption costing is variable costing, which is often used for internal decisions. See also *variable-costing system*. Synonymous with *full costing*.

abusive tax shelters. N. See *tax shelters*.

Academy of Accounting Historians. N. A professional association that encourages teaching and research about all phases of accounting history and its relationship to business and economics. http://accounting.rutgers.edu/raw/aah.

accelerated cost-recovery system. N. A cost-recovery method used for tax purposes for assets used after 1980, but before 1987, in a business or trade. Cost recovery means that the business can deduct the cost of the asset on the tax return, thereby saving tax payments. The accelerated cost-recovery system allowed businesses to write off the asset's cost over a shorter time period than the economic life. The purpose was to stimulate capital investment, because when further deductions were unavailable, companies would buy new assets. ABBRV. *ACRS*.

accelerated depreciation. N. Methods of allocating the cost of an asset against income. Accelerated-depreciation methods charge off more of the cost in the early years of the asset's use. Accelerated depreciation is mainly used for tax accounting because it can result in the company paying lower taxes in the early years of asset use. See also *depreciation*.

accelerated share repurchase. N. A company agrees to buy back a large quantity of its own stock at a particular price on a particular date from an investment bank. Usually the investment bank does not own all the necessary shares but will acquire them over a period of time. The company sees an immediate reduction in shares outstanding and an increase in earnings per share. However, the company also must account for the obligation associated with the investment bank's forward contract. If the forward contract is dilutive, the effects must be reflected in earnings per share. ABBRV. *ASR*.

acceleration clause. N. A term in a debt agreement that allows the lender to demand payment prior to maturity. Objective acceleration clauses specify precise actions or a lack of actions that trigger the acceleration clause. Subjective acceleration clauses do not specify the triggering event.

acceptable quality level. N. The point at which the cost of additional quality-control activities exceeds the decrease in the costs of poor quality and failure costs. Acceptable quality level is a traditional view of quality.

acceptance sampling. N. A method of determining whether a batch of items is of acceptable quality. Based on a statistically valid sampling plan, only a few of the batch are checked for quality. The quality of the sample is assumed to be the overall quality of the batch, and the entire batch is then accepted or rejected.

account. N. A structure for showing the effect of business events on a particular asset, liability, equity, revenue, or expense. The effects are measured in terms of dollars. The account acts as a collection point during the processing of all the transactions involving the balance sheet or income-statement item, providing the value that appears on the financial statement. All the increases and decreases to a company's cash are collected in the cash account, which appears on the balance sheet.

accountable plan. N. A method of managing business expenses and reimbursements to employees. An accountable plan requires the employee to verify and support expenses in order to receive reimbursement from the employer; any excess reimbursement must be returned to the employer. An accountable plan is important to both the employer who wants to track expenses, and to the employee who does not want to pay income taxes on reimbursement money. If the employee receives reimbursement through an accountable plan, then the reimbursement is not included in the employee's wages, and the employer can deduct the costs as a business expense.

account analysis. N. A process of reviewing all the entries in an account to determine the balance or to discern patterns. Account analysis is useful in cost accounting to build a model of standard costs or to predict costs. Auditors use it to find unusual patterns for further investigation.

accountancy. N. Another word for accounting, usually used to designate the profession; it is used more often in the United Kingdom or former British colonies.

accountant. N. A person who performs accounting for a career. The types of activities vary significantly. Some accountants are clerks who do bookkeeping functions, and some are business advisors to large corporations.

Accountants for the Public Interest. N. A professional organization that encourages accountants to volunteer to help people who cannot afford their services. www.geocities.com/api_ woods/api/apihome.html.

Accountants' Index. N. A bibliography of accounting research articles from 1920 to 1991.

Accountants International Study Group. N. The predecessor to the International Accounting Standards Board.

Accountant's Magazine, The. N. The publication of the Institute of Chartered Accountants of Scotland.

account form of the balance sheet. N. A presentation format of the balance sheet that lists assets on the left side of the sheet and liabilities and equities on the right side. Contrast with the report form of the balance sheet, in which assets are listed first, followed vertically by liabilities and equities.

account groups. N. A set of accounts used in governmental accounting that keeps track of general long-term assets and general long-term liabilities. This set of accounts is not required, but is a convenient way to keep records.

accounting. N. The process of representing business transactions in financial reports.

Accounting and Auditing Enforcement Release. N. A report on Securities and Exchange Commission (SEC) actions against an organization violating securities laws. The reports are available on the SEC's website. ABBRV. *AAER*.

Accounting and Tax Database. N. An online compilation of articles from three hundred publications. The Accounting and Tax Database is indexed and contains abstracts. http://library.dialog.com/bluesheets/html/bl0485.html#top.

accounting anomalies. N. A symptom of fraud. Accounting anomalies can involve unusual characteristics of source documents, such as alterations or photocopies rather than originals. Accounting anomalies can also be evident in journal entries and ledgers.

accounting change. N. See *cumulative effect of change in accounting principle*.

accounting cycle. N. The set of procedures that record business events into the accounting records and culminate in the production of financial statements. The accounting cycle involves first entering the transaction into the company's journal. The journal entry consists of the date and the amount of increases or decreases to the accounts involved. The second step in the accounting cycle is to show the effect of increases and decreases on each account through a process of posting to the ledger accounts. After all journal entries are posted, the third step is to prepare a trial balance to check for errors. The fourth step is to adjust the ledger accounts for year-end transactions. The next step is to prepare the financial statements and then finally close the temporary (income statement) accounts.

accounting entity. N. The object of the accounting process. The accounting entity is the organization or part of the organization for which the process of representing business transactions in financial reports is separated from the other parts. The accounting entity is necessary for meaningful information. A sole proprietor must separate the business part of life from the personal part of life. The business is the accounting entity, and to measure performance, only the transactions associated with the business are counted in revenues and expenses. Personal income, such as inheritances or gifts, cannot be added to the revenues of the accounting entity.

accounting equation. N. See *balance sheet equation*.

accounting estimate. N. An educated guess made to facilitate the recording of expenses or revenues. Generally accepted accounting principles allow the estimation of things like uncollectible accounts, warranty costs, useful lives of fixed assets, and some other items. These accounting estimates, which make it possible to match expenses with revenues, are based on historical patterns of bad debts, warranty costs, or machine usage.

Accounting Hall of Fame. N. Located at the Ohio State University in Columbus, Ohio. Honors scholars who have completed significant research in accounting and professionals who have made significant contributions to accounting. http://fisher.osu.edu/departments/accounting-and-mis/the-accounting-hall-of-fame.

Accounting Historians Journal. N. The publication of the Academy of Accounting Historians.

accounting income. N. A term used to distinguish the income number on the income statement (measured using generally accepted accounting principles) from taxable income (measured using tax laws). See also *accounting profit*.

accounting information systems. N. The systems within a company for collecting and communicating information. Accounting information systems collect information from various areas in the entity and make it available for processing into reports. They are concerned with security, accuracy, and completeness. The information is usually financial in nature, but it may be another type of data that supports the financial data. For example, in addition to collecting the cost of inventory purchases that are processed into payments to suppliers, an accounting information system would also collect data on the quantity of inventory units. Processing that data could provide management with stock out warnings. ABBRV. *AIS*.

accounting period. N. The period of time covered by the income statement. Companies with publicly traded stock must prepare quarterly statements and one statement covering the entire year. The year can be either the calendar or the fiscal year. For internal purposes, financial statements can cover any time period needed.

accounting principles. N. The rules, conventions, and methods of accomplishing accounting for an organization. See also *generally accepted accounting principles*.

Accounting Principles Board. N. Created by the American Institute of Certified Public Accountants (AICPA) in 1959 to replace the Committee on Accounting Procedure. The purpose of the Accounting Principles Board was to organize the theory and concepts for accounting rules so that companies would use the same procedures for similar events. Unlike the Committee on Accounting Procedure, the AICPA managed to force companies to comply with the Opinions issued by the Accounting Principles Board. Independent accountants are members of the AICPA and are subject to the organization's ethics rules, which require members to apply generally accepted accounting principles (GAAP), the Accounting Principles Board Opinions. Companies wanting to sell stock to the public had to have audits by independent accountants who were obligated to enforce GAAP, so compliance with the Accounting Principles Board Opinions was unavoidable. In 1972 the Financial Accounting Standards Board replaced the Accounting Principles Board as the rule-making body for accounting. ABBRV. *APB*.

accounting profit. N. The net income reported on the income statement. Accounting profit is calculated using accrual accounting and is in contrast to cash flow measures of performance. Synonymous with *net income, accounting income*.

accounting rate-of-return method. N. A measure used in capital budgeting decisions. The accounting rate of return is calculated by dividing the projected net income by the forecast asset book value for each year of the asset's use. The average of the calculated rates is equal to the accounting rate of return. This method uses accrual numbers rather than cash flows and does not adjust for the time value of money. Synonymous with *accrual-accounting rate-of-return method*.

Accounting Research Bulletins. N. The publications of the Committee on Accounting Procedure (1939–1959) that set forth the rules for financial disclosure. Companies were not required to follow the *Accounting Research Bulletins*. ABBRV. *ARB*.

Accounting Review, The. N. An academic journal that focuses on basic scholarship, published by the American Accounting Association.

accounting standard. N. Usually refers to one of the official pronouncements of the Financial Accounting Standards Board that gives the required method of accounting for a particular topic. Accounting standards are necessary to provide relatively uniform ways of recognizing income and expenses, so that people outside the organization can compare the financial statements of companies and make decisions. See also *Financial Accounting Standards Board*.

Accounting Standards Executive Committee. N. An American Institute of Certified Public Accountants committee consisting of fifteen members representing various constituencies. The Accounting Standards Executive Committee can set accounting standards through Statements of Position. It focuses on industry-specific standards. ABBRV. *AcSEC*.

accounting system. N. The structure used to accumulate and organize the accounting data of a business. It may be either manual or computerized.

Accounting Trends and Techniques. N. A reference book published by the American Institute of Certified Public Accountants that presents the results of an annual survey of businesses regarding the accounting procedures they use.

account reconciliation. N. See *bank reconciliation*.

accounts payable. N. A current liability on the balance sheet representing the amount of goods or services that the company has bought on credit. Usually these amounts are paid quickly and no interest is involved. This account is similar to a consumer charge account where the balance is paid off every month. It is different, however, in that the company can sometimes take a discount if it pays within a very short time. The company balances the value of the discount against the use of the cash and manages cash carefully by not paying too early. Synonymous with *trade accounts payable, trade credit.*

accounts payable turnover. N. A ratio for analyzing the level of accounts payable in relation to the amount of inventory purchases. The formula is inventory purchases divided by average accounts payable. The higher the turnover, the faster the company is paying for inventory purchases.

accounts receivable. N. A current asset on the balance sheet representing the amount customers owe and have promised to pay (without any formal written agreement). Usually these amounts, which arise from credit sales, are paid quickly and do not involve interest. Accounts receivable are one type of trade receivable. See also *accounts receivable, net; bad-debt expense; allowance for doubtful accounts; trade receivables.*

accounts receivable, net. N. A current asset on the balance sheet representing the actual cash the company expects to collect from customers who have purchased goods or services using credit. The gross amount of accounts receivable is reduced by an allowance for uncollectible accounts. See also *accounts receivable.*

accounts receivable turnover. N. A ratio for analyzing the level of accounts receivable in relation to the amount of credit sales. The formula is net credit sales divided by average accounts receivable. A high turnover indicates faster collection.

accredited investor. N. An entity meeting Securities and Exchange Commission criteria of position, net worth, and income level. The designation of accredited investor is used in the sale of securities because different, less stringent registration requirements exist for securities that are sold only to accredited investors.

accretion basis. N. A theoretical method of recognizing revenue based on the increasing value of the asset because of growth or the passing of time. Timberland, wines, and farm animals, for example, become more valuable, theoretically, as they grow or age, resulting in higher revenue. Adding revenue during the growth or aging process (the accretion basis) is not acceptable for generally accepted accounting principles but may be used for internal decision making.

accrual accounting. N. A method of recognizing revenue and expenses based on criteria other than the receipt or payment of cash. An entity includes revenue in income when the earnings process is substantially complete, even if the customer has not paid yet. This usually means the product has been shipped or the service has been performed. Then, after all the earned revenues are identified, the company includes all the expenses it took to produce those revenues, even if the company has not paid for those expenses.

accrual-accounting rate-of-return method. N. See *accounting rate-of-return method*.

accrual bond. N. See *deep-discount bonds*.

accrual earnings. N. Net income based on accrual accounting, in which revenues are included in income when earned, not when cash is received, and the expenses for the period are all the costs necessary to produce the revenues that are included in income.

accrue. V. Recording an increase or accumulation based on a business transaction or event. To accrue something means that it will affect the financial statements for the accounting period. If the bookkeeper is going to accrue the cost of utilities, then an entry increasing utility expense and a liability for the payment is made.

accrued expense. N. A type of adjusting entry. Recording accrued expenses increases the expenses for the current accounting period even though the cash payment for the expense will not be made until a future period. See also *accrued liability*.

accrued liability. N. Usually a current liability on the balance sheet that shows up because the company had to match an expense and record it on the income statement before the payment was due. A common example is utilities. A company must include the phone, gas, and electric expense for December in the annual income statement, but the bill does not have to be paid until January. The accumulated depreciation company records the expense, reducing income, and then, rather than reducing cash, increases the accrued liability on the balance sheet. In January when the company pays the bill, the liability and cash are reduced. See also *accrued expense*.

accrued pension cost. N. A liability on the balance sheet. The amount by which the net periodic pension cost, sometimes called pension expense, exceeds the cash funding by the company. See also *prepaid pension cost*. Synonymous with *accrued pension liability*.

accrued pension liability. N. See *accrued pension cost*.

accrued revenues. N. A type of adjusting entry. Recording accrued revenues increases revenue for the current accounting period even though the cash has not yet been received. The other half of the entry is usually an increase to accounts receivable.

accumulated adjustments account. N. Used when an S corporation has been a C corporation. The accumulated adjustments account keeps track of the S corporation earnings that have not been distributed. Usually the distributions of S corporations are not taxable because the shareholders pay taxes on the pass-through income every year. However, if distributions exceed the earnings of the S corporation and extend to amounts from the C corporation's retained earnings, then that part of the distribution is just like a dividend from a C corporation and is taxable.

accumulated benefit obligation. N. The present value of all pension benefits earned by employees as calculated by an actuary. This calculation includes all employees and all benefits, even if the employee is not guaranteed those benefits because of vesting. It is based on current salary levels, even though the final benefits may be based on higher salaries in later years. Accumulated benefit obligation is usually the most conservative estimate of the pension obligation of the company. ABBRV. *ABO*.

accumulated depreciation. N. A contra account that appears with a fixed asset account in the noncurrent asset section of the balance sheet. Accumulated depreciation is the sum of all the depreciation expense taken on the assets owned. Deducting the dollar value in the accumulated depreciation account from the historical cost of the assets, which is the balance in the fixed asset account, results in the book value of the fixed assets. See also *book value*.

accumulated E&P (earnings and profits). N. The sum of all the current E&P amounts from previous years, less all dividends distributed. The accumulated E&P amount represents all undistributed E&P. Any dividends that are in excess of accumulated E&P are a return of capital. E&P can be negative only from operating losses, not from paying out liquidating dividends. Accumulated E&P is similar to the balance sheet account retained earnings, but calculated differently and based on taxable income. While retained earnings is equal to net income from all income statements less all dividends paid over time, accumulated E&P is the sum of all taxable income from the tax returns less all taxes paid and all dividends paid.

accumulated earnings tax. N. A penalty tax on corporations that do not pay dividends to shareholders to help them avoid tax on dividends at ordinary income rates. The result is that the stock price appreciates and shareholders pay capital gains tax when the shares are sold. Capital gains are taxed at a lower rate than dividends, which are part of ordinary income. When the 2003 tax act was passed, eliminating some tax on dividends, several companies that had never paid dividends changed that practice and began paying dividends.

accumulated other comprehensive income. N. An account on the balance sheet that appears in the stockholders' equity section. Accumulated other comprehensive income is increased or decreased by events that increase or decrease equity—other than investment by owners and dividends—but is not included on the income statement. Examples of the type of things that change equity without being on the income statement include unrealized gains or losses on the revaluation of some types of investments.

accumulation bond. N. A bond sold at less than the maturity value. See also *bonds issued at a discount*.

ACE. ABBRV. Adjusted current earnings.

ACFE. ABBRV. Association of Certified Fraud Examiners.

acid test ratio. N. See *quick ratio*.

ACL. ABBRV. Audit command language.

acquired surplus. N. Net worth that is not stock, obtained in a pooling of interests.

acquisition cost. N. The price paid to buy an asset. For a building, the acquisition cost is the purchase price. For a gold mine, it could be the amount paid to explore a plot of land for gold, or it could be the purchase price to buy an existing gold mine. The acquisition cost is included in the depletable or depreciable base of the asset.

ACRS. ABBRV. Accelerated cost-recovery system.

AcSEC. ABBRV. Accounting Standards Executive Committee.

activity analysis. N. The part of process-value analysis that focuses on the actual activities that are performed, the people working in those activities, the time it takes to do the activities, and the contribution of the activities to the success of the entity.

activity-based budgeting. N. A method of budgeting that bases selling expenses, administrative expenses, and overhead costs on activities rather than on departments. For example, the overhead budget includes the costs of purchasing applied on the basis of the number of required purchase orders rather than on the traditional basis of direct labor hours.

activity-based costing. N. A method of assigning overhead costs to products. The first step is to analyze the cost of various activities. This approach looks at activities (such as changing specifications for a computerized painting machine or the cost of processing customer orders) as distinct parts of labor. These activities are then identified as cost drivers. Activity-based costing uses cost drivers to assign overhead costs to products or services. Traditionally, manufacturing companies have used the number of direct labor hours as the method of allocating overhead. Activity-based costing compels manufacturing companies to analyze what is contributing to the cost of the product beyond the usual labor and materials. See also *cost driver*. ABBRV. *ABC*.

activity-based management. N. A type of management accounting system that focuses on the costs of activities and then assigns those activity costs to products and customers. The efficiency analysis focuses on reducing the cost through the analysis of cost drivers. See also *functional-based management*. ABBRV. *ABM*.

activity-based responsibility accounting. N. A system for measuring and rewarding performance based on activities or processes using both financial and nonfinancial measures. Activity-based responsibility accounting is needed in a dynamic environment that has advanced information systems and a high level of technology (if the organization is large). See also *functional-based responsibility accounting*.

activity capacity. N. The number of times a set of actions can be performed in a given time period or with a given set of resources.

activity driver. N. A factor in the cost of a product. Activity drivers can be associated with the number of units produced (a unit-level activity driver) or with some facet of the production process (a nonunit-level activity driver). See also *unit-level activity drivers*, *nonunit-level activity drivers*.

activity inputs. N. The efforts and resources necessary to execute the steps or actions that make up the activity. Identifying activity inputs is part of process-value analysis, which is trying to determine what causes the costs in the activity. If the activity is designing landscapes, the inputs would be a designer, a computer, software, paper, and a printer.

activity output measure. N. The count of the resulting product of an activity. If the activity is designing landscapes, the activity output measure would be the number of landscape designs produced. The activity output measure counts the number of activity outputs that are completed.

activity outputs. N. The results of performing the steps or actions that make up the activity. Identifying activity outputs is part of process-value analysis, which is trying to determine the causes of the costs associated with the activity. If the activity is designing landscapes, the output would be a landscape design.

activity ratios. N. Financial analysis tools that measure how effective companies are at using their assets. Activity ratios are calculated using amounts from the financial statements and give information about the relationship between these amounts. Analysts then compare the relationships from different companies to evaluate the asset use. Common activity ratios are receivable turnover, inventory turnover, and asset turnover.

activity volume variance. N. A measure of manufacturing costs that do not add value to the product. The activity volume variance is the difference between the actual activity level and the value-added standard.

actual costing. N. A method of measuring and assigning production costs to determine the unit cost. Actual costing assigns the real cost of materials, labor, and overhead to production. Compare with normal costing, which uses a predetermined rate to assign overhead to production costs. Actual costing is rarely used because actual overhead costs are not available in time to calculate the needed unit cost. See also *normal costing, predetermined overhead rate*.

actual return on plan assets. N. A component of pension expense. This component is the increase in pension fund assets due to the earnings or returns, not because of cash contributions by the employer to the fund. Actual return on plan assets is adjusted for the unexpected return component, resulting in the expected return on plan assets being part of pension expense, rather than part of actual return. This component decreases pension expense.

actuarial cost method. N. The technique used to determine the amount of contributions required to meet pension benefit needs in the future.

actuarial gains/losses. N. An item included in calculating projected benefit obligation. The assumptions associated with the calculation may change and result in changes to the projected benefit obligation that are not the result of service cost, interest cost, or benefit payments. The changes increase, through actuarial losses, or decrease, through actuarial gains, the projected benefit obligation of the pension plan.

actuary. N. A professional who is skilled in using mathematics and statistics to solve risk problems. Actuaries provide accountants with estimates of pension and other postretirement benefits.

additional depreciation. N. See *excess depreciation*.

additional funds needed. N. Used in forecasting to identify the dollars that the company must raise through borrowing or stock sales. ABBRV. *AFN*.

additional paid in capital. N. A part of contributed capital in the stockholders' equity section of the balance sheet. Only one additional paid in capital account is required, even though increases and decreases to the account arise from different types of stock transactions. The most common increase to additional paid in capital is for the amount above par value in the sale of stock. Additional paid in capital is also increased when treasury stock is sold above cost. Synonymous with *capital in excess of par, paid in capital in excess of par value*.

additional pension liability. N. A liability on the balance sheet representing the difference between the fair market value of the investments underlying the pension plan and the most conservative measure of the pension plan obligations. See also *minimum pension liability*.

additions. N. A term used for asset expenditures when an existing asset is increased or extended. Expenditures for additions are capitalized, meaning the asset is increased. The cost is then allocated to future use periods through depreciation. This spreads the cost out over future accounting periods rather than recording an expense that would reduce income in the accounting period when the company made the outlay.

add-on-basis installment loans. N. Loans that include principal and interest in the face amount of the loan. Many consumer loans do this, which increases the effective rate of interest.

adjunct account. N. An account that increases its partner account. An adjunct account can increase an asset, liability, or equity account. Premium on bonds payable, an adjunct account, is added to the amount in the bonds payable account to get the balance sheet value for bonds payable.

adjustable rate loan/mortgage. N. A type of loan in which the interest rate changes periodically based on some other rate, such as the rate on treasury bills or the prime rate. Usually, adjustable rate loans have a maximum rate, but the borrower takes on some of the risk of interest rate changes. Because of the risk sharing, adjustable rate loans have a lower beginning rate than fixed rate loans. Synonymous with *variable rate loan/mortgage*. ABBRV. *ARM*.

adjusted balance method. N. A procedure for calculating the interest on a debt—usually something like a credit card balance—in which the interest rate is applied to the amount owed after all payments, purchases, and adjustments are made to the balance. Usually this method results in the lowest interest charges. Contrast with the average daily balance method, in which the charges are calculated on a weighted-average calculation of the outstanding amount. Also contrast with the previous balance method, in which the charges are calculated on the balance at the end of the last period. The previous balance method usually produces the highest amount of finance charges.

adjusted basis of an asset. N. Used to compute gains or losses when the asset is sold or abandoned. Adjusted basis is equal to the initial value at acquisition plus any capital expenditures to improve or extend the life of the asset less any depreciation taken. The proceeds are compared to the adjusted basis and if they exceed the adjusted basis, a gain results. If the proceeds are less than the adjusted basis, then a loss results.

adjusted book value. N. The balance sheet amounts for assets and liabilities that are current market values. Normally the amounts on the balance sheet for assets and liabilities are the historical cost, adjusted for depreciation in the case of assets.

adjusted cost of goods sold. N. The cost of goods sold amount that includes an adjustment for the difference between applied overhead and actual overhead costs.

adjusted current earnings. N. A calculation for alternative minimum tax that starts with alternative minimum taxable income (AMTI)—before the adjusted current earnings (ACE) adjustment—and adds tax exempt income, 70% of the dividends-received deduction, life insurance proceeds, increase in the cash surrender value of insurance policies, amortization of organization expenses, and the difference between the last in, first out (LIFO) and first in, first out (FIFO) costs of goods sold (if the business is using LIFO and deducts losses on related party sales). The result is adjusted current earnings. Then to arrive at the ACE adjustment, deduct the original AMTI. The resulting amount is then multiplied by 75% to get the adjusted current earnings adjustment. ABBRV. *ACE*.

adjusted gross income. N. A tax item on a personal tax return that is the taxable income after adjustments and before deductions. Adjusted gross income is used as a threshold for some deductions like miscellaneous expenses and medical expenses.

adjusted net capital gains. N. Net long-term capital gains less net short-term capital losses, less collectibles gain, less part of the gain from the sale of certain small business stock, and less excess depreciation on some real estate sales.

adjusted-rate preferred. N. A type of stock that pays a dividend based on some money market rate in effect during the quarter rather than paying a flat stated rate.

adjusted trial balance. N. The second trial balance that is prepared after adjusting entries are journalized and posted. The dollar amounts in each account on the adjusted trial balance appear on the financial statements. See also *trial balance*.

adjusting entry. N. A journal entry made at the end of an accounting period that adjusts the revenues or expenses so that they comply with generally accepted accounting principles. Adjusting entries may increase or decrease revenues, depending on if they are earned during the period or deferred to a future period. The adjustments may also increase or decrease expenses so that the income measurement includes all the resources it took to generate the recognized revenues. Synonymous with *year-end adjustment*.

administrative costs. N. Nonproduction costs that usually include product design and development, and other administrative costs of the entity. Administrative costs are expenses that reduce income in the period in which they occur and are not in inventory. These expenses are not associated with any one product or service line, but are needed to manage the entire company. See also *nonproduction costs*.

administrator/administratrix of an estate. N. A male/female person appointed by a probate court to assume the fiduciary responsibility for management of a will. The court appoints a fiduciary if a will does not name one or if the named person is unable or unwilling to serve.

adoption credit. N. A type of nonrefundable personal tax credit that reduces the amount of taxes the taxpayer must pay. To be eligible to take the adoption credit, the taxpayer must have paid the qualified adoption expenses to adopt a child under 18 or with special needs. No tax credit is available prior to the final adoption. The maximum tax credit is $11,390, and the credit is taken in the year or the year after the adoption is final. The total amount of all personal tax credits taken by a taxpayer in one year cannot be more than the tax owed plus the tentative alternative minimum tax.

ADRs. ABBRV. American depository receipts.

advance pricing agreement. N. An agreement between the Internal Revenue Service and a company on the acceptability of transfer prices, which are the prices different parts of the company charge each other for goods or services. ABBRV. *APA*.

advances from customers. N. See *unearned revenue*.

advancing issues. N. Stocks that have increasing prices. Business news reports may say, "Advancing issues exceeded declining issues," indicating that more stocks had price increases that day than had price decreases.

adverse audit report. N. The formal judgment made by a certified
public accountant firm after auditing an organization. The adverse
audit report is a red flag for readers of the report. It signals that the
organization did not follow generally accepted accounting principles (GAAP) and does not provide adequate disclosure. The difference between a qualified and an adverse report is the materiality
and persistent use of non-GAAP accounting rules. The audit report
is included in the required Securities and Exchange Commission
filings and in the annual report of the organization. See also
*unqualified audit report, qualified audit report, disclaimer-of-
opinion audit report.* Synonymous with *adverse opinion.*

adverse opinion. N. See *adverse audit report.*

affiliate. N. A related company. An affiliate is usually a company in
which another company owns less than 50% of the outstanding
stock. If Ash Company owns 35% of the stock of Birch Company,
Birch is an affiliate of Ash.

affiliated group. N. A group of related corporations that can file one
tax return for the group. To be defined as an affiliated group, one
corporation must own 80% of the stock or votes in another corporation that is a parent-subsidiary group. Shares of other corporations are acquired by either the parent or the subsidiary; when the
group ownership of the new corporation exceeds 80%, it becomes
part of the affiliated group. The key is the collective ownership of
the shares. The requirement is not that the 80% is owned by an individual corporation, but rather that the members of the affiliated
group together hold 80% of the votes or stock. An affiliated group
has a stricter definition than a parent-subsidiary group. The affiliated group cannot include tax-exempt organizations, foreign corporations, life insurance companies, or S corporations.

affirmative covenants. N. The restrictions and agreements associated with long-term debt that specify what the borrower must do.

Examples of affirmative covenants are using the borrowing for the agreed-upon project, maintaining insurance, and allowing the lender the right of inspection. Affirmative covenants protect the lender.

AFN. ABBRV. Additional funds needed.

after-hours trading. N. Buying and selling securities when the organized markets are closed. After-hours trading is done through electronic communication networks to match buyers and sellers.

aftermarket. N. Security trades between investors. The securities are purchased from an owner rather than from the company issuing the security, with the owner receiving the proceeds. The only time the corporation receives the proceeds is the first time the stock is sold. See also *secondary market.*

AGA. ABBRV. Association of Government Accountants.

agency fund. N. A type of fiduciary fund used in governmental accounting. The agency fund is used to hold money collected or withheld that must be paid or sent at a later date. When the government withholds amounts from employees' checks, the amounts are put in the agency fund so that the Social Security amounts, insurance premiums, income tax amounts, etc., can later be sent to the appropriate party.

agency theory. N. A set of concepts that describes conflicts and behaviors associated with relationships in which the principals or owners of an organization hire a person or another organization, called the agent, to act on behalf of the principal. The agent can make decisions, spend money, and sign contracts for the principal. Agency theory suggests that the agent will not always act in the best interests of the principals without monitoring or incentives. Agency theory applies to the corporate environment in which the stockholders (the principals) hire the managers (the agents) to run the company in a way that maximizes the wealth of the stock-holders.

agency transactions. N. Events in which a nonprofit organization acts as a conduit for funds from another source. Government grants of financial aid awarded to students are agency transactions for a college or university, because the institution is acting as a means of distribution for the financial aid.

aggregate theory of partnerships. N. A framework for viewing partnerships. The aggregate theory of partnerships looks at partnerships as if only the partners exist. The partnership does not own the assets—the partners do. Contrast this with the entity theory of partnerships, which views the partnership like a corporation.

aggressive growth fund. N. A type of mutual fund in which the goal is to maximize the share price rather than to receive dividends. Aggressive growth funds invest in industries or companies that are riskier than average because they are in developing or unstable industries. The logic is that these new industries will provide big share price appreciation.

aging receivables. N. See *aging schedule*.

aging schedule. N. A schedule of accounts receivable classified by due dates. An aging schedule is used to estimate bad-debt expense using the percentage-of-receivables approach. A probability of noncollection is applied to each total in each age group. The sum is the amount of bad debts on the books. Synonymous with *aging receivables*.

AICPA. ABBRV. American Institute of Certified Public Accountants.

AIS. ABBRV. Accounting information systems.

all-events test. N. One of two tests that determine if an item is included in income for the year or if it is deductible as an expense for the year. The all-events test requires that every action has been performed that sets the amount and right or obligation of the taxpayer. The standard for deduction of expenses is economic performance, which means the property or service has been provided to the taxpayer. The wages due to employees cannot be deducted as a business expense until the employees work the hours to earn the wages. If a contract specifies a certain number of hours per week and a wage per hour, the deduction cannot be taken until the employee actually works the hours.

allocation. N. A general term used to describe means of distributing cost to the income statement. The key issues are how much of the cost is assigned to any one accounting period and over how many accounting periods the cost should be apportioned. In cost accounting, allocation is the assignment of indirect costs to cost objects; it is some logical way of apportioning costs when the precise amount is unknown. Allocation is an issue because of the matching principle. To accurately measure income, the income statement must reflect all the expenses it took to generate the revenue on that income statement. That means some allocation is necessary for items like buildings. Allocation is also a problem because measures are not precise enough to match expenses easily.

allowance for bad debts. N. See *allowance for doubtful accounts*.

allowance for doubtful accounts. N. A contra-asset account on the balance sheet that reduces the amount of accounts receivable to the net realizable value, the amount the organization actually expects to collect. The allowance for doubtful accounts is increased by the bad-debt expense for the period and decreased when an account is actually written off after becoming uncollectible. See also *bad-debt expense*. Synonymous with *allowance for bad debts, allowance for uncollectible accounts*.

allowance for uncollectible accounts. N. See *allowance for doubtful accounts*.

allowance method. N. The method of accounting for bad debts that complies with generally accepted accounting principles. The expense of providing credit to customers, bad-debt expense, is included in the same period as the sales revenue from those credit sales. The company estimates the amount of bad-debt expense and records it as a decrease to income for the period. That decrease is offset by an increase in the allowance for bad debts, a contra-asset account. When the company identifies a particular account as a bad debt and as uncollectible, accounts receivable is reduced and the allowance for bad debts is reduced, with no effect on income. Contrast with the direct write-off method in which the expense of bad debts is only on the income statement when a particular account is identified as uncollectible. This violates the matching rule because that determination is usually in an accounting period after the sale is recorded. See also *bad-debt expense*.

allowance to reduce inventory to LIFO. N. See *LIFO reserve*.

alpha risk. N. See *risk of incorrect rejection*.

alternate valuation date. N. Estate property can be valued as of the American depository receipt's date of death or any date up to six months after the death. The choice of valuation date is important for tax purposes.

alternative minimum tax. N. A system of tax rules that applies after the regular tax laws to ensure that companies or individuals pay their fair share of taxes. The alternative minimum tax reduces or eliminates some deductions, exclusions, and tax credits very profitable companies and wealthy individuals use to reduce their taxable income. ABBRV. *AMT*.

alternative minimum taxable income. N. A term used to distinguish the entity's income for alternative minimum tax purposes from regular taxable income. The alterative minimum taxable income is always equal to or greater than the taxable income because the alternative minimum tax system does not allow deductions for certain preference items that are allowed for regular tax calculations. ABBRV. *AMTI*.

American Accounting Association. N. A professional organization with a membership of mainly postsecondary accounting instructors. The organization emphasizes teaching skill development and, through a peer review process, provides important outlets for scholarship. ABBRV. *AAA*.

American Association of Public Accountants. N. A predecessor to the American Institute of Certified Public Accountants. It was established in 1887 as a professional organization for accountants. The name was changed to the American Institute of Accountants in 1917, and to the American Institute of Certified Public Accountants in 1957. See also *American Institute of Certified Public Accountants*.

American depository receipts. N. A way for U.S. investors to own foreign stocks that are not listed on the U.S. stock exchanges. American depository receipts represent shares of foreign stocks held in trust by banks. The banks issue the certificates that are traded mainly on the over-the-counter market. ABBRV. *ADRs*.

American Institute of Accountants. N. A predecessor to the American Institute of Certified Public Accountants. The original organization was established in 1887, with the name American Association of Public Accountants, as a professional organization

for accountants. The name was changed to American Institute of
Accountants in 1917, and to American Institute of Certified Pubic
Accountants in 1957. See also *American Institute of Certified
Public Accountants.*

American Institute of Certified Public Accountants. N. The professional organization for accountants. To become a member, an individual must have passed the Uniform Certified Public Accountant
Exam. The original organization was established in 1887 as a
professional organization, with the name American Association of
Public Accountants. The name was changed to American Institute
of Accountants in 1917, and to American Institute of Certified
Public Accountants in 1957. ABBRV. *AICPA.*

American option. N. An option contract that can be settled anytime
before the specified date. This is in contrast to a European option,
which is only exercisable at the specified date.

American Society of Women Accountants. N. A professional association of women in all types of accounting careers.
www.aswa.org. ABBRV. *ASWA.*

American Stock Exchange. N. An alternative market to the New
York Stock Exchange (NYSE), also located in New York City. The
American Stock Exchange has less rigorous size requirements for
the listing of companies. Founded in 1842 as the New York Curb
Exchange, the American Stock Exchange provided a market for
smaller companies that could not meet the NYSE's requirements.
This market actually traded outside, on the curb, until 1921.
Synonymous with *Curb, the.* ABBRV. *AMEX.*

American Taxation Association. N. A professional organization
for tax professors. The organization's objectives are to foster
research in taxation, to provide tax education at the university
level, and to instruct the public through the publication of tax
information. The *Journal of the American Taxation*

Association is published three times a year and contains mainly academic research articles. www.atasection.org/index2.html. ABBRV. *ATA*.

AMEX. ABBRV. American Stock Exchange.

amortization. N. The process of spreading dollar amounts of cost across future accounting periods. Amortization is similar to depreciation, but is not used for tangible assets. Rather, it is used for intangible assets, bond discounts, and bond premiums.

amortization of gain or loss in pension accounting. N. An allocation of unexpected returns on pension plan assets to pension expense. The amortization of gain or loss only affects pension expense when the amount of net unexpected returns is too large, or is more than 10% of the projected benefit obligation or the pension plan assets at the beginning of the year. When the unexpected returns, net unrecognized gains or losses, are too large, then a minimum amount must be included in pension expense. The minimum amount is calculated as the amount of net unrecognized gains or losses in excess of the 10% threshold, divided by the average years to retirement of the current employees.

amortization of premium. N. Systematically reducing the excess of the original selling price of a bond payable over the par value when interest is recorded. Interest expense is less than the cash paid for interest by the amount of the premium. Straight line amortization allocates an equal portion of the premium to each interest payment. Effective interest amortization calculates interest expense using the book value of the bonds and the market rate at the time the bond was sold. The difference between the calculated interest expense and the cash paid for interest is the amount of amortization.

amortization of prior service cost. N. The allocation of the prior service cost to pension expense. Rather than include the entire amount of the prior service cost in the year of the plan change, employers are required to spread it out over the remaining working time of the current employees. The logic is that the employer grants the retroactive benefits to get better future service from the existing employees. Therefore, the cost of those benefits should be matched with the future revenues.

amortized cost. N. The balance sheet value for debt investments purchased at a premium or discount. See also *amortized-cost method of accounting for debt investments.*

amortized-cost method of accounting for debt investments. N. Used for debt securities that the owner intends to hold until maturity. The acquisition cost of the investment is adjusted for any premium or discount amortization during the holding period. Interest income is on the income statement when earned. The mechanics are similar to accounting for bonds payable. No year-end revaluation to market value is required; therefore, no unrealized gains or losses are on the income statement.

amortized loan. N. A loan that is repaid with equal payments over the life of the loan. Each payment contains a different proportion of principal and interest. Early payments have a higher percentage of interest included in the payment than later payments. Most consumer car loans are amortized loans. Contrast with a bond in which only interest is paid over the term of the borrowing and the entire principal is paid at maturity.

AMT. ABBRV. Alternative minimum tax.

AMT adjustments. N. Amounts that can be added or deducted to arrive at alternative minimum taxable income. Alternative minimum tax (AMT) adjustments usually include depreciation adjustments, amortization adjustments for pollution-control facilities and mining costs, an adjusted gain or loss on property dispositions, adjustment to the percentage of completion for long-term contracts, an installment sales adjustment, and an adjusted current earnings adjustment.

AMT base. N. Alternative minimum taxable income after the alternative minimum tax (AMT) exemption. Used to calculate the tentative minimum tax.

AMT exemption. N. The amount deducted from alternative minimum taxable income (AMTI) to get the amount on which alternative minimum tax (AMT) is calculated.

AMTI. ABBRV. Alternative minimum taxable income.

AMT preferences. N. Amounts of deductions or tax credits that increase alternative minimum taxable income. These amounts are otherwise nontaxable, but according to alternative minimum tax (AMT) rules, they are considered taxable, for purposes of the AMT. The AMT preferences include tax-exempt interest from private activity bonds, excess percentage depletion, excess intangible drilling costs, and accelerated depreciation of real estate.

analytical anomalies. N. A symptom of fraud. Analytical anomalies are circumstances that are too unusual to be real. For instance, a sharp increase in debit or credit memos must have an explanation other than it just being a normal occurrence, and that could be fraud.

analytical procedures. N. Methods of investigating the relationship between account balances on financial statements. The analysis of the relationships informs the auditor how the account balances compare to expectations. Using analytical procedures in this way assumes that financial relationships are stable. Two types of analytical procedures used in auditing are ratio analysis and trend analysis.

analytical review. N. An auditing procedure that consists of comparing ratios and amounts from the current year to those of past years to see if the pattern has changed.

announcement date. N. See *declaration date*.

annual compounding. N. See *compounding*.

annual gift tax exclusion. N. The amount per person that an individual can give as gifts and not be subject to the gift tax. As of 2007, the amount is $12,000 per recipient. For a married couple, the exclusion amount is $24,000 per recipient. If an individual gives four people $10,000 each, none of the $40,000 is subject to gift tax. If the individual gives $40,000 to one person, then the giver must pay tax on $28,000 ($40,000 less the per person annual exclusion of $12,000).

annualize. V. A mathematical procedure that extends an item to cover one year. If the six-month rate is 4%, then the annualized rate is 8%. The process usually simplifies the calculation and ignores compounding in interest rates.

annual percentage rate. N. The interest rate charged on a loan. Interest rates for consumer loans are listed as an annual rate even if the duration of the loan is less than one year. ABBR. *APR*.

annual report. N. A document produced by a business once per year that contains financial information and other information about the company. The annual report must include the financial statements and notes to them, the audit report, management's analysis, and other items that help convey information useful to people outside the company.

annual return. N. The percentage of increase in the value of an investment over a year.

annuitize. V. To begin receiving payments of defined amounts at defined intervals from an investment.

annuity. N. Payments of a fixed amount made or received at fixed, regular intervals. See also *ordinary annuity, annuity due.*

annuity due. N. Payments of a fixed amount made or received at the beginning of regularly spaced time intervals. Monthly rent payments are an example of an annuity due.

antidilution provision. N. See *preemptive right.*

antidilutive. N. Identifying the positive effect on earnings per share of the conversion of a convertible security. For example, if convertible bonds were all converted into stock, the income would increase because the company would not have an interest expense. The number of shares would increase by the additional shares the company would issue. The new earnings per share, calculated with the higher net income and the higher number of shares, are compared to the basic earnings per share. If the new earnings per share are higher, then the convertible bonds are antidilutive and would not be included in calculating diluted earnings per share.

antitrust laws. N. Federal laws that restrict businesses from growing so large that they have the power to drive out competitors. The Sherman Antitrust Act of 1890, the Clayton Antitrust Act of 1914, and the Federal Trade Commission Act of 1914 form the basis of antitrust laws. Microsoft has had several antitrust lawsuits filed since 2000. The company settled many out of court with large payments, but admitted to no wrongdoing.

APA. ABBRV. Advance pricing agreement.

APB. ABBRV. Accounting Principles Board.

APB Opinions. N. Official rules set by the Accounting Principles Board (APB). APB Opinions are analogous to Financial Accounting Standards Board standards and, unless superseded by subsequent standards, still remain in effect.

applet. N. A small program on the World Wide Web that runs in conjunction with a user's Internet browser to perform a certain activity, such as playing a game or answering a survey. The applet may contain a virus that can be transmitted to the user's computer.

applicable federal rate. N. An interest rate that changes monthly and is based on what the federal government pays to borrow funds. The applicable federal rate is used to calculate the imputed interest for tax purposes.

application controls. N. The procedures and measures a company takes to make sure that the computer processing of data is safe and accurate. The goal is to have information that is free of both intentional and accidental errors. Application controls cover all three aspects of information technology—input, processing, and output—and are part of the internal control environment of the entity. See also *input controls, processing controls, output controls, internal control.*

application software. N. Computer programs that allow users to complete various activities or tasks. Quick Books and Quicken are examples of application software that perform accounting and bookkeeping functions. Application software is designed to do a specific task and is distinguished from the operating system software that makes a computer run.

applied overhead. N. The dollar amount of production costs in a normal costing system. Applied overhead is calculated by multiplying the overhead rate by the actual amount of unit-level activity driver used. See also *underapplied overhead*, *overapplied overhead*.

apportionment of business income among states. N. The dividing up of a corporation's income among all the states that have nexuses with the corporation, meaning the state has the right to tax the corporation because of the way it does business in the state. Generally, states can only tax income from activities within the state.

appreciation. N. The amount of increased value of an asset. If you buy shares of stock for $150 on Monday and the market price of those shares later in the week is $200, the $50 difference is the appreciation.

appropriated retained earnings. N. The portion of retained earnings that is not available for dividends. To appropriate retained earnings, the company must record the partitioning of retained earnings. The company can use appropriated retained earnings for contingencies or big projects. Appropriating retained earnings does not involve setting aside any cash. It only sends a signal to balance sheet readers that dividends cannot be equal to the total retained earnings. See also *unappropriated retained earnings*.

appropriations. N. The term used in governmental accounting to identify amounts that the governmental unit is authorized to spend for operating activities, debt repayment, and asset acquisition. The appropriations account is a budgetary account that acts as a control account for all budgeted expenditures. More generally, appropriations refer to any funds dedicated to a particular purpose. For example, at the beginning of the period, the planned amount of expenditures is entered as the budget amount to the appropriations control account. The appropriations control account has a subsidiary account for each type of expenditure, such as salaries or supplies. The budgeted amount of each type of appropriation is entered as a credit to the corresponding subsidiary account; the budgeted amount of salaries is entered in the salary expenditures subsidiary account. During the accounting period, the actual amount of expenditures for salaries is entered as a debit to the appropriate subsidiary account. At any point in time, the actual amount spent on salaries (the debit balance) can be compared to the budgeted amount (the credit balance).

APR. ABBRV. Annual percentage rate.

APT. ABBRV. Arbitrage pricing theory.

ARB. ABBRV. *Accounting Research Bulletins*.

arbitrage. N. Earning a risk-free return by buying and selling the same asset in two different markets at the same time. Because the markets are different, the price is different. Obviously, the arbitrageur buys in the lower priced market and sells in the higher priced market.

arbitrage pricing theory. N. An alternative to the capital asset pricing model that estimates stock price as a function of factors in addition to risk. ABBR. *APT*.

ARM. ABBRV. Adjustable rate mortgage. See *adjustable rate loan/mortgage*.

arm's length transactions. N. Transactions in which everyone involved acts in their own self-interest, rather than for the benefit of one of the other participants. Arm's length transactions ensure that the prices involved in the exchange are genuine market prices. See also *related party transactions*.

ARO. ABBRV. Asset retirement obligation.

arrearages. N. See *dividends in arrears*.

articles of incorporation. N. The documentation that an entity submits to a state to obtain a corporate charter. Corporate charters are granted by states, making the corporation similar to an individual in the state and subject to state laws and taxes. State laws regarding corporations differ, and companies choose the state for incorporation that has favorable laws or tax advantages. A company is incorporated in only one state, not in every state in which it operates. Synonymous with *corporate charter.*

articulate. N. The interrelationships between the financial statements of a company. The statement of cash flows explains why the cash account on a comparative balance sheet changed. The income statement and statement of stockholders' equity describes why the balance in retained earnings changed.

artificial intelligence. N. The processing of data by a computer that mimics the human thinking process. Artificial intelligence is usually applied to complex processes like robotics, speech recognition, and problem-solving situations.

A shares. N. A class of mutual fund shares that are available to anyone and are front-end loaded, carrying a charge to purchase. The letter "A" designates the class of the shares.

ask price. N. The lowest selling price of a stock offered by an investor who owns a stock. See also *spread.*

ASR. ABBRV. Accelerated share repurchase.

assessed value. N. The dollar amount on which taxes are based. Property owners receive a notification of assessed value, which determines the amount of property taxes the owner must pay. The property owner has an opportunity to appeal the assessed value. Assessed value is rarely higher than the market value of a property.

asset. N. Owned by an entity, something that provides benefits and whose cost can be measured. The measure of the value of assets in dollars appears on the balance sheet. For something to be classified as an asset, and to appear on the balance sheet, it must provide probable future benefits, be owned by the entity as a result of a past transaction, and have a value that is measured using generally accepted accounting principles. Examples include cash, land, and patents.

asset allocation. N. The mix of types of investments in a portfolio. The portfolio includes not only different stocks, but also bonds, real estate, cash, and other investments. The mix is determined by the goals of the investor, which are usually to reduce risk and earn a return.

asset-allocation funds. N. Mutual funds that hold both stocks and bonds. Some asset-allocation funds follow specified allocation percentages, and others take advantage of current conditions. Those that take advantage of current conditions are higher risk, because the fund manager tries to adjust the allocations to take advantage of predicted conditions.

asset-backed security. N. A debt instrument that is collateralized by cash flows from a bundle of assets such as mortgages.

asset-based lending. N. See *asset-based loan.*

asset-based loan. N. A type of loan made to businesses in which the business pledges company assets as collateral for the loan. The assets may be inventory, receivables, or something else that is fairly liquid. Synonymous with *asset-based lending, commercial finance.*

asset class. N. A category or type of investment. Common asset classes include stocks, bonds, real estate, and cash. See also *asset allocation.*

asset coverage. N. A ratio of net assets to liabilities and/or preferred stock. Net assets are equal to total assets minus total liabilities. Asset coverage measures the proportion of equity to debt.

asset depreciation range. N. Time over which an asset can be depreciated for tax purposes. The time is given as a range of years applicable to classes of assets.

asset fraud. N. A type of fraud in which financial statements over-state assets.

asset-linked bonds. N. See *commodity-backed bonds*.

asset-management ratios. N. Financial analysis tools that measure how well a firm manages assets. The key is to have adequate, but not more than adequate, assets on hand. If a firm has too many assets, it spends too much on financing charges, which reduces profits. Common asset-management ratios include inventory turnover, fixed asset turnover, total asset turnover, and days sales outstanding.

asset retirement obligation. N. Significant costs associated with the disposal of an asset. Accounting for asset retirement obligations requires estimating the cost and discounting the estimate. The present value is added to the asset's depreciable base and a liability is recorded for the obligation. Each year, interest expense is added to the liability so that when the asset is retired, the value in the liability is equal to the cost estimate. ABBRV. *ARO*.

asset substitution. N. Switching from one investment—usually a low-risk investment financed with borrowed money at a rate reflecting the low-risk—to a different investment with higher risk.

asset turnover. N. A ratio used in financial statement analysis to investigate how efficiently assets are used to generate earnings.

The numerator is usually sales for the period and the denominator is the average value of the specific assets held during the period covered by the sales. A higher ratio is better, but the exact number depends on the industry and should be compared to industry norms.

assignment of accounts receivable. N. Using accounts receivable to obtain a loan. The company signs a note with the bank using the accounts receivable as collateral for the loan. If the company does not repay the loan, the bank gets the cash paid by customers on the accounts receivable. The note can be general, in which no particular accounts receivable are identified. Or, specific accounts receivable may be identified as available for repayment of the loan. See also *factoring*.

assignment of income doctrine. N. A legal doctrine that prescribes that income belongs to the entity that owns the underlying asset producing the income. Even if a property owner directs the renters to pay the rent to someone with a lower tax rate, such as a child or parent, the owner of the property has to pay income on the taxes.

Association of Certified Fraud Examiners. N. A professional organization whose mission is to prevent and detect white-collar crime and fraud. www.acfe.com. See also *certified fraud examiner*. ABBRV. *ACFE*.

Association of Government Accountants. N. A professional association of accountants working in government. www.agacgfm.org. ABBRV. *AGA*.

assurance services. N. A set of activities that involve investigating an object about which a group or individual needs some type of guarantee or reassurance. It usually involves inspection and evaluation to see if something is correct, is being complied with, or is appropriate. Assurance services are broader than audits, compilations, and reviews and the attestation services of certified public accountants (CPAs) or other types of professionals who provide assurance in their areas of expertise. CPAs may review payments on a loan and provide assurance that the company is complying with the loan terms. Attestation services are specifically associated with audit procedures, while assurance services can be any type of examination.

ASWA. ABBRV. American Society of Women Accountants.

asymmetric information. N. Circumstances in which company insiders (managers) have better and more complete information about the firm's future performance than do company outsiders (investors).

asymmetric return profile. N. A description of a financial derivative that does not result in a gain for one party equal to the loss for the other party. This occurs in option contracts because the holder of the option pays for that option and can limit the amount of loss to that payment by not exercising the option.

ATA. ABBRV. American Taxation Association.

at par. ADJ. The price of the financial security is the same as the face value. For bonds, that is the maturity value. For stock, it only applies if a par value is assigned to each share of stock.

at-risk amount. N. The amount a taxpayer would lose if the business failed. Usually this is relevant in a small, closely held business. In a real estate–investment environment, the at-risk amount is the actual cash invested plus any debts for which the taxpayer has personal responsibility. See also *at-risk rules*.

at-risk rules. N. Tax rules that limit (to the at-risk amount) the amount of loss a taxpayer can use. At-risk rules prevent taxpayers from offsetting regular income with huge losses from other activities. See also *at-risk amount*.

attest function. N. The service provided by certified public accountant (CPAs) in which the accounting information of an organization is reviewed, tested, and verified for completeness, accuracy, and existence through various audit procedures. After performing these activities, the CPA issues an audit opinion attesting to the fairness of the financial statements. See also *audit*, *audit report*. Synonymous with *attest services*.

attest services. N. See *attest function*.

at the bell. N. A measure of time indicating right after the opening of trading in the stock market or right before the close of trading.

at-the-money. N. A situation in which the exercise or strike price of an option is equal to the market price of the security. Being at-the-money provides no benefit for the holder of the option because the item could be purchased for the same price with or without the option. If an executive held an option to buy 100 shares of stock for $14 per share prior to December 31, 2004, the executive would be at-the-money if the market price for the stock was $14.

attorney's letter. N. A letter, used as part of an audit's activities, sent by the certified public accountant (CPA) to the client's attorney to inquire about any lawsuits involving the client. The letter serves to verify that the client is not involved in any additional lawsuits or claims that could affect the company's financial well-being. See also *contingent loss*.

attribution rules. N. The standards for determining indirect ownership of stock. Stock owned by siblings, spouses, children, grandchildren, or ancestors is "attributed" to the individual and considered indirectly owned for sales of property.

audit. N. A term usually referring to a financial audit, which is a set of procedures performed by accountants from a certified public accountant (CPA) firm. The procedures are designed to investigate and verify the accounting information that management puts in financial reports. When the audit is completed, the accounting firm issues an opinion on the fairness of the financial statements, not on how well the company is performing. The Securities and Exchange Commission requires all companies that have publicly traded stock to present their annual financial report with audited financial statements. The financial statements are supposed to give investors the information necessary to evaluate the company's performance and make good investment decisions. The audit lends credibility to the financial statements presented by managers of the company, who may be motivated to shade the truth. Many financial institutions also require audited financial statements before lending money to an entity. See also *audit report, internal audit, compliance audit, external audit.*

audit command language. N. Data mining software used to investigate fraud by checking accounting transactions. ABBRV. *ACL.*

audit committee. N. A subgroup of the board of directors composed of directors who are independent of an organization and not employed by it. The committee acts on behalf of the full board and all stockholders to check on management actions, and it has responsibility for the soundness of the financial statements and reporting processes of the organization. The audit committee has become more important in the post-Enron financial reporting environment.

audit evidence. N. The information gathered by audit procedures that substantiates the auditor's report. The auditor plans the audit to gather sufficient and relevant information regarding the financial statements on which to base an opinion. The methods used to obtain audit evidence include physical observation, pattern and account balance analysis in relationship to previous years, and control procedure testing.

audit guide. N. A book from the American Institute of Certified Public Accountants setting out the practices for a particular industry. Audit guides offer not just suggestions, but also authoritative literature considered binding as Statements on Auditing Standards.

auditing around the computer. N. Audit procedures that ignore the actual computer processing part of business activities. A sample of inputs is tested and verified through standard audit techniques, and the output is checked. Auditing around the computer assumes that if the output is right, then the processing is right. Auditing around the computer is only effective for transactions in which the right output is obvious; for unusual transactions, these procedures are inadequate.

Auditing Standards Board. N. A fifteen-member board that is part of the American Institute of Certified Public Accountants, which has the responsibility of establishing the rules, procedures, and guidance for audits.

auditing through the computer. N. Audit procedures that check for processing controls. The auditor performs the normal procedures, following the audit trail to the point of processing, then checks the processing controls and the output of the processing. Usually, the auditor assumes that the equipment is working properly and focuses on the aspects where human error intersects with the accounting data. See also *processing controls*.

auditing with the computer. N. Using the computer to perform audit procedures. In a nearly paperless environment, this is the only way to perform an audit, because hard copies of source documents are not available. Auditors use several types of software to accomplish this.

audit opinion. N. See *audit report*.

audit program. N. A list of audit objectives and the activities that will be performed to achieve those objectives. The audit program is really the plan for performing the audit, and that plan is based on an analysis of the risks involved with the audit. If the risk of misstatement is high, specific accounts are targeted for a more extensive investigation.

audit report. N. A signed letter from the auditor of a company, included in the annual report, that states whether or not the financial statements fairly present the results of operations and the financial position of the company. An annual audit is required by the Securities and Exchange Commission for firms selling stock to the public. The audit report has consistent wording and can state an opinion on the quality of the numbers on the financial statements, or it can indicate that the auditor is unable to give an opinion for some reason. See also *adverse audit report, disclaimer-of-opinion audit report, qualified audit report, unqualified audit report.* Synonymous with *audit opinion.*

audit risk. N. The possibility that the auditor will not catch a material misstatement in a client's financial report and will mistakenly give an unqualified opinion. The level of audit risk is set by the auditor after assessing the engagement risk, inherent risk, control risk, and detection risk. The auditor evaluates the level of this risk to determine the type and amount of audit activities. Higher risk means more audit work.

audit risk model. N. A model that explains the relationship between the types of risk involved in an audit. The audit risk is equal to the product of the inherent risk stated as a probability, the control risk stated as a probability, and the detection risk stated as a probability. Because the elements of the model are difficult to measure precisely, the quantitative application is limited.

audit sampling. N. A way to reduce the number of audit procedures by performing only those procedures regarding the client organization's processes, accounts, or transactions. The auditor cannot check every transaction or process but instead checks some of the items. The size of the sample is determined through statistical methods based on how confident the auditor wants to be.

audit software. N. Computer programs auditors use to perform various audit procedures. These programs simplify investigating and analyzing client records and practices.

audit trail. N. The evidence of a business transaction's path through the accounting system. Auditors should be able to trace financial statement amounts back to source documents. For example, the audit trail that verifies salary expense on the income statement would include paychecks to employees connected to the employees' time cards.

authentication. N. Security and privacy techniques used by businesses in electronic commerce to identify a computer's communication with the system.

authorized-share capital. N. See *authorized stock.*

authorized shares. N. See *authorized stock.*

authorized stock. N. The maximum number of shares of stock that a corporation can issue. This number is specified in the charter or articles of incorporation. The corporation can change the number proportionately through a stock split, but then the par value of the stock must also be adjusted proportionately. For example, if a company's balance sheet indicates that it has 21 million shares of stock authorized, then the maximum number of shares that can be issued is 21 million. If the company needs additional stock, it can issue a new class of stock by going through an investment banker. See also *issued stock*. Synonymous with *authorized-share capital*, *authorized shares*.

automatic termination. N. The ending of a partnership because 50% or more of the ownership has been sold or exchanged in the past twelve months. The quantity of partnership interest sold or exchanged determines this termination. Gifts of partnership interests or transfers to heirs do not count as sales or exchanges.

available-for-sale investment. N. An investment classification based on the purpose of the investment. Usually this type of investment is less than 20% of the outstanding shares of the investee company, but it may also be a debt investment that will not be held until maturity. The dividends or interest from an available-for-sale investment are included in income. At year-end, the investments in this classification are adjusted to the year-end market value using an adjustment account. If an investment is classified as "available-for-sale," then year-end market value changes are not included in net income, but in other comprehensive income and as an unrealized gain or loss in the equity section of the balance sheet.

average age of inventory. N. See *average days to sell inventory*.

average collection period. N. The time between the sale and the receipt of payment. Calculated as average accounts receivable divided by average daily sales. A high average collection period indicates that customers are slow to pay. A very low average collection period indicates that credit policies may be too strict. A change in the average collection period should reflect a change in credit policy.

average cost method. N. An inventory cost flow method in which costs are assigned based on the prices of all similar items available for sale during the accounting period. The costs of the beginning inventory and purchases are combined and spread over all costs available for sale during the accounting period. See also *weighted-average cost method, moving-average-cost method*.

average daily balance method. N. A procedure for calculating the interest on a debt—usually something like a credit card balance or a bank account—in which periodic charges are calculated on a balance figured from a weighted-average calculation of the daily outstanding amount. Contrast with the adjusted balance method, in which the interest rate is applied to the amount owed after all payments, purchases, and adjustments are made to the balance. Usually this method results in the lowest interest charges. Also contrast with previous balance method, in which the charges are calculated on the balance at the end of the last period. The previous balance method usually produces the highest amount of finance charges.

average days to collect receivables. N. A financial analysis tool that is also a component of the cash conversion cycle model. Average days to collect receivables can be calculated by dividing receivables turnover by 365 or by dividing average receivables by average sales per day. The average days to collect receivables can indicate how effective collections are by representing the time it takes to collect cash from a sale. Synonymous with *days sales outstanding, receivables collection period*.

average days to sell inventory. N. A financial analysis ratio that is also a component of the cash conversion cycle model. The formula for average days to sell inventory is inventory turnover divided by 365 or average inventory divided by cost of goods sold divided by 365. Some publications use sales rather than cost of goods sold.

The average days to sell inventory can estimate the time to produce and sell products. Synonymous with *days of inventory, inventory conversion period, average age of inventory*.

average tax rate. N. A calculation that represents the overall percentage of taxable income that an entity pays in taxes. The amount of the taxes that the entity pays for the year divided by the taxable income.

avoidable interest. N. The amount of interest that an organization would have avoided if it had not made the expenditures for an asset. Avoidable interest is usually calculated when an entity is self-constructing an asset. The cost of the asset can include materials, labor, and overhead plus some interest. The company is allowed to capitalize the lesser of the actual interest on borrowings for the project, or the avoidable interest. The business calculates avoidable interest based on weighted-average expenditures for the project and on a rate. For the amount up to the actual borrowing, the entity uses the actual borrowing rate, and for the remainder it uses a weighted-average rate. Interest cannot be capitalized if the entity takes on debt to purchase the completed asset; it can only be capitalized in the case of self-constructed assets. The Financial Accounting Standards Board allows this because a contractor would borrow to build the project, adding the interest into the cost of the project, so a purchased asset may include the builder's interest cost.

away-from-home requirement. N. The standard for determining if travel expenses are deductible. Travel expenses are deductible if the taxpayer is temporarily away from his or her tax home overnight. The standard is subject to interpretation by the Internal Revenue Service as to what is considered temporary and where the tax home is located. Generally, work assignments of less than one year are temporary.

B

b2b. N. Activity between two businesses. Usually it involves one business selling to another business in an electronic commerce environment. Compare this to b2c, which is business to consumer. Synonymous with *business-to-business commerce*.

b2c. N. Activities between a business and a consumer. Usually they involve a business selling to a consumer in an electronic commerce environment. Compare this to b2b, which is business to business. Synonymous with *business-to-consumer commerce*.

baby bond. N. A bond with a par value of less than $1,000. Most bonds carry a par value, or a maturity value, of $1,000.

backdating options. N. The practice of dating options at a more favorable date than the actual grant date. The result is built in compensation rather than incentive compensation. This practice was allowed because companies could delay notifying the Securities and Exchange Commission about granting stock options. New rules require notification within a short period of time, eliminating the opportunity to significantly backdate options.

back-end load. ADJ. Describes a mutual fund's fee structure. A back-end load fund charges a commission when the investor sells the shares.

back-office server. N. The computer system of an organization that contains the programs, applications, and controls necessary to process business activities. Contrast with the Web server, which is the computer system that keeps transactions involving the Internet or World Wide Web separated from other computer systems in the organization (to avoid viruses or other outside attacks).

back-to-back transactions. N. Transactions in which two companies agree to buy and sell the same product to each other. If Company X agrees to sell a product worth $2 to Company Y on

Tuesday, and then agrees to buy it back for $2 from Company Y a
short time later, both companies have increased their revenues
without any real increase in business. Companies engage in this
earnings management technique to meet quarterly revenue projec-
tions, believing that the real increase in revenue will take place in
a later quarter.

back up. V. To make a second copy of important information and
store it in a safe place, in case the original is lost or destroyed.
Accounting information systems use back-up procedures to avoid
losing data.

bad-debt deduction. N. A tax deduction for the losses that result
from debtors being unable or unwilling to repay the debt to the
taxpayer. Nonbusiness bad debts are deductible as short-term
capital losses. Business bad debts are deductible as an ordinary
loss.

bad-debt expense. N. The estimate of credit sales that a company
will not collect. To comply with generally accepted accounting
principles, companies must include the expense for credit sales in
the same period in which the sales revenue is on the income statement. The problem is that companies do not know precisely which
customers will not pay. If they did, they would not sell to them in
the first place. Companies must estimate bad-debt expense using
several methods based on historical patterns. See also *allowance
for doubtful accounts, allowance method.*

balance. N. (1) The net amount left in an account after adding the
increases and deducting the decreases. (2) The situation in which
debits equal credits.

balanced budget. N. A plan for operating a government unit in
which expenditures do not exceed income items.

balanced funds. N. Mutual funds that are invested in both stocks and bonds.

balanced scorecard. N. A performance measurement system that uses multiple measures, both financial and nonfinancial, to determine the effectiveness and efficiency of a unit. Four perspectives structure the balanced scorecard. The first, financial perspective, measures the profitability. The second, customer perspective, looks at customer satisfaction and market share. The third perspective, internal business process perspective, evaluates the entire process from design to after-sales service. The fourth perspective, learning and growth, focuses on employees and long-run performance. The advantage of using the balanced scorecard approach is that it allows the evaluator to determine if the unit is operating in a manner consistent with company values that are not directly measured by financial numbers. In addition to the financial measures, the balanced scorecard looks at the unit's ability to operate in the future, by evaluating the unit's potential for learning and growing—the internal processes—and by evaluating relationships with customers. The balanced scorecard approach rewards units that keep the long-run success of the entity in mind.

balance of trade. N. The total value of exports minus the total value of imports for a country.

balance sheet. N. A listing of the assets, liabilities, and equity of an entity at a point in time, usually the end of a month, quarter, or year. It is one of the four financial statements required in a full financial report. The balance sheet tells the reader what the entity owns (assets) and what the entity owes (liabilities) at that moment. The difference between the two is equity.

balance sheet account. N. Any account that is listed on the balance banker's acceptance sheet—an asset, liability, or equity.

While they may be part of a transaction involving a revenue or an expense, balance sheet accounts do not directly affect income the way a revenue or an expense does. Synonymous with *permanent account, real account.*

balance sheet equation. N. States that the total dollar value of the assets must equal the sum of the dollar value of liabilities plus the dollar value of equities. The balance sheet equation is the basis for double entry bookkeeping and underlies the "debits must equal credits" rule. Synonymous with *accounting equation.*

balloon payment. N. The final payment in a partially amortized loan. The balloon payment repays the entire remaining principal and is usually larger than previous payments on the loan. Loans that are set up with balloon payments allow the borrower to make the purchase and have a lower payment than if the loan were fully amortized. The borrower will often refinance the remaining loan rather than pay the balloon payment.

bank confirmation. N. A standard audit procedure in which the auditor requests information on account balances, loan terms, collateral, interest payments, etc., from the client's bank. The purpose of the procedure is to establish the existence of assets and liabilities and to verify the accuracy of expenses and revenues.

bank discount yield. N. The rate of return on treasury bills that is quoted in the financial papers. The bank discount yield is calculated as (selling price–par value) (360/days to maturity). For a six-month treasury bill, the days to maturity equal 182. This yield is lower than the effective annual rate on a six-month treasury bill, which is calculated as the difference between the par and the selling price divided by the selling price, and that result multiplied by two (((par–selling price)/selling price) x 2).

banker's acceptance. N. A security that starts as an instrument similar to a check, in which a customer asks the bank to pay the designated amount to a payee in the future. The bank accepts this order, becoming responsible for payment, because the customer actually has the money to back the check, and then that instrument can be sold by the holder to get the cash immediately. Because the bank has agreed to pay it—no matter what—the instrument is easier to sell than if it were simply a check written from a customer to the payee.

Bank for International Settlements. N. A bank that acts to promote international cooperation in monetary policy. The Bank for International Settlements is governed by an international board made up of eleven countries. It provides banking services for other banks internationally. www.bis.org.

bank holding company. N. A company that owns more than one bank. Bank holding companies are required to register with the Federal Reserve System.

bankmail. N. A strategy to achieve a takeover in which the company doing the takeover arranges agreements with banks that promise not to finance any other takeover.

bank overdrafts. N. The result of writing a check for more than the amount of cash in the checking account. Bank overdrafts are shown as current liabilities on the balance sheet.

bank reconciliation. N. A procedure for coming up with the true cash balance in a business. The monthly bank statement is compared to the records the company keeps, and totals rarely match. Like personal checking accounts, businesses have outstanding checks and deposits in transit. In the business environment, banks may collect debts for the business and automatically deposit the amount in the checking account. The notification of the collection is on the bank statement. The company adjusts the bank statement balance for deposits in transit, outstanding checks, and any errors the bank may have made. The company also adjusts the balance in the company records for any collections made by the bank, bank charges, automatic payments, interest earned, errors, or anything else that is not reflected in the company records. The two corrected cash balances have to be equal.

bankruptcy. N. A legal process that allows a debtor, either a business or a person, to eliminate some or all of the debt. The normal process involves selling assets and using the proceeds to pay off creditors in an order and/or in an amount determined by a judge. Some types of bankruptcy involve arranging a payment schedule, rather than selling the assets of the filer. Business bankruptcy happens when the amount of debt is greater than the market value of the assets of the business. Personal bankruptcy is an option for individuals or married couples unable to pay their debts. The bankruptcy laws do not allow individuals to have their debt discharged more often than every six years. See also *Chapter 7, Chapter 11, Chapter 13*.

bank transfer schedule. N. An audit procedure used to test for the existence of kiting. The auditor lists all transfers between company subunits that occur near the end of the year, noting the date of deposit and withdrawal and comparing it to the bank dates. The withdrawal dates should be in the same accounting period as the deposit dates, or in the accounting period before the deposit dates, to avoid double counting the cash.

Bardahl formula. N. A method of predicting the amount of working capital an organization needs for an operating cycle. The Bardahl formula first calculates an average operating cycle as a percentage of a year and then applies that to the sum of the cost of goods sold and the operating expenses for the year. The Bardahl formula is used to justify accumulated earnings and to avoid the accumulated earnings tax to which corporations are subjected.

bargain element. N. Used to determine the taxable amount of compensation when an employee exercises a stock option. The bargain element is the difference between the market value of a share of the stock and the strike price of the option.

bargain purchase. N. The acquisition of an asset for less than market value. Usually this happens when the seller is under pressure to raise cash and has to sell quickly, such as in a liquidation situation.

bargain-purchase-option test. N. One of the four capitalization criteria for leases. If a lease contains the opportunity for the lessee to buy the asset at the end of the lease for a price that is significantly lower than the market value, the lease is considered a capital lease, because it contains a bargain purchase option.

bargain renewal option. N. An extension of the lease by the lessee at a rental below market value. The effect is to structure a lease that is longer than it first appears. For example, if Company L is leasing a piece of equipment for $300 per month for two years, with the option to renew the lease for another two years at $25 per month, the lease is considered to be four years. Bargain renewal options are significant when applying the economic life test to determine if the lease is a capital lease.

barometer stock. N. See *bellwether*.

barren money. N. Funds available for investment because they are not currently earning interest or a return.

base-case NPV. N. The starting point for sensitivity analysis, in which the inputs are the values most likely to occur. Then, using sensitivity analysis, the input values are changed and compared to the base-case to see how sensitive the outcome is to those changes.

baseline budgeting. N. See *incremental budgeting*.

base salary. N. A component of a compensation package that occurs at regular intervals as payment for the employee's time and skills.

basic earning power. N. A financial analysis tool that measures the amount of earnings produced by assets without leverage or taxes. The formula is earnings before interest and taxes (EBIT) divided by total assets. EBIT is calculated from the income statement by taking the net income and adding the back taxes and interest expense. Total assets can be found on the balance sheet. ABBRV. *BEP*.

basic earnings per share. N. A financial statement analysis ratio that appears on the income statement. Basic earnings per share can be calculated using net income reduced preferred dividends, and dividing that result by the weighted-average number of common shares outstanding during the time period covered by the net income. See also *antidilutive earnings per share*.

basic research credit. N. A tax incentive to encourage businesses to engage in research activities. The basic research credit is a tax credit of 20% of the amount paid by the business to organizations doing basic research, such as universities.

basis. N. A tax term for identifying the cost used to determine capital gains or losses. The basis is the purchase price plus commissions and expenses necessary to get the asset in use. If the asset is received as a gift, the basis is whatever the donor's basis was. If the asset is inherited, the basis is the fair market value, on the date of death. The term "basis" is used because it often includes more than just the purchase price of the asset. Synonymous with *cost basis*.

basis adjustment. N. The increase or decrease in the balance sheet value of an asset or liability due gains or losses associated with a fair value hedge. A basis adjustment is required for fair value hedges and prohibited for cash flow hedges.

basis point. N. A measurement division of an interest rate. One basis point is .01% or one hundredth of a percent. If an interest rate is 4.62% and it goes up 5 basis points, the new rate is 4.67%.

basket purchase. N. The purchase of a number of different assets for one price. The purchase of a building usually includes some land. The purchase price is allocated between the land and the building based on their relative market values. Another example is a builder who buys acreage to divide into home sites. The lots are different sizes and the builder has to make a reasonable allocation of the cost to each lot. Synonymous with *lump-sum price*.

batch-level activities. N. Actions that are done for every batch of a product that an entity produces. Batch-level activities are distinct from unit-level, product-level, and facility-level activities. Activity-based costing systems identify the level of an activity to build homogeneous cost pools, because costs in a homogeneous pool must be associated with activities performed at the same level. Activities that use overhead costs in the same proportion can be combined into the pool rate. Examples of batch-level activities include setup of the assembly process and setup of the painting machines for a particular lot of custom-produced products.

bearer bonds. N. Bonds that pay interest to the person presenting the coupon or holding the bond. The bond can be sold without notifying the issuer, and ownership transfers with the delivery of the bond. Synonymous with *coupon bonds*.

bear market. N. Describes a stock market in which the stock prices are moving lower. The term "bear" comes from frontier bearskin jobbers, who sold bearskins before the bear had been caught. The connection to the market is through investors who are selling short, or betting that the price will go down. Contrast with a bull market, in which stock prices are moving higher.

beginning inventory. N. The value in dollars, and the number of units, that are in inventory at the beginning of the accounting period. Beginning inventory is used to calculate the cost of goods sold. The dollar amount is shown on the balance sheet for the previous year, and the units associated with that value are used for internal decision making.

Beige Book. N. The Federal Reserve Board report on economic conditions in the Federal Reserve regions. The report is published eight times per year and is released two weeks prior to the open market meeting. Analysts use the report to predict what action the Federal Reserve Board will take at its open market meeting.

bellwether. N. A descriptor for a stock or bond that is believed to provide a signal of future economic and market trends. The U.S. Treasury twenty-year bond is considered a bellwether of interest rate movements. The term is derived from the days when shepherds put a bell on a male sheep, a wether, during a storm or in the fog, and the sound of the bell led the way for the flock. Synonymous with *barometer stock*.

below the line. N. Items on the income statement that come after income from continuing operations. These are nonrecurring items such as discontinued operations, extraordinary items, and the cumulative effect of change in accounting principle. See also *nonrecurring items*.

benchmarking. N. A way to improve performance that investigates the way several different entities do the same activity and finds the best way to accomplish the activity. The best way then becomes the standard, or the benchmark, for all the entities.

benchmark test. N. The process of testing a new software program using actual data and comparing the results to the alternative software. The alternative can be new software or the organization's existing system. The test should examine the software's accuracy and efficiency.

beneficiaries. N. The recipients of the benefits of a trust or insurance policy.

Benford's law. A mathematical rule that identifies the frequency of numbers appearing in certain positions in strings of real life data. For example, in a list of account numbers, the digit 1 will appear in the first position about 30% of the time. The digit 2 will appear less than the digit 1, but more than numbers 3 through 9. Benford's law can be useful in detecting fraudulent accounting transactions. Synonymous with *first-digit law.*

BEP. ABBRV. Basic earning power.

bequest. N. See *legacy.*

best efforts offering. N. A type of contract with an investment bank for the sale of a new stock issue. A best efforts offering only requires that the investment bank do the best it can at selling the stock, with no guarantee of proceeds. The issuing company bears the risk of the sale. Contrast with a firm commitment offering, in which the investment bank actually buys the shares from the company, thereby guaranteeing the price and the sale of a specified number of shares.

best practices. N. See *benchmarking*.

Beta Alpha Psi. N. An honorary organization that invites the top accounting students at accredited business schools into membership. Membership is based on excellence in scholarship as evidenced by grades.

beta coefficient. N. A stock's risk measure that indicates how closely the individual stock's return follows the entire market's return. If the beta of a stock is one, then the stock price moves in the same direction and nearly the same magnitude as the entire stock market—or one of the market indices—and is considered a stock with average risk. If the beta of a stock is two, the individual stock is twice as risky as the average stock.

beta risk. N. See *risk of incorrect acceptance*.

betterments. N. See *improvements and replacements*.

bid-ask spread. N. The difference between the bid price and the ask price, or between how much a buyer of a stock is willing to pay and how much a seller of a stock is willing to sell for.

bid pooling. N. A type of fraud that occurs in a competitive bidding environment with a limited number of bidders. Bidders coordinate bids on different contracts so that each gets a contract. For example, if a company is soliciting bids for raw materials, the vendors can each agree to be the low bidder on one type of raw material, thereby guaranteeing that each gets part of the sales.

bid price. N. The highest price offered by the buyer of stock. The bid price is used to compute the spread. See also *spread*.

bid rigging. N. A general category of fraud that occurs in a competitive bidding environment and eliminates or reduces the competitive nature of the bidding process. Bid rigging can take several forms, such as bid pooling or bid splitting.

bid splitting. N. A type of fraud in which a large project is split into small parts so that the total dollar value of the part is below the threshold that requires competitive bidding. The result is that an employee can award the contract to a favored vendor rather than through the process that would produce the lowest or best price.

big bath. N. Taking huge, additional—not necessarily closely related—losses once the decision is made to take a loss. The logic is that the current accounting period is going to be bad because of the loss, so to save future negative amounts, as many losses as possible are taken in the current period. Some managers believe that investors do not use one-time charges in determining stock price. Arthur Levitt identified big bath restructuring charges as an earnings management device in 1998.

big board. N. See *New York Stock Exchange.*

Big Four. N. The largest certified public accountant firms in the world. The current Big Four include Deloitte & Touche, Ernst & Young, KPMG, and PricewaterhouseCoopers.

big GAAP versus little GAAP. N. The controversy that exists around the use of a single set of generally accepted accounting principles (GAAP) regardless of the size of the entity. The Financial Accounting Standards Board believes that accounting information is better if all companies use the same methods. Opponents believe that the cost of complex accounting for deferred taxes, leases, and pensions, for example, far outweighs any benefit received by small companies that do not have publicly traded stock.

bill-and-hold sale. N. A type of sale in which the selling company records the sale, includes the revenue in income, and increases accounts receivable on the balance sheet, but does not ship the goods until a later date. If legal title passes to the buyer at the time revenue is recorded, the sales are real. The problem is the timing of the revenue recognition. Bill-and-hold sales can represent next period's revenue that has been accelerated into the current period.

billing scheme. N. A type of fraud in which an invoice is used to steal from a company. The invoice can be altered or completely false. Billing schemes can be deterred by requiring purchase orders and receiving reports prior to the authorization for payment.

billings on construction-in-progress. N. A contra-inventory account used in the percentage-of-completion method of recognizing revenue on long-term contracts. This account is deducted from the construction-in-progress account.

bill of lading. N. A document used to keep track of goods transferred by a separate delivery service from one place to the next. When the goods are picked up, the delivery person gives the shipper a copy of the document that specifies what the goods to be delivered are, where they will be delivered, who will receive them, and when the delivery will take place.

bill of material. N. The itemized specification of all raw materials and parts needed to make a product. ABBRV. *BOM*.

bill of sale. N. A document that indicates the terms of a sale, including the transfer of title, the amount, the payment terms, and any warranties, return rights, or other conditions.

bird-in-the-hand theory. N. A theory that suggests that firms that pay high dividends will have higher stock prices because investors prefer dividends today versus gains in the future.

Black Friday. N. A historically significant day in the history of the stock market. Black Friday occurred on September 24, 1869, and the market crash led to an economic depression.

Black Monday. N. A historically significant day in the history of the stock market because of the huge decline, which, while devastating, did not lead to the deep depression that had followed such events in 1869 and 1929. Black Monday occurred on October 19, 1987, when the Dow Jones Industrial Average fell 22%.

blackout period. N. A defined time period in accounting for stock options. During the blackout period, the person granted the option is not allowed to exercise it. This usually occurs just after the granting of the stock options and allows the price of the stock to increase above the exercise price.

Black-Scholes Option Pricing Model. N. See *option pricing model*.

Black Tuesday. N. October 29, 1929, when stocks lost 13% of their value in one day. The economic effects were devastating, and the United States fell into the Great Depression.

blank check. N. A check that is signed by the account holder but no date, payee, or amount is filled in.

blank check offering. N. An initial public offering for a shell corporation that plans to invest the funds from the stock sale. Blank check offerings are subject to all Securities and Exchange Commission regulations for new stock issues, but have a reputation for being scams.

blanket purchase order. N. A contract that allows agents of a company to purchase predetermined items at specified prices over a period of time and eliminates the need for the preparation of new authorization forms for every order.

blind pool offering. N. An initial public offering for a shell corporation that plans to invest the funds from the stock sale in a specified project. Blind pool offerings allow small companies to finance large projects or acquisitions. Because the use of the funds is specified in the registration statements, blind pool offerings are not as risky as blank check offerings, which do not specify the purpose for which the funds will be used.

blockage rule. N. A term used in business valuation that discounts the value of large quantities of a single stock, because selling many shares in a short time pushes the market price down.

block trade. N. A large number of shares in one buy/sell transaction. A block trade involves at least ten thousand shares.

blue chips. N. The largest and most profitable companies over the long term. Blue chip stocks get their name from blue poker chips, which are the most valuable color chip. IBM is considered a blue chip company.

Blue Sky Laws. N. State laws that apply to any investments sold in the state. The actual company selling the security does not have to be located within the state, but the purchaser does.

board of directors. N. Representatives of interested parties or owners of an organization elected to govern the management of the organization. In a corporate setting, shareholders elect representatives to the board of directors. The board has the authority to set policies, declare dividends, and choose top management, plus other similar activities that guide the operations of the corporation.

Board of Examiners. N. A committee of the American Institute of Certified Public Accountants that has the responsibility for creating and grading the certified public accountant exam. The members of the board come from the accounting profession and from education.

boilerplate. N. A term used to describe typical language used in legal documents. Boilerplate is usually unvarying fine print that appears in contracts.

BOM. ABBRV. Bill of material.

bond. N. A financing instrument in which the borrower promises, in writing, to repay with interest the amount borrowed (on a specified schedule involving interest payments and the principal amount) at the end of the term of the bond. Bonds usually have a face value, or maturity value, of $1,000. The stated rate of interest, or coupon rate, determines the amount of the interest payment. See also *bonds payable*.

bond anticipation notes. N. A type of debt used by governments in which the government borrows against bonds it is planning to sell. Having the cash available allows the project to begin before all the bonds are sold. This is especially important in building projects where the climate affects the progress. The borrowing is repaid when the bonds are sold.

bond conversion. N. The term used to describe the process associated with convertible bonds. Bond conversion is the exchange of the bond for the number of shares of stock that the conversion feature specifies.

bond discount. N. See *discount on bonds payable*.

bond indenture. N. The contract that specifies the terms and acts as a promise to pay the principal and the interest at specified times.

bond issue costs. N. Costs such as printing, legal fees, accounting fees, promotion fees, and commissions that a company incurs when it decides to issue bonds. Consistent with the matching principle, these costs may be capitalized and will appear on the balance sheet as an asset in the other asset section. The asset is then amortized over the time the bonds are outstanding.

bonds issued at a discount. N. The sale of bonds when the stated rate is lower than the effective yield, resulting in a selling price that is lower than the maturity value.

bonds issued at a premium. N. The sale of bonds when the stated rate is higher than the effective yield, resulting in a selling price that is higher than the maturity value.

bonds issued at par. N. The sale of bonds when the effective yield is the same as the stated rate for the bond. The selling price equals the maturity value.

bonds payable. N. A form of long-term debt that appears in the liabilities section of the balance sheet. A company sells bonds as a way to borrow large amounts of cash. The buyer pays for the bond and receives regular interest payments, usually annually or semiannually, for the duration of the bond and receives the principal at the maturity date of the bond. This type of long-term debt allows more than one lender to hold part of the debt. Bonds are used when the amount needed by the borrower is too large for one lender to risk. Each bond, which normally has a maturity value of $1,000, represents a portion of the total debt. The bond agreement regarding repayment is called the bond indenture and specifies the terms that determine the repayment. See also *discount on bonds payable*, *premium on bonds payable*.

bond yield. N. The return received by the purchaser of a bond investment. The current yield equals the interest received annually divided by the market price of the bond. See also *yield to maturity*.

bond-yield-plus-risk-premium approach. N. A method for estimating the cost of using retained earnings to finance a project. The bond-yield-plus-risk-premium is equal to the rate a firm must pay on long-term debt plus 3–5 percentage points. See also *cost of equity*.

book. V. To record a journal entry, as in "book an expense."

book an expense. V. See *capitalize*.

book balance. N. The amount shown in the accounting records or on the balance sheet for a particular account. The book balance is used specifically in the bank reconciliation and compared to the balance on the bank statement. The book balance is the amount according to the accounting records and is almost never the same as the bank statement amount, because of outstanding checks and deposits in transit.

book capital accounts. N. The tax terminology used by Subchapter K regulations to identify the partners' capital accounts. Normally when "book" is applied to an account title, it means whatever shows up on the financial statements using generally accepted accounting principles. In this case, it is the account balance applying the tax rules for capital accounts.

book income. N. A company's income calculated using generally accepted accounting principles (GAAP) and appearing on the income statement. The term "book income" is usually used to distinguish it from other income numbers. Other income numbers include taxable income, which is based on Internal Revenue Service code, and pro forma income, which is calculated according to shifting rules. Pro forma income usually excludes some expenses and losses that must be included according to GAAP. See also *pro forma financial statements, taxable income*. Synonymous with *net income*.

bookkeeping. N. The process of recording business transactions in the journals and ledgers of the business. Bookkeeping is the procedural basis of accounting.

book tax rate. N. See *effective tax rate*.

book value. N. The dollar amount recorded on the balance sheet for an asset, liability, or equity. Subtract the accumulated depreciation from the historical cost to get the book value of an asset. Adjust the maturity value of the liability for any discount or premium to calculate the book value of a liability. The book value of a liability is usually the amount of cash required to pay off the obligation at that point in time, and the amount at which the asset or liability is "carried on the books." The book value of an asset represents the cost of the asset that has not been put on the income statement as an expense. Synonymous with *carrying value*.

book-value method of accounting for convertible debt. N. The stock is recorded at the book value of the debt. The convertible debt is removed at the book value, the number of shares times par is added to the stock account, and the remaining amount is plugged into additional paid in capital. Contrast with the market value, in which the new stock is recorded at the market value of the new shares, and any difference between that amount and the book value of the debt is a gain or loss.

book value per share. N. A financial ratio that is calculated as common stockholders' equity divided by the number of outstanding shares. Common stockholders' equity is the total stockholders' equity less the par value of any preferred stock. This ratio is refined further if preferred stock is redeemable, has dividends in arrears, or has a participating feature. In those cases, part of retained earnings is deducted so that the equity really represents that which is available to common shareholders.

boot. N. The amount of cash, or another monetary asset, involved in an exchange of assets. If Company A gives Company B $1,000 plus a 2000 pickup truck, and Company B gives Company A a 2002 pickup truck, the boot is the $1,000. Boot is significant in the accounting treatment of the transaction because it may signal a gain or loss on the trade.

borrowing base. N. Current assets that serve as collateral for short-term borrowing.

bottlenecks. N. The part of the production process that is at capacity. The bottleneck affects the speed of all subsequent processes.

bottom line. N. See *net income*.

bounced check. N. A check that is not paid because the account holder does not have sufficient funds deposited. The check is then returned to the payee as unpaid. Synonymous with *rubber check*.

bracket creep. N. Moving into a higher tax bracket because of inflation rather than because of higher earnings.

break-even point. N. The operating level at which the total sales revenue equals the total cost. Total sales revenue is equal to the price per unit times the number of units sold. Total cost equals the total variable cost, the number of units sold times the variable cost per unit, plus the total fixed cost. Break-even can be calculated either in terms of units sold or the sales revenue. To find the break-even in units, divide fixed costs by the contribution margin per unit. To find the break-even sales revenue, divide the fixed cost by the contribution margin ratio.

bridge loan. N. Short-term borrowing that will be paid back quickly when long-term financing is available. The short-term loan "bridges" the time between when the funds are needed and when the final long-term financing process is completed. Synonymous with *swing loan*.

brokerage fee. N. The amount charged by a professional who acts as an intermediary between buyers and sellers. The brokerage fee is usually a percentage of the transaction total, called a commission.

broker-assisted cashless exercise. N. A technique that allows the holder of a stock option to receive the difference between the exercise price and the market price, net of any taxes, without actually using cash to initially exercise the options. The transaction involves coordinating the exercise of the option with the sale of the shares obtained in the exercise. This is useful for the person exercising the option because it requires no cash outlay.

brother-sister group. N. A type of controlled group of corporations with significant overlap of ownership. A brother-sister group has five or fewer shareholders who own 80% or more of the stock value or voting power in both corporations. The sum of the lowest percentages of ownership for each owner in either corporation must exceed 50%. The definition of a brother-sister group is used for tax purposes to designate maximum income amounts within brackets and to limit certain benefits. If Steve owns 25% of B and 50% of G, Tim owns 40% of B and 20% of G, Aaron owns 35% of B and 10% of G, and Amy owns 0% of B and 20% of G, B and G can be considered a brother-sister group, by virtue of meeting both ownership tests. First, five or fewer shareholders have 80% of the stock in both corporations. Second, Steve's lowest percentage of ownership is 25%, Tim's is 20%, Aaron's is 10%, and Amy's is 0%. The lowest percentages of ownership totaled equal 55%, which exceeds the minimum of 50%.

B shares. N. A class of mutual fund shares that are available to anyone and are back-end loaded, carrying a charge at the time the shares are sold. The "B" indicates the class of shares. Contrast with A shares, which are front-end loaded.

budget. N. A financial plan for a future period of time. The budgeting process translates the strategic plan for an entity into financial terms and identifies the steps for achieving the goals of the plan.

budgetary accounts. N. Accounts used in governmental accounting to record the budget amounts, but not the actual amounts. For example, at the beginning of the accounting period, the planned amounts of tax revenue, revenue from licenses, and inflows from fines would be recorded as one amount in the budgetary account for estimated revenues of a city. During the accounting period, no other entries would be made to the budgetary account for estimated or real revenues. Then, at the end of the accounting period, the budget entry would be reversed. Each budgetary account has subsidiary accounts associated with it. The estimated revenue budgetary account may have subsidiary accounts that identify the individual sources of the revenues by type, such as property taxes, fines, licenses, etc. The budget amount is entered in the subsidiary accounts with a debit. The actual cash collections are entered as a credit in the subsidiary accounts, with the debit for the total to cash. The budget (the debit amount) is easily compared with the actual (the credit amount) at any point in time.

budgetary entry. N. The journal entry made in governmental accounting to record the budget amounts in the budgetary accounts and the subsidiary accounts. This entry is made once, at the beginning of the accounting period. The budgeted amount of estimated revenues is entered in the control account with a debit, and into the subsidiary accounts—each type of revenue—with a credit. The budgeted amount of estimated expenditures is entered in the control account with a credit.

budgetary slack. N. A problem in participative budgeting in which managers set revenue targets too low (therefore ensuring that they will meet the budget) or set cost targets too high (making it easy to stay within the budgeted costs).

budgeted balance sheet. N. The part of the master budget that projects what the balance sheet will look like at the end of the year if activities go as planned in the budget. Synonymous with *projected balance sheet*.

budgeted income statement. N. The part of the master budget that uses information from other budgets to prepare an estimate of operating income. For example, the sales revenue amount is taken from the sales budget.

budget for capital expenditures. N. The part of the master budget that identifies asset acquisitions.

budget variance. N. The difference between the actual result and the budgeted amount. The budget variance can be further analyzed to look at the components of the variance, such as price differences, variations in volume produced from the budgeted volume, and differences in quantity used from the budgeted amount for a given level of production.

buffer. N. A holding area for computer information that adjusts for different speeds of processing. When running a video or audio file from the Internet, the delay between the click on the link to show the video or audio file and the beginning of the picture or sound exists because the buffer is filling with enough information for the viewing computer to process into a picture or sound.

buffer stock. N. See *safety stock*.

built-in gain or loss. N. Related to allocations in partnerships when a partner has contributed property with a fair market value different from the partner's basis (cost minus tax deductions taken to date). The built-in gain or loss is the difference between the fair market value and the partner's basis.

built-in gains tax. N. Levied on S corporations that have not always been S corporations. The built-in gains tax is 35% of some built-in gains and is paid at the entity level. This tax is considered a sting tax because it is painful to the entity.

bullet dodging. N. The setting of a grant date for a stock option just after a planned announcement of bad news. The result is option grants that are more favorable to the grantees.

bull market. N. A stock market in which the stock prices are moving higher, which is the opposite of a bear market. The term "bull" comes from the frontier practice of baiting bears with bulls.

bundled product. N. Several items of merchandise or several services that are sold separately, but are also sold as a package of products or services. Las Vegas resorts sell vacation packages including airfare, hotel rooms, meal coupons, show tickets, and car rentals. You can buy these things separately, but the combination package is almost always cheaper.

burn rate. N. See *cash burn rate*.

business combinations. N. A method of expanding or growing a corporation quickly. A business combination is the union of two or more companies through a merger, consolidation, or acquisition. All the assets of one entity are acquired by another.

business cycle. N. A repeating pattern of economic conditions. The cycle moves from a peak in the economy, through a downturn, through a recession, to a low point, and then continually improves through a recovery to a new peak.

business energy credit. N. A type of general business credit that rewards businesses that invest in energy-conserving devices or building improvements. The tax credit is equal to 10% of the costs. The business energy credit is one of several general business credits, and the total of all these credits cannot be more than an amount based on the net income for the year. The amount of excess can be carried back one year and forward twenty years.

business meal expense. N. A tax deduction that is deductible for adjusted gross income if the taxpayer is self-employed, and is deducted from adjusted gross income if the taxpayer is an employee and the expense is not reimbursed. For the employee, the business meal expense deduction is part of the miscellaneous itemized deduction. The business meal must be directly related to business activities and only 50% is deductible. Complete documentation is required. An easy way to document business meal expenses is to write the discussion items and participants on the back of the receipt.

business plan. N. A formal document prepared by company managers indicating the current and proposed activities of the company, with the purpose of obtaining additional financing.

business processes. N. A group of action steps related to a business activity. For example, the payroll process consists of the steps of collecting timecards, recording earnings, preparing and distributing checks, and completing the government reporting for employees.

business-purpose doctrine. N. A doctrine that requires a real business reason for the existence of transactions that provide for tax savings. The sole purpose of the transaction cannot be the avoidance of taxes.

business reengineering. N. See *process improvement*.

business risk. N. The sources of possible losses, dangers, or hazards to a business. In addition to theft, businesses are at risk from poor planning and bad decisions.

business-to-business commerce. N. See *b2b*.

business-to-consumer commerce. N. See *b2c*.

bustout. N. A bankruptcy that is planned in advance. The fraudster takes on a large amount of debt, hides the proceeds, and then files bankruptcy, relieving him- or herself of the obligation to repay the debt.

buyback. N. A company's purchase of its own stocks or bonds. See also *treasury stock*.

buyback agreements. N. See *sales with buyback agreements*.

buying on margin. N. Using a margin account to buy stock. See *margin account*.

buying power. N. See *purchasing power*.

buy-sell agreement for stock. N. A restriction on the ability of a shareholder to sell an equity interest that is usually associated with closely held corporations.

buy-sell agreements. N. See *sales with buyback agreements*.

bypass trust. N. A type of trust designed to distribute property to children without going through the estate. Synonymous with *credit shelter trust*.

by-product. N. An item that is part of the production process and is produced along with a main product, but has a low selling price compared to the main product. A by-product is rarely produced without the main product. For example, turkey processing produces several high-value products: whole turkeys, breasts, drumsticks, etc. A by-product of the process is taking all the leftover bits of the turkey carcass and producing poultry meal, an animal feed.

byte. N. A unit of computer storage. One byte is one character: a letter, number, or symbol. A kilobyte, abbreviated KB, is about a thousand bytes. A megabyte, abbreviated MB or called a meg, is about a million bytes.

C

C2C. ABBRV. Cash to cash.

CA. ABBRV. Chartered accountant.

CAATs. ABBRV. Computer-assisted audit techniques.

cafeteria plan. N. A type of fringe benefit for employees that allows the employees to choose between receiving cash or a type of nontaxable fringe benefit. If an employee chooses the cash, then the cash is included in gross income. If an employee chooses the fringe benefit, then the amount is not included in gross income. Medical expense accounts are a common example of a fringe benefit included in cafeteria plans. The employee agrees to have an amount put into a medical expense account and then uses that account to pay medical expenses. The employee does not pay taxes on that amount, but cannot deduct the medical payments on the tax return. Often, if the employee does not spend all the dollars in the account by the end of the year, those dollars are lost. Synonymous with *flexible spending account*.

callable bonds. N. Bonds that allow the issuer, i.e., the debtor, to retire the bonds before they mature. If the issuer calls the bond, the holder of the bond must sell it to the issuer, usually for a predetermined price that is higher than the par value. The additional amount is the call premium. The call provision of the bond contract specifies the details of the redemption. Most callable bonds have a deferred call, meaning the call provision is not enforceable for several years after the sale. Synonymous with *redeemable bonds*.

callable preferred stock. N. Preferred stock that allows the issuing company to buy back the security at a set price and a designated time. The buy-back price is usually higher than the original selling price of the preferred stock. Because callable preferred stock has characteristics similar to debt, not equity, companies selling callable preferred stock should not include it in stockholders' equity, but rather should put it just before that section on the balance sheet. Synonymous with *redeemable preferred stock*.

call feature. N. See *call provision*.

call option. N. A contract giving the right to buy a specified quantity of an asset at a specified date, or during a specified time period, for a specified price. A call option is not an obligation to buy, but gives the opportunity to do so. Contrast with a put option, which is the right, but not the obligation, to sell a specified quantity of an asset at a specified date, or during a specified time period, for a specified price.

call premium. N. The difference between the maturity value and the price a company must pay when it redeems a security before the maturity date. Bonds and preferred stock may be callable, meaning that the issuing company has the right to buy back the security. The price to redeem is usually more than the maturity value of a bond and more than the par value of the preferred stock. The excess over the maturity value or the par value is the call premium.

call price. N. The specified price at which the issuer will buy back the callable, or redeemable, preferred stock or bond. The call price is usually higher than the original selling price of the instrument. The result of setting a call price, though, is to limit the upper end of the selling price to an amount less than the call price.

call provision. N. The characteristic of a bond that allows the issuer to buy back the bond. See also *callable bonds*, *callable preferred stock*. Synonymous with *call feature*.

canceled check. N. A check that has been cashed by the payee and returned to the bank on which it was drawn. The writer had funds to cover the check, and they were transferred to the payee's bank. The writer of the check may receive the actual check with an indication that it has been cashed, may receive a photocopy of it, or may have to request a copy if proof of payment is needed.

canned software. N. Computer application programs that are not custom products developed specifically for a company. The company instead buys a program that is already written and adjusts its information system to work with the software. Contrast with custom software, in which a business contracts with a programmer or a consulting firm to develop computer software specifically designed for the needs of the business and the existing information system.

cannibalization. N. The reduction in sales of an existing product by the introduction of a new product from the same company. IBM did not fully develop its personal computer because it feared that the personal computer would take sales from the main frame business.

CAO. ABBRV. Chief accounting officer.

CAP. ABBRV. Committee on Accounting Procedure.

capital. N. Cash or other types of funds available for use in business.

capital account. N. An account used in a partnership to record an individual partner's investment in the partnership plus the individual's share of any undistributed partnership income. In a corporation, the equity section has two parts: the contributed capital, which is the amount of shareholder investment, and the retained earnings, which is the undisturbed income of the firm. In a partnership, the equity section has a capital account for each partner that combines that partner's investment and share of undistributed income.

capital-account maintenance rules. N. The regulations for computing partners' capital accounts. Generally, capital accounts are increased by the partner's share of partnership revenues and gains, and decreased by the partner's share of expenses, losses, and distributions.

capital asset. N. Another term for "fixed asset," which is anything that is used in the production process or in the generation of revenues, but is not itself sold. Inventory is not a capital asset, but machinery used in producing a product is.

capital-asset pricing model. N. A model based on the idea that any stock's rate of return is the sum of the return on a risk-free investment plus a premium that represents the risk that cannot be diversified away. ABBRV. *CAPM*.

capital budgeting. N. Plans made by a firm for investing in assets that will provide cash flow over future years. Capital budgeting involves the analysis of the cost of capital and the expected return from the investment to determine which assets will provide the best investment. The word "capital" means the assets used in production.

capital components. N. The ways in which a firm finances the acquisition of assets. Capital components are various types of liabilities or stock.

capital expenditure. N. Expenditure that increases the dollar amount of fixed assets on the balance sheet. These outlays either add additional assets or increase the value of assets already owned. The payments increase the future benefits of an asset by extending the life of the asset, increasing productivity, or increasing quality. If the payment does this, then the cost is recorded as an asset rather than as an expense. Capital expenditures do not reduce income all at once. Instead, the cost is allocated through depreciation expense over the time the asset is used to produce revenues. See also *revenue expenditure*.

capital flight. N. The movement of investment dollars between investment opportunities. Investors sell one investment and buy another, looking for a lower risk and better returns. Capital flight can occur between countries, so countries with risky political conditions or unstable economies may experience capital flight.

capital gain. N. The increase in value that the owner of a capital asset receives when the asset is sold. The owner pays taxes on that increase, or gain, at a lower rate if the assets that are sold are capital assets, such as factory buildings, rather than assets that are sold in the normal course of business, such as inventory. Capital gains are usually associated with the sale of investments or property used for personal reasons, such as cars or houses. If the asset was held for more than one year, the gain is a long-term capital gain, and the tax rate is 20%, or 10% if the taxpayer is in a low tax bracket. If the asset was held for less than one year, the gain is taxed like ordinary income.

capital gain dividends. N. Distributions from a mutual fund that result from the fund selling investments. Capital gain dividends are considered long-term.

capital-gain property. N. A tax term used to describe a type of property donated to a charity. Capital-gain property is property the owner-donor has owned for more than one year and sold outright, which results in a capital gain. If capital-gain property is donated to a public charity, the value is its fair market value. If it is donated to a private nonoperating foundation, the value is the adjusted basis, usually the original purchase price. Contrast with ordinary-income property, which, if sold, results in income included in the owner-donor's ordinary income.

capital in excess of par. N. See *additional paid in capital.*

capital-intensity ratio. N. A financial ratio that represents the dollar amount of assets required to generate one dollar in sales. The formula for the capital-intensity ratio is the assets directly used to generate sales divided by the sales. The capital-intensity ratio reflects the business's need for financing. Companies with high capital-intensity ratios (i.e., companies needing many assets to produce one dollar of sales) will need more financing in order to acquire additional assets to support increased sales.

capitalization criteria for leases. N. The standards for determining if a lease is a capital lease or an operating lease. If none of the criteria are met, then the lease is an operating lease. If the terms of the lease contract meet one of the four standards, then the lease is a capital lease. A capital lease requires the lessee to record the asset and a liability for the lease on the balance sheet. The four criteria are transfer-of-ownership test, bargain-purchase-option test, economic-life test, and recovery-of-investment test. Even if the transaction is called a lease, if the contract meets one of these criteria, the lessee and lessor must treat it just like a purchase or sale. See also *transfer-of-ownership test, economic-life test, bargain-purchase-option test, recovery-of-investment test.*

capitalize. V. To increase an asset—rather than to reduce income—through an expense, for the entire amount of the expenditure. This is done correctly when the purchased item will be used for more than one year. The entire cost of a factory building should not reduce income in the year of purchase, but should be capitalized and the cost spread out over the years that the factory is used. Because this results in smoother, more predictable income, companies may try to capitalize things with questionable future value. Only material amounts are capitalized, and companies will have a policy that identifies the minimum dollar amount of capitalization. Synonymous with *book an expense.*

capitalized expenses. N. Expenditures that are recorded as an asset.

capitalize earnings. V. To transfer amounts from retained earnings to contributed capital through stock dividends. The effect is to decrease retained earnings and increase the stock accounts. Stock dividends also permanently retain the earnings in the corporation by moving it out of the retained earnings account—which is used for dividend payments—and into the contributed capital section of the balance sheet. To reduce contributed capital, the corporation would have to declare liquidating dividends.

capital lease. N. A lease that is treated like a purchase of an asset even if it is called a lease. If the lease requirements meet one of four criteria, then the company leasing the asset must account for it just like a purchase. The following are the four criteria: (a) the title to the asset transfers to the lessee at the end of the lease; (b) the lessee can exercise a bargain purchase option at the end of the lease; (c) the lease term is equal to or greater than 75% of the useful life of the asset; and, (d) the present value of the lease payments is equal to or greater than 90% of the cash selling price of the asset (at the time the lease is made). If the lease meets any one of these criteria, the lessee must record the asset and the lease liability on the balance sheet. See also *operating lease.* Synonymous with *financial lease.*

capital loss. N. The decrease in the value of a capital asset that the owner of the asset realizes when the asset is sold. The owner can deduct up to $3,000 per year in capital loss. If the loss is greater than that, it is carried forward to future years. Capital gains are usually associated with the sale of investments or property used for personal reasons, such as cars or houses.

capital maintenance. N. A method of calculating income that subtracts net assets at the beginning of the accounting period from net assets at the end of the accounting period and then adjusts that amount for dividends and additional owner investment. While this method can use any measure of net assets—not just historical cost—it provides only an amount. No information on the elements or sources is possible.

capital markets. N. A physical or virtual location in which entities seek funds through borrowing—with a duration longer than one year—or through the sale of stock. Contrast with money markets, in which the funds are only from borrowing and the length of the debt contract is less than one year.

capital projects fund. N. The part of governmental funds that accounts for service activities to citizens. The capital projects fund accounts for the acquisition of land, buildings, equipment, or other major facilities. The acquisition may be through purchase or construction. Once the asset is in service, it is transferred to either the general fixed assets account group or to a proprietary fund.

capital rationing. N. Circumstances that make it impossible for a firm to undertake all profitable projects because of an inability to obtain the necessary financing, either through debt or equity. Start-up companies, small firms, and firms with a weak credit history have to allocate capital to the best projects, requiring careful analysis.

capital recovery. N. Another term for the depreciation deduction on the tax return.

capital stock. N. A general term referring to all the stock, both common and preferred, of a corporation.

capital structure. N. The way assets are financed as evidenced by the balance sheet. Capital structure is made up of the liabilities and equity of a company. The mixture of the two components is the capital structure of a company. See also *simple capital structure, complex capital structure.*

capital surplus. N. Another name for additional paid in capital, an equity account on the balance sheet. The use of the term "surplus" is declining, probably because it is not as descriptive and implies that the amount is extra and not really necessary.

CAPM. ABBRV. Capital-asset pricing model.

carried interest. N. Compensation taken by investment fund managers that was previously taxed as capital gains at a lower rate than ordinary earned income. Federal legislation to change this situation is in progress.

carryback loss. N. On the income statement, the dollar amount of a net loss that the company can use to offset past taxable income. The loss offsets taxable income from previous years and results in a tax refund for taxes paid in those years. See also *income-tax-refund receivable.* Synonymous with *loss carryback.*

carryforward loss. N. On the income statement, the dollar amount of a net loss that the company can use to offset future taxable income. Because it will reduce a company's tax payments in the future, it appears on the balance sheet as an asset. A carryforward loss is useful only if the company anticipates having income to offset, and it expires after a period of time determined by the tax laws. This is similar to carryback loss, in which the loss offsets taxable income from previous years and results in a tax refund for taxes paid in those years. See also *carryback loss.* Synonymous with *loss carryforward.*

carrying costs. N. An inventory cost when materials are available prior to sale or use in production. Carrying costs include insurance, handling costs, storage costs, the opportunity cost of funds tied up in inventory, and spoilage.

carrying value. N. See *book value*.

carryover basis. N. The value of an asset received in exchange for a corporation's stock that equals the original owner's basis plus any gain that the original owner recognized when receiving the stock.

cartel. N. An organization made up of sellers that tries to regulate the prices of a good through restricted production and/or price fixing. For example, the Organization of Petroleum Exporting Countries is a cartel.

carve-out. V. Raising capital by selling shares in a subsidiary, but still maintaining control of the subsidiary by limiting the number of shares to a minority interest.

cash balance pension plan. N. A type of defined-benefit pension plan that promises the employee a certain contribution to a pension account and guarantees a certain return on that account. The total pension benefit is stated as a total account balance. Often cash balance pension plans allow either a lump sum payout or an annuity at retirement.

cash basis. N. A method of determining the performance of an entity by defining revenues as being earned and included in income when the cash is received, and expenses as included when the cash is paid. This method distorts performance, because a company can just avoid including expenses by delaying the payment of bills.

cash budget. N. A plan for the cash coming into and going out of a business. Based on the sales forecast, management budgets the timing and amounts of cash receipts. Based on forecasts of resources necessary to meet the sales forecast, management budgets the cash disbursements. This process identifies periods of excess cash or insufficient cash and allows management to budget for the short-term investing of idle cash or for short-term financing. Usually a cash budget is part of a master budget.

cash burn rate. N. A ratio used to measure the rate of negative cash flow, often associated with Internet companies. A formula for calculating the burn rate is the cash used by operations (found on the statement of cash flows), plus the net cash used for capital investments and business acquisitions, divided by the number of months the statement of cash flows covers. Another way to calculate the cash burn rate is to divide earnings (loss)—before interest, taxes, depreciation, amortization, and nonrecurring gains and losses—by the months covered by the income statement. Synonymous with *burn rate*.

cash conversion cycle. N. An estimate of the time between cash outflows and inflows. The cash conversion cycle is the sum of the time it takes to manufacture products and sell them and the time it takes to collect the cash from sales, less the amount of time that the company uses before paying for material and labor purchases. Stated another way, the cash conversion cycle equals the average days to sell inventory plus the average days to collect receivables, less the payables deferral period. The shorter the cash conversion cycle, the less financing the company will have to use (resulting in less interest expense).

cash coverage of debt. N. A financial analysis tool that measures if the company's operating cash flow is able to meet long-term obligations. The formula is cash flows from operating activities divided by noncurrent liabilities. A higher ratio is better.

cash coverage of growth. N. A financial analysis tool that measures the need for financing. The formula is the cash flow from operating activities divided by the cash paid for long-term assets. Cash paid for long-term assets can be found on the statement of cash flows, in the investing-activities section. A low ratio indicates a need for additional financing for more growth. A high ratio indicates that cash flows are adequate, but it can also suggest that opportunities for growth are limited.

cash cow. N. A part of a company's operations that consistently provides cash but operates in an area that has little opportunity for growth.

cash-debt coverage. N. A financial analysis ratio that indicates the long-term solvency of a company. The formula is the net cash from operating activities divided by the average total liabilities.

cash disbursements. N. Payments made within a business. Cash disbursements may be to suppliers, employees, creditors, or any other payees. The controls in this function are important to protect the cash of the organization.

cash-disbursements journal. N. A journal that contains a chronological record of all cash payments made by a company. See also *journal*.

cash discounts. N. See *sales discounts*.

cash equivalents. N. Items that can be turned into cash very quickly. On the balance sheet and statement of cash flows, it usually means investments such as treasury bills or money market funds, which can quickly be sold for their cash value. Cash equivalents do not include accounts receivable.

cash flow. N. Actual dollars that are received by an organization or paid out by an organization. Cash flow is the difference between the inflows and outflows. In capital budgeting, the cash flows are the dollar amounts coming in and going out that relate to the project. If the net cash flows are negative, that means more cash is going out than is coming in, a sign of financial distress.

cash flow adequacy ratio. N. A financial analysis tool for evaluating if a business is a cash cow. The formula is cash from operating activities divided by cash used by investing activities.

cash-flow hedge. N. A type of hedge that covers the risk of unfavorable future cash flows due to an existing asset or liability. For example, if a frozen-food processor knows that a given quantity of corn is needed to meet the production budget, the company is at risk for increased prices for the corn because weather problems might occur. To hedge this risk, the company could buy an option to buy a specified quantity at a specified price in the future. With the price established, the company has covered the risk of increased prices for the corn.

cash flow per share. N. A financial analysis ratio equal to cash from operating activities divided by common shares outstanding.

cash flows from financing activities. N. A section on the statement of cash flows. Cash flows from financing activities are those that increase or decrease noncurrent liabilities or stockholders' equity accounts. Borrowing and repaying funds, transactions involving the stock accounts, and the payment of dividends are examples of financing activities.

cash flows from investing activities. N. A section on the statement of cash flows. Cash flows from investing activities are those that increase or decrease noncurrent assets. Cash purchases and sales of investments; purchases and sales of property, plants, and equipment; and, the loaning of funds and receiving of repayments are examples of investing activities.

cash flows from operating activities. N. The first section of the statement of cash flows. Cash flows from operating activities include transactions (involving cash) that relate to the normal business activities of the entity. Cash flows in this section usually involve cash and other current asset or current liability accounts. Examples include cash received from cash sales, cash paid to employees for wages and salaries, and cash paid to suppliers for inventory.

cash-flow statement. N. See *statement of cash flows.*

cash flow to assets. N. A financial analysis tool (similar to return on assets) that measures the cash generated by assets. The formula is cash flow from operating activities divided by total assets.

cash flow to net income ratio. N. A financial analysis tool that evaluates the effect of accrual adjustments on income. Usually greater than one.

cash flow to sales. N. A financial analysis tool that measures how well sales generate cash. A higher ratio is better. The formula is cash flow from operating activities divided by net sales.

cash-flow yield. N. A financial analysis tool that measures cash flow as a percentage of net income. The formula is cash from operating activities divided by net income.

cashier's check. N. A check that a bank writes from its own account.

cash larceny. N. Fraud that steals cash after it has been recorded in the accounting records of the company. Taking money from a cash register is an example of cash larceny.

cash merger. N. A business combination in which the acquiring corporation buys all the assets of the target, recording them at fair market value. The target is absorbed into the acquiring corporation, and has gains on the sales of the assets that appear on its last tax return. In addition, the target shareholders—who receive the distributions from the liquidation—must pay tax on the difference between their original investment and the amount of the distribution. A cash merger results in double taxation.

cash on delivery. N. The terms of sale in which the buyer must have cash or a certified check to pay for the goods when they are delivered. ABBRV. *COD*.

cash out. V. To liquidate an item or items of value for cash or to distribute the cash amounts that are in an account.

cash overdraft. N. See *bank overdrafts*.

cash-payments journal. N. See *cash-disbursements journal*.

cash-receipts journal. N. A journal that contains a chronological record of all cash received by the company. See also *journal*.

cash sale. N. An exchange transaction between two parties in which one party gives the other cash in return for the immediate receipt of a valuable good or service.

cash shortage/overage. N. An income statement item that represents the difference between the actual cash amount and an accounting measure of how much cash there should be. The most common example exists in a retail situation where the cash in the cash register is compared to the register tape. Any difference is entered in the cash shortage/overage account, and that account appears on the income statement.

cash surrender value. N. The amount of cash that would be received if a life insurance policy were canceled before the death of the insured (or before maturity if the policy is a whole-life type). The cash surrender value appears on the balance sheet as a noncurrent asset if the company has life insurance on the top executives.

cash times interest earned ratio. N. A financial analysis tool that indicates the interest payment ability of an entity. The formula is the sum of cash from operations plus cash paid for taxes plus cash paid for interest divided by cash paid for interest.

cash to cash. N. A financial tool for analyzing how efficiently a company is using cash. It calculates the number of days cash is in the cash conversion cycle. ABBRV. *C2C*.

casualty loss. N. A loss of personal-use property that is caused by an identifiable event such as a fire, storm, earthquake, or theft. Lost items are not included, since they do not represent an identifiable event. The amount of a casualty loss is measured as the difference between the fair market value, right before and right after the identifiable event. If the property is completely destroyed, then the loss is limited to the basis or original cost of the property. The portion of the loss that is deductible on the tax return is limited to the portion over and above insurance proceeds.

cause-and-effect diagram. N. Used to investigate quality problems after a Pareto diagram finds the most common defect. A cause-and-effect diagram is used to identify the causes of the major quality problem. The causes may be human-related, machine-related, design-related, or material-related.

CBOT. ABBRV. Chicago Board of Trade.

C corporation. A type of corporation whose income is taxed through the corporation rather than the corporation's individual shareholders under subchapter C of the Internal Revenue Code.

CD. ABBRV. Certificate of deposit.

CDE. ABBRV. Community development entities.

ceiling. N. The maximum price or value. See also *lower of cost or market*.

cell. N. A location in a software spreadsheet. A cell is identified by a letter and a number indicating the column and the row of the sheet where the cell is located.

central bank. N. Another name for the Federal Reserve System of the United States, which is the organization that has the responsibility for the monetary policy. The "central bank" can refer to the analogous agency in any country.

Central Index Key. N. A unique number assigned to a company by the Securities and Exchange Commission. ABBRV. *CIK*.

centralized decision making. N. The practice of having plans and actions decided by the top-level executives of an organization, with managers implementing the decisions made above them.

central processing unit. N. The part of a computer that does the calculations, sorting, classifying, or other processes and stores the data and programs. The two main parts of the central processing unit are the RAM and the microprocessor. The data and programs are stored in the RAM and the microprocessor does the calculations, sorting, and classifying of the data. Usually this part of the computer is not visible like the monitor and keyboard, but is instead housed in a case that also holds disk drives. ABBRV. *CPU*.

CEO. ABBRV. Chief executive officer.

certificate authority. N. A third party that verifies the identity of a participant to electronic commerce through a digital certificate.

certificate of deposit. N. A type of debt security investment in which cash is tied up for a specified period of time and an early withdrawal is penalized. Certificates of deposit, available from banks, are low-risk and low-return investments that mature in short and medium time frames. ABBRV. *CD*.

certified check. N. A check drawn on an account holder's account with payment guaranteed by the bank.

certified financial planner. N. A professional certification awarded by the Certified Financial Planner Board of Standards to individuals meeting experience, education, ethics, and examination requirements. Certified financial planners help individuals and organizations analyze investment and savings options to prepare for their financial needs. www.cfp.net. ABBRV. *CFP*.

certified fraud examiner. N. A certification awarded by the Association of Certified Fraud Examiners upon the passing of a two-day exam. Certified fraud examiners are instrumental in uncovering white-collar crime. ABBRV. *CFE*.

certified information systems auditor. N. A certification awarded by the Information Systems Audit and Control Association. To receive the certification, the candidate must pass an exam and meet an experience requirement. ABBRV. *CISA*.

certified information technology professional. N. A certification awarded by the American Institute of Certified Public Accountants to certified public accountants who pass an additional examination on information-systems strategy, implementation, and management. Certified information technology professionals must also meet an experience requirement and take continuing professional education to keep the designation. ABBRV. *CITP*.

certified internal auditor. N. A certification awarded by the Institute of Internal Auditors to individuals who have passed an exam and have met experience qualifications. ABBRV. *CIA*.

certified management accountant. N. A certification awarded by the Institute of Management Accountants. To receive the certification, the candidate must pass a comprehensive exam and meet an experience requirement. To keep the certification, the individual must take continuing education. ABBRV. *CMA*.

certified public accountant. N. A certification given by the American Institute of Certified Public Accountants to accountants in the United States who pass the Uniform Certified Public Accountant Exam. State boards of accountancy determine other qualifications for the licensing of certified public accountants (CPAs). Only CPAs can perform audits of companies that sell stock to the public. ABBRV. *CPA*.

CESA. ABBRV. Coverdell Education Savings Account.

ceteris paribus. ADV. *(Latin)* All other things held constant or all other things being equal.

CFE. ABBRV. Certified fraud examiner.

CFO. ABBRV. Chief financial officer.

CFP. ABBRV. Certified financial planner.

change in accounting estimate. N. Occurs when a company uses information to adjust a previously made approximation. The approximation could be the percentage of credit sales that will prove to be uncollectible, the useful life of an asset, or any other estimate used in preparing the financial statements. The accounting for a change in estimate is done prospectively. In other words, the company makes no change to previously published financial statements nor does it restate as if the new estimate had always been used. Instead, the company just begins to use the new estimate in the statements. Note disclosure of the change in estimate is required.

change in accounting principle. N. Occurs when a company changes from one correct method of accounting to another correct method. The reporting entity must restate the financial statements for all years presented in the annual report as if the new method had always been used. A cumulative adjustment to retained earnings for the earliest year presented is made for all previous years.

change in equity. N. A term used to describe the comprehensive income in which all changes (other than those with owners) are reflected in the income.

change in reporting entity. N. Occurs when the companies combined in the financial statements change. A change in reporting entity usually involves adding a new subsidiary or eliminating an existing one. A change in reporting entity is accounted for by restating the financial statements for all the periods presented, to show how the statements would have looked if the change had occurred from the earliest period shown forward.

channel stuffing. N. A method of increasing current period sales by encouraging customers to buy more product in the current period. Channel stuffing is the term used in the computer software industry. The software developer offers incentives to the wholesale customers to buy excess inventory in the current accounting period, thereby increasing the seller's income for the current period. The problem is that the seller cannot sell to the same wholesale customers in the next period because the "channels are stuffed."

Chapter 7. N. A type of bankruptcy available to individuals and businesses in which the assets of the individual or business filing bankruptcy are sold, and the proceeds are used to repay debts. Assets are exempt from liquidation if they are necessary to life, e.g., an individual's shelter, transportation, and clothing. Chapter 7 bankruptcy liquidates the business assets, after which the business no longer exists.

Chapter 11. N. A type of bankruptcy available to businesses in which the assets are not sold and the business continues on, making payments—usually reduced in amount—to the creditors.

Creditors agree to the reduced amounts, figuring they will get more that way than through the liquidation of the assets and payoff from the proceeds. Chapter 11 bankruptcy is more like a reorganization than a bankruptcy.

Chapter 13. N. A type of bankruptcy available to individuals in which creditors give up the right to interest and penalties and agree to receive the principal over time according to a specified payment plan. The individual's assets are not liquidated to pay off creditors as they are under Chapter 7 bankruptcy.

charge off. V. To reduce income through the recording of an expense.

charitable-contribution deduction. N. A tax deduction from adjusted gross income (on Schedule A) for an organization that meets the tax code criteria for being a qualified charity. Donations directly to individuals, no matter how needy, are not deductible. The contribution may be cash or property and is limited to a percentage of the taxpayer's adjusted gross income, depending on the type of contribution and the type of charity. See also *ordinary-income property, capital-gain property.*

charitable remainder trust. N. A type of trust in which the earnings from the trust assets are dispersed and—at a designated point in time—the trust assets are donated to a charity. Usually the designated point in time is the death of the donor.

chartered accountant. N. The British equivalent of the certified public accountant. ABBRV. *CA.*

chart of accounts. N. A list of the assets, liabilities, equity accounts, expenses, and revenues that are on the company's financial statements. The chart of accounts serves as the structure for categorizing and organizing the transactions of the business. See also *account.*

chattel mortgage. N. A loan for personal property rather than for real property, using the financed goods as collateral.

checkbook register. N. The record of all deposits, checks, charges, and withdrawals from a checking account maintained by the account holder. The bank's record of transactions, the bank statement, is used to reconcile the account.

check tampering. N. A type of fraud involving the employee preparation of fraudulent checks or the employee conversion of checks meant for the employer.

cherry picking. V. See *gains trading*.

Chicago Board of Trade. N. An organized exchange for grain, gold, futures, and options trading located in Chicago. ABBRV. *CBOT*.

chief accounting officer. N. An executive-level employee with responsibility for interpreting and translating the effects of accounting rules on a business. Chief accounting officers often have the responsibility for compliance with all the provisions of the Sarbanes-Oxley Act. ABBRV. *CAO*.

chief executive officer. N. Usually the top executive in a business who is in charge of all aspects of the firm. ABBRV. *CEO*.

chief financial officer. N. An executive in a large organization who is responsible for all the financial operations of the entity. Synonymous with *finance director*. ABBRV. *CFO*.

chief operating officer. N. The executive responsible for a company's day-to-day-operations. In some companies, this position is the same as the chief executive officer or the president. ABBRV. *COO*.

child and dependent care credit. N. A type of nonrefundable personal tax credit that reduces the amount of taxes the taxpayer must pay. To be eligible to take the child and dependent care credit, the taxpayer must be employed, and the care services must be necessary in order for the taxpayer to work. The amount of the credit is determined by the adjusted gross income, the amount of qualifying child care or dependent care expenses, and the number of children. The maximum amount of the credit is $3,000 for one child and $6,000 for two or more children. The total amount of all personal tax credits taken by a taxpayer in one year cannot be more than the tax owed plus the tentative alternative minimum tax.

child tax credit. N. A type of personal tax credit that reduces the amount a taxpayer must pay. The child tax credit is $1,000 (in 2008) for each child meeting the criteria. To meet the criteria, the child must be a U.S. citizen, national, or resident under 17, a dependent of the taxpayer, and a child, grandchild, stepchild, or foster child of the taxpayer. For taxpayers with earned income below $10,500, the child tax credit is refundable up to 10% of the income under $10,500. The tax credit is phased out for taxpayers with modified adjusted gross incomes over $75,000 (for single taxpayers), $110,000 (for couples), and $55,000 (for married couples filing separately).

Chinese Wall. N. The precautions taken by a firm dealing in securities to avoid illegal use of information for insider trading.

churning. N. Actions taken by a broker that result in higher commissions because of excessive trading in a customer account.

CIA. ABBRV. Certified internal auditor.

CIK. ABBRV. Central Index Key.

CISA. ABBRV. Certified information systems auditor.

CITP. ABBRV. Certified information technology professional.

classical variables sampling. N. See *mean-per-unit sampling*.

classified balance sheet. N. A balance sheet that uses subdivisions of assets, liabilities, and equity. The usual subdivisions are current and noncurrent for assets and liabilities and paid in capital, and retained earnings for equity. A classified balance sheet is useful for assessing liquidity because current assets and liabilities are identified.

classified stock. N. Common stock of a company that has different class designations such as Class A, Class B, etc.

clear. V. A term used for part of the process involved in using checks to make payments. A check clears when the funds are transferred from the account holder's institution to the payee's institution because the account has enough funds to pay the check.

clearly and closely related criterion. N. Relates to the determination of the accounting for an embedded derivative. If the embedded derivative is nearly alike in risk and characteristics to the host instrument, then with a few exceptions, the instrument is not subject to hedge or derivative accounting. Instead the instrument is accounted for as a single asset.

clientele effect. N. A consequence of a firm's dividend policy that results in the investors having similar dividend preferences. The clientele effect may result in a firm being less able to alter dividend policy significantly without suffering major stock price reductions.

client/server computing. N. A scheme for organizing an entity that allows individuals to access, manipulate, analyze, and change data and allows the resulting data to be available to others in the organization. Client/server computing allows clerks to enter payments into customers' accounts. Then, the collections department is able to view the account balances and payment histories in order to establish credit limits, which they add to the system. The sales force can look up the credit policies when making sales. In contrast, in a centralized system, the information is not available immediately because the data entry is not processed right away, and it is saved up in batches that are usually run at night.

closed corporation. N. A business that is organized as a corporation, whose stock is held by a small number of people (usually family), and is not available for purchase by the public. Synonymous with *private enterprise, nonpublic corporation*.

closed-end credit. N. A loan that must be repaid in full by a certain date. Contrast with revolving credit, which specifies the interest rate and the maximum amount that can be borrowed.

closed-end mutual fund. N. A type of mutual fund that limits the number of shares that will be sold. Shares in closed-end mutual funds are traded over-the-counter or on a stock exchange. Managed investment companies pool investors' money to buy assets for investment purposes. Investors in closed-end funds must sell their shares to other investors to get out of the investment. Contrast with an open-end fund, in which the investment company buys back the shares of investors wanting to get out.

closely held C corporation. N. A C corporation in which five or fewer stockholders own more than 50% of the stock. A corporation that meets this definition is allowed to use passive losses as an offset to the corporation's income from operations.

closing bell. N. The end of trading at an exchange.

closing entries for governmental accounting. N. A three-step process. The first step is to simply reverse the budget entry involving the control accounts, leaving the subsidiary accounts open. The second step is to close the operating accounts that act as control accounts for revenues and expenditures, leaving the subsidiary accounts open. This step is similar to closing in financial accounting, except that instead of using the income summary account, governmental accounting uses "fund balance" to equalize the expenditures and the revenues. The third step is to analyze the budget versus the actual amounts in the subsidiary accounts, and close those.

closing entry for financial accounting. N. A journal entry that moves the effects of revenues or expenses to the owners' equity account. Only temporary accounts, those that are on the income statement, are closed. The purpose of a closing entry is twofold. First, it moves income to retained earnings on the balance sheet. Second, it zeros out the income statement accounts. The temporary accounts are used to collect revenues and expenses for the accounting period. To do that correctly, they must start with nothing and then be increased or decreased by the business transactions for the period. Then, at the end of the period, those accounts must be made ready for the next accounting period by getting the balance to zero.

closing tick. N. A measure of market price movement. The closing tick is calculated as the number of shares increasing in price minus the number decreasing in price during the trading day. A positive number means more stocks increased in price than decreased in price. No information on the magnitude of the change is included in the measure.

CMA. ABBRV. Certified management accountant.

CMO. ABBRV. Collateralized mortgage obligations.

COBIT. ABBRV. Control Objectives for Information and Related Technology.

COBRA. ABBRV. Consolidated Omnibus Budget Reconciliation Act.

COD. ABBRV. Cash on delivery.

coefficient of correlation. N. A statistical measure of goodness of fit for a regression equation. The coefficient of correlation can range between negative one and positive one. If it is positive, the bigger the independent variable, the bigger the value for the dependent variable. The variables move in the same direction. A negative coefficient of correlation means the variables move in opposite directions. The closer the value is to one, the higher the correlation between the variables.

coefficient of determination. N. See *R-squared*.

Cohan rule. N. A procedure that allows business tax deductions for expenditures that have been paid but are lacking good documentation. The Cohan rule is based on a court ruling involving George M. Cohan. That court case involved travel and entertainment expenses—which now must be thoroughly documented—but the ruling still applies to other business expenses.

coinsurance clause. N. A way to spread the risk of covering a total loss. Coinsurance requires the covered entity to have more than one policy (with different carriers) and the total coverage to equal a specified percentage of the value.

collar. N. A restriction on stock market trades that goes into effect when the Dow Jones Industrial Average moves more than 210 points in one direction. A collar limits the price for index arbitrage orders, which require buying or selling all the stocks in a particular index. The selling price must either be higher than the last trade or at the last price if the price was moving up. Individuals can set up a collar by owning both a put and a call option for the asset and effectively establishing a price range over which they will continue to own the stock. The call option limits the loss on the sale, while the put option limits the gain.

collateral. N. Items that a borrower pledges to the lender, allowing the lender to take those assets if the borrower does not repay the loan. Examples of collateral include real estate, accounts receivable, and inventories. Collateralized loans usually have a lower interest rate than unsecured loans.

collateralized mortgage obligations. N. Types of bonds sold by investment banks that are secured by the mortgages the banks own. The borrowers pay their mortgages to the bank, and the banks use the payments to cover the interest payments to the bond holders. ABBRV. *CMO*.

collateral trust bond. N. A debt instrument that is backed by stocks and bonds owned by the borrower. The securities are transferred to a trust and held as collateral.

collectibles gain. N. Occurs when valuables like antiques, stamps, art, or rugs are sold and exchanged. The excess of the proceeds over the adjusted basis, usually the acquisition price, is called collectibles gain. Collectibles gain is taxed at a higher rate than other long-term capital gains and is excluded from net long-term capital gains to get adjusted net capital gains.

collusion. N. The cooperation of two or more people to commit fraud.

collusive pricing. N. A method of restraining trade that involves companies in one industry agreeing on pricing and production decisions. The result is prices that are artificially high. Customers have no alternative if most companies in the industry have set a similar price. Collusive pricing is a violation of antitrust laws.

combined attributes–variables sampling. N. See *probability-proportional-to-size sampling*.

combined group. N. A type of controlled group of three or more corporations in which one is both the parent of a parent-subsidiary group and a member of a brother-sister group. The definition of a combined group is used for tax purposes to designate the maximum amounts of income in brackets and to limit certain benefits.

COMEX. ABBRV. The Commodity Exchange in New York, which trades futures in precious metals.

comfort letter. N. A letter from a public accounting firm that accompanies a prospectus and Securities and Exchange Commission registration documents. A comfort letter says that the financial information in the prospectus follows generally accepted accounting principles, and that no subsequent events have occurred that significantly change the financial position indicated in the prospectus.

comment letters. N. The public's response to Financial Accounting Standards Board (FASB) exposure drafts. Comment letters are available from the FASB. www.fasb.org. Synonymous with *letters of comment.*

commercial credit. N. Loans to businesses for business purposes, rather than to individuals for personal purposes.

commercial finance. N. See *asset-based loan.*

commercial paper. N. A type of short-term loan for large amounts of cash that is available to only the largest, strongest corporations. Commercial paper is usually in increments of $100,000, and the interest rate is below the prime rate.

commercial substance. N. A term used to determine the accounting for nonmonetary exchanges. An exchange has commercial substance if an entity expects cash flows to change as a result of the exchange. Previously, nonmonetary exchanges involved the classification of similar or dissimilar productive assets. The use of commercial substance as the identifying factor is consistent with international accounting standards.

commission. N. A form of incentive compensation in which the agent receives pay based on volume, the dollar level of sales, or a percentage of the sales amount.

Committee of Sponsoring Organizations. N. The organization that defined internal control and its components through a report in 1992. The committee was organized after the National Commission on Fraudulent Financial Reporting studied the cause and the control of fraudulent financial reporting. ABBRV. *COSO*.

Committee on Accounting Procedure. N. Created by the American Institute of Certified Public Accountants in 1939 to establish the rules for financial disclosure. See Accounting Research Bulletins. ABBRV. *CAP*.

commodities futures. N. An agreement between parties to buy or sell a specified amount of a specified item at a specified price at a date in the future. The agreement is called a contract and involves items, like agricultural products, in which an individual item is the same as any other item. Commodities futures contracts are bought and sold to lock in gains or to limit losses and reduce the risk for producers and buyers.

commodity. N. A product that is difficult to differentiate because the standards for the product are narrowly defined. Commodities include cement, steel, gold, wheat, and eggs.

commodity-backed bonds. N. Bonds that may be paid in a quantity of a commodity, such as barrels of oil, ounces of gold, or bushels of grain, rather than in dollars. Synonymous with *asset-linked bonds*.

commodity futures. N. See *futures contracts*.

common costs. N. Costs that are not directly associated with a unit of product, but are necessary for operating and are shared by more than one user. Common costs are allocated using either the stand-alone cost-allocation method or the incremental cost-allocation method. Common costs include the cost of a corporation's human resource department.

common fixed expenses. N. The costs of doing business that stay the same in total over a normal range of activity and are associated with more than one segment of a company. Common fixed expenses continue even if one of the segments is eliminated. For example, if a company has two divisions—garden furniture and kitchen cabinets—and sanding machines are used by both, the depreciation on those machines is a common fixed expense.

common-life approach. N. See *replacement-chain approach*.

common-size analysis. N. A financial analysis tool that expresses all items on a financial statement as a percentage of one item. Common-size analysis is useful to spot trends within a single company or to compare companies of different sizes. See also *common-size balance sheet, common-size income statement*. Synonymous with *percentage analysis*.

common-size balance sheet. N. All the amounts on a balance sheet stated as a percentage of total assets. A common-size balance sheet is useful for analyzing the financial structure of a company. See also *common-size analysis*.

common-size income statement. N. All the amounts on an income statement stated as a percentage of sales. A common-size income statement is useful for analyzing the structure of a company's revenues and expenses. Contrast with a trend income statement in which several years of data are all expressed as a percentage of a base year's amounts. See also *common-size analysis*.

common stock. N. A balance sheet account in the stockholders' equity section representing investment by owners. Common stock is distinguished from preferred stock in that common stockholders have a vote but receive dividends after preferred stockholders. The dollar amount in the common-stock account is equal to the number of shares issued times the par value of one share. See also *preferred stock, par value of stock, stated-value stock, equity shares*.

common stock equivalent. N. Security with provisions allowing it to be exchanged for common stock under certain conditions or at a specified time (at the choice of the holder of the security) that meets a yield test requiring inclusion in diluted earnings per share. The yield on the security must be less than two-thirds of the corporate Aa bond yield. Convertible bonds, convertible preferred stock, options, and warrants are the most common examples. Options always meet the yield test because they have a yield of zero.

common stock subscribed. N. A stockholders' equity account representing common stock that is sold with a receivable instead of immediate payment.

common stock subscriptions receivable. N. Stockholders' equity accounts that reduce total stockholders' equity. Common stock subscriptions receivable represent amounts owed to the company from the sale of stock and are not classified as a current asset.

community development entities. N. An organization, usually a partnership or corporation, that is set up to serve low-income communities or individuals. Community development entities are certified by the Internal Revenue Service if they comply with the primary mission requirement and if they have members of the low-income community on the board of directors. Investors in community development entities receive tax credits (over a seven-year period) that equal about 39% of the original investment. ABBRV. *CDE*.

company-specific risk. N. See *diversifiable risk*.

comparability. N. A secondary quality of accounting information. Accounting information is comparable if it is recognized, processed, and reported in a way that allows the reader to figure out the differences and similarities, or to evaluate the performance of the entities being compared. Comparability is an important characteristic if the user is trying to evaluate different businesses. It is easiest to compare the performance of two companies when both use similar methods of determining amounts on the financial statements.

comparable-profits method. N. A method of determining transfer prices by applying the same profit on the intercompany sale as exists on the nonintercompany sale.

comparable-uncontrolled-price method. N. One of three Internal Revenue Service–allowed methods of determining transfer prices. The comparable uncontrolled price is equal to the market price less any costs that will be avoided because the sale is internal. These avoidable costs are things like selling commissions and marketing.

comparative analysis. N. A method of analyzing the trends in a single company. Financial data is compared over time to discern inclinations, movements, or subtle changes. Companies often include comparative data in their annual reports so that readers can perform the comparative analysis.

comparative statements. N. Financial statements that present more than one year's information so that the reader can compare the current performance to the past performance. Comparative statements allow users to identify trends. Many corporations present the current year and the previous four years in their financial statements.

compensated absences. N. A liability on the employer's balance sheet representing amounts of vacation, illness, or holiday pay due to employees. Compensated absences increase compensation expense and increase liabilities if the pay is based on past service by the employee; if the amount accumulates from year to year or must be paid if the employee leaves; if it is probable that it will be paid; and, if the amount can be estimated. The entry must be recorded in the year that the employee earns the benefit—not necessarily in the year that it is paid.

compensating balances. N. Amounts of cash that are minimum required amounts in checking and savings accounts. These amounts support borrowing arrangements with the bank or act as payment for bank services without overt charges, such as check processing. Compensating balances also increase the interest rate on the borrowing arrangements they support.

compensating controls. N. Part of the internal control system of an organization that makes up for a weakness in another area. When auditors find an internal control weakness, they continue investigating and analyze the system as a whole, determining if other controls offset the identified weakness.

compensation committee. N. A group of directors from the board of directors responsible for determining the pay for the organization's executives.

compensation discussion and analysis. N. A required disclosure regarding compensation policies to be used in context with the compensation information for the top five officers of a corporation. The compensation discussion and analysis is part of the Securities and Exchange Commission filings.

compensatory stock options. N. Stock options that are given to employees in place of part of their wages. The corporation accounts for compensatory stock options as a compensation expense by determining the difference between the market price and the option price of the stock (when the employee receives the option).

competitive advantage. N. A situation in which a company earns a rate of return that is above the floor return for the industry. The floor is the risk-free rate adjusted for the risk of the industry. If perfect competition existed, all companies in an industry would earn the floor rate.

compilation. N. A service provided by certified public accountants (CPAs). The CPA puts the report together using information from management. No opinion or assurance that the report is in compliance with generally accepted accounting principles is provided without verifying or auditing it. While the CPA must follow American Institute of Certified Public Accountants rules for accounting and review services, a compilation is not an audit, and the CPA does not verify or investigate the information. The purpose of a compilation is to put the information in the proper form and to check for obvious mistakes. It represents a type of accounting service performed by CPA firms that is the lowest level of assurance service. A compilation involves putting together the financial statements from information supplied by the organization. This service offers no assurance about the fairness of the statements and no report or opinion is included. CPA firms can only do this for nonpublic companies. CPAs are careful not to provide any assurance that gives the impression that audit procedures have been performed.

completed-contract method. N. A method of recognizing all revenue and expenses on long-term contracts when the contract is completed. However, if it appears during the contract as though the contract will be a loss, that loss has to be included on the current-period income statement, even though the contract is not complete. While this method has the advantage of involving no estimates, it does not accurately present the results of operating activities. The American Institute of Certified Public Accountants Statement of Position 881–1 advises that companies use the completed-contract method only if they are unable to use the percentage-of-completion method. See also *percentage-of-completion method.*

completion-of-production basis. n. A method of recognizing revenue prior to sale. The completion-of-production basis is used in the mining of precious metals and in agriculture. This method is justified in these instances because an organized market for these products exists, so a selling price is nearly certain.

complex capital structure. N. The term used to describe the mix of liabilities and equity that includes items that could reduce earnings per share, such as convertible securities and stock warrants.

complex trust. N. Any trust that does not meet the criteria for a simple trust is, by default, a complex trust. A simple trust holds the donated property and distributes all the income to the beneficiaries. It does not sell any of the corpus (the donated property) and makes no donations to charities.

compliance audit. N. A special report by either an external or internal auditor indicating that the entity is operating within a set of restrictions or policies. The management of a corporation may have internal auditors determine if the corporation is obeying restrictions that may be associated with debts or regulation requirements. See also *audit.*

compliance testing. N. Audit procedures that check to determine if controls are operating effectively. Auditors do these tests after reviewing the internal control system and finding controls in place. The next step is to verify that the controls actually work. If auditors can rely on controls, that may reduce the amount of time and cost involved in the audit.

composite cost of capital. N. See *weighted-average cost of capital.*

composite depreciation method. N. Allocating the cost of a set of dissimilar assets by applying a rate to the total depreciable base of the collection. The rate is an average of all items in the collection. Instead of depreciating each individual item, the collection is depreciated. The key difference between this method and the usual single asset depreciation is that no gain or loss is recorded when an individual item in the set is retired. The cash is recorded, the original cost of the individual item is removed from the account, and the difference is either an increase or a decrease in the accumulated depreciation account. See also *group method of depreciation*.

composite unit. N. A theoretical unit constructed of a mixture of all products, with the contribution margin weighted according to the product mix. If a business has three products (products A, B, and C) with contribution margins of .20, .30, and .40, respectively, and the sales mix is 80% product A, 10% product B, and 10% product C, the composite unit would consist of eight As, one B, and one C. The contribution margin for the composite unit would be $1.60 + $0.30 + $0.40 = $2.30.

compounding. N. The process of finding the future value of an investment at a specified rate over a defined period of time. Annual compounding adds interest once a year. Semiannual compounding adds interest every six months, or twice a year.

compound interest. N. A method of calculating interest in which the interest for each period is determined by multiplying the rate by the sum of the original amount borrowed plus any unpaid interest. Compound interest charges interest on unpaid interest. Simple interest is computed using only the rate times the principal for each period that amount is owed.

comprehensive budget. N. See *master budget*.

comprehensive income. N. All changes in equity for the accounting period, except investments by owners and dividends. Comprehensive income includes changes in equity that are not included in income. Examples of items that are not included in the determination of net income but are part of comprehensive income include unrealized gains or losses on some investments. These gains or losses result from changes in the market value of the investment, but because the investment has not yet been sold, the gain or loss does not affect net income.

comptroller. N. Another name for a controller—an organization's top accountant.

COMPUSTAT. N. A research database product presented by Standard & Poor's. COMPUSTAT has financial information on thousands of companies in a computer database.

computer-assisted audit techniques. N. All methods of gathering audit evidence in a computerized information system. ABBRV. *CAATs*.

computer crime. N. A crime committed using a computer in some way, either directly or indirectly.

computer-facility controls. N. Measures that keep the hardware, software, and data safe. Computer-facility controls include choosing a safe location for the processing center and limiting access. Insurance does not protect the facility from loss. It can only offset the loss from a damaged computer facility.

computer hacker. N. A person who uses a computer to gain unauthorized access to files on another computer.

computer virus. N. A program that is secretly placed on a computer to slow or upset normal processing. Once established in a host, it often sends itself to contacts in the host's address book files and then repeats the process, slowing down processes through volume.

concealment. N. One of the three elements of fraud in which the fraudster covers up the existence of the fraud. False accounting entries, phony invoices, and doctored receipts are examples of concealment. See also *elements of fraud*.

concentration-of-credit risk. N. A situation that exists if a company's receivables have a common characteristic that could result in nonpayment. Geographical location is an example of a common characteristic that could result in a concentration-of-credit risk. A weather situation such as a drought or flood in a particular location could affect many of the company's debtors, causing a higher risk of nonpayment.

conceptual framework. N. A project of the Financial Accounting Standards Board that resulted in six concept statements identifying the theoretical framework of accounting.

concurring partner review. N. A requirement for all public companies in which an audit is examined and analyzed by a partner—an owner or executive in a certified public accounting firm—who is not involved with the audit. The concurring partner review is similar to the quality inspection function in a manufacturing company. The partner should understand the client's industry and be looking for adequate support for the audit opinion.

condensed financial statements. N. Financial statements that present less detail than regular financial statements. Usually the specific current assets and current liabilities are not displayed, and only the total for each category is displayed. Property, plant, and equipment (net of accumulated depreciation) is identified, but other long-term assets are combined.

conditional obligation. N. A requirement or duty for one party to act if some condition is met. A company may issue redeemable stock that must be repurchased from the stockholders if and when the Standard & Poor's 500 index reaches a certain level. The obligation to redeem the stock is conditional on the level of the index.

conditional pledges. N. Promises by donors to make contributions to a not-for-profit organization that will be fulfilled when some donor-identified requirements occur. A donor may make a pledge of $10,000 toward a scholarship fund if the university can match that amount through the contributions of other donors. When the $10,000 matching amount is raised, then the pledge is no longer a conditional pledge (and instead becomes unconditional).

confirmation of receivables. N. A required audit procedure in which the auditor contacts customers to "confirm" the amount that the customer owes the client.

conflict of interest. N. Circumstances in which an employee has a secret relationship that will allow him or her to benefit from a transaction with a company. For example, if an employee owns a lawn-care service and influences his or her employing company to use that lawn-care service without disclosing the ownership, the employee will be unable to act in an unbiased way for both him- or herself and the employing company.

conformance quality. N. An aspect of quality that emphasizes how well the product meets the production specifications.

conglomerate. N. Business combinations involving entities that are in different industries or business activities. A conglomerate allows a corporation to enter a new business area quickly, through an already established organization, and to diversify risk from being in only one line of business. If McDonald's restaurants bought Gold's Gym, it would be considered a conglomerate because the two organizations are in totally different businesses.

conservatism. N. A guide to deciding between equally acceptable alternative accounting solutions. Conservatism dictates choosing the solution with the smallest chance of overstating assets or income. Conservatism does not suggest that assets or income should be understated.

consideration. N. The good or service given up in exchange for an action or a promise to act.

consignment. N. A method of marketing and selling items through another entity in which that entity does not have title to the items at any time. Usually this arrangement has the original owner, the consignor, physically distant from the selling agent, the consignee. The items are shipped to the consignee, and the consignee has no obligation other than to protect the items. The consignee receives a commission for selling the item. The issue in consignment sales is which organization has the dollar value of the consigned items included in their assets. Because title never passes to the consignee, the items are in the consignor's inventory, even though they are physically at the consignee's location.

consistency. N. A secondary quality of accounting information. Accounting information is consistent if the same method is used from year to year. Consistency is important when evaluating one company over time. See also *conceptual framework*.

consolidated financial statements. N. A unification of the financial statements of the parent company with all the subsidiaries. The assets, liabilities, and results of operations are combined to make it appear like one big company. Consolidated financial statements are required if the parent owns more than 50% of the subsidiary. The consolidation process eliminates any transactions between the parent and the subsidiary.

consolidated group. N. An affiliated group that files one tax return for the group, called a consolidated return. The first year the group files a consolidated return, each member must affirm inclusion in the group. The parent corporation must remain the same, but subsidiaries can change without affecting the tax status of the consolidated group.

Consolidated Omnibus Budget Reconciliation Act. N. A law that gives employees who leave a company the right to continue receiving health benefits through the company for an extended period of time. The insurance that provides for the continuous coverage is commonly known as COBRA Health Insurance. ABBRV. *COBRA*.

consolidated taxable income. N. The total of the separate incomes of all members of a consolidated group, less the group-level adjustments. Complications lie in the need to adjust each separate income for transactions with members of the consolidated group and in the group-level adjustments. ABBRV. *CTI*.

consolidation. N. This method of accounting unifies the financial statements of a parent company with its subsidiaries to make it look like one company. The parent company must control each subsidiary that is combined through ownership of more than 50% of the voting stock. Any transactions that occur between the parent and the subsidiaries is eliminated to give an accurate picture of assets, liabilities, equity, cash flow, and results of operations.

constant-dollar accounting. N. Restating financial statements so that the dollar amounts represent equal purchasing power. The basis for the measurement is the cost. Each cost is adjusted using a price index relevant to the date of the original expenditure. Constant-dollar accounting is useful during periods of high inflation. See also *inflation accounting*.

constant-growth model. N. A method of calculating the intrinsic value of a particular stock. The constant-growth model calculates the price an investor will pay based on the expected dividends, the investor's required rate of return, and the expected growth rate of the dividends. The formula is price equals expected dividends per share per year, divided by the difference between the required rate of return and the expected growth rate of the dividends. This model is only meaningful if the required rate of return is greater than the expected growth rate of the dividends. Because dividend growth rates are not stable or constant for many companies, including those in new industries or start-ups, the constant-growth model works best for mature corporations. Synonymous with *Gordon model*.

construction-in-progress. N. The current asset account on the balance sheet of companies engaged in long-term construction contracts. This account is increased by the amount of expenditures for the contract plus any profit recognized during construction. When displayed on the balance sheet, i.e., the contra account, billings on construction-in-progress is deducted from it. At the end of the project, this account is closed out like any inventory account. See also *billings on construction-in-progress*.

constructive capitalization. N. A financial analysis tool that discounts the operating lease disclosures in order to adjust all balance sheets to include all leases, not just capital leases. Constructive capitalization allows for a more effective comparison of companies having mainly operating leases with those having mainly capital leases.

constructive dividends. N. Payments from S corporations to shareholders that really are dividends, but are disguised as business activities to avoid double taxation. The situation must involve a legitimate business activity that makes good business sense.

constructive receipt. N. A category of income that a taxpayer may not have taken physical possession of, but could have. Because taxpayers must report income on the tax return, a strategy to avoid receiving it could be not cashing a check or not redeeming an interest coupon. Constructive receipt eliminates this strategy because it states that income is received if the taxpayer refuses to accept it until a later tax year.

consumer credit. N. Borrowings to individuals for personal use (e.g., for houses, cars, and credit card charges).

consumer price index. N. A number that measures the change in the cost of a fixed set of items that most households use, including utilities, housing, food, and transportation. The cost of those items is recalculated every month, and the change is reported by the U.S. Bureau of Labor Statistics. Synonymous with *cost-of-living index*. ABBRV. *CPI*.

contingency. N. A business event that may or may not happen depending on the outcome of some other event. An ongoing product liability lawsuit creates a contingency for the company being sued. The payment of damages is contingent on the outcome of the lawsuit. See also *contingent gain*, *contingent liability*, *contingent loss*.

contingency planning. N. A necessary part of a reliable accounting information system that provides a strategy for dealing with a disaster that may disrupt that system. Contingency planning usually includes regular archiving of accounting data to back up the system.

contingent gain. N. The possibility of a company experiencing a gain as the result of some future event. Generally accepted accounting principles prohibit companies from increasing income by the amount of contingent gains. A company would have a contingent gain if it purchased a stock that was expected to increase in value. The gain is contingent on the future sale price of the stock. Synonymous with *gain contingency*.

contingent issue agreement. N. A contract, usually part of a business combination, in which one party, usually the acquiring company, agrees to issue additional shares of common stock if something occurs or arrives (e.g., a particular date, a level of earnings, a market price for stock, etc.). If the threshold for the contingent agreement is met, then those shares should be added to the denominator of basic earnings per share when calculating diluted earnings per share.

contingent liability. N. A liability on the balance sheet that represents an obligation that may exist depending on the outcome of an event. Generally accepted accounting principles require organizations to reduce income for contingent losses if those losses are probable and can be measured. The other half of that entry is an increase in a contingent liability. In addition to lawsuits, warranties are an example of a contingent liability. In the period of the sale, warranty expense reduces income, usually before any costs for providing warranty service are incurred. The other half of that expense entry is an increase to a contingent liability, for providing service or products in the future under warranty agreements.

contingent loss. N. The possibility of a company experiencing a loss as the result of some future event. Generally accepted accounting principles (GAAP) require companies to reduce income if the contingent loss can be estimated and is probable. If the loss is only possible rather than probable (or cannot be measured), the company must disclose the nature of the possible loss in the notes to the financial statements. If there is only a remote possibility of the loss happening, then the company does not have to reveal the information. GAAP do not give specific probability numbers to determine what is probable, possible, or remote, so companies and their auditors use careful judgment when accounting for contingent losses. Synonymous with *loss contingency*.

continuity. N. See *going concern*.

continuity-of-business-enterprise requirement. N. A requirement for tax-deferred business combinations that the business activities of the target continue, either through the operation of the target as a subsidiary or by the use of the target's assets in the acquiring corporation.

continuity-of-interest requirement. N. The regulation that determines if a merger or consolidation can qualify as a tax-deferred reorganization. The continuity of interest requirement states that the compensation paid to shareholders in the target corporation must consist of at least 50% stock in the continuing corporation.

continuous auditing. N. Audit procedures that are performed throughout the year, usually by triggers set up within the organization's information system. For example, any check that pays an employee for more than a designated number of hours might be listed in a file. The auditors would then review that file during the year-end audit.

continuous budget. N. A philosophy of adding a month to the twelve-month budget, to take the place of the month that just ended. In using continuous budgeting, the budget does not always include January 1 to December 31. Rather, in January, the budget includes January 1 to December 31, but in February, the budget includes February 1 to January 31 of the next calendar year.

continuous compounding. N. Calculating compound interest over infinitely short time periods.

continuous improvement. N. A way of operating in which employees are always looking for a better way of doing things, so that efficiency and effectiveness are improved. Continuous improvement requires good information to identify areas of improvement and to evaluate the effects of new activities or methods.

continuous replenishment. N. The method of acquiring inventory in contributions to not-for-profit entities in a just-in-time environment. Continuous replenishment delegates the order function to the supplier, who suggests orders that the buyer approves. Electronic data interchange is important for the smooth functioning of this method. The supplier has access to the buyer's inventory data.

contra account. N. An account that decreases its partner account. A contra account can decrease an asset, liability, or equity account. Accumulated depreciation is deducted from the amount in the property, plant, and equipment account to get the balance sheet value for property, plant, and equipment.

contra-asset account. N. An account that reduces the asset account with which it is paired. Accounts receivable is reduced by the allowance for doubtful accounts, a contra-asset account. Property, plant, and equipment is reduced by accumulated depreciation, a contra-asset account.

contract rate for a bond. N. See *stated rate for a bond.*

contributed capital. N. A category within the stockholders' equity section of the balance sheet. Contributed capital is the total of the common- and preferred-stock accounts and additional-paid-in-capital accounts. It represents the total cash received from the initial sale of equity shares. Synonymous with *paid in capital.*

contribution margin. N. The difference between the sales revenue and all variable costs. The contribution margin represents what is contributed toward covering the fixed costs.

contribution-margin income statement. N. An income statement that classifies cost by fixed and variable costs, rather than by functional descriptors. The sales revenue is first reduced by all variable costs, resulting in the contribution margin. The fixed costs are then deducted to arrive at the net income. The contribution-margin income statement is useful for internal decision making, but is not acceptable for official financial reporting purposes.

contribution-margin ratio. N. An analysis statistic calculated by dividing sales revenue by the contribution margin. The contribution-margin ratio represents the part of every dollar of sales that is available to cover fixed costs and produce profit.

contributions to not-for-profit entities. N. A type of revenue, recognized in a not-for-profit organization, in which cash or other assets are transferred to the organization from a person (or from another organization) without expecting anything in return. A contribution is also recognized if another organization or person settles or forgives a debt of a not-for-profit organization. Contributions may also be in the form of volunteer services or free or reduced-cost facilities.

contributory pension plan. N. Pension plans to which both the employer and the employee contribute.

control account. N. A ledger account that summarizes transactions in subsidiary accounts. The subsidiary accounts are part of the control account. Accounts receivable is a control account for all of a company's customer accounts. The individual customers' accounts are the subsidiary accounts.

control activities. N. One of the five components of an internal control system. Control activities are the actual practices that prevent a problem, detect a problem, or correct a problem.

control chart. N. Used to detect quality problems. A control chart is a plot of defect rates relating to an average defect rate. If the plot has a rate much higher than the average, the defects are considered nonrandom and need investigation. The average defect rate is referred to on a control chart as the "mean" or "mu." The term for a much higher defect rate is "standard deviation" or "sigma." If an observed defect rate is more than two standard deviations from the mean, it is considered nonrandom.

control costs. N. The costs of actions or efforts necessary to discover or avoid poor quality in products or services.

control deficiency. N. The least serious type of deficiency in the system of internal control over financial reporting. A control deficiency means that the procedure or technique designed to prevent or find either accidental or intentional errors in financial statements does not operate correctly or has been designed badly. A combination of control deficiencies may result in a significant deficiency or a material weakness in the internal control over financial reporting. See also *significant deficiency, material weakness*.

control environment. N. Various aspects of the situation and atmosphere in which an organization operates that affect the likelihood that intentional or accidental errors will occur in the accounting. Control environment factors include management philosophy and style, organizational structure, organizational ethics, and employee competence. The board of directors, the audit committee, and the human resource function also play a role. The auditor assesses the control environment as one part of the audit planning process. This is one of the five components of an internal control system. The control environment determines the commitment and attentiveness of employees to internal control.

controllable costs. N. The costs a manager can affect through decisions and planning. For example, the production manager can control labor costs through hiring and work schedules, but cannot control selling commissions. The production manager should not be judged on making or missing sales forecasts.

controlled group. N. A tax term referring to a set of corporations with overlap of ownership. The controlled group rules prevent corporations from forming new corporations in order to spread income across more units (thereby avoiding the higher rates at higher income levels). The definition of a controlled group is used for tax purposes to designate maximum amounts of income in brackets and to limit certain benefits. Several different types of controlled groups are brother-sister groups, parent-subsidiary groups, and combined groups.

controller. N. A staff position in an entity that supervises all accounting functions in the entity. The controller deals with both the internal and external accounting needs, including taxes, cost accounting, internal control, internal auditing, and financial accounting. The treasurer has a related position managing the finance function. The treasurer raises capital through borrowing and through the selling of stock, and manages cash and investments.

controlling. N. The activity that monitors the implementation and the outcome of specified steps in a plan to check if the plan is working.

controlling interest. N. One shareholder that owns more than 50% of the outstanding voting stock of a corporation. If one corporation holds more than 50% of the voting stock of another corporation, the investor is called the parent, and the investee is called the subsidiary.

controlling ownership. N. An investment in which the investor owns more than 50% of the voting stock of a company and can control the board of directors.

Control Objectives for Information and Related Technology. N. A structure of objectives and guidelines for information systems auditors to use in assessing the risk associated with the IT environment and in designing controls to lessen those risks. ABBRV. *COBIT*.

control premium. N. An increase in the price of an equity interest in a corporation because the interest will give the owner control.

control risk. N. An element of audit risk. Control risk is the chance that an accidental or intentional error will be undetected by the internal control system of the client.

conventional-retail-inventory method. N. The retail-inventory method that calculates the cost-to-retail ratio only using net markups in the retail value and ignoring markdowns and cancellations of markdowns. The cost-to-retail ratio is equal to the cost of goods available for sale, valued at the wholesale or purchase price, divided by the goods available for sale valued at retail. The conventional-retail-inventory method includes markups and markup cancellations in this retail value. The result is a lower percentage that approximates the lower-of-cost-or-market valuation of inventory.

conversion. N. One of the three elements of fraud in which the fraudster transforms the gains from the fraud into cash, real estate, jewelry, or other desirable things. Cashing stolen checks or selling stolen inventory or office assets are examples of conversion.

conversion cost. N. The total direct labor cost plus the overhead cost. Conversion cost is a concept used in manufacturing accounting.

convertible bonds. N. Bonds that allow the holder to exchange the bond for another security, usually stock of the issuer. When the issuer receives the proceeds from convertible bonds, the amount is classified as a liability on the balance sheet. Even though this type of bond may become stock, it is still classified as a liability on the balance sheet. When the bonds are converted, the bonds payable and any premium or discount on the bonds are reduced. The common stock account is increased for the par value of the shares issued and additional paid in capital is increased for the difference. If some additional compensation is offered to increase the likelihood of conversion, that amount is recorded as a conversion expense and reduces income in the period of conversion. This feature may allow the company selling the bonds to pay a lower interest rate because of the possibility of future stock returns that are higher than the bond interest.

convertible preferred stock. N. Preferred stock that carries with it the option for the owner to swap the preferred shares for common shares at a specified exchange rate. Convertible preferred stock provides investors with a great opportunity to initially be guaranteed a dividend when the investment is preferred stock, and, as the company becomes more successful and the returns to common shareholders improve, to then change the investment to common shares, which have no limit on the return.

COO. ABBRV. Chief operating officer.

cooking the books. N. Intentionally misstating the financial statements to make firm performance look better than it really is.

copyright. N. An intangible asset that gives the owner the exclusive right to publish, produce, or sell intellectual property such as music, art, or books. A copyright lasts for the life of the artist plus fifty years. Copyrights are valued at the historical cost, if purchased, plus the cost of successful defenses of the copyright. If a defense is unsuccessful, the copyright is worthless and must be written off. The cost is written off through amortization expense over the economic life of the copyright, which is usually less than the legal life. If the creation to which the copyright applies was developed through research, then—although the copyright is in force—the balance sheet value is only the cost of successful defenses. All the research and development costs are expensed during the creation phase.

corporate charter. N. See *articles of incorporation*.

corporate governance. N. The structures and processes involving control and oversight functions of the board of directors monitoring the management of an organization. Corporate governance is not limited to corporations, but is necessary in all large organizations. The board of directors is a key component of corporate governance, because that group determines policy, compensation, and interacts directly with management.

corporate liquidation. N. The process of ending the existence of a corporation. The corporation sells all assets and uses the proceeds to pay all liabilities. Any cash remaining is distributed to owners; then the procedures specified in the state of incorporation determine the remaining steps in ending the business.

corporate risk. N. See *within-firm risk*.

corporate stock. N. See *share of stock*.

corporate welfare. N. A collective term for the tax incentives that benefit businesses and special groups. Two provisions, the general-business-credit limitation and the alternative minimum tax, curb the effect of tax incentives. See also *general business credit*.

corporation. N. A form of business that allows multiple owners who are not involved in the day-to-day operations of the company and who are personally liable for all the debts of the company. The maximum amount an owner of a corporation can lose is the amount invested. A corporation receives a charter from a state and is treated like an individual. It can own property, acquire debts, and pay taxes; it becomes a legal entity. Several types of corporations exist. See also *public sector corporation, nonstock* *corporation, closed corporation, listed corporation, over-the-counter corporation.*

corpus. N. The principal or property that is donated to the trust.

correction of error in the financial statements. N. Accounting for the correction of an error requires that the beginning of retained earnings be adjusted for the effect of the error.

corridor approach in pension accounting. N. A method for recognizing unexpected returns on pension plan assets. The corridor approach does not account for unexpected returns if the amount falls within a "corridor" that equals 10% of the projected benefit obligation, or 10% of the pension plan assets at the beginning of the year—whichever is larger. If the amount of accumulated gains or losses on the plan assets are greater than that threshold, then a portion of the gain or loss must be included in the pension expense.

COSO. ABBRV. Committee of Sponsoring Organizations.

cost. N. The sacrifice to acquire, either through purchase or production, something that will bring future benefit to the entity making the sacrifice. Cost is distinct from expense, because while the dollar amount may be the same, the term "cost" is used before the entity receives the benefits. A cost is often an asset during this time, like inventory or prepaid insurance. Then, when the inventory is sold or the insurance time period expires, the assets become expenses (in the cost of goods sold or insurance expenses).

cost accounting. N. The part of accounting that involves keeping track of how much it costs the company to provide products or services. Several different systems exist to accomplish this goal, each being suitable for different types of products or services. Cost-accounting information is used by both management accounting and financial accounting. See also *activity-based costing, job-order costing, process costing, standard-cost system.*

Cost Accounting Standards Board. N. An independent board consisting of ten members from government and industry that sets the cost-accounting standards for government contracts. It is part of the Office of Management and Budget.

cost accumulation. N. The collection of cost information in an organized way so that it can be assigned to products or another cost object.

cost allocation. N. See *cost assignment*.

cost assignment. N. Allocating direct costs and indirect costs to products or to some other cost object. Synonymous with *cost allocation*.

cost-based transfer pricing. N. A method of determining the transfer price for a product. Three cost-based methods exist. Full-cost transfer pricing sets the transfer price at the cost of direct materials, direct labor, variable overhead, and a portion of fixed overhead. Full-cost-plus-markup pricing sets the transfer price at the cost of direct materials, direct labor, variable overhead, a portion of fixed overhead, plus a margin for the selling division. Variable-cost-plus-a-fixed-fee transfer pricing sets the transfer price at the cost of direct materials, direct labor, variable overhead, plus a fixed transfer fee.

cost basis. N. See *basis*.

cost behavior. N. The pattern of change in a cost when activity (either production or service) changes. Understanding cost behavior is important for forecasting income under different levels of production. If production is significantly increased, the materials cost might change because of quantity discounts.

cost-benefit analysis. N. A comparison of the positive aspects of a course of action and the negative aspects of the action. Usually the evaluation focuses on aspects measured in dollars. The decision resulting from this method is only as good as the values assigned to costs and benefits and is useful in situations where those numbers are readily available. A simple example of a cost-benefit analysis is the evaluation of whether to replace human painters in a manufacturing plant with robots. The cost of the machines and increased electricity is compared to the wage savings and increased productivity.

cost center. N. A responsibility center in which the manager is held accountable only for controlling costs. The housekeeping department in an organization is usually a cost center, because it cannot generate any revenue.

cost driver. N. An activity or material that is part of business activity, and that generates a cost associated with that business activity. It is something that causes the cost of a product or service to increase. For example, in a cabinet-making business, the carpenter's labor hours are a cost driver.

cost-flow assumption. N. The term applied to the method a company uses to decide which purchase prices of goods in inventory remain in inventory, and which are included in the cost of goods sold. The cost-flow assumption is meaningful if the cost of inventory items changes during the accounting period.

cost formula. N. See *cost function*.

cost function. N. A procedure for calculating total costs at a particular level of output or activity. Total cost is equal to the fixed cost plus the product of the variable cost per unit, times the number of units produced. Symbolically, TC = a + bx, where "a" is the fixed cost, "b" is the cost per unit, and "x" is the number of units of either a product or a service. Synonymous with *cost formula*.

cost hierarchy. N. Used in activity-based costing systems to catego-rize costs based on the level at which the activity occurs. The four levels, from lowest to highest, are output unit level, batch level, product level, and facility level.

cost incurrence. N. The point in time when a resource is used up in the production process.

costing system. N. Part of the accounting system that focuses on collecting and monitoring information on organizational costs. The management of the organization uses that information to measure performance and to establish policy. See also *standard-cost system*.

cost-leadership strategy. N. A strategy used by businesses that depends on having a lower price than competitors.

cost method. N. One of two acceptable ways to account for treasury stock. When the stock is acquired, a contra-equity account, or treasury stock, is increased for the amount paid. If that stock is reissued later for an amount different than the cost, the treasury stock account is reduced by the original price paid, and additional paid in capital is increased if sold for a higher price. If sold for a lower price, treasury stock is still decreased for the price paid, and additional paid in capital is decreased for the difference. If additional paid in capital is inadequate, then retained earnings is reduced for the remainder. See also *treasury stock*.

cost object. N. The customers, products, divisions of an organiza-tion, etc., about which cost data is collected in a management accounting system. Cost objects are used in both functional-based systems and activity-based systems. A department in a university is a cost object. The school's management accounting system collects cost information on all expenditures for the department.

cost of capital. N. The charges for raising money. A firm needs money to grow and can obtain it from borrowing or from selling stock. The cost of capital is the interest rate on the borrowing or the rate of return that will entice investors to buy the stock.

cost of debt. N. The interest rate charged for borrowing. Because interest expense is deductible for tax purposes, the real cost of debt reflects the tax savings and is calculated as the interest rate times the difference between one and the tax rate of the corporation.

cost of equity. N. The rate of return required by purchasers of a corporation's stock. The cost of equity represents the charge for financing through the sale of stock rather than through borrowing and paying interest. The capital-asset pricing model can be used to calculate the cost of common equity. The cost of preferred stock is equal to the dividend divided by the current share price. The cost of retained earnings is equal to the return that shareholders could earn on a similar investment. The cost of new common equity equals the cost of retained earnings plus the cost of selling it. See also *bond-yield-plus-risk-premium approach, dividend-yield-plus-growth-rate approach.*

cost of goods available for sale. N. In a retail environment, calculated by the formula beginning inventory plus net purchases. This total represents the cost of all products available for sale during the period. In a manufacturing business, goods available for sale can be calculated as beginning-finished-goods inventory plus goods completed during the accounting period.

cost of goods manufactured. N. The total of materials, labor, and overhead put into production, plus the costs of items already in production at the beginning of the period, less the costs of unfinished items.

cost of goods sold. N. Calculated by the formula beginning inventory plus net purchases less ending inventory. This total is an expense on the income statement. In a manufacturing setting, the cost of goods sold is the cost of direct materials, direct labor, and overhead associated with the units sold. In a retail setting, the cost of goods sold is the wholesale cost of the items sold, plus any transportation cost to get the items to the warehouse. Synonymous with *cost of sales*.

cost-of-goods-sold budget. N. Part of the master budget that calculates the cost of goods sold that will appear on the income statement for the year.

cost-of-living index. N. See *consumer price index*.

cost of new common stock. N. See *cost of equity*.

cost of preferred stock. N. See *cost of equity*.

cost of retained earnings. N. See *cost of equity*.

cost of sales. N. See *cost of goods sold*.

cost-plus method. N. One of three Internal Revenue Service–allowed methods for determining transfer prices. The cost-plus method sets the transfer price at the cost, adjusted for any additional costs of delivery or transfer.

cost reconciliation in process costing. N. Accounting for all the manufacturing costs for the accounting period by comparing the costs in the beginning work-in-process plus the costs added during the period with the costs continuing in the work-in-process plus the costs transferred out. When the two are equal, the cost reconciliation is complete and all costs have been accounted for.

cost-recovery method. N. A method of revenue recognition, usually used when payment for the sale is received over a long period of time and the likelihood of collection is unknown and undeterminable. All cash collections are first applied to the cost of goods sold. After that amount has been collected, the seller recognizes profit. The deferred profit is a liability account on the balance sheet.

cost segregation. N. The process of allocating the cost of an asset to various useful life classifications.

cost smoothing. N. See *peanut butter costing*.

costs of quality. N. The cost of the actions or efforts necessary to correct quality problems that exist—or are thought to exist—in products or services. Costs of quality can sometimes be observable and available in accounting records, such as the cost of inspecting finished goods. Some costs of quality, however, are hidden, such as lost sales, which are recorded because they are opportunity costs. Estimation techniques can quantify hidden quality costs. Costs of quality represent the costs to detect substandard quality products and the costs to remedy the problem, either before or after the sale. Costs of quality are classified as prevention costs, appraisal or detection costs, internal failure costs (which are the costs associated with a low-quality product prior to sale), and external failure costs (which are the costs associated with a low-quality product following sale).

cost-to-cost basis. N. The method of figuring what percentage of a long-term contract is finished. The costs incurred so far are compared with the total estimated costs to get the percentage complete. The cost-to-cost basis is the recommended method when using the percentage-of-completion method of revenue recognition on long-term contracts.

cost-to-retail ratio. N. Used in inventory valuation when using the conventional retail inventory method to get to the lower-of-cost-or-market value. The formula for the cost-to-retail ratio is the cost of goods available divided by the original retail price of goods available, plus net markups. Then this ratio is multiplied by the ending inventory at retail to get the lower-of-cost-or-market value.

cost tracing. N. The process of connecting direct costs to a product or some other cost object.

cost-volume-profit analysis. N. A procedure for investigating the relationship between the cost of a unit, the quantity of units sold, and the selling price of a unit to estimate the components for different levels of profit. To use cost-volume-profit analysis, costs must be separated into fixed and variable costs. Cost-volume-profit analysis can be used to calculate the required sales in either units or sales dollars. To find the volume in units, the formula involves solving the equation that sets the desired profit equal to the selling price times the number of units minus the variable cost per unit times the number of units minus the fixed cost. Finding the volume in sales revenue needed involves dividing (the fixed cost plus the desired profit) by the contribution margin ratio. In a multiple product situation, sales mix data defines the single product, a package containing units of all products. See also *sales mix*. ABBRV. *CVP*.

cost-volume-profit graph. N. A graph that plots two lines with the horizontal axis indicating the number of units sold and the vertical axis representing dollars—either revenue or cost. One line is the relationship between the number of units sold and the dollars of revenue. The other line is the relationship between the number of units sold and the dollars of cost. The point at which the two lines intersect is the break-even point.

counterbalancing errors. N. Accounting errors that will self-correct over a two-year period. Synonymous with *offsetting errors*.

counterparties. N. The other entities involved in an arrangement or contract.

coupon bonds. N. See *bearer bonds*.

coupon rate for a bond. N. See *stated rate for a bond*.

covenants. N. The restrictions and agreements associated with long-term debt that are set up to protect the lenders and the borrowers. Examples include maintaining a certain level of working capital, limiting the amount of dividends, describing collateral, etc.

coverage ratios. N. Financial analysis tools that measure a company's long-term solvency. Coverage ratios are calculated using amounts from the financial statements and provide information about the relationship between these amounts. Analysts then compare the relationships of different companies to assess the risk to long-term creditors. Common coverage ratios are the debt-to-total assets ratio, times-interest-earned ratio, cash-debt-coverage ratio, and book-value-per-share ratio. Synonymous with *solvency ratios*.

Coverdell Education Savings Account. N. An education savings device that allows taxpayers with adjusted gross incomes under $110,000 (or $220,000 for those filing a joint return) to contribute $2,000 per year for each beneficiary under 18 years old. Although the contributions are not deductible, the beneficiary can withdraw the amounts tax-free if they will be used for education expenses at the elementary, secondary, or college level. ABBRV. *CESA*.

covered option. N. An option (the right to sell a quantity of an asset at a specified price during a specified time period) in which the seller already owns the quantity of the asset to be delivered if the option is exercised. Contrast with a naked option, in which the seller does not own the asset at the time when the contract for the option to sell is made.

CPA. ABBRV. Certified public accountant.

CPA2Biz. N. A service for accountants that markets products and services to certified public accountants. CPA2Biz is in partnership with the American Institute of Certified Public Accountants. www.cpa2biz.com.

CPA Journal. N. A monthly publication of the New York State Society of CPAs. Available at www.cpajournal.com.

CPI. ABBRV. Consumer price index.

CPU. ABBRV. Central processing unit.

credit. N. An entry in the accounts of an entity that increases a liability, revenue, or equity account. A credit can decrease an asset or expense. An entry on the right side of a T-account. See also *debit*.

credit balance. N. In the accounting records of an entity, an account with a balance on the credit (or right) side of a T-account. That is the normal balance for liabilities and equities, but it is a negative balance for assets.

credit crunch. N. A reduced availability of loans making it difficult for businesses and individuals to borrow. Causes of a credit crunch include higher rates of payment delinquencies, unfavorable economic numbers, and a perception of poor economic conditions in the future.

credit for the elderly and disabled. N. A type of personal tax credit that reduces the amount of taxes an elderly taxpayer must pay. To qualify for the elderly and disabled credit, the taxpayer must be 65 or older, must be retired because of a disability, and must receive very low Social Security payments. The total amount of all personal tax credits taken by a taxpayer in one year cannot be more than the tax owed plus the tentative alternative minimum tax.

credit memo. N. A document notifying the receiver that his or her account is being increased. A bank will issue a credit memo to

notify an account holder that interest for the period is being added
to the savings account.

creditor. N. The person, bank, company, or organization that has
loaned funds and is entitled to repayment.

credit risk. N. The possibility that the borrower will not pay the
interest or principal on time. Synonymous with *default risk*.

credit-risk rate of interest. N. A component of a lender's interest
rate that compensates the lender for the possibility of nonpayment.
The credit-risk rate of interest increases as the likelihood of
nonpayment increases.

credit sale. N. An exchange transaction between two parties in
which one party promises to pay cash in the future in return for
receiving a valuable good or service at present.

credit shelter trust. N. See *bypass trust*.

credit spread. N. The amount above the risk-free rate of interest
that a borrower must pay. The credit spread is dependent on the
riskiness of the borrower's repayment. Synonymous with *sector
spread*.

credit unions. N. Banking entities in which members save and
borrow. Usually members have something in common, such as an
employer or profession, and nonmembers cannot use the services.
Loans are usually for houses, cars, or other consumer-type
purchases.

critical event. N. The point in the earnings process necessary for
revenue to be recognized. A practical example of the critical event
is subscriptions (and the recognition of revenue from subscriptions). The critical event is not the receipt of the cash, which
occurs before the revenue is earned. Rather, the subscriptions
revenue is earned when the publisher mails out the magazines, and

the critical event is the provision of the good to the customer, not the payment by the customer.

critical terms of a derivative. N. Characteristics of a derivative that determine its ability to be an effective hedge. The critical terms are the nature of the underlying, notional amount and settlement date. The more closely the derivative terms match that of the hedged item, the more effective the hedge will be.

cross-footing. N. An audit activity in which the auditor uses the results from footing columns to get a grand total.

cross-hedging. N. Using derivatives with critical terms different from the hedged item. Cross-hedging usually involves different underlyings, such as different currencies.

crossover rate. N. See *net-present-value profile*.

cross-sectional analysis. N. A financial analysis tool that focuses on comparing different companies at a point in time. Cross-sectional analysis requires financial statements from the same time period for all companies under consideration. Contrast with time-series analysis, which looks at a single company over several years.

Crummey trust. N. A type of trust to which contributions qualify for the annual gift tax exclusion of $12,000 per individual or $24,000 per married couple (according to the 2007 rates). The beneficiary of the trust, who does not have to be a child, can demand distributions from the trust. The creator of the trust, however, wants the contributions to build and can stop the contributions if the beneficiary demands distributions. The Crummey trust can be terminated at any time and is more flexible than the qualified trust in benefiting a minor.

C shares. N. A class of mutual fund shares that have annual fees such as 12b-1 fees.

CTI. ABBRV. Consolidated taxable income.

Cumulative Bulletin. N. The annual publication by the Internal Revenue Service listing revenue rulings and revenue procedures.

cumulative effect of change in accounting principle. N. An adjustment to retained earnings for the earliest year of financial statements presented. It represents the amount by which retained earnings must change because of a change in the way the entity was accounting for something. See also *change in accounting principle.*

cumulative-monetary-amount sampling. N. See *probability-proportional-to-size sampling.*

cumulative preferred stock. N. A preferred stock that carries the right to receive a dividend for every year the stock is owned. If dividends have not been declared for a few years, then, when the board of directors declares a dividend, owners of cumulative preferred stock receive payment first. The preferred shareholders get paid for all past years in which they have not received dividends (called dividends in arrears), plus the current-year dividend, before common shareholders receive any dividends.

cumulative voting. N. A voting system in which a voter can cast a number of votes for the same candidate. If a state is electing a governor, an assistant governor, and a treasurer, a voter would normally vote for each position, making three votes. Cumulative voting allows the voter to cast three votes for a single person. Positions are assigned based on total votes. Cumulative voting in corporations gives small shareholders more power to elect their board members.

Curb, the. N. See *American Stock Exchange.*

currency appreciation. N. The situation that occurs when a given amount of Country A's money is exchanged for more of Country B's money than in the past. Country A's currency is said to be getting stronger.

currency depreciation. N. The situation that occurs when a given amount of Country A's money is exchanged for less of Country B's money than in the past. Country A's currency is said to be getting weaker.

currency risk management. N. The actions or efforts necessary to control the effects of change in exchange rates.

current assets. N. Assets on the balance sheet that represent amounts that are cash or will be converted to cash, or that will be used up during the next year or during the operating cycle of the entity, whichever is longer. Examples of current assets include inventory, accounts receivable, and prepaid expenses.

current asset turnover. N. A financial analysis ratio that evaluates the efficiency of an organization. Calculated by average current assets during the period divided by sales for the period, the current asset turnover illustrates how well the company manages accounts receivable and inventory.

current cash-debt ratio. N. A financial analysis ratio that indicates how easily a company can pay its current bills. The formula is the net cash from operating activities divided by the average current liabilities.

current-cost accounting. N. Restating financial statements so the dollar amounts represent the cost to replace the identical asset. If the replacement cost is higher than the original cost, the entity has a holding gain. If the replacement cost is lower, then it is a holding loss. See also *inflation accounting*.

current-cost/constant-dollar accounting. N. An accounting technique that adjusts amounts for the changing price of an asset due to technology, additional features, etc., and then adjusts that current replacement cost for inflation.

current distribution in a partnership. N. Amounts—usually cash—given out by a partnership to a partner that are less than the total amount in the partner's capital account. Contrast with a liquidating distribution, which reduces the capital account to zero so that the partner no longer has ownership in the partnership. The partner's capital account cannot be negative.

current E&P. N. Current earnings and profits. Taxable income plus or minus some adjustments and minus the federal income tax.

current liabilities. N. A type of liability on the balance sheet that represents amounts that will require payment in cash, will use other current assets to satisfy the obligation, or will require the creation of another liability within the next year, or within the operating cycle of the entity, whichever is longer. Examples of current liabilities include accounts payable and unearned revenues. Any account including the word "payable" is either a current or noncurrent liability. The classification depends on how soon the payment is due.

currently attainable standards. N. A type of standard that assumes efficient operation but not perfection. Currently attainable standards are challenging because they assume efficiency, but they are achievable.

current maturities of long-term debt. N. A current liability on the balance sheet representing the amount of a debt the debtor will pay within the next year. Only the principal amount that will be repaid is included. The remaining debt—which will not be paid in the next year—is still classified as a noncurrent liability. In some situations, the current maturities of long-term debt are not classified as a current liability, because no current assets will be used to pay them off.

current ratio. N. A common tool for analyzing the ability of an entity to pay its bills. The formula is total current assets divided by total current liabilities. Generally, a higher current ratio is better than a lower one, but good analysis compares a company's ratio to the industry standard to determine if the ratio is adequate. See also *quick ratio*.

current yield. N. The return on an investment calculated as the annual income from the investment divided by the current price.

CUSIP number. N. Committee on Uniform Securities Identification Procedures number. A nine-digit identification number for every security, stock, or bond. The Committee on Uniform Securities Identification Procedures, a committee set up by the American Bankers Association, assigns the numbers and organizes the classification scheme.

customer-profitability analysis. N. Evaluating the profit from individual customers. Customer-profitability analysis is useful for price-discounting decisions and resource-allocation decisions. Obviously, businesses want to sell to the customers that contribute the most to the overall profit.

customer-response time. N. The amount of time between a customer's order and delivery.

customer value. N. The difference between what a customer gets and what the customer gives up. The customer gets both tangible and intangible benefits from purchasing a good or service. He or she gives up the purchase price, and often time (to learn to use the product), effort (to arrange for delivery and setup), etc. Businesses can increase customer value by increasing what the customer receives or by reducing what the customer gives up. For example, in online shopping, the customer not only pays for the purchase, but he or she also has to learn to use the website, gives up the opportunity to touch or try the product, and pays shipping charges. However, for some customers, the benefit of avoiding a busy shopping center is valuable enough to offset the sacrifices.

cutoff bank statement. N. A company's bank statement that is sent by the bank directly to the auditor, shortly after the official year-end date. The purpose of the cutoff bank statement is to confirm that all checks written during the accounting period were mailed and cashed, and that all deposits in transit were actually deposited. The company could inflate the cash on the year-end balance sheet by not mailing the checks or by recording fictitious deposits and claiming they were in transit.

cutoff tests. N. Audit procedures performed to see if sales, cash receipts, and sales-returns transactions are recorded in the right accounting period. Auditors check on transactions occurring near (just before and just after) the end of the accounting period.

CVP. ABBRV. Cost-volume-profit analysis.

cycle billing. N. A technique for spreading cash inflows throughout the cycle by having different groups of customers with different payment dates.

database. N. A collection of facts and figures that are related in some way. Businesses may have a database of customers that contains information on location, payment history, credit rating, and other characteristics useful for planning.

database design. N. The process of structuring the data within a database so that it is complete but still manageable, secure, and nonredundant.

data-communications protocol. N. Used in sharing data between computers that are in separate locations. These settings ensure that both parties have data in a compatible format and that the computers can share the data. Examples include the speed of transmission, the parity used, and the transmission type.

data-compression techniques. N. Procedures that modify data in a computer so that more can be stored on the same size disk. While data is still available for use, it is harder for accountants to review.

data encryption. N. A security measure used by entities to limit access to electronic data when sending it between computers. Data encryption is the scrambling of electronic data so that only someone with the right decryption key installed on his or her computer can unscramble and read the data.

data mining. N. Using data from several different parts of the information system to make decisions about marketing or entity strategy. Data mining usually involves using large amounts of data concerning the past behavior of customers to discern preferences and patterns that influence the future activities of the entity. Auditors use data mining to look at patterns of transactions and use that information to determine audit procedures.

data processing. N. Transforming transaction data into information. An example of data processing is having data entry operators type in sales data, and processing that data to produce a list of customer accounts and balances.

data transcription. N. The process of putting data in a form that can be processed by a computer. Data entry operators do this when they type in numbers or text from a document at a workstation.

data warehouse. N. A method of integrating all aspects of business information. A data warehouse is one large database of all the information held in an entity, rather than many separate databases, each with a single purpose. A data warehouse allows for the production of reports with information from several functional areas, and it reduces the duplication of information storage. For example, marketing strategy and credit and collections activities can use the same customer information.

date of record. N. A significant date for corporations that pay dividends. The date of record is the date on which the owners of shares are identified. Whoever owns the stock on that day will receive a dividend check. The declaration date gives the market a little time to complete transfers and paperwork, so that the dividend checks go to the proper owners. Synonymous with *holder-of-record date*.

DAX. N. The German stock market index.

day order. N. The duration of a stop order or limit order that tells the broker that the order is canceled if it is not filled that day.

days accounts payable outstanding. N. An analysis tool that indicates the average number of days it takes a company to pay for inventory purchases. The formula is 365 divided by the accounts payable turnover. Comparing the days accounts payable outstanding number over time can help analysts spot trends in a company's payment pattern. Synonymous with *days payable outstanding*.

days accounts receivable outstanding. N. See *days in receivables*.

days in receivables. N. An analysis tool that indicates the average number of days it takes a customer to pay. The formula is 365 divided by the accounts receivable turnover. Comparing the days in receivables over time can help analysts spot trends in payment patterns. See also *accounts receivable turnover*. Synonymous with *days accounts receivable outstanding*.

days of inventory. N. See *average days to sell inventory*.

days payable outstanding. N. See *days accounts payable outstanding*.

days sales outstanding. N. See *average days to collect receivables*.

dealer market. N. A virtual stock exchange in which securities are traded via technology. Contrast with the physical location markets of the New York Stock Exchange or the American Stock Exchange. The National Association of Securities Dealers Automated Quotations (NASDAQ) is an example of a dealer market.

death tax. N. A tax paid on inheritance or estate property.

debenture bond. N. A bond that does not have collateral to back it. Synonymous with *unsecured bond*.

debit. N. An entry in the accounts of an entity that increases an asset or expense. A debit can decrease a liability, a revenue, or an equity account. An entry on the left side of a T-account. See also *credit*.

debit memo. N. A document notifying the receiver that his or her account is being decreased. A bank will use a debit memo to notify an account holder that the cost of printing checks is being deducted from the checking account.

debt. N. Owing something of value to another. In business, a debt is usually the obligation to pay for a service or good already received. Debts may be short-term, meaning they must be paid within the next year, or long-term.

debt capacity. N. The amount of borrowing a firm can support based on its ability to repay from stable cash flows. Firms with unstable cash flows are less able to borrow to expand operations, because the risk of bankruptcy is higher.

debt covenants. N. The restrictions imposed by the lender on the borrower to protect the repayment ability. Debt covenants usually require a specified level of liquidity as measured by a minimum current ratio. The borrower must keep enough current assets, like cash, in relation to short-term debts, making it more likely that the debt payments will be made. Debt covenants often restrict the amount of additional debt a borrower can take on by specifying a maximum debt ratio.

debt-for-debt swap. N. A transaction between a company and its bondholders in which current bondholders trade in their bonds for new bonds.

debt-for-equity swap. N. A transaction between a company and its bondholders in which current bondholders trade in their bonds for shares of stock.

debt instrument. N. Any written agreement to repay a loan. Bonds, certificates of deposit, and promissary notes are examples of debt instruments.

debtors. N. The term used for accounts receivable on a British company's balance sheet.

debt ratios. N. Measures of a company's long-term solvency. The amount of debt carried by the company is compared to various totals, such as total equity, total assets, and total tangible assets. Debt is measured as either total liabilities or long-term liabilities. Generally, a higher debt ratio indicates a greater solvency risk, but good analysis compares the calculated value to the industry standard.

debt securities. N. A financial instrument that represents borrowing. The individual instrument is part of a group of similar ones. Corporate and municipal bonds are common examples of debt securities.

debt service. N. Another term for payments made on loans. Debt service usually refers to the cash amount of the payment, including both principal and interest.

debt-service fund. N. Part of the governmental funds that account for service activities to citizens. The debt-service funds account for payments of interest and principal on general long-term debt.

debt-to-total assets ratio. N. A measure of the portion of assets that are financed. The formula is total liabilities divided by total assets. A high debt-to-total-assets ratio signals a high level of debt for the company. To interpret the calculated ratio, though, it should be compared to industry averages, since what is considered high depends on the industry. Sources for industry averages include Moody's and Standard & Poor's Index.

decentralization. N. The delegation of authority for plans, priorities, and decisions to lower-level managers in an organization. One of the advantages of decentralization is that information is local, and decisions made closer to information allow for better information gathering and increased competition in the local market. Decentralization also allows top levels of the organization to focus on long-range plans and strategy.

decentralized decision making. N. The practice of having managers make plans and set priorities for themselves, rather than at the top level of the organization.

decision model. N. A set of procedures that serves as a guide to decision making. Usually the first step is defining the problem. The next steps usually involve identifying various alternatives and the costs, benefits, advantages, and disadvantages of each alternative, as well as assessing costs and benefits that are not quantitative. The final step is the decision.

decision rule. N. A method of choosing an action by setting up criteria that the alternative must meet. Establishing decision rules eliminates some choices automatically. A person could establish a decision rule for buying a car with the criteria that the car must not cost more than $15,000.

decision support systems. N. Information-processing systems that provide information to help people make decisions regarding unstructured questions. If a manager wants to know how much interest a company is paying on the mortgage, the information system can easily provide the answer. A decision support system, however, can determine if the company would be better off refinancing the mortgage from an adjustable to a fixed-rate loan. Answering this unstructured question requires investigating various combinations of rates and durations, as well as including fees for refinancing and penalties for early payoff.

decision tree. N. An illustration representing all the possible results of a choice or decision. Each result is one branch in the tree.

declaration date. N. A significant date for corporations that pay dividends. The declaration date is the date when the board of directors approves the dividend amount and that information is released to the press. Synonymous with *announcement date*.

declining-balance depreciation. N. A method of allocating the cost of an asset to the periods in which it is used in order to generate revenue. A percentage is applied to the book value of the asset. The most common percentages are 200%, called "double declining balance," and 150%, called "150% declining balance." The amount of depreciation expense each year is a percentage of the book value, cost minus depreciation taken so far. When using declining balance, the book value cannot be less than the estimated salvage value of the asset.

declining issues. N. Stocks that have decreasing prices.

deductible amounts. N. Dollar amounts from transactions or events that reduce taxable income.

deductible temporary difference. N. Dollar amounts from transactions or events that are not fully allowed as a tax deduction in the current period, but will be in the future.

deductions for adjusted gross income. N. One of two types of deductions on tax returns indicating where on the return the deduction is made. Deductions of this type reduce the amount of adjusted gross income, an important measure for other tax items. Most deductions for adjusted gross income are related to business expenses. Examples of deductions for adjusted gross income are reimbursed employee expenses, contributions to individual retirement accounts, alimony paid, moving expenses, and interest on education loans.

deductions from adjusted gross income. N. One of two types of deductions on tax returns indicating where on the return the deduction is made. Deductions of this type are made after adjusted gross income is calculated and include either the standard deduction or itemized deductions and personal exemptions.

deductions in respect of a decedent. N. Tax-deductible amounts to which the deceased is entitled that have not been used prior to the time of death. Examples include property taxes and state income taxes owed, but unpaid at the time of death. ABBRV. *DRD*.

deep-discount bonds. N. Bonds that pay no regular interest, but are purchased for much less than the maturity value and provide all the interest at maturity. Synonymous with *zero coupon bonds, zeros, accrual bond.*

DEF 14A. N. A form filed with the Securities and Exchange Commission by a company intending to have a shareholder meeting. The form gives details of the agenda and proposals requiring a shareholder vote.

defalcation. N. Misappropriation of an organization's funds or assets by an employee. Defalcation is a broader term than embezzlement, which is one type of defalcation, and usually involves using the accounting system to hide the misappropriation.

default. N. The term used when a debtor fails to repay a creditor. The borrower is in default or the loan is in default if the repayment is not made.

default risk. N. See *credit risk*.

deferrals. N. A collective term for accounting items that a company puts off to future income periods, because requirements for recognition in the current period are not met. For example, a company may defer revenue to a future accounting period, even if cash has been received, because the goods or services have not been provided. Rather than increasing income in the current period, the recognition of income is deferred, or put off, to the future period in which the revenue is earned by providing the goods or services. See also *deferred charge*.

deferred annuity. N. A series of equal payments at regular intervals beginning sometime in the future. Determining the present value of a deferred annuity involves discounting the annuity to the time when the payments begin, then discounting that amount as a single sum back to the present.

deferred call. N. See *callable bonds*.

deferred charge. N. One type of deferral. An expenditure that is not expensed but will be in the future. Instead, the deferred charge is shown as a noncurrent asset on the balance sheet, and a portion of the charge reduces income as an expense over a logical allocation period. The costs of issuing bonds can be listed in noncurrent assets on the balance sheet as bond issue costs. A portion of that amount reduces income as an expense each year the bonds are outstanding. See also *deferrals, other assets*.

deferred compensation. N. A situation in which the employee performs the services at present and receives payment later (e.g., in retirement).

deferred-cost accounting. N. A method of recording expenditures as capitalized assets rather than expenses. Deferred-cost accounting allows the expense to be spread over several accounting periods, resulting in a higher net income in the current year.

deferred pension cost. N. An intangible asset recorded to offset the required minimum pension liability. The deferred pension cost cannot exceed the unamortized prior service cost. If the amount needed to record the minimum pension liability is greater than the unamortized prior service cost, the excess is reported as a contra equity amount and included in other comprehensive income.

deferred revenue on the balance sheet. N. See *unearned revenue*.

deferred revenues. N. A type of adjusting entry. Recording deferred revenue decreases revenue in the current accounting period because the earnings process is not complete. Usually the entity has already received payment, but has not performed the services or provided the product. This adjustment records a liability for the unearned revenue. See also *unearned revenue.*

deferred tax asset. N. An asset account on the balance sheet representing taxes the entity has already paid on income that have not appeared on the income statement because of deductible temporary differences.

deferred tax benefit. N. The decrease in the deferred tax liability account during the accounting period. Deferred tax benefit occurs when taxable temporary differences reverse.

deferred tax expense. N. The increase in the deferred tax liability during the accounting period. Deferred tax expense occurs when taxable temporary differences exist.

deferred tax liability. N. A liability account on the balance sheet representing the taxes that the entity has put off paying until a future date because of taxable temporary differences.

deficiency dividend. N. Used by corporations that are unaware of their status as personal holding companies to comply with the dividend-distribution requirements. A deficiency dividend avoids the penalty by making a cash distribution within ninety days of the date that the corporation becomes aware of the classification.

deficit. N. See *retained deficit.*

deficit-restoration obligation. N. Applies to general partners in partnerships that generate losses. After losses are distributed among the partners, if the capital accounts have a negative balance and the partnership is liquidated, the partners have the obligation to contribute enough to return their capital account to zero. Limited partners do not have this application, so losses that result in negative capital balances are not usually allocated to the capital accounts of limited partners.

defined-benefit pension plan. N. A plan in which the amount of the employee's retirement benefit is specified and the employer has to contribute enough to make that happen. The employee has a guaranteed amount of pension benefits. Employers bear higher risk than the employees because there is no limit on the amount the employer has to contribute to this type of plan.

defined-contribution pension plan. N. A plan in which the amount the employer puts into the pension fund is specified. There is no guarantee to the employee on the amount of the benefits, only on the amount of the employer's contribution. Employees have more risk than the employers in this type of plan because the amount of the benefits is dependent on economic conditions, which produce varying returns on the invested funds. The employer's contribution is limited to the specified amount.

deflation. N. Economic conditions in which prices in general are falling. While falling prices sound good, they are usually the result of a significant cut in spending. The lower demand for products (the cut in spending) usually triggers increases in unemployment.

degree of operating leverage. N. A measurement calculated by dividing the contribution margin by the profit.

delist. N. The removal of a company's stock from an exchange. Stocks are delisted if they no longer meet certain financial requirements or if the company violates regulations or laws.

delta ratio. N. A measure of hedge effectiveness equal to the change in the fair value of a derivative to the change in the value of the hedged item. A ratio between .8 and 1.25 is considered effective and hedge accounting is allowed. A ratio outside those values means the hedge is not effective and both instruments are accounted for separately. Synonymous with *offset ratio*.

demand-based management. N. See *demand-pull system*.

demand deposit. N. An account in which the account holder can withdraw amounts without waiting for a maturity date or providing notice to the institution. Contrast with a time deposit, from which withdrawals are not allowed without waiting for the maturity date or giving the financial institution notice of the intent to withdraw. Checking accounts are an example of demand deposits.

demand flow. N. See *demand-pull system*.

demand-pull system. N. A term used to describe just-in-time manufacturing. Because goods are produced only when needed, the demand pulls the process along. Contrast with a push-through system, which produces goods to meet anticipated customer demand. Synonymous with *demand flow, demand-based management*. See also *just-in-time manufacturing system*.

de minimis benefits. N. A category of fringe benefits that a taxpayer can exclude from income. De minimis benefits are small benefits such as free coffee, holiday fruit baskets, etc. Usually these benefits must be available to virtually all employees in order to avoid being classified as compensation.

demonstrative legacy. N. A distribution of personal property involving an item from an identifiable source, according to the provisions of a will. This type of legacy usually involves a specified dollar amount, and if the identified source of the legacy cannot satisfy the dollar amount, then the estate makes up the difference from general assets. An example would be a gift identified as $10,000 in jewelry. If the jewelry was not worth $10,000, then the estate would provide cash or other items to meet the $10,000 threshold.

denial-of-service attacks. N. A type of risk faced by organizations that rely on the Internet for some aspect of business operations. Denial-of-service attacks are situations in which the organization's computer system is overwhelmed by activity and shuts down. The most familiar denial-of-service attack is a virus that replicates itself and automatically sends itself to all contacts in an address book. The volume of email shuts down the system. For businesses that rely on electronic commerce, a denial-of-service attack can cause bankruptcy quickly.

denominator-level variance. N. See *fixed-overhead volume variance.*

dependency exemption. N. Similar to personal exemption, except it applies to children or other dependents of the taxpayer. At higher income levels, the amounts are reduced. The Internal Revenue Service has rules governing who can claim a dependent, because only one dependency exemption is allowed per person. The taxpayer must supply over half of the dependent's support, and the dependent must be related to the taxpayer, a citizen of the United States, and either single or not filing a joint tax return with a spouse. In addition to having a Social Security number, if the dependent is over 19, his or her income must be less than the exemption. See also *personal exemptions.*

dependent. N. A tax term for an individual who is not financially self-supporting. The person who provides more than half the support for the living expenses of the individual can claim the individual as a dependent on a tax return.

dependent variable. N. A part of a function or formula that is determined by the independent parts of the function. In the cost function, total cost equals the fixed cost plus the variable cost per unit,

times the number of units of activity. The total cost is the
dependent variable because it is determined by the level of output
chosen.

depletion. N. The allocation of the cost of natural resources. The
depletable base, which includes the acquisition costs, exploration
costs, development costs, and restoration costs, is allocated to the
units of the natural resource. The depletable base is divided by the
total estimated units of the resource that the owner expects to
produce from the property. That depletion per unit is multiplied by
the number of units sold to arrive at the cost of goods sold. The
term "depletion" is similar to depreciation on property, plant, and
equipment, except that depletion is always part of the cost of goods
sold.

deposit. N. Additions made by an account holder to a checking or
savings account.

deposit method. N. A method of accounting for payments received
before a sale takes place. Cash received from a customer is classified as a liability on the balance sheet before the revenue is recognized on the income statement. For example, if a lawn service
company offers customers a discount for paying in November, year
one, for the entire contract for year two's summer service, that
payment would not be on the year one income statement, but
instead on the year one balance sheet as a liability. The revenue
would be on year two's income statement.

deposits in transit. N. Additions to a checking account that have
been sent to the bank but do not appear on the latest bank statement (because the most recent transactions are not on the bank
statement).

depreciable base. N. The dollar amount of an asset's historical cost
that becomes the depreciation expense and reduces income over
the time the entity uses the asset. The depreciable base is equal to

the historical cost, which includes all costs necessary to put the asset into use, less the estimated salvage value at the end of the asset's useful life.

depreciable cost. N. See *depreciable base*.

depreciated cost. N. See *depreciated historical cost*.

depreciated historical cost. N. An asset's carrying value measured by the original cost of the asset less any depreciation taken on the asset. Synonymous with *depreciated cost*.

depreciation. N. The method for allocating the cost of a fixed asset to the time periods in which it is being used. Several different methods of calculating the amount of depreciation exist. Some methods spread out the allocation evenly, and others front-end load the depreciation. Depreciation is not intended to reduce the value of the fixed asset to its market value.

derivative financial instruments. N. Complicated financial instruments that get their value based on some underlying asset, such as commodities or bonds, or some indicator, such as interest rates or the Dow Jones Industrial Average. A derivative is a contract in which one party has an obligation to make a payment to the other party, and the amount of the payment depends on some other underlying price or value. The payment amount may be caused by the underlying price rising above a certain value or it may be caused by a quantity of the underlying item changing in value. According to the Financial Accounting Standards Board, a derivative is a financial instrument that has three characteristics: (a) an underlying price or value and a notional or principal amount, or specified payments; (b) no or little initial investment is required; and, (c) settlement is in cash or is easily converted to cash or another derivative.

Derivatives Implementation Group. N. A task force created by the Financial Accounting Standards Board to resolve problems and address questions relating to the implementation of SFAS 133, Accounting for Derivative Instruments and Hedging Activities.

derived service period. N. A service period that must be determined through the use of mathematical models because the ability to exercise the options is based on some market performance measure. For example, an employee is granted options that can be exercised during the next three years, but only if the share price increases by 10%. The valuation models would estimate the time it would take for the stock price to increase by 10%, which would be the derived service period for allocating the compensation expense from the stock options. See also *service period for stock options, explicit service period, implicit service period, requisite service period*.

designated fund balance. N. Part of the unreserved fund balance that identifies amounts that the governmental unit intends to use in a specified way. The designated fund balance appears after liabilities on the balance sheet of the city or state. The designated fund balance is different than the reserved fund balance in that the designated fund balance is not usually legally required. The city council may vote to buy a new snow plow and designate some of the fund balance for that purpose. However, if a major emergency arises, the council could use the funds for another purpose—such as equipment in the waste treatment facility. Reserved fund balance, on the other hand, must be used for the item identified.

designed-in costs. N. See *locked-in costs*.

detachable stock warrants. N. Stock warrants that are part of another security purchase and can be sold separately from the other parts of the security. Companies may include detachable warrants on their bonds to make the bonds more desirable to investors. The company must allocate part of the proceeds from the sale of the bonds to the warrants, because the buyers really bought two securities—the bonds and the warrants. The allocation is based on the relative market value of the bond without the warrants, and the warrants alone. If the company cannot determine the market value of either the bond or the warrants, then the allocation is based on first determining a value for one part, whichever is more reliable, and assigning it to that part of the security. Whatever amount is left from the proceeds is allocated to the remaining part.

detailed testing. N. A classification of audit procedures in which the auditor verifies the accuracy of an account balance through appropriate techniques. See also *vouching of transactions, tracing of transactions.*

detection risk. N. A component of audit risk. Detection risk is the chance that an error will go undetected by the audit procedures. The auditor controls the level of detection risk by planning the type, timing, and quantity of audit activities. If detection risk is set very low, then more audit procedures are necessary.

development costs. N. The costs that a company incurs to remove a natural resource from a particular territory. Development costs must be associated with one particular location, and cannot be associated with another location. For example, development costs could be used for the drilling costs for an oil well, but not for the tanker trucks to transport the oil to the refinery. Development costs are included in the depletable base of the asset.

development-stage enterprises. N. Companies that are in the organizational stages, whose business operations have not really started. Instead, the activities of the entity are focused on getting the new business started. The same rules for the capitalization of costs that apply to businesses already operating apply to development-stage enterprises.

devise. N. A distribution of real property according to the provisions of a will. The person receiving the property is called a devisee. Contrast with a bequest or legacy, which is a distribution of personal property. The person receiving the property is called the legatee.

differential cost. N. A cost used in decision making. Differential cost is the difference in total costs between two alternatives.

digital signature. N. An identifying mark that is sent electronically. Digital signatures are encrypted and used to attest or authenticate whatever they are attached to.

diluted earnings per share. N. A financial-statement analysis ratio that appears on the income statement. The effect of any potential common stock, such as convertible securities or stock warrants, is included in diluted earnings per share. Net income is adjusted for any effect of conversion, such as the absence of interest expense if convertible bonds are converted into stock. The denominator is increased from weighted-average shares outstanding by any additional shares that the company issues. Those additional shares could be from the conversion of convertible securities, or from the exercise of warrants. If issuing the new shares brings in cash (such as when executives exercise stock options), then it is assumed that the company will use the cash to buy back some shares, and only the incremental shares are added to the denominator. Only the effect of potential common stock items that reduce basic earnings per share are included.

direct costing. N. See *variable-costing system*.

direct costs. N. Costs that can be traced to an identifiable product, department, or other cost object.

direct financing lease. N. A type of lease for a lessor. A direct financing lease meets one of the four capitalization criteria and means that the lessor has no uncertain costs associated with the lease and the lessee is likely to pay. A direct financing lease is distinguished from a sales type lease by the absence of a seller's profit. If a lease is a direct financing lease, the lessor removes the asset from the balance sheet and records a receivable. The rental payments received are split between the receivable and interest revenue using the effective interest method. The lessor records no depreciation expense for assets leased on a capital lease.

direct fixed expenses. N. A cost of doing business that stays the same in total over a normal range of activity and is associated with only one segment of a company.

directional testing. N. Audit procedures for checking the amount by which a balance in an account is above or below the account's predetermined balance. Directional testing checks one direction at a time, looking only for overstatement to determine the existence of transactions, or only for understatement to determine the inclusion of all necessary transactions (completeness).

direct labor. N. The cost of the labor associated with the actual manufacture of goods. The direct labor costs become part of the inventory value of the finished goods and are transferred to the income statement as the cost of goods sold, when the items are sold. An example of direct labor is the cost of a carpenter's wages in a cabinet-making shop. See also *indirect labor*.

direct-labor budget. N. Part of the master budget that plans the number and cost of direct-labor hours needed to meet the production budget.

direct materials. N. The cost of raw materials used in the actual manufacture of goods. Direct materials are observable and measurable, so the cost of direct materials can be traced to the product.

The cost of direct materials becomes part of the inventory value of the finished goods and is transferred to the income statement as the cost of goods sold, when the items are sold. For example, the wood used in cabinet making is a direct material. The wood is visible in the finished cabinet, and the quantity used is measurable. See also *indirect materials*.

direct-materials inventory. N. See *raw materials inventory*.

direct-materials purchases budget. N. Part of the master budget that plans the timing and quantity of direct materials and estimates the cost of materials needed to meet the production-budget requirements. The desired ending inventory of direct materials is also factored into the plan.

direct method of allocation. N. A method of allocating support-department costs to products. The direct method assigns those support-department costs only to producing departments. Contrast with the sequential method of allocation and the reciprocal method of allocation, which both allocate support-department costs to other support departments before allocating the total support cost to producing departments. See also *sequential method of allocation, reciprocal method of allocation*.

direct method of determining cash from operating activities. N. One of two acceptable methods of determining cash from operating activities, on the statement of cash flows. It is the method encouraged by the Financial Accounting Standards Board. All the operating items on the income statement are converted from their accrual amounts to cash amounts. Companies use this method in the operating activities section, and must also disclose a reconciliation from net income to cash from operating activities. Synonymous with *income-statement method*.

direct tracing. N. A technique used in assigning costs to products. Direct tracing allocates costs based on clear, usually observable relationships between the cost and the product, and is easily done for direct materials and direct labor. For example, a truck uses an observable amount of steel, plastic, tires, etc. The manufacturing of a truck also uses an observable amount of labor.

direct write-off method. N. A procedure for determining bad-debt expense. The direct write-off method makes no estimate, but records bad-debt expense only when a bad debt is identified. At that time, the receivable is removed from the balance sheet and the bad-debt expense is recorded and included in income. The direct write-off method does not comply with generally accepted accounting principles and violates the matching principle because the expense is usually taken in an accounting period after the sale is recorded on the income statement. This method is used for tax purposes in determining the amount of bad-debt deduction. Synonymous with *specific write-off method.*

disabled-access credit. N. A type of general business tax credit for up to $5,000 on modifications made to business facilities to accommodate disabled employees, customers, or others. The amount of the credit depends on the amount of the expenditures. The disabled-access credit is one of several general business credits, and the total of all these credits cannot be more than an amount based on the net income for the year. The amount of excess can be carried back one year and forward twenty years.

disaster recovery plan. N. The procedures for continuing operations if an organization's facilities are not operational. An important component of a disaster recovery plan is the strategy for restoring computer facilities and the information and data necessary to operate. Back-up disks and off-site storage, plus a location for computers and processing, are key pieces of the plan.

disbursement. N. A payment of a debt or an expense.

discharge of debt income. N. The amount of debt a creditor forgives a business. The debtor must include this amount as income for tax purposes. If the debtor is not in bankruptcy, and the amount of the debt forgiveness is less than the difference between the fair market value of the business assets and the liabilities, then the debtor can avoid this inclusion.

discharge of indebtedness income. N. Taxable income that arises when an individual has a debt forgiven without repayment. The excess of the mortgage over the value of the property is taxable income in a foreclosure. ABBRV. *DOI*.

disclaimer of an opinion. N. A type of audit opinion in which the auditor expresses no opinion because the auditor does not have enough information to form an opinion. The disclaimer of an opinion does not indicate that the financial statements are bad, but only that the auditor cannot issue any opinion.

disclaimer-of-opinion audit report. N. The formal judgment made by a certified public accountant (CPA) firm after auditing an organization. A disclaimer-of-opinion report states that the auditor was not able to determine if the statements are fair. A disclaimer is issued when the auditor is unable to gain access to all necessary aspects of the business or is unsure of the going-concern status of the client organization, or when the CPA firm is not independent. The audit report is included in the required Securities and Exchange Commission filings and in the annual report of the organization.

disclosure. N. Including information in the financial statements and notes of a business. If the accounting standard requires disclosure, the transaction must either be recorded in an account or a written explanation must be included in the notes to the financial statement.

disclosure fraud. N. Releasing misleading information in press releases or missing or fraudulent notes to the financial statements.

discontinued operations. N. A readily identifiable part of a business that the company decides to dispose of. To qualify as discontinued operations, the part of the company eliminated must have separate assets, activities, and operations. If eliminating a segment qualifies as discontinued operations, the company can put the results of operations and the gains or losses on disposal in the nonrecurring section of the income statement—after the earnings number that follows the provision for taxes. Analysts often ignore the results of discontinued operations, which is usually advantageous for the company eliminating an underperforming segment. If the disposal does not meet the requirements for discontinued operations, then the revenues and expenses remain in the operating section, and the gains or losses are part of continuing operations.

discounted cash flow. N. The process of identifying the amount and timing of cash inflows and outflows and then using time-value-of-money techniques to measure them at one point in time.

discounted-cash-flow method of determining cost of equity. N. See *dividend-yield-plus-growth-rate approach.*

discounted payback period. N. A decision rule for accepting or rejecting capital budgeting projects that is a modification of the payback period rule. Instead of using the estimated annual profit, the discounted-payback-period method adjusts each cash flow to its present value and then determines the time (in years) necessary to cover the original cost. The discount rate is the cost of capital for the project. See also *payback period.*

discounting. N. The process of finding the present value of a specified amount at a designated time in the future, using a specified interest rate.

discount-interest loans. N. Loans in which the interest is deducted from the proceeds at the beginning of the loan term. The borrower signs a contract for the face amount of the loan but receives less than that amount in cash. The interest on the loan is paid at the beginning of the loan term.

discount on bonds payable. N. A contra-liability account associated with bonds payable on the balance sheet. It is equal to the difference between the face value of bonds and the amount of cash received, when that amount is less than the face value. A discount results when the interest payments on the bonds are at a rate less than bonds with similar risk characteristics. Investors are willing to buy the bonds with the lower interest but will not pay the face value. The effect is to increase the interest rate. See also *bonds payable*. Synonymous with *bond discount*.

discount rate. N. The interest rate used to calculate the present value of dollars to be paid or received in the future. The choice of a discount rate is critical. The higher the discount rate, the lower the present value. That means that when calculating the present value of cash outflows, businesses would rather use a higher discount rate, because that would produce the lowest liability.

discovery basis. N. A theoretical method of recognizing revenue based on the increasing value of the asset because of a discovery of a natural resource as part of the asset. Theoretically, land becomes more valuable if oil is discovered or estimates or reserves increase, resulting in higher revenue in the future. The Securities and Exchange Commission requires some disclosure of oil reserves, but discovery basis is not an acceptable method of revenue recognition for generally accepted accounting principles.

discovery sampling. N. A method of drawing inferences about a population based on the occurrences of something in a sample from the population. For example, an investigator can draw a sample of checks from a company's accounts. The discovery of a number of fraudulent checks in the sample can be used to estimate the total amount of fraudulent checks.

discretionary costs. N. Those costs that are not directly caused by output increases and are associated with the time period. Examples of discretionary costs include advertising and sales training.

discretionary income. N. The amount of earnings that remains after tax payments and essentials (such as food, clothing, shelter, insurance, utilities, etc.). Discretionary income is either spent on nonessential items or saved.

discussion memorandum. N. The first public presentation of a proposed Financial Accounting Standards Board (FASB) standard. The FASB seeks reaction to the discussion memorandum through public hearings. The public reaction is used to craft the exposure draft of a proposed statement. See also *exposure draft*.

disguised sale. N. A distribution from a business to an owner that really represents a sale. Usually the return of investment is not taxed, but if an owner receives cash in the same transaction as an exchange of assets, it will have some tax ramifications for the owner.

disposable income. N. The amount of earnings that remains after tax payments. Disposable income is spent on discretionary items or necessary items such as food, clothing, or housing, or it is saved.

disposal date. N. The date the assets of a segment of an organization are sold, or the date operations cease, if no sale is involved.

dissimilar nonmonetary asset. N. Assets other than cash, receivables, or investments that are not similar. That is, the assets are not alike or do not fulfill the same purpose in the business. The classification of nonmonetary assets as dissimilar is important in an exchange. In an exchange of dissimilar nonmonetary assets, any gain or loss in the amount of the difference between the fair value of assets received and the book value of assets given up is recorded on the income statement. This treatment is unlike the exchange of similar nonmonetary assets, in which only loss—not gain—is recorded. See also *nonmonetary-asset exchange*.

distributions. N. Withdrawals from businesses. This term is used in tax topics.

distributive share. N. The amount of partnership income, gain, deduction, loss, or credit that is allocated to a partner for tax purposes on Schedule K-1. The partnership agreement determines the allocation. The tax allocations have to be similar to the capital account allocations.

diversifiable risk. N. The part of a stock's risk (the uncertainty of its return) that can be removed if the stock is held as part of a set of stock investments containing at least forty different stocks. Diversifiable risk is caused by events that are specific to a company, and if enough different stocks are held, the good and bad events will balance out. Synonymous with *unsystematic risk, company-specific risk*.

divestiture. N. A general term to indicate the sale of a company's assets. Spin-offs, carve-outs, and liquidations are types of divestitures.

dividend-irrelevance theory. N. A theory that states that the dividend policy has no effect on the stock price or cost of capital. The basis for the dividend-irrelevance theory is that a stockholder can create any desired dividend by selling or buying shares. A dividend viewed as too low can be increased by selling shares, and one that is too high can be decreased by buying shares. The theory is based on simplifying assumptions that include no taxes or brokerage costs. Empirical tests of this theory have not been conclusive.

dividend payout ratio. N. The percentage of net income paid as dividends to shareholders. Calculated as dividends per share divided by earnings per share.

dividend-reinvestment plan. N. A way to receive dividends in the form of additional shares of stock. A dividend-reinvestment plan is an opt-in plan for shareholders that allows them to have their cash dividends automatically purchase more shares of stock. The shareholder must pay taxes on the dividends, even though the cash is never received. ABBRV. *DRIP.*

dividends. N. Distributions, usually cash, to stockholders. Dividends represent a portion of the corporation's earnings, and they reduce retained earnings. The corporation's board of directors votes on the dividends and as soon as they are approved, a liability, dividends payable, is created. Not all companies pay dividends, even companies with strong earnings. Instead, those dollars are reinvested in the company and stockholders receive their return in the form of a higher stock price when they sell their shares. Dividends paid to holders of common stock are called common dividends, and those paid to holders of preferred stock are called preferred dividends. No dividends are paid on treasury stock. See also *property dividends, scrip dividends, stock dividends, stock splits, declaration date, date of record, payment date.*

dividends in arrears. N. The dividends on cumulative preferred stock that have not been paid but are guaranteed to the shareholders. See also *cumulative preferred stock.* Synonymous with *arrearages.*

dividends in kind. N. See *property dividends.*

dividend-yield-plus-growth-rate approach. N. A method for estimating the cost of retained earnings equal to the dividend rate plus
the expected growth rate. The dividend rate is equal to the dividend
per share divided by the price per share. The growth rate can be
determined by using an average rate from analysts or by multiplying the retention rate, one minus the payout rate, times the
return on equity. See also *cost of equity*. Synonymous with
discounted-cash-flow method of determining cost of equity.

DJIA. ABBRV. Dow Jones Industrial Average.

documentary evidence. N. One type of evidence gathered in a
fraud investigation. Documentary evidence originates with documents, either paper or electronic. Examples of documentary
evidence include computer reports, public record searches, and
financial statement analysis. See also *evidence square*.

DOI. ABBRV. Discharge of indebtedness income.

dollar-unit sampling. N. See *probability-proportional-to-size
sampling*.

dollar-value LIFO. N. Dollar value last in, first out. A cost-flow
assumption based on last in, first out (LIFO) that adds new LIFO
layers only if the value of ending inventory, indexed to the
purchasing power at the beginning of the accounting period, is
greater than the value of beginning inventory. That difference,
measured in dollars of equal purchasing power, represents the real
increase. Then, to get the ending inventory balance, the difference
is adjusted for the change in purchasing power during the year and
added to beginning inventory.

domain address. N. The text that identifies a particular Internet
location. The form of an Internet address is account@site.code. A
specific computer can be inserted following @, separated by a
period from the site. The code at the end of the address indicates

the type of user—"com" stands for commercial, "edu" stands for educational organization, etc. Synonymous with *universal resource locator*.

donation. N. Assets that have been given to an entity and recorded at market value.

donor-imposed restrictions. N. Qualifications put on a contribution to a not-for-profit organization that determine the classification of the amount as unrestricted, temporarily restricted, or permanently restricted net assets. If the donor puts no restrictions on the contribution, then the amount is unrestricted. If the donor specifies a particular program or time period, the amount is temporarily restricted, and the restriction expires when the program is done or the time period is over. Some contributions that are classified as temporarily restricted are reclassified as unrestricted little by little over a long time period. If the donor sets up an endowment for a particular purpose, the contribution is permanently restricted.

double-entry accounting system. N. The system underlying the recording of transactions in which the dollar value of an entry's debits must be equal to the dollar value of the entry's credits.

double extension. N. Calculating dollar-value LIFO (last in, first out) using complete base-year prices and end-of-year prices for individual inventory items. Simplification is possible through the use of a price index.

double-loop feedback. N. Information about performance that tells managers how well the performance matches the measure and how well the measure relates to the actual goal.

Dow Jones Industrial Average. N. A measure of stock market performance. The Dow Jones Industrial Average is the sum of the prices of thirty high-quality stocks, divided by a leveler to account for splits and other changes. The calculation takes into account stock splits that have occurred in the past, which is why the number can be greater than 9,000. By choosing companies in various sectors of the economy, the average is a good indicator of the overall economy. If the average is high, it means that stock prices are high, indicating that investors are viewing companies' future earnings as good. www.dowjones.com. ABBRV. *DJIA*.

downsizing. N. Reducing the number of employees through layoffs.

downward-demand spiral. N. The result of pricing decisions based on decreased volume and excess capacity that reduces sales, causing more and more price decisions based on decreased demand and excess capacity, and so on. Selling prices are raised when volume decreases, because the sales revenue from fewer units has to cover the same fixed costs.

drawing account. N. An account in the equity section of an unincorporated business's balance sheet. All withdrawals that the owner makes from the business are recorded in the drawing account, reducing the business's equity.

DRD. ABBRV. Deductions in respect of a decedent.

DRIP. ABBRV. Dividend-reinvestment plan.

driver analysis. N. The investigation of an activity to determine the causes of costs associated with the activity. Part of process-value analysis, the goal of which is to continuously improve the performance of an entity. For example, if an activity is transferring work-in-process from one department to the next, the underlying cost may be the factory layout.

driver tracing. N. A technique used in assigning costs to products. Driver tracing allocates costs based on some factor (the driver) related to the amount of resources used by the product. In a business that produces headboards, the costs of stain, varnish, sandpaper, and brushes could be allocated based on the driver—the bed size. Logically, a twin-size headboard would use less of these materials than a king-size headboard.

dual-purpose test. N. An auditing procedure that tests both an internal control activity and the correctness of the account balance.

due diligence. N. An evaluation of a company's ability to repay debt. The extent of the procedures depends on the amount of the loan and the loan history. Due diligence is also performed prior to a company's issuance of stock.

due process procedure. N. The steps in establishing accounting standards that involve public participation in decision making. In the first step, the Financial Accounting Standards Board (FASB) issues a discussion memorandum that identifies the issues and the initial views of board members. The public can provide comment letters or attend public hearings, if held. In the next step, an exposure draft is issued. The FASB presents the proposed accounting treatment in the exposure draft, which is the result of research and public comment on the discussion memorandum. The public is again encouraged to comment. In the last step, the final standard is issued, following a vote of the FASB.

due professional care. N. A term used in auditing standards to describe how auditors should perform audits. Due professional care means competence but not perfection.

dummy company. N. See *shell company*.

dumping. N. An illegal pricing method in which goods are sold below cost in another country. In the 1980s, American car companies believed that Japanese car companies were dumping because the prices were so low.

Du Pont equation. N. A financial analysis tool that measures the return on assets. The formula is profit margin multiplied by total assets turnover. The profit margin is equal to net income divided by sales, and it represents the amount of profit each dollar of sales produces. The total assets turnover is calculated by dividing sales by total assets, and it indicates how many dollars in sales each dollar of assets produces. The extended Du Pont equation combines the profit margin, total assets turnover, and equity multiplier to calculate the return on equity. The basic equation for return on equity is net income divided by total common equity, but the Du Pont equation shows the interaction of profit margin, asset turnover, and leverage in producing the return on equity. The formula for the extended Du Pont equation is profit margin times total assets turnover times the equity multiplier.

duration. N. The measure of a bond's susceptibility to value change because of interest rate changes and the holding period. Duration is a built-in function in Microsoft Excel as part of the Analysis ToolPak.

Dutch auction. N. A method of trading securities in which the amount of securities available for sale is announced, and then prospective buyers or sellers submit the price at which they trade. Treasury bills are sold in this way, and investors wanting to buy propose their purchase prices. The sale takes place at the highest price bid. Companies may repurchase their stocks using a Dutch auction. The company announces how many shares it wants to buy, and shareholders submit the selling price they will take. All shares are purchased at the lowest price bid.

E&P. ABBRV. Earnings and profits.

early extinguishment of debt. N. The repayment of borrowings before the due date. A company may choose this option in order to refinance at a lower interest rate.

earned capital. N. See *retained earnings*.

earned income. N. Wages, salaries, tips, commissions, and other forms of compensation for services received by an individual taxpayer.

earned income credit. N. A type of refundable credit, meaning that the credit can offset the taxpayer's tax liability, and if the credit exceeds the liability, the taxpayer will receive a refund for that excess. Taxpayers with earned income of under $39,783 in 2007 may be eligible for the credit depending on the number of children they have. The earned income credit is designed to provide an incentive for low-income people to work. While primarily designed for taxpayers with children, a taxpayer without children may qualify for the earned income credit if he or she is living in the United States for at least half the year, is between the ages of 25 and 64, and is not a dependent of another taxpayer. ABBRV. *EIC*.

earned surplus. N. Another name for retained earnings, an account in the stockholders' equity section of the balance sheet. The term is not used much now because the accounting profession prefers "retained earnings."

earnest money. N. A sum of money put down on a contract to illustrate to the other party the serious intent to go through with a transaction.

earnings. N. The net income of a company.

earnings and profits. N. The theoretical measure of a corporation's ability to pay dividends without liquidating the shareholders' investments. ABBRV. *E&P*.

earnings before interest and taxes. N. Calculated as net income plus interest expense, plus provision for income taxes. All the variables are found on the income statement. ABBRV. *EBIT*.

earnings-conservatism ratio. N. A rough measure of earnings quality that looks at the relationship between pretax income on the income statement adjusted for permanent differences, divided by taxable income on the tax return. Managers have incentives to reduce taxable income to the lowest possible level and to increase net income to the highest possible level. The closer the earnings-conservatism ratio is to one, the more conservative the firm's accounting policies.

earnings forecast. N. An estimate of future earnings. The estimate may be made by management or by analysts.

earnings management. N. Manipulating the inclusion of revenues, expenses, gains, and losses to achieve a desired effect, such as meeting analyst expectations, the earnings forecast, or bonus thresholds.

earnings multiplier. N. See *price-earnings ratio*.

earnings per share. N. The dollar amount of the period's net income that is available to each share of common stock. Basic earnings per share (EPS) are calculated by deducting any preferred dividends due to preferred stock shareholders for the period, and dividing by the weighted average number of common shares of stock outstanding during the period. Diluted earnings per share include an adjustment for common stock equivalents, resulting in lower earnings per share than basic EPS. See also *simple capital structure, basic earnings per share, diluted earnings per share, complex capital structure, common stock equivalent, antidilutive.* ABBRV. *EPS.*

earnings surprise. N. A term used to describe a situation in which a company reports earnings that are not what investors predicted. Investors use forecast earnings to establish the stock price, and if the actual earnings are different than the forecast, investors use that new information to set a new stock price.

EBIT. ABBRV. Earnings before interest and taxes.

EBITDA. N. Earnings before interest, taxes, depreciation, and amortization.

EBITDA-coverage ratio. N. Earnings before interest, taxes, depreciation, and amortization coverage ratio. Measures the ability of a company to service its debt. The formula includes EBITDA plus lease payments in the numerator. The denominator is the interest expense plus principal payments plus lease payments. The EBITDA-coverage ratio is used by lenders for short-term lending, and times interest earned is used for long-term lending.

eco-efficiency. N. The concept that businesses do not have to sacrifice production of goods and services to reduce pollution or other negative environmental effects. Basic to this concept are the beliefs that profits and good environmental stewardship go together, and that environmental stewardship is a necessary component for competitive advantage.

e-commerce. ABBRV. Electronic commerce.

economic-entity assumption. N. A basis for accounting in which business transactions are separated from personal and nonbusiness transactions. The economic-entity assumption is especially important for a small business or sole proprietor. It would be hard to determine the success or failure of a business if the owner counted personal expenses as business expenses. Synonymous with *entity concept*.

economic extortion. N. A type of fraud in which an employee demands payment from someone outside the company to make a decision that favors the payer.

economic growth. N. An increased level of production of goods and services within a country. Economic growth includes the increase in value resulting from inflation and the real growth resulting from innovation, technology improvements, and external factors.

economic-life test. N. One of the four capitalization criteria for leases. If the term of the lease, including any bargain renewal option, is equal to or greater than 75% of the useful life of the asset, the lease is a capital lease because it has met the economic-life test.

economic nexus. N. A substantial business relationship between residents of a state and a business that is not located or incorporated in the state, which allows the state to tax the corporation. The relationship involves the corporation selling to residents of the state. If the sale is of tangible goods, economic nexus is not established, according to federal law.

economic-order quantity. N. A mathematical computation used to determine the size of an inventory order to minimize the cost of ordering and carrying inventory. The economic-order quantity is equal to the square root of two, times the cost of placing and receiving an order, times the annual demand for the inventory item, divided by the cost of carrying one unit of inventory for a year. The economic-order quantity can help determine how much inventory to order whenever an order is placed. ABBRV. *EOQ*.

economic performance. N. The standard for determining the tax deductibility of expenses. If a business wants to deduct an amount that has not been paid—that is, an unconditional liability—the actual service or good must be provided for the expense to be tax deductible. For example, if Karen contracts with Kathy on September 1 to provide $50,000 of design services, and by the end of the year Kathy has only provided half the services, Karen can only deduct $25,000.

economic-performance test. N. One of two tests to determine if an item is included in income for the year or if it is deductible as an expense for the year. The economic-performance test requires that the service or property involved be provided by the other party to the taxpayer.

economic value added. N. A financial analysis tool that measures the difference between after-tax operating income and the average cost of capital. A positive difference indicates that economic value is being added to the organization. ABBRV. *EVA.*

EDGAR. ABBRV. Electronic Data Gathering, Analysis, and Retrieval system.

EDI. ABBRV. Electronic data interchange.

edit tests. N. A method for checking the accuracy of data transcription in which a program compares entered data with a specified value or format and rejects entries that do not comply.

education-expense deduction. N. A tax deduction applicable if the education is a necessary part of the taxpayer's business. The education costs are deductible if they are required by law or an employer, and if the education is associated with improving or maintaining the taxpayer's skills—but not if it is used to meet minimum qualifications. If the expenses meet the requirements, the deduction may be for adjusted gross income if the taxpayer is self-employed, but from adjusted gross income if the taxpayer is an employee. See also *Hope Scholarship Credit, Lifetime Learning Credit.*

Education IRA. N. See *Coverdell Education Savings Account.*

effective-interest method. N. Used to allocate the discount or premium from a bond sale to interest expense. First, calculate the carrying value of the bond, which is the maturity value of the bond less the unamortized discount or plus the unamortized premium. Then, calculate the interest expense as the product of the carrying value at the beginning of the period and the effective rate of the bond, adjusting if necessary for a period less than a year. Next, compare the interest expense to the cash-interest payment, the product of the maturity value and the stated rate, adjusting if necessary for a period less than a year. The difference is the amount by which the premium or discount is decreased, resulting in a carrying value closer to the maturity value of the bond than existed at the beginning of the period.

effective rate for a bond. N. See *effective yield on a bond.*

effective tax rate. N. A calculation that represents the percentage of total economic income that the entity pays in taxes. The tax liability for the year is divided by the measure of total economic income. Total economic income is not strictly defined, but usually includes nontaxable interest and business deductions, but not personal deductions. The effective tax rate is calculated as the total income tax expense for the period divided by the pretax financial accounting income. Synonymous with *book tax rate.*

effective yield on a bond. N. The rate of interest actually earned by the bondholders, taking into account the interest payments and maturity value received versus the purchase price of the bond. Synonymous with *effective rate for a bond, market rate (in relation to bonds).*

efficiency variance. N. See *usage variance*.

efficient markets hypothesis. N. A theory that the price of stocks is based on all available information, resulting in investors being unable to beat the market over time.

EFT. ABBRV. Electronic funds transfer.

EIC. ABBRV. Earned income credit.

EIN. ABBRV. Employer identification number.

EITF. ABBRV. Emerging Issues Task Force.

eldercare services. N. A line of services provided by certified public accountants for older people and their families. Eldercare services include handling the finances for the elderly, checking that income is deposited and accurate, and verifying that bills are appropriate and correct.

electronic commerce. N. Selling products or services over the Internet. ABBRV. *e-commerce*.

Electronic Data Gathering, Analysis, and Retrieval system. N. An electronic database of Securities and Exchange Commission filings that is available to the public. www.sec.gov/edgar.shtml. ABBRV. *EDGAR*.

electronic data interchange. N. A type of communication between entities that replaces paper documents with information transmitted between computers. Transmission takes place through phone lines or high-speed dedicated communication (integrated services digital network) lines. This is sometimes called a paperless system. A company may send a digital purchase order to a supplier. If it has the capability, the seller can process the order and do the billing without any manual data entry. This may complicate the audit trail. Another example is a phone company sending bills to customers via email. ABBRV. *EDI.*

electronic funds transfer. N. A method of paying or receiving cash without the actual, physical transfer of cash or a check to the payee. The payer directly increases the bank account of the payee through an electronic transaction between the banks involved. Employers may use electronic funds transfer to increase employees' bank accounts rather than issue a paycheck. ABBRV. *EFT.*

elements of fraud. N. The three aspects that are part of every fraud: the theft act, concealment, and conversion.

elephant. N. An institutional investor that is so large that any trade by that entity affects the market price of the stock being traded.

Elijah Watt Sells Award. N. An award given to the three candidates with the top scores on the certified public accountant exam. The candidates must have taken and passed all four parts in one sitting. The American Institute of Certified Public Accountants (AICPA) makes the award in honor of Elijah Watt Sells, a founding partner of Haskins & Sells—now called Deloitte & Touche—who helped found the AICPA.

email. N. Electronic mail, or a way of communicating via the Internet. The recipient must have an email address, which is an account on a particular domain. The sender types in the recipient's account followed by "@" and the domain address.

embedded audit module. N. An audit procedure for collecting data for the audit through a program code added to applications. Embedded audit modules allow the auditor to collect data as the processing is taking place, rather than at the time of the audit.

embedded derivative. N. A term used to identify an aspect of a derivative financial instrument. The embedded derivative is part of another nonderivative financial instrument. For example, Company A loans Company B $1 million to be repaid in three years. Instead of interest, Company A will receive the difference between the market price of 1,000 shares of Company A stock today, at $40 per share, and the price at the end of each of the next three years. No other interest is paid. The embedded derivative is the annual payment based on the increase in share price. The host contract is the $1 million loan.

embezzle. v. To steal from an employer (by an employee who has custody of the asset being stolen). A bookkeeper could embezzle cash by lapping of accounts receivable.

emerging company. N. A company that is newly organized and needs to borrow to acquire the fixed assets it needs. Emerging companies often have net losses from operations.

Emerging Issues Task Force. N. A creation of the Financial Accounting Standards Board with representatives from public and corporate accounting firms. The charge of the Emerging Issues Task Force is to determine how to account for unusual or new kinds of financial transactions. ABBRV. *EITF*.

employee contribution. N. Pretax dollars put into a company pension plan that are withheld from employees' paychecks.

employee expense deduction. N. Part of the miscellaneous itemized deduction that appears on Schedule A and is limited to the amount over 2% of adjusted gross income. Employee expenses include uniforms, union dues, professional journals, professional organization dues, small tools and supplies, and employment agency fees.

Employee Retirement Income Security Act of 1974. N. A federal law that affects the pension plans of nearly all companies in the United States. The law establishes requirements meant to make pension plans fair to employees and financially sound—even in the event of the employer going out of business. ABBRV. *ERISA*.

employee-stock-ownership plans. N. A benefit provided to employees in which they can purchase stock in the employer corporation. The plan can be part of the pension package offered to employees. ABBRV. *ESOP*.

employee stock purchase plan. N. A benefit offered by some companies in which an employee can purchase the stock of the company at a discount through a payroll deduction. The employee does not have to recognize the discount as income at the time of purchase if the discount is less than 15% from the market price. ABBRV. *ESPP*.

employer identification number. N. A number assigned by the Internal Revenue Service and used by a company for various reporting functions, including employee withholding and income taxes. ABBRV. *EIN*.

employer matching contribution. N. Dollars put into a pension plan for employees. The amount is based on the amount employees contribute to the plan.

employment taxes. N. See *payroll taxes*.

empowerment-zone employment credit. N. A tax incentive for small businesses in empowerment zones that provides a tax credit for employees who live and work in the zone. While the tax credit offsets the amount of tax payable, it also reduces the deduction for salary paid to those employees.

empowerment zones. N. Designated geographical areas that meet certain criteria in terms of poverty and unemployment. Businesses operating in an empowerment zone are eligible for tax incentives for employing residents of the zone and for buying business property in the zone. Businesses can also use special tax-exempt financing to buy property located in an empowerment zone. Empowerment zones can be located in either urban or rural areas.

enacted future tax rate. N. Tax rates that will be in effect in the future as a result of laws already passed by Congress. When calculating the deferred-tax expense or deferred-tax benefit, the entity must use the rates that will be in effect when the temporary differences reverse.

encryption. N. Similar to the use of secret codes during wartime, the process of disguising the real meaning of data through a coding process. Organizations use this process with sensitive data that needs privacy and security protection. The data is coded, entered into the accounting information system, and stored or transmitted in the coded state. The user has to have the right encryption key to decode the data.

encryption key. N. The solution to the code used to input data into the accounting information system of an organization. See also *encryption*.

encumbrance system. N. A method of keeping track of planned expenditures in a governmental accounting system. The encumbrances account is a control account that is debited (increased) for every amount that will have to be paid. The encumbrances account acts like a running total of all credit purchases made during the period and it is credited (reduced) when payment is made. The encumbrances account is also linked to subsidiary accounts representing all the types of expenditures. The individual amounts are recorded in the subsidiary accounts, too. At the end of the accounting period, the encumbrances account reduces the undesignated fund balance. The encumbrance system is an effective way to keep track of spending because each subsidiary account has a record of the budgeted amount, the amount spent, and the amount spent but not yet paid for.

ending-finished-goods-inventory budget. N. Part of the master budget that identifies the costs in the ending-finished-goods-inventory that appears in the current asset section of the year-end balance sheet.

ending inventory. N. The value in dollars, and the number in units, in inventory at the end of the accounting period. Ending inventory is used to calculate the cost of goods sold. The dollar amount is shown on the balance sheet as a current asset. The number of units in inventory is used in internal decision making. Ending inventory from one year becomes the next year's beginning inventory.

endowment. N. A sum of money given to an organization that is invested and whose return on the investment is used for a specific purpose. An alumnus may donate an endowment to a college and the interest may be used to fund a scholarship every year.

engagement letter. N. An agreement between an accounting firm and a client on procedures, extent, fees, and responsibilities associated with accounting services. The engagement letter clarifies not only the accounting firm's role, but also the information and support the client will provide if the services are performed at the client's office.

engagement risk. N. A type of risk faced by accounting firms that is based on the characteristics of the client. The risk of accepting a bad client includes lawsuits, loss of reputation, inability to collect fees, or defection of other clients. The engagement risk sets the context for determining audit risk.

engineered costs. N. Costs directly caused by output. Engineered costs increase as output increases, and an increase in output causes an increased cost. Engineered costs can be either direct or indirect. Direct materials are clearly an engineered cost. Indirect costs, such as equipment, also are engineered costs because if output increases above an existing capacity, it is necessary to purchase more machinery.

enrolled agent. N. An individual who has passed an exam covering tax law administered by the U.S. Treasury Department. An enrolled agent advises individuals and businesses on tax matters and can represent them in a claim against the Internal Revenue Service.

enterprise communities. N. Designated geographical areas that meet certain criteria in terms of poverty and unemployment. Businesses operating in communities are eligible for tax incentives for employing residents of the community and for buying business property in these communities. Businesses can also use special tax-exempt financing to buy the property located in the enterprise community. Most enterprise communities are in rural areas, but they can be in urban areas.

enterprise fund. N. A type of fund used in governmental accounting that is a proprietary fund, meaning it performs a business-type function with users paying for the service. Enterprise funds provide business-type services to the general public. Contrast with internal service funds, which provide business-type services within the government.

enterprise network. N. A system of connecting all the parts of an entity so that information is always available. Usually this involves client/server computing that allows any computer in the network to access, manipulate, analyze, and change data. See also *client/server computing*.

enterprise-resource-planning software. N. Computer programs that allow entities to share and use data throughout the organization. This application software is useful for coordinating accounts receivable, inventory, and marketing after a sale is made. The real advantage is that all the functional areas are using the same information rather than maintaining their own information, which may differ from area to area. ABBRV. *ERP*.

entertainment expense. N. A tax deduction deductible for adjusted gross income if the taxpayer is self-employed, and deducted from adjusted gross income if the taxpayer is an employee and the expense is not reimbursed. For the employee, the entertainment-expense deduction is part of the miscellaneous itemized deduction. Entertainment expense is limited to 50% of the cost, must have complete documentation, and must be directly associated with business activities. Any costs considered lavish or extravagant are not allowed. The cost of club dues is not deductible.

entity concept. N. See *economic-entity assumption*.

entity theory of partnerships. N. A framework for viewing partnerships. The entity theory of partnerships looks at partnerships like corporations as if the partnership were distinct from the partners. Contrast this with the aggregate theory of partnerships, which views the partnerships as nonexistent and as simply a collection of partners.

entity view of the firm. N. A perspective that emphasizes the assets used by a firm. The defining characteristics of a company are the assets that are used to carry out business activities. The accounting equation for the entity view is assets = liabilities + owners' equity. Contrast with the proprietary view of the firm, which focuses on equity and emphasizes the owners' investments as the defining characteristics. The accounting equation for the proprietary view is assets – liabilities = owners' equity.

entrepreneur. N. A businessperson who creates a successful business through hard work, creativity, innovation, and big-picture thinking.

entry. N. A journal entry, or the recording of events in a business's accounting system.

entry cost. N. The replacement cost.

environmental costs. N. The costs that result from detecting or causing environmental damage.

environmental detection costs. N. The costs of actions or efforts to establish conformity with environmental laws and standards. An example is testing the air around a power plant for pollution.

environmental external-failure costs. N. The costs of actions or efforts to deal with contaminants already released into the environment. Environmental external-failure costs may be paid by the company or by society. Examples include cleaning up oil spills or managing increased medical problems due to pollution.

environmental internal-failure costs. N. The costs of actions or efforts to handle contaminants before their release into the environment, in accordance with laws or standards. Examples include installing filters on smokestacks and chilling heated water before discharging it into a lake.

environmental prevention costs. N. The costs of actions or efforts necessary to avoid environmental damage. Examples include recycling and designing processes that do not pollute or damage the environment.

environment risk. N. Part of audit risk. Environment risk is the chance that a material error, intentional or unintentional, is present in the financial records and will not be caught by the internal control system. Environment risk, a combination of inherent risk and control risk, is determined by the attributes of the client and cannot be controlled by the auditor. Rather, the auditor designs procedures to react to the environment risk.

EOQ. ABBRV. Economic-order quantity.

EPS. ABBRV. Earnings per share.

equilibrium. N. A state in which things are in balance and opposing forces counterbalance each other. In economic terms, equilibrium results when the expected rate of return equals the actual, resulting in a stable share price.

equity. N. (1) A section of the balance sheet that is equal to the difference between the total assets and total liabilities. It represents contributions by owners plus earnings, less any distributions to owners, and it is called stockholders' equity in a corporation and owner's equity for a sole proprietor. (2) An ownership right, such as equity in real estate, that represents the amount of the property value that is not financed. Synonymous with *net assets*.

equity funds. N. A type of mutual fund with an investment policy that stipulates that stocks will be the majority of the investment.

equity investor. N. An entity that supplies capital in exchange for an ownership right. A shareholder or stockholder of a company is an equity investor. An investor that buys shares of stock is an equity investor.

equity kicker. N. An opportunity to buy stock that is somehow attached to the purchase of a debt security. The opportunity becomes real if certain conditions exist (e.g., a particular date arrives or a merger occurs). Bonds with detachable warrants are an example of a bond with an equity kicker.

equity method of accounting for investments. N. Used when the investor has significant influence—but not control—over the investee. Significant influence is presumed if between 20% and 50% of the outstanding stock is owned by one investor. Three important issues in equity-method accounting include the original cost versus the underlying assets, the treatment of dividends received, and the investment income. The first issue, the cost versus value, arises if the investor pays more for the investment than the investee's book value for the proportionate share purchased. That difference is amortized over a logical period of time. The second issue is the treatment of dividends. When using the equity method, the investor does not record the dividends received as investment income. Instead, the amount of the dividends reduces the balance-sheet value of the investment. The third issue, the recognition of investment income, is handled by allowing the investor to include in income a proportionate share of the investee's income. Because no cash is received for this, the investment account is increased to balance the revenue transaction.

equity multiplier. N. A financial analysis tool that adjusts the return on assets to get return on equity. The equity multiplier represents the effect of debt on the return. The formula for the equity multiplier is total assets divided by common equity. Common equity is calculated by adding the amount in the common stock account plus any additional paid in capital from common stock plus retained earnings.

equity-residual method. N. A technique for establishing the value of a target company in a merger situation. The equity-residual method uses a discounted cash flow technique applied to the target's postmerger net cash flows. This method requires estimates of the earnings for the target, and deducts the amounts needed for growth to get the net cash flow. Those cash flows are then discounted over the time period at the cost of equity to arrive at the value for the target company.

equity shares. N. Shares of stock, either common or preferred, that represent an ownership of the company. See also *common stock*, *preferred stock*.

equivalent units of output. N. A practical technique for calculating unit costs in a process-costing system. Because some units are not complete at the end of the period, a process will have an ending work-in-process inventory with costs that were transferred in, and some added costs. These costs must be factored in when calculating the per unit cost, so the concept of equivalent units of output is used. An estimate determining how complete the unfinished units are is then translated into an estimate determining how many units could be finished if all energy were put into finishing the units. The equivalent units of output are added to the completed units during the period, and that sum is divided into total costs to arrive at the cost per unit. For example, if 500 units are 30% complete at the end of the accounting period, the equivalent-units-of-output figure is 150 units.

ERISA. ABBRV. Employee Retirement Income Security Act of 1974.

ERP. ABBRV. Enterprise-resource-planning software.

escalator clause. N. A stipulation within a contract that allows a change in price tied to some other event, such as an increase in inflation.

escheat property. N. A property in which the ownership passes to a governmental unit upon the death of the owner because no heirs exist and no will directs the ownership transfer. Governments account for escheat property in fiduciary funds called private-purpose trust funds, because if an heir or legal claimant comes forward, the property is returned.

ESOP. ABBRV. Employee-stock-ownership plans.

ESPP. ABBRV. Employee stock purchase plan.

estate. N. The structure set up when a person dies that serves to manage, protect, and distribute the decedent's assets in a manner specified by the decedent.

estate tax. N. The tax paid by an estate to the federal government. Estate tax is calculated starting with the fair market value of the estate, reducing it by deductions, and increasing it by all taxable gifts made by the deceased. This total taxable-transfers amount is multiplied by the appropriate rate to get a preliminary tax amount. Gift taxes already paid and the estate tax credit are deducted from the preliminary tax amount. The remainder is the estate tax payable.

estimated liability. N. An obligation of an identified entity that is of an uncertain amount. Estimated liabilities are not contingent liabilities because the amount of the obligation is the only uncertainty, not the actual obligation. Warranties are an example of estimated liabilities.

estimated other financing sources/uses. N. Accounts used in governmental accounting that represent the budgeted amounts of other financing items. See also *other financing uses*.

ETF. ABBRV. Exchange-traded fund.

euro. N. The currency used in the European Union in general circulation since January 1, 2002.

eurodollars. N. Deposits of U.S. currency in banks outside the United States, exempt from Federal Reserve Board regulations.

European option. N. An option contract that must be settled on the specified date. This is in contrast to an American option, which can be settled anytime before the specified end date.

European Union. N. An organization of European countries trying to create a free market throughout Europe that is similar to the market that exists in the United States.

EVA. ABBRV. Economic value added.

events of default. N. The section of a loan agreement that describes when the lender can end the agreement because of actions by the borrower and what the lender can do in that situation.

event subsequent to the balance sheet. N. See *subsequent event.*

evidence square. N. A method of organizing the results of a fraud investigation. The investigation can collect four types of evidence: documentary evidence, testimonial evidence, physical evidence, and evidence gathered through personal observation.

eWallet. N. A software application that buyers use to make purchases over the Internet. The buyer enters credit card and shipping information once, and the software stores the information on the buyer's computer. Then, the buyer uses the eWallet reference at participating e-commerce sites rather than entering the information directly into the seller's online order form.

exante return. N. The estimated return on an investment that will be received in a future period.

exception report. N. A report that is generated, often by a computerized system, to highlight something out of the ordinary. For example, a low level of a raw material vital to the manufacturing process would trigger an exception report.

excess capacity. N. A term used to describe a situation in which an entity could produce more of an activity or product and still be operating efficiently.

excess depreciation. N. The difference between the accelerated depreciation amount taken over the time the asset has been in service, and the amount that would have been taken if the owner had used the straight-line method of depreciation. Excess depreciation is significant because it changes the tax treatment of part of the gain on the sale of the asset. Normally, if the asset was held for more than a year, the gain would be a long-term capital gain, which is taxed at a lower rate than ordinary gains. However, if excess depreciation is evident, the part of the gain from the sale is treated as an ordinary gain. Synonymous with *additional depreciation.*

excess net passive income tax. N. Levied on S corporations that have not always been S corporations. The excess net passive income tax is paid at the corporate level on the amount of passive income that is greater than 25% of the gross receipts. This tax is considered a sting tax because of the pain it inflicts on the S corporation.

excess returns. N. Positive abnormal profits. Excess returns are returns on an investment that are higher than predicted returns. This terminology is used in financial research.

exchange gain. N. The receipt of more of a foreign currency at the time of exchange than was anticipated at the time of transaction. An exchange gain occurs because the home currency is getting stronger, or appreciating. Assume the exchange rate today is 105 yen for $1, and two weeks ago the rate was 109 yen for $1. A U.S. company sold products for 2.5 million yen to a Japanese firm, with payment due in two weeks. When the sale was made, the U.S. firm expected to receive $22,936 (2.5 million÷109). However, today, the U.S. firm can convert that amount into $23,810 (2.5 million÷105), resulting in an exchange gain of $874.

exchange loss. N. The receipt of less of a foreign currency at the time of exchange than was anticipated at the time of transaction.

An exchange loss occurs because the home currency is getting weaker, or depreciating. Assume the exchange rate today is 9.97 pesos for $1, and two weeks ago the rate was 9.90 pesos for $1. A U.S. company sold products for 4 million pesos to a Mexican firm, with payment due in two weeks. When the sale was made, the U.S. firm expected to receive $404,040 (4 million÷9.90). However, today the U.S. firm can convert that amount into $401,204 (4 million÷9.97), resulting in an exchange loss of $2,386.

exchange-rate quotes. N. The measure of value of one currency versus another. A direct quote indicates the dollar amount that one unit of the foreign currency is equal to. An indirect quote indicates how much of the foreign currency $1 will buy.

exchange rate risk. N. The ambiguity about cash flows that occurs when assets and liabilities are denominated in foreign currency. Because exchange rates change over time, the precise dollar amount is unknown until settlement.

exchange rates. N. The amount of foreign currency received in exchange for a given amount of U.S. dollars.

exchange-traded fund. N. An investment in which shares can be traded like any stock, but the underlying asset is dollars invested in a portfolio that mirrors a particular stock index, such as the Standard & Poor's 500 or the Dow Jones Industrial Average. While fees for exchange-traded funds are lower than those for mutual funds and shares can be traded anytime during the day, rather than only at the end of the day for most mutual funds, exchange-traded funds are only available through brokers, not through the fund itself, so there is always a commission involved in the trade. ABBRV. *ETF*.

exchange transactions. N. Events in which participants trade items of similar value. This distinction is important in not-for-profit accounting to separate program revenues from contributions. A charitable organization has a contract with the county to provide housing for homeless youths. The organization receives a daily allowance for each person in the facility. The transaction between the county and the organization is an exchange transaction.

excise tax. N. A tax on a particular product, such as alcohol, gasoline, and tobacco. Federal and state governments impose excise taxes, and often the tax is earmarked for a particular activity. In many states, the gasoline tax goes to maintain roads.

exclusion. N. Items that are included in gross income, but are not taxable. An exclusion is different from a deduction in that an exclusion is an income item, and a deduction is an expense item. Both exclusions and deductions reduce taxable income. Examples of common exclusions include gifts, life insurance proceeds, child support payments, some scholarships, and some interest on Series EE savings bonds.

ex-dividend. N. A term used to describe a stock that has had a dividend declared recently that the stock buyer will not receive. The buyer will have to wait for the next quarter's or next year's dividend.

executor/executrix of an estate. N. The male/female person named in a decedent's will who has the fiduciary responsibility for managing the will.

executory contract. N. See *mutually unperformed contract*.

executory costs. N. Costs included in rental payments for things like insurance, maintenance, and taxes. If the lessor is responsible for these costs, then part of each rental payment is allocated to the executory costs. This is an important allocation because executory costs are not included in minimum lease payments, which are used to check the recovery-of-investment test and to find the initial value on the lessee's balance sheet for the leased asset.

exempt security. N. See *private placement*.

exercise price. N. See *strike price*.

exit value. N. The selling price.

expectations gap. N. The difference between what the public believes accountants can do and what accountants actually can do. Principally, this gap is related to uncovering fraud, cheating, and illegal actions by company management.

expected-activity capacity. N. The estimate of the quantity of the unit-level activity driver used to apply overhead in a normal costing system. The expected-activity capacity is the quantity that the company expects to produce or use in the next year; this amount may vary considerably from year to year. See also *unit-level activity drivers, predetermined overhead rate, normal costing*.

expected-inflation rate of interest. N. A component of the interest rate charged by a lender that offsets the loss of purchasing power over the term of the loan due to inflation.

expected misstatement. N. The amount of error that the auditor anticipates is present based on last year's audit findings, the results of other tests, and the audit judgment. Auditors may slightly overstate the expected misstatement to be conservative in choosing a sample for actual testing.

expected return on plan assets. N. A component of the pension expense calculated by multiplying the pension fund assets at the beginning of the year by the return that the fund is expected to earn over the long-term. This component decreases the pension expense.

expected value. N. Used in statistical probability analysis, it is the weighted average of the outcomes using the probabilities of each outcome as the weighting scheme. If the outcomes are measured in money, then the expected value will be a dollar amount equal to the sum of the outcome values multiplied by their probabilities.

expendable trust funds. N. See *special-revenue funds*.

expenditure. N. A term used to describe transactions that result in a decrease in the financial resources of an entity. Expenditure is used in governmental accounting to designate outflows for operating activities, capital asset acquisition, and debt repayment (both principal and interest).

expense. N. A cost that has expired or brought benefit to the owning entity. Expenses are classified into different types and are found on the income statement. Expenses reduce income, but they are different from losses, which are costs that provide no benefit to the owner. V. To put the cost on the income statement as a reduction of income. Sometimes the terminology gets confusing, and prepaid expenses appear on the balance sheet in the asset section. These are usually things like insurance or rent that must be paid in advance. After the coverage period of the rent or insurance elapses, then the prepaid expenses are moved to the income statement and reduce income.

experience curve. N. The application of the learning-curve concept to various areas in an organization (e.g., to marketing). The experience curve measures the decrease in cost per unit as the total number of units produced increases. The unit may not necessarily be the unit of production; it might be the number of purchase orders processed, or the number of times a delivery route has been followed.

expert systems. N. A type of artificial intelligence in which computer software programs use data to solve problems usually solved by experts in the problem area. A bank could use an expert system to analyze loan applications and decide the size of the loan.

expert witness. N. Someone who testifies at a trial and can provide persuasive opinions about a subject because of his or her particular experience or education in the subject.

expired costs. N. Another name for expenses. Expired costs are the value of the assets that are used up in the earning of revenues during the accounting period.

explicit service period. N. A service period associated with stock options that has a specifically defined length of time before the employee can exercise the options. For example, an employee is granted options that can be exercised after three years of full-time employement. The explicit service period is three years and the compensation associated with the stock options is allocated to those three years. See also *derived service period, service period for stock options, implicit service period, requisite service period.*

exploration costs. N. The costs that a company incurs to look for a natural resource on a piece of territory. Exploration costs are included in the depletable base of the asset.

exposure draft. N. The second public presentation of a proposed Financial Accounting Standards Board standard that incorporates public reaction into the discussion memorandum (the first draft of the proposed standard).

extendable swap. N. A swap in which one of the parties can choose to continue the arrangement beyond the initial time period.

eXtensible Business Reporting Language. N. A format for reporting financial information that allows analysis and exchange without interpreting and re-entering the data from financial statements. While not useful for transactions, eXtensible Business Reporting Language provides investors, regulators, and analysts with an easy way to use the data on financial statements by defining how the items on the statements relate to one another. www.xbrl.org. ABBRV. *XBRL*.

external audit. N. Distinguishes the audit function from the internal audit. The external audit is the financial audit that provides assurance by the auditors that the financial statements fairly represent the actual status and performance of the entity. See also *audit*.

externalities. N. A consideration in project or investment analysis that examines the changes that might occur in other parts of the business if a project is undertaken. If a downtown business opens a suburban office, some of the customers of the suburban office may be people who had patronized the downtown location. The effect of opening the suburban office may include a reduction in downtown business.

external linkages. N. The relationships a company has with its suppliers and customers. A company with better external linkages has a competitive advantage because it has a stable source of materials and satisfied customers.

external measures. N. Types of targets used to evaluate performance. External measures focus on things outside the entity such as community support and shareholder satisfaction.

extinguishment of debt. N. The repayment of debt. If the repayment is at the maturity of the debt, then no gain or loss is recorded, because the market value is the maturity value. If the debt is repaid before maturity, then the maturity value plus any premium or discount is removed, as well as any unamortized costs such as bond issue costs. Any difference between the net of those amounts and the cash paid is either a gain or loss. The gain or loss is classified as an extraordinary item on the income statement. If the debt is repaid before maturity, the company must also disclose the source of the funds, a description of the transaction, any income tax effects, and the per share amount of gain or loss. Synonymous with *retirement of debt*.

extranet. N. A network of computers that allows access to limited users outside the entity. This is useful for businesses that want established links between themselves and suppliers, customers, or other groups.

extraordinary gain. N. See *extraordinary items*.

extraordinary items. N. A separate section on the income statement after the provision for taxes. Extraordinary items are nonrecurring items that the entity must separate out from the continuing operations of the company, shown at net of tax effects, to help users predict future income. Extraordinary items are defined as unusual and infrequent. Some items are automatically classified as extraordinary, such as the effects of early retirement of long-term debt. Synonymous with *extraordinary gain, extraordinary loss*.

extraordinary loss. N. See *extraordinary items*.

face amount. N. See *face value*.

face value. N. The amount of a debt that is stated on the instrument. For a bond, the face value is the dollar amount that the owner of the bond will receive at the maturity date of the bond. The face value of a bond, though, is often different than the issue price, resulting in a premium or discount on the balance sheet. Face value is not the same as par value for stock. Synonymous with *face amount, maturity value of a bond*.

face value of a bond. N. See *maturity value of a bond*.

facility-level activities. N. Actions that are done at the factory level. Facility-level activities are distinct from unit-level, batch-level, and product-level activities. Activity-based costing systems identify the level of an activity to build homogeneous cost pools, because costs in a homogeneous pool must be associated with activities performed at the same level. Usually, facility-level activities are not combined in homogeneous cost pools but are allocated using a logical allocation system. Examples of facility-level activities include security and plant depreciation.

factoring. N. Selling accounts receivable to another party. Businesses can sell the receivables with recourse or without recourse, which determines if the bank or the business takes the risk of nonpayment. If the accounts are sold without recourse, then the collection is not guaranteed, and the other party bears the risk of nonpayment. The company selling the accounts receivable does not receive the full value, but instead receives a lower amount to compensate for getting the cash immediately and to cover any uncollectibles. When selling receivables to a bank or finance company, the entity receives cash from the buyer, and the buyer collects the receivables from the customers. The difference between the cash received and the amount of the receivables is the fee for factoring. The advantage is that the business receives the cash immediately. Factoring usually involves only two parties, the seller and the buyer, and the seller does not collect the payments. See also *assignment of accounts receivable, with recourse, without recourse.* Synonymous with *sale of receivables.*

factory burden. N. See *overhead.*

factory supplies inventory. N. A type of inventory found in the current asset section of the balance sheet for a company that makes the products it sells. The costs of miscellaneous items used to make the product are included in factory supplies. Factory supplies are things like sandpaper, oil, and screws, or cleaning products that are necessary for production but are not major visible components of the product. Synonymous with *manufacturing supplies inventory.*

FAF. ABBRV. Financial Accounting Foundation.

FAFSA. N. Free Application for Federal Student Aid, a form used to apply for federal education assistance. The information provided on a FAFSA is used to determine how much a student's family can contribute to his or her education expenses and for which federal programs the student is eligible.

failure activities. N. Actions and efforts taken in reaction to detected quality problems. These activities can take place prior to sale (internal failure activities), e.g., reworking products that fail quality inspection, or the activities can occur after the sale (external failure activities), in response to customer dissatisfaction.

failure costs. N. The cost of performing the actions or efforts necessary to find or fix poor quality products.

fair market value. N. The price a buyer would pay and the price a seller would take if neither were forced by time or circumstances to make the exchange.

fair value. N. The price at which an asset is bought or sold in an arm's-length transaction, in which neither party is forced to act. Fair value is used in several accounting procedures and is sometimes called market value or fair market value.

fair-value hedge. N. A hedge that covers the risk that the market value of an asset, a liability, or a contract will move in an unfavorable direction. For an asset, that would be a lower market value. For a liability or purchase-commitment contract, that would be a higher market value. For example, if a company has in-inventory oil, the market value of the oil changes the value of the inventory. If the company has agreed to buy a certain quantity of oil at a specified price in the future, the value of that contract changes with the market price of oil. The company can hedge the risk of an unfavorable outcome by entering into a contract to sell a specified quantity of oil at a specified price in the future (a futures contract), and the selling price that the company receives covers the decrease in inventory value or the purchase price of the contract to buy oil.

fair-value method of accounting for stock options. N. A procedure for calculating and allocating the compensation expense of stock options. When an employee receives the option, an option pricing model calculates the value of the options. That value is the compensation expense that is allocated over the service period.

fair value of plan assets. N. See *market-related value of pension plan assets*.

family limited partnership. N. A method of transferring partial ownership of property without being subject to gift tax. A family limited partnership is usually established by parents who exchange assets for general partnerships. Then, the general partners give limited partnership interests to children and grandchildren over time. If the amounts of the annual limited partnership gifts are less than the annual gift exclusion, then no gift tax is paid. Eventually, the limited partners will have most of the interest in the property, and when the general partners die, only that part of the partnership is included in the estate.

family of funds. N. A mutual-fund investment company that has several different types of mutual funds available to the investor. The investor can move money among the funds at a low cost and can receive one combined statement with the results of all investments in the funds. Synonymous with *mutual fund family*.

Fannie Mae. N. A government agency that buys home mortgages from banks and transforms them into an investment opportunity for the public. The investors receive the payments made on the mortgages, and the banks continue to service the borrowers. Synonymous with *Federal National Mortgage Association*. ABBRV. *FNMA*.

FAS. ABBRV. Statement of Financial Accounting Standards.

FASB. ABBRV. Financial Accounting Standards Board.

FASB Interpretations. N. Documents produced by the Financial Accounting Standards Board (FASB) that clarify or explain Statements of Financial Accounting Standards or other official generally accepted accounting principles. As of the end of 2007, the FASB has issued forty-eight interpretations. They are available at www.fasb.org.

fault-tolerant system. N. A structure for successfully accomplishing a goal even if an error or problem occurs. The design of a fault-tolerant system includes features that are only needed if another feature fails. For example, in an accounting information system, data can be written to two disks so that if one disk fails, the other can be used. The system tolerates a disk failure.

favorable M-1 adjustments. N. Items included on Schedule M-1 (the reconciliation of net income to taxable income) that reduce net income. These items include income or gain amounts that are not taxable, and expense and loss amounts that are deductible but not included on the income statement. These adjustments are considered favorable because they decrease net income to get taxable income.

favorable variances. N. The difference between the actual cost and the standard cost when the standard cost is larger. A favorable variance happens if the quantity used or the price paid is less than the standard permits.

favored tax treatment. N. A term used to indicate that the taxes on an item are better than ordinary income. Taxpayers pay taxes at a lower rate on capital gains, an example of favored tax treatment.

FBM. ABBRV. Functional-based management.

FCPA. ABBRV. Foreign Corrupt Practices Act.

FDIC. ABBRV. Federal Deposit Insurance Corporation.

Fed. ABBRV. Federal Reserve System.

Fed chairman. N. The presidential-appointed head of the Federal Reserve System. The current chairman is Ben Bernanke.

Federal Deposit Insurance Corporation. N. An agency of the federal government that insures an individual's savings or checking account up to $100,000 if the account is at a financial insurance company that has Federal Deposit Insurance Corporation insurance. ABBRV. *FDIC*.

federal funds rate. N. The interest rate that banks charge other banks for the use of federal funds. The federal funds rate is not the rate charged to consumers, but it indicates the trend in interest rates charged to consumers.

Federal Home Loan Mortgage Corporation. N. See *Freddie Mac*. ABBRV. *FHLMC*.

Federal ID Number. N. A number assigned to a business for tax reporting purposes. The Federal ID Number is used on wage statements provided to employees; dividend, interest, and miscellaneous income statements provided to investors and independent contractors; and, the actual business tax return. ABBRV. *FIN*.

Federal Insurance Contribution Act. N. Usually refers to the amount of withholding for old-age, survivor, and disability insurance administered by the federal government. Employees pay half the premium, and it is deducted from their paychecks. Employers pay the other half. Synonymous with *old-age, survivor, and disability insurance*. ABBRV. *FICA*.

Federal National Mortgage Association. N. See *Fannie Mae*. ABBRV. *FNMA*.

Federal Reserve Bank. N. See *Federal Reserve System*.

Federal Reserve Board. N. See *Federal Reserve System*.

Federal Reserve System. N. The central banking arrangement in the United States. Twelve regional banks—Federal Reserve Banks—act as banks for other banks in the area. The Federal Reserve Board, which consists of seven members appointed by the president of the United States, sets interest rates and reserves requirements to adjust monetary policy so that the economy stays strong. The Federal Reserve System controls the money supply in the United States by specifying the percentage of deposits that banks must keep on hand, rather than lend to other customers. If reserve requirements are raised, less money is in the economy. If reserve requirements are lowered, more money is in the economy. Synonymous with *Fed*.

Federation of Schools of Accountancy. N. An organization of university accounting programs with the goal of improving education. Membership requirements include Association to Advance Collegiate Schools of Business (AACSB) accounting accreditation and business accreditation. www.thefsa.org. ABBRV. *FSA*.

feedback value. N. An aspect of the primary qualitative characteristic of accounting information—relevance. Accounting information has feedback value if it helps decision makers correct or assess past predictions.

FEI. ABBRV. Financial Executives International.

FFO. ABBRV. Funds from operations.

FHLMC. ABBRV. Federal Home Loan Mortgage Corporation. See *Freddie Mac*.

FICA. ABBRV. Federal Insurance Contribution Act.

fidelity bond. N. A type of insurance that a company obtains to cover losses from criminal or negligent acts by an employee. Securities firms often have fidelity bonds on traders.

fiduciary. N. See *trustee*.

fiduciary funds. N. A set of accounts used in governmental accounting to monitor assets for which the government is acting as a trustee. An estate's gardens might be donated to a city as a park, and the city would use fiduciary funds to account for the garden.

field audit procedure. N. A type of Internal Revenue Service investigation of a taxpayer or corporation in which more than one item on the tax return is focused on. To facilitate access to information, field audits are located at a taxpayer's home or office or at a corporation's business location.

FIFO. ABBRV. First in, first out.

file server. N. Part of a computer network used to store software and data files used by all the computers on the network.

filing status. N. One of five categories that a taxpayer chooses. The filing status determines tax rates and limitations on certain items. The five categories are joint, surviving spouse, head of household, single, and married filing a separate return.

FIN. ABBRV. Federal ID Number.

finance director. N. See *chief financial officer*.

financial accounting. N. A type of accounting with the main objective of providing information about a company that is useful to decision makers outside the company. Financial accounting involves a process of measuring the effect of events on the company and recording and reporting them in the financial statements.

Financial Accounting Foundation. N. The source of funding for the Financial Accounting Standards Board, composed of a nine-person board chosen by the American Institute of Certified Public Accountants (AICPA). Organizations that financially support the Financial Accounting Foundation are the AICPA, Financial Executives Institute, Financial Analysts Federation, National Association of Accountants, Securities Industry Association, and American Accounting Association. ABBRV. *FAF*.

Financial Accounting Standards Board. N. The entity, established in 1972, that sets generally accepted accounting principles (GAAP) through the publication of Statements on Financial Accounting

Standards. While it is not a government board, its publications are recognized as binding by the Securities and Exchange Commission and the American Institute of Certified Public Accountants. Certified public accountant (CPAs) must use GAAP in their work, which means that companies using CPA services must comply with GAAP. www.fasb.org. ABBRV. *FASB.*

financial analysis. N. The process of examining the information on financial statements (and other sources) to draw conclusions about the performance of a company. Various ratios form the basis for financial analysis. The ratios are calculated using numbers on the income statement, balance sheet, and statement of cash flows. Comparing a company's ratio to the previous years' ratios or to the average for similar firms allows an analyst to assess how well a company will do in the future.

financial budget. N. Part of the master budget concerning cash flows and what is owned and owed by an entity. Components of the financial budget are a cash budget, a budgeted balance sheet, and a budget for capital expenditures.

financial condition. N. The proportions and amounts of an organization's assets, liabilities, and owners' equity amounts at a specific point in time. The balance sheet is sometimes titled "Statement of Financial Condition."

financial engineering. N. Designing securities with the characteristics desired by investors. Financial engineering bundles, or combines, several simple investment opportunities to give investors flexibility and lower risk. This type of engineering also unbundles existing securities into components that meet the needs of a set of investors. A simple example of bundling is the selling of bonds with detachable warrants that allow the investor to buy common stock at a specified price. The security combines both debt and equity features. A simple example of unbundling is the separation of interest payments and principal payments in some collateralized mortgage obligations.

Financial Executives International. N. A national professional organization that was originally named the Controllers Institute of America, with the mission to help financial executives meet new challenges. Financial Executives International publishes the magazine *Financial Executive* nine times a year. ABBRV. *FEI*.

financial flexibility. N. The ability of a company to raise cash through activities outside of sales, such as selling off assets, borrowing, or selling stock.

financial forecast. N. A set of financial statements for a future accounting period with estimates instead of historical data. A financial forecast is based on what a knowledgeable person would expect the future financial position, results of operations, and cash flows to be. A financial forecast is distinguished from a financial projection because a forecast is not based on any particular change. The financial forecast is a comparative tool to look at the situation as is, versus what it would be with a new action. See also *financial projection.*

financial futures. N. See *futures contracts.*

financial highlights. N. Part of a company's annual report that presents parts of the financial statements that the company thinks will be of interest to readers of the report. The financial highlights are not complete financial statements.

financial instruments. N. Devices for managing the risk of business problems related to economic changes such as higher interest rates, higher oil prices, higher inflation, or fluctuating foreign exchange rates. Financial instruments are cash, ownership interests, or a contract between two entities. The first entity is obligated to deliver cash or another financial instrument or to exchange financial instruments under unfavorable terms with the second entity. The second entity has the right to receive the cash or financial instrument from the first entity or to exchange financial instruments under favorable terms with the first entity. Simple financial instruments include accounts receivable and bonds payable.

financial intermediaries. N. Organizations that arrange and aid in the transfer of capital from providers to borrowers. Banks, pension funds, life insurance companies, and mutual funds are financial intermediaries. Financial intermediaries are necessary to give households with small investment amounts the opportunity to invest by combining many small amounts into a large loan to a corporation or large organization. See also *savings and loan associations, mutual savings banks, credit unions.*

financial lease. N. See *capital lease.*

financial measures. N. A type of target used to evaluate performance. Financial measures are in terms of dollars.

financial planning models. N. Computer application software that does the calculations for analyzing the outcome if changes in costs are made. Any spreadsheet application can be used to build a planning model. The relationships necessary for building the spreadsheet are found in the master budget.

financial position form of the balance sheet. N. A presentation format of the balance sheet that lists assets first and then deducts liabilities. The final section of the financial position form is equity. Few organizations use this format.

financial productivity measure. N. The ratio of outputs to inputs, with inputs and outputs being measured in terms of dollars. To determine changes in efficiency, the current year's ratio is compared to one from a previous year. If the ratio has increased, then efficiency has increased. See also *operational productivity measure*.

financial projection. N. A set of financial statements for a future accounting period with estimates based on the occurrence of one or more actions or events. A financial projection determines what the financial statements would look like if a company followed a certain course of action. A financial projection is distinguished from a financial forecast by the existence of that assumption or action, which drives the estimates. The financial forecast just estimates future financial outcomes based on business as usual with no change. See also *financial forecast*.

financial reporting. N. Accounting based on the Securities and Exchange Commission requirements. Financial reporting follows generally accepted accounting principles (GAAP) and is used by those outside the company. Contrast with managerial accounting, which is based on the information needs of managers and is not required to follow GAAP.

financial risk. N. The chance that the financial statements contain incorrect amounts. The purpose of internal controls is to reduce the possibility of this happening.

financial-statement analysis. N. See *ratio analysis*.

financial statements. N. Reports with a defined format containing accounting information. The financial statements include the balance sheet, income statement, statement of stockholders' equity, and statement of cash flows. The Securities and Exchange Commission requires companies to prepare financial statements annually.

financing activities. N. A section on the statement of cash flows that includes cash from long-term borrowing and the repayment of those amounts. Financing activities also include the sale of the company's stock, treasury stock transactions, and the payment of dividends. If borrowing is for a specific purpose and the company does not have any choice over the use of the borrowing, the amount is listed in significant noncash transactions. Financing activities usually involve long-term liabilities and equity accounts. Any interest payments resulting from borrowings are not financing activities, but are included in the operating activities section of the statement of cash flows. See also *investing activities, significant noncash transactions.*

finished-goods inventory. N. A type of inventory found in the current asset section of the balance sheet of a company that makes items for sale. Finished-goods inventory contains the costs of producing items that are completed and ready to sell.

firewall. N. A computer security technique that limits access to the computer system. A firewall can prevent access through the Internet by analyzing characteristics of the computer trying to access the system. Firewalls are an important tool for protecting the financial information stored in the accounting information system; they make it difficult for hackers to break in and steal credit card numbers, passwords, and other valuable information.

firm commitment offering. N. A type of contract with an investment bank for the sale of a new stock issue. A firm commitment offering guarantees the proceeds to the issuing company, because the investment bank actually buys the shares and resells them, bearing the risk of not achieving the price. Contrast with a best efforts offering, which only requires that the investment bank do the best it can to sell the stock, with no guarantee of proceeds.

first-digit law. See *Benford's law.*

first in, first out. N. A method of determining the cost of ending inventory that puts the oldest costs in the cost of goods sold and the newest costs in the ending inventory. This method of assigning costs results in the value of inventory on the balance sheet approximately representing replacement cost. The choice of costing method is only significant if prices are rising or falling rapidly. ABBRV. *FIFO*.

fiscal year. N. A twelve-month period that ends on a date other than December 31. Businesses may choose to use a fiscal year rather than a calendar year because it evens out the work involved with preparing year-end reports. For example, retail businesses usually do not use a calendar year because their busiest time is December. It is difficult for them to serve customers, have adequate inventory, and complete all the year-end reporting activities by December 31. Rather, a retail company may choose to end the reporting year during a slow time, like the end of January or February, coinciding with the natural business cycle. See also *natural business year*.

five-year look back rule. N. A provision applying to gains and losses on Section 1231 property that limits the use of long-term capital gains. If in a given tax year Section 1231 gains exceed Section 1231 losses, the amount of the net gain is treated on the current year tax return as ordinary rather than as long-term capital gain, if the taxpayer does not have net 1231 losses in the previous five years.

fixed assets. N. See *property, plant, and equipment*.

fixed cost. N. A cost of doing business that stays the same in total over a normal range of activity. The per unit cost, though, changes with the level of activity. An example of a fixed cost is the property tax on the workshop building of a cabinet-building business. Until a larger or newer workshop must be opened, the cost is fixed each year. But, the cost per cabinet will change depending on how many cabinets are made during the year. Classification is important for planning and pricing.

fixed-income funds. N. Mutual funds invested in assets that produce a specified payout, such as bonds.

fixed-overhead spending variance. N. The difference between actual fixed overhead and the budgeted, or standard, fixed overhead.

fixed-overhead volume variance. N. The difference between budgeted fixed overhead and applied fixed overhead. This difference results from a variance between budgeted output and actual output. Synonymous with *production volume variance, output-level overhead variance, denominator-level variance.*

fixed-price tender offer. N. A type of stock repurchase in which a company publicizes the number of shares it will buy back at an announced price with an ending date specified. Stockholders then offer to sell at that price.

flash memory. N. A small, thin, rectangular card that functions as a storage device for items like digital cameras and personal data assistant devices. The card holds four to six million bytes of information.

flat tax. N. A tax in which the rate is the same on all income. Sales taxes are flat taxes. Synonymous with *proportional tax.*

flexible budget. N. A master budget prepared for a range of output. Flexible budgets are useful for comparing actual costs to budgeted costs, because the differences reflect the efficiency of the production, not a different volume of production. Synonymous with *variable budget.*

flexible-budget variance. N. The difference between the actual cost at the actual level of output and the budgeted amount based on that actual level of output. The flexible-budget variance is due to the efficient or inefficient use of resources at that given level of output.

flexible spending account. N. See *cafeteria plan*.

flip-flop note. N. A type of debt security that allows the lender or investor to change from one kind of debt to another.

flipping. N. Buying and then immediately selling shares of stock. Flipping occurs when an individual has an option to buy shares at a discount from the current price. The gain is the difference between the proceeds from the sale less any taxes and the purchase price. Some companies do not allow flipping.

float. N. Equal to the checkbook balance minus the bank balance for the checking account. Float represents all the checks that have not yet cleared the bank and all the deposits that have not yet been recorded by the bank. The dollar amount available for use because of the time lag between checks being written and funds being deducted is called the disbursement float. Float works to the detriment of the account holder in the case of deposits. Although the deposit has been made, the funds are not always available immediately, and that is called collections float.

floating an issue. N. Offering bonds for sale to the public.

floating-rate debt. N. Loans that specify the rate of interest not as an absolute amount, but in relation to some other measure. The result is a debt investment with a value that is unaffected by rate changes in the capital markets.

floor. N. See *lower of cost or market*.

flotation costs. N. The costs associated with selling new issues of common stock. Flotation costs are the costs of using an investment banker to design the stock and underwrite it. The flotation costs reduce the proceeds of the sale of the stock to the issuing corporation. The flotation costs can be stated in absolute dollar terms, or as a percentage of proceeds of the sale.

FNMA. ABBRV. Federal National Mortgage Association. See *Fannie Mae.*

FOB. ABBRV. Free on board.

FOB destination. N. Free on board destination. A term that determines who has title to goods in transit. If goods are shipped FOB destination, then title passes when the goods are delivered to the buyer. That means that for ending inventory purposes, those goods are still on the seller's inventory. The seller owns the goods until they are delivered and has to follow up with the insurance and delivery companies if the items are destroyed.

FOB shipping point. N. Free on board shipping point. A term that determines who has title to goods in transit. If goods are shipped FOB shipping point, then title passes to the buyer as soon as the goods are released from the seller to the company doing the delivery—a trucking company, for example. That means that for ending inventory purposes, the goods are included in the buyer's inventory. If the item is destroyed during shipping, the buyer has to deal with his or her insurance company and the delivery company.

footing. N. The process of calculating the balance of an account. The debits and credits are totaled, and the two are combined to get the balance. An audit activity in which the auditor reads a column of figures to check the client's answer.

footnote disclosure. N. Information appended to the financial statements to provide more information about the statements. Explanations of accounting policies, information on events that could negatively affect the company (such as lawsuits), and specifics of some statement items are vital to using financial statements to make good investment decisions.

footsie. N. See *FTSE*.

Forbes 500. N. Published by *Forbes* magazine every year, a list of the five hundred largest public U.S. companies based on various measures.

forecast. N. Estimates or educated guesses about what will happen in the future. Businesses usually base forecasts on budgets. Professional analysts base forecasts on their investigations of the company's financial information.

Foreign Corrupt Practices Act. N. A federal law passed in 1977 requiring large public corporations to implement internal control systems that safeguard assets and record transactions in compliance with generally accepted accounting principles. The Foreign Corrupt Practices Act was designed to prevent corporations from paying bribes to foreign governments. ABBRV. *FCPA*.

foreign currency transaction. N. Any business event in which the amount is denominated in a currency other than the one used in the financial records. For example, if Best Buy buys cell phones from Nokia, the transaction may be in Finnish currency, even though Best Buy's accounting records are kept in dollars.

foreign currency translation. N. The process of stating the economic effect of a transaction that took place using a foreign currency into the home-country currency. Foreign currency translation involves using exchange rates to adjust the measurement; the changes in exchange rates between the date of the transaction and the date of the translation are gains or losses.

foreign-source income. N. Income that is considered part of foreign taxable income, meaning it was earned in a foreign country. The motivation for corporations is to increase this number in order to increase the maximum amount of foreign tax credit. Basic rules indicate that service income belongs to the geographic area where the service was performed. Rental income belongs to the place where the property is located. Royalty income belongs to the country where the intangible property is used. Interest income belongs to the debtor's country. Dividend income belongs to the home country of the payer. The rules for the sale of property and inventory vary.

foreign tax credit. N. A deduction in the amount of taxes a corporation must pay. The foreign-tax-credit maximum is the product of the percentage of foreign taxable income to total taxable income times total taxable income. If the corporation paid more during the year than this maximum amount, then the excess can be carried back two years and forward five years. The maximum still applies in those carryback and carryforward years. Key to this calculation is determining foreign taxable income. The larger that amount, the larger the maximum credit. Individuals may take a credit for foreign taxes paid, or exclude income earned in a foreign country.

foreign trade zones. N. Areas in the United States near ports of entry that allow foreign goods to enter without paying the tariff until the goods leave the zone. Production facilities located in foreign trade zones can put off paying the tariffs on imported goods. This has a real advantage because it means that the tariff is only paid on useable goods, not on waste or defective goods.

forensic accounting. N. Procedures conducted to prevent and detect fraud and white-collar crime in organizations, usually focusing on the accounting aspects of the entity.

Form 1041. N. A U.S. tax form used by estates and trusts.

Form 1065. N. The Internal Revenue Service tax form for use by partnerships and limited liability companies. Form 1065 is informational only because the partnership does not pay tax. Synonymous with *information return*.

Form 1120. N. A U.S. tax form used by corporations.

Form 20-F. N. The Securities and Exchange Commission form used to convert non-U.S. generally accepted accounting principles (GAAP) financial statements into financial statements that meet U.S. GAAP requirements. Form 20-F is necessary if foreign companies want to be listed on the U.S. stock exchange.

Form 990. N. A U.S. tax form used by not-for-profit organizations.

Form S-1. N. See *registration statement.*

Form SS4. N. The Internal Revenue Service form used to request an employer identification number.

Fortune 500. N. A list of the five hundred largest industrial companies in the United States, published by *Fortune* magazine every year.

forward contract. N. A type of derivative financial instrument that is an agreement to exchange a specified amount at a specified rate on a specified future date. Forward contracts are used as hedges to protect against foreign currency exchange rate changes and other price changes. Synonymous with *forwards.*

forward date. N. The specified date at which a forward-contract transaction is measured.

forward price or rate. N. The specified price of the asset or specified rate in a forward contract.

forwards. N. See *forward contract.*

forward triangular merger. N. A merger that dodges the requirement of shareholder approval. The acquiring corporation forms a subsidiary by contributing its stock in exchange for all the subsidiary's stock. Then, the subsidiary merges into the target, using the contributed stock as payment. The acquiring company, as the only owner of the new subsidiary that was merged into the target, really owns the target as a controlled subsidiary.

franchise. N. (1) The rights to use a name to sell a product or service. The franchisee purchases those rights from the franchisor and records the franchise as an intangible asset on the balance sheet. The cost is amortized over the useful life, the term of the franchise, or a maximum of forty years. (2) The arrangement between a government and a company giving the company the exclusive right to provide a service involving public property, such as TV broadcasting, ferry service, or bus service.

fraud. N. A deliberate act to embezzle funds for personal gain or to present financial reports that misrepresent the performance of an organization in order to increase stock price or bonuses.

fraud auditor. N. See *forensic accounting.*

fraud diamond. N. The four elements that are necessary for a person to commit fraud: pressure, opportunity, rationalization, and capability. Capability refers to the position of the fraudster and his or her intellect, ego, coercion skills, ability to lie effectively, and resistance to stress. See also *fraud triangle.*

fraud risk factors. N. The aspects of organizations and the employees of those organizations that increase the chances that fraud will occur in the organization. The three fraud risk factors are the characteristics of management and their influence over the control environment, the characteristics of the industry in which the organization operates, and the characteristics of the business transactions and financial stability of the organization.

fraud triangle. N. The three elements that are necessary for a person to commit fraud: pressure, opportunity, and rationalization. The person must have some financial pressure, the control environment in the business must have a weakness that allows the person to believe the fraud will not be detected, and the person must rationalize that the fraud is not really wrong. See also *fraud diamond*.

fraudulent financial reporting. N. A deliberate act to misrepresent the performance of an organization in order to increase stock prices, inflate bonuses, or set aside amounts to manage future earnings in a way that will increase stock prices or bonuses.

Freddie Mac. N. A government agency that buys home mortgages from banks and transforms them into an investment opportunity for the public. The investors receive the payments made on the mortgages, and the banks continue to service the borrowers. Synonymous with *Federal Home Loan Mortgage Corporation.* ABBRV. *FHLMC.*

free cash flow. N. A financial analysis ratio that assesses the company's capability to take advantage of new opportunities while maintaining current dividend levels and asset replacement. The formula is net cash from operating activities, minus dividends, and minus purchases of fixed assets.

free on board. ADJ. Indicates that the product will be delivered by an independent carrier. It is usually followed by the point at which title for the shipped items changes hands. ABBRV. *FOB.*

freight-in. N. The delivery cost associated with getting purchased inventory items from the source to the company that will resell them. Freight-in is a cost that is included in inventory and is reflected in the cost of goods sold.

freight-out. N. The cost of delivering products to the buyer. Freight-out is classified as a selling expense.

frequency analysis. N. A method of determining if a hedge will be effective by looking at how often it has been effective in the past.

friendly takeover. N. A corporate acquisition in which the target and the acquiring parties negotiate in relative harmony. The target is generally agreeable to the takeover.

fringe benefit. N. A benefit that is in addition to wages or salaries. Employers provide employees with fringe benefits as a way of increasing compensation. Fringe benefits commonly include health insurance and life insurance and, if offered to all employees, they usually are not taxable. In a partnership, some fringe benefits for partners are just like guaranteed payments, and the partner must pay self-employment and income tax on them. Some fringe benefits are included in the wage and salary expense, such as the cost of medical or life insurance. Others, such as sales discounts or free parking, are not.

front-end load. ADJ. Describes a mutual fund's fee structure. A front-end load fund charges a commission when the investor purchases the shares.

front money. N. The initial investment to start a business.

FSA. ABBRV. Federation of Schools of Accountancy.

FTSE. ABBRV. A stock market index made up of one hundred large stocks from the London Stock Exchange. The FTSE is printed in the *Financial Times*. Synonymous with *footsie*.

full-cost accounting for natural resources. N. One of two acceptable methods of calculating the depletable base in the oil and gas industry. This method capitalizes all costs of exploration, including the searches that did not find any oil, as part of the depreciable base.

full costing. N. See *absorption costing*.

full-disclosure principle. N. The rule for deciding what to include in the financial reports. The full-disclosure principle requires that entities include information that will make a difference in decision making. The character and quantity of information in the financial reports is balanced with the need to make it comprehensible to the user.

full environmental costing. N. Assigning all environmental costs— prevention, detection, handling, and cleanup—to products. Full environmental costing includes the company's cost and society's cost of protecting and preserving the environment.

full private costing. N. Assigning all environmental costs borne by an organization to products. Full private costing includes the costs of prevention, detection, handling, cleanup, and litigation that an organization incurs. It excludes environmental damage's cost to society.

fully depreciated. ADJ. Describes an asset whose book value equals the estimated salvage value. All the cost associated with the purchase of the asset has been allocated to the depreciation expense over preceding accounting periods.

functional-based management. N. A type of management accounting system that focuses on the costs of departments and then assigns those department costs based on production. The efficiency analysis focuses on how well the departments are containing costs. See also *activity-based management*. ABBRV. *FBM*.

functional-based responsibility accounting. N. A system for measuring and rewarding performance based on functional concepts, such as departmental and financial measures of performance.

Functional-based responsibility is appropriately used in a stable environment. See also *activity-based responsibility accounting*.

functional currency. N. The currency used for business transactions. In the United States, the functional currency is the dollar.

fund accounting. N. The accounting system used by governments and not-for-profit organizations. The objectives of fund accounting are to provide financial reports that emphasize accountability for resources and to assess interperiod equity, which measures how well revenue sources covered current-year expenditures, and whether future resources will be needed to cover current-year expenditures.

fund capital assets. N. Assets used in a governmental unit that are part of a proprietary or fiduciary fund. The garbage trucks used by city trash collectors are fund capital assets because they are used in the proprietary fund that accounts for waste-management activities. That fund is supported by charging users, the way a business operates. The city hall is not a fund capital asset because it is used for general government activity and supported through tax levies.

funding of pension plans. N. The cash contributions made by an employer to a pension fund. The retirement benefits are paid out of the pension fund.

funding policy. N. The strategy established by a company for determining the contributions to the company's pension plan.

funds-flow statement. N. See *statement of cash flows*.

funds from operations. N. Terminology used by Standard & Poor's to designate the net income adjusted for depreciation and amortization. ABBRV. *FFO*.

fungible. ADJ. A descriptor meaning that one item is just like another. For example, a bushel of corn is a fungible good. One bushel is almost exactly like another bushel, and the two are interchangeable.

furniture and fixtures. N. A noncurrent asset on the balance sheet representing the costs of office furniture, display cases, and other business furnishings. Furniture and fixtures are depreciable assets.

futures contracts. N. A type of derivative financial instrument that is similar to a forward contract, except that it is traded on an organized exchange resulting in more standardization than forward contracts. A futures contract is a deal made today for an exchange to take place at a specified date in the future, for a specified quantity, at a specified price. Commodities futures involve the exchange of things, and are used to protect against unfavorable changes in the price of materials or inputs. Financial futures involve exchanges of treasury bills, certificates of deposits, or other financial instruments.

futures markets. N. A physical or virtual location in which buyers and sellers agree to take part in an exchange transaction on a future date. Contrast this with a spot market, in which the exchange transaction takes place immediately, or on the spot.

future value. N. The future value of a single invested amount—or any number of amounts—assuming compound interest. It is always larger than the single amount or the total of all the amounts invested over time.

fuzzy logic. N. A characteristic of an expert system, which mimics the intuition of an expert. Fuzzy logic relies on assigning probabilities to outcomes.

G

G-7. N. The Group of Seven, including the United States, Japan, Great Britain, France, Germany, Italy, and Canada—or the largest industrialized countries in the world. See also *G-8*.

G-8. N. The Group of Eight, or the largest industrialized countries in the world. Includes the United States, Japan, Great Britain, France, Germany, Italy, and Canada—the nations that comprise the G-7—plus Russia. See also *G-7*.

GAAP. ABBRV. Generally accepted accounting principles.

GAAP convergence. N. The process of changing U.S. accounting standards to more closely conform to international accounting standards. This change could provide a more efficient flow of investment capital by allowing investors to easily compare financial information. See also *International Accounting Standards Board, International Financial Reporting Standards, Norwalk Agreement*. Synonymous with *harmonization of accounting standards*.

GAAS. ABBRV. Generally accepted auditing standards.

gain. N. The positive difference between the selling price of an asset and the original cost (or the value recorded in the accounting records) for asset sales that are not part of normal business operations. Contrast with profit, which is the difference between the selling price and the cost of the goods or services the business sells as part of operating activities. Also contrast with loss, which is the negative difference resulting when the selling price is less than the cost. The gain on an investment is the difference between the original cost of that investment and the proceeds from the sale.

gain contingency. N. See *contingent gain*.

gain sharing. N. A form of motivational compensation that is tied to quality and productivity improvement. The cash to all employees is based on the savings from the achievement of a quality goal or a productivity goal.

gains trading. N. Manipulating earnings numbers by selling investments that are doing well and keeping the ones that are not. Other than trading securities, the loss on bad investments only reduces income in the period in which the losing investments are sold. The accounting rules can motivate companies to make bad investment decisions (i.e., keep the losing investments in order to avoid the decrease in income). Requiring all changes in market value to be included in income (whether or not the security is sold) makes income very volatile. Synonymous with *cherry picking*.

Gantt chart. N. A representation of a project's progress through time, comparing estimated completion dates for the stages of the project to the actual completion dates. Gantt charts are useful for projects that have few simultaneous steps and many sequential ones. The comparison of actual time taken to estimated time taken gives the project director information on new completion dates, if things go faster or slower than the original estimate.

GAO. ABBRV. U.S. Government Accountability Office.

GAS. ABBRV. Generalized audit software.

GASB. abbrv. Governmental Accounting Standards Board.

GDP. ABBRV. Gross domestic product.

general business credit. N. A collection of tax credits available to businesses. The annual total amount of these credits is limited by legislation. The tax credits for research, low-income housing, disabled access, rehabilitation, work opportunity, welfare-to-work, empowerment-zone employment, new markets, alcohol fuels, enhanced oil recovery, renewable electricity production, American Indian employment, employer Social Security, and orphan drugs are the credits included in the general business credit. A business totals all the amounts available from these credits for any one year and applies the limitation rules. The maximum amount of annual tax credit that a business is allowed for all the tax credits included in the general business credit is equal to the taxes payable before the credit minus either a minimum tax amount or 25% of the taxes payable (before the credit) over $25,000. The amount of the credit over this maximum can be carried back one year and forward twenty years.

general capital assets. N. Assets used in a governmental unit that are not part of a proprietary or fiduciary fund but are used for common governmental function. The city hall is an example of a general capital asset. The garbage trucks used by city trash collectors are not general capital assets because they are associated with the proprietary fund that accounts for trash collection. The proprietary fund operates by charging users.

general expenses. N. A category of expenses on the income statement that includes costs directly associated with running the entity and not included in other more descriptive categories. The precise expenses included depend on the type of business or organization. The key characteristic is that the costs are closely related to generating the revenues of the entity and are not identified by any other category of expenses in the operating section of the income statement.

general-fixed-assets-account group. N. A part of governmental accounting that keeps track of the general capital assets of the governmental unit. Special assets that are part of a proprietary fund or a fiduciary fund are not included in this group. Examples of assets included in this group are city hall buildings, street maintenance vehicles, and repair shop equipment. An example of an asset that is excluded (because it is a fund capital asset associated with a proprietary fund or fiduciary fund) is garbage trucks used by city trash collectors.

general fund. N. Part of the governmental funds that account for service activities to citizens. The general fund contains the unrestricted revenues and is used for operating activities that do not belong in another fund. Every state and local government uses a general fund.

generalized audit software. N. Software used by auditors to perform certain procedures on any client's files. Generalized audit software is compatible with the client's existing computer system. The software sorts, compares, and combines information in the client files so that the auditor can be efficient and effective. ABBRV. *GAS.*

general journal. N. A journal that contains miscellaneous entries that do not fit in any specialized journal. A company uses special journals for routine transactions, but uses general journals for uncommon transactions and for the entries associated with the end of the accounting period, i.e., adjusting and closing entries. See also *journal, special journal.*

general ledger. N. An accounting device for collecting all the increases and decreases to each account in the chart of accounts. Information from the journal is separated into the effects on each asset account, liability account, equity account, revenue, and expense that appears on the financial statements of the company. See also *journal, ledger, subsidiary ledger.*

general legacy. N. A distribution of personal property according to the provisions of a will that states a value or dollar amount, but no source, e.g., "a gift of $10,000 to my friend." Giving no indication of the estate's source for the $10,000 makes it a general legacy.

general long-term debt account group. N. Liabilities of governmental units that will be paid from general governmental funds, not from a specific source. The term "general" indicates that the repayment source is not limited to any particular type of revenue. "Long-term" refers to repayment that will occur over a time period longer than a year. Bonds payable, amounts of compensation earned, but not received, by employees, such as compensated absences, and capital leases are included in the general long-term debt account group.

generally accepted accounting principles. N. The system of rules, procedures, and concepts developed by the accounting profession. Generally accepted accounting principles are the approved methods of accounting for business activities and are used as the basis for evaluating the fairness of financial statements. The Financial Accounting Standards Board determines generally accepted accounting principles. ABBRV. *GAAP*.

generally accepted auditing standards. N. Rules and procedures developed by the American Institute of Certified Public Accountants for performing audits. ABBRV. *GAAS*.

general obligation bond. N. A municipal bond that is repaid using the taxing authority of the governmental unit issuing it.

general partnership. N. A type of partnership in which all partners can be called on to use personal assets to repay partnership debt.

generation-skipping transfer tax. N. A tax on gifts from a grandparent to a grandchild. If a very wealthy person wants to help his or her child avoid paying estate taxes on an inheritance that will be passed along to the grandchild, the grandparent's will or gift can specify the grandchild as the recipient. The generation-skipping transfer tax is at a higher rate than a normal gift or estate-tax rate.

generic interest rate swap. N. See *plain vanilla interest rate swap*.

GFOA. ABBRV. Government Finance Officers Association.

ghost employee. N. A person who is listed on the payroll records of a company and receives a paycheck, but does not actually perform any work or is not an actual employee of the company. Fraudsters create ghost employees to perpetrate payroll fraud.

ghosting. N. An illegal activity in which market makers cooperate to manipulate stock prices.

gift-splitting election. N. A choice made by married couples to treat all gifts as if they were made together, and so the annual gift tax exclusion per person is $24,000 per recipient (as of 2007).

gift tax. N. A tax paid by the gift giver, not the recipient of the gift. As of 2007, an individual giver can transfer up to $12,000 per recipient before being subject to gift tax. A married couple's maximum is $24,000. The gift can be in many forms, including cash, stocks, bonds, real estate, personal property, artwork, or equity interests in a closely held business. Gift-tax liability is calculated based on cumulative taxable gifts, applying a rate to that total, deducting any gift tax paid previously, and then deducting the unified credit. The remaining amount is the gift tax for the year.

Ginnie Mae. N. A government agency that buys home mortgages from banks and transforms them into investment opportunities for the public. The investors receive the payments made on the mortgages and the banks continue to service the borrowers. Ginnie Mae securities are based on mortgages with similar maturities. Synonymous with *Government National Mortgage Association*. ABBRV. *GNMA*.

GNMA. ABBRV. Government National Mortgage Association. See *Ginnie Mae.*

goal congruence. N. A situation in which a manager's ambition is the same as the organization's ambition.

going concern. N. The concept that a business will continue to engage in its activities for the foreseeable future. This concept justifies cost measurement in terms other than liquidation value. If the auditors of a company doubted that the company would exist for at least the next year, the audit opinion would include an extra paragraph explaining this concern. Synonymous with *continuity.*

going private. N. Eliminating public ownership of equity shares by buying back outstanding stock. The company, its employees, or its management may finance the buyback.

going public. N. See *initial public offering.*

golden handcuffs. N. Compensation, benefits, rewards, and penalties that are given to certain employees so that they do not leave the company for a competitor.

golden parachute. N. A way to avoid a hostile takeover, in which compensation contracts specify huge payoffs to certain employees—usually executives—if the company is taken over and the executives are replaced. The amounts of the payoffs are so large that the acquiring firm could not afford to continue with the takeover.

Goldilocks economy. N. Economic conditions that are not too hot and not too cold, but are just right.

goodness of fit. N. A measure of the reliability of a statistically derived function. The goodness of fit is measured by the coefficient of determination and the coefficient of correlation. If a cost function is derived from a set of existing data, the goodness of fit indicates how consistent the function's predicted values are with the actual values. The "least squares" regression line may be the best available, but it may not be very good.

good 'til canceled. ADJ. Indicates the duration of a stop order or limit order, telling the broker to keep the order in effect until it is completed or until the investor cancels it.

goodwill. N. Occurs when one company buys another and pays more than the market value of the net assets. It appears on the balance sheet as an intangible asset. Goodwill represents something valuable about the purchased company that is not tangible, like a reputation for good service or a loyal, well-trained workforce. To calculate the dollar amount of goodwill, first adjust the book value of the assets to the market value of those assets. Then subtract the net assets of the acquired company from the purchase price. Prior to 2001, companies amortized goodwill over forty years or fewer. Current standards do not allow the amortization of goodwill. Instead, the value of the goodwill is tested and any impairment is written off.

Gordon model. N. See *constant-growth model*.

Government Accountability Office. N. See *U.S. Government Accountability Office*.

Governmental Accounting Standards Board. N. The organization established to address financial-reporting issues at all levels of government. The Governmental Accounting Standards Board issues standards for use by state and local government units through a process similar to the Financial Accounting Standards Board. ABBRV. *GASB*.

governmental funds. N. A set of categories used for the accounting of state and local government service activities that are supported by taxes. The five funds are general funds, special revenue funds, capital projects funds, debt service funds, and permanent funds. Governmental funds only contain current assets and liabilities.

Government Finance Officers Association. N. A professional association for people who perform the financial functions in a city, state, or province in the United States and Canada. Membership is open to interested persons. Prior to 1984, a subgroup of this organization established the accounting and auditing rules for governmental units. ABBRV. *GFOA*.

Government National Mortgage Association. N. See *Ginnie Mae*. ABBRV. *GNMA*.

government paper. N. An investment in the form of a debt security in which payment is guaranteed by the U.S. government. The traditional view is that government paper has almost no default risk associated with it. Treasury bills are an example of government paper.

graduated payment. N. A method of repayment in which payments made early in the repayment period are actually smaller than those at the end. Those lower, early payments may not cover the entire cost of the interest during the period, resulting in an increase in the loan principal. This type of payment schedule is especially beneficial to borrowers who are young and just beginning their careers. Their earnings increase and they can afford the higher payments that are made later in the term of the loan.

graduated security. N. A change in the exchange market in which an investment opportunity is traded. The term implies that a stock moves up, or graduates, from the over-the-counter market to the New York Stock Exchange.

grant date of a stock option. N. The date when an employee receives a stock option. This date is significant if the fair-value method of accounting for stock options is used, because it is the date on which the value of the options is based.

graphical user interface. N. Computer operating systems that use pictures and menus instead of complicated commands to run software. ABBRV. *GUI.*

greenmail. N. A method of defending against a hostile takeover. The company that is the target of the acquisition offers to buy back shares of stock at a premium price. Greenmail is the money paid to avoid losing the company, like blackmail is the price paid to keep individual secrets.

gross domestic product. N. The value of all spending by consumers, investors, and governments, plus exports minus imports. The change in gross domestic product is the significant aspect of it, rather than the absolute value, so the measure is adjusted for inflation. The gross domestic product is announced quarterly, and it is the measure of spending for the previous twelve months. ABBRV. *GDP.*

gross income. N. A tax term that is equal to income less exclusions. Income includes wages, tips, interest income, dividends received, and earned inflows from any other source. Exclusions are the items of income that are not taxable.

gross margin. N. The difference between the sales revenue and cost of goods sold. Synonymous with *gross profit.*

gross-margin method. N. See *gross-profit method.*

gross-margin percentage. N. Calculated by the formula gross margin divided by net sales revenue. Synonymous with *gross-profit percentage.*

gross method for purchase discounts. N. A way of accounting for purchase discounts that highlights the dollar amount of discounts taken. A company records purchases at the amount on the invoice (the gross amount), increasing accounts payable. Then, when it makes the payment within the discount's specified time period, it reduces the accounts payable for the original invoice amount, reduces cash for the amount of payment, and records the discount amount. At the end of the accounting period, the company reduces purchases by the amount of the discount. This method does not account for any discounts the company missed out on because of late payment. See also *purchase discounts*.

gross profit. N. See *gross margin*.

gross-profit method. N. A method of estimating inventory that can be used for interim accounting periods or when records are destroyed. It is not acceptable for the annual report. The method is based on the concept that if you know the percentage of the selling price that is the profit, then you can calculate the amount that is the cost of goods (sales minus the gross-margin percentage times sales). Starting with beginning inventory, add the purchases during the period then deduct the calculated cost of goods sold. What remains is an estimate of ending inventory. The estimate is only as good as the data used to calculate the gross-margin percentage. Synonymous with *gross-margin method*.

gross-profit percentage. N. See *gross-margin percentage*.

gross sales. N. The total amount of sales revenue before adjusting for sales returns, sales allowances, or sales discounts.

group depreciation. N. Calculating depreciation on all similar assets as if the collection were one asset. Depreciation is based on the average life of the group.

group method of depreciation. N. Allocating the cost of a group of similar assets that have similar lives by applying a rate to the depreciable base of the group. The rate is an average for all items in the group. Instead of depreciating each individual item, the collection is depreciated. The key difference between this method and the usual single-asset depreciation is that no gain or loss is recorded when an individual item in the group is retired. The cash is recorded, the original cost of the individual item is removed from the account, and the difference is either an increase or a decrease to the accumulated-depreciation account. See also *composite depreciation method*.

groupware. N. Software that allows multiple users (those in the group) to send email, share calendars to schedule meetings, share files and databases, and develop specific functions for the group. Examples of groupware are Exchange, Lotus Notes, and Outlook.

growth funds. N. Mutual funds invested in stocks that will provide most of the return through appreciation, resulting in capital gains. Contrast with income funds, which invest in stocks that pay high dividends and have a much smaller potential for capital gains.

growth stock. N. Companies that focus on earnings growth and do not pay much in dividends. Investors in growth stocks rely on the appreciation of the stock for their return.

guaranteed payment. N. The compensation paid to partners who work in the partnership's business. These payments, which are like salary, are income to the recipient and a business deduction to the partnership, but no payroll taxes are paid by the partnership. The recipient must pay self-employment taxes on these payments. This only applies to paychecks to partners and not to regular employees.

guaranteed residual value. N. The asset value or dollar amount that the lessee promises to the lessor at the end of the lease. A guaranteed residual value motivates the lessee to care for and keep up the leased asset.

GUI. ABBRV. Graphical user interface.

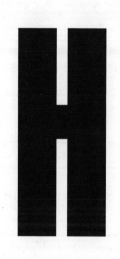

hacker. N. An unauthorized user of a computer system. Hackers gain entry through modems and by guessing passwords.

half-year convention. N. The custom of depreciating a newly acquired asset as if it were owned for only half the year, regardless of when it was purchased. The half-year convention simplifies depreciation calculations and is required for Modified Accelerated Cost Recovery System depreciation for taxes if assets are acquired relatively evenly throughout the year.

Hang Seng Index. N. A measure of the strength of the Hong Kong stock market. The Hang Seng Index is based on the stock prices of the thirty-three largest companies in the Hong Kong stock market.

hard currency. N. The money that is trusted by investors. Hard currency may not be a country's own currency if the country is unstable or if the economy is weak.

hard disk. N. The part of a computer used to store data. A hard disk consists of a flat, circular object that is magnetized to record information.

harmonization of accounting standards. N. See *GAAP convergence.*

head of household. N. A tax return filing status that is applicable to unmarried taxpayers who have relatives living in the home, whose relatives are not dependents of the taxpayer. To qualify, the taxpayer must be single on the last day of the year (but must not be a widow or widower), must be a citizen or resident of the United States, must have a relative living in the home, and must pay half the cost of the household (e.g., rent, property taxes, mortgage interest, utilities, etc.) If the relative is a dependent parent, then the in-home living is not required. Because the costs of the household do not include education expenses, medical expenses, clothing, or transportation for those living there, this filing status can be used by divorced parents. The tax rates for head of household filers are less than those for single filers.

Health Insurance Portability and Accountability Act. N. Protects individuals from losing health insurance coverage when they change jobs, which can be especially problematic if the individual has a medical condition that makes insurance expensive. ABBRV. *HIPAA*.

health reimbursement account. N. A device used by employers to reimburse employees for medical costs. If the arrangement meets Internal Revenue Code specifications, the employees do not pay taxes on the reimbursement but the employer can claim the reimbursement as a compensation deduction.

health savings account. N. A vehicle for taxpayers to put aside pretax dollars to use for medical costs, in particular those associated with high deductible medical insurance. ABBRV. *HSA*.

HECM. ABBRV. Home equity conversion mortgage.

hedge. N. A financial arrangement that protects against an unfavorable outcome in an existing contract or agreement because of price changes, interest rate changes, or foreign currency exchange rate changes.

hedge effectiveness. N. The degree to which a hedge achieves its purpose of offsetting either the gains or losses of the hedged risk. If a hedge is successful at covering the risk, a company can use hedge accounting, which limits the variability of income from the hedges. When the hedge is ineffective, all gains and losses are immediately included in income.

hedge fund. N. A type of investment fund that has limited government regulation because only accredited investors can participate. Hedge funds use many different investment strategies because of the limited regulation. While not characteristic of all hedge funds, many are aggressively managed and provide volatile returns to the investors.

hedging. N. Arranging contracts that offset the potential loss on other contracts from an economic outcome. If an entity signs a contract to buy 100 units of product W at a price of $5 per unit in the next six months, the entity would be worse off if the price of W went down. So to offset this possible loss, the entity tries to arrange a contract in which it will sell 100 units of W at a price of $5 in six months.

held-to-maturity. ADJ. A classification of an investment in a debt security that requires the owner of the debt security to intend to hold the investment until maturity and to demonstrate the ability to do so. Amortized cost is the accounting method used for held-to-maturity investments.

high-low method. N. A method of estimating the cost function and separating fixed cost from variable cost. Two data points with the total cost and level of activity are necessary inputs. First, variable cost per unit is determined by comparing the change in cost to the change in volume. That will reveal the cost per unit for the additional units produced. Then, the variable cost is removed from the total cost and only the fixed cost remains. Assume that total cost is $5,000 for 200 units and $7,000 for 300 units. The variable cost must be the $2,000 for the additional 100 units, or $20 per unit. So, if of the $5,000, $20 times 200 (or $4,000) is variable, then the fixed cost must be $1,000.

HIPAA. ABBRV. Health Insurance Portability and Accountability Act.

historical cost. N. A way of valuing assets that is measured by the amount of cash it takes to buy the asset and get it into use. Delivery costs, installation costs, sales tax, and calibration costs for technical equipment are included.

hobby losses. N. A category of business expenses that are deductible if the activity meets the definition of a business with a profit motive rather than a hobby. The expenses are deductible if the activity has shown a profit in three of the last five years.

holder-of-record date. N. See *date of record.*

holding gain/loss. N. The increase or decrease in the selling price of an asset that occurs only because time has passed. Holding gains or losses usually apply to investments that are owned but are not yet sold. The price increases or decreases are a result of market changes, not of anything the owner of the investment has done to increase or decrease the value.

holding period. N. The time an entity owns an asset. The holding period determines the tax treatment of gains or losses resulting from the sale or disposal of the asset. If the holding period is more than one year (even a single day more), the gain or loss on the disposal is long-term. If the ownership period is exactly one year or less, it is considered short-term.

home equity conversion mortgage. N. A type of reverse mortgage insured by the Federal Housing Administration and designed by the U.S. Department of Housing and Urban Development. Home equity conversion mortgages cap the amount of cash available to the homeowner at an amount less than the market value. Homeowners must be at least 62 years old to qualify, but the loan is most beneficial to older homeowners. Details are available at www.hud.gov/offices/hsg/sfh/hecm/hecm—df.cfm. ABBRV. *HECM*.

home-equity debt. N. A loan that is based on the difference between the market value of a home and the remaining mortgage balance. Home-equity debt uses the home as security for the loan. Subject to certain limitations, the interest on home-equity debt is tax deductible just like mortgage interest.

home-office deduction. N. A tax deduction if the office in a home is the primary place of business. The requirements for taking home-office deductions are very strictly enforced.

home page. N. Part of a website—usually the first screen the viewer sees—that acts like the base for the website. Usually a user can get to the home page from any part of the website, and the home page acts as a map to get to different parts of the website.

homogeneous cost pool. N. Used to reduce the number of overhead rates in an activity-based cost system, which assigns overhead to products based on how much of an activity the product uses. Homogeneous cost pools are made up of the sum of the costs associated with related activities that go into producing the product. This sum is then divided by the practical capacity of the activity driver to calculate the pool rate, which is used to assign the overhead costs from the related activities to the products.

Hope Scholarship Credit. N. A type of personal tax credit that reduces the amount of taxes the taxpayer must pay. The Hope credit is available to taxpayers, their spouses, and their dependents, and has a maximum amount of $1,800 per student during the first two years of higher education. The student must be considered at least a part-time student. The amount is based on tuition and required fees, but not other education expenses like books, activity fees, or room and board. This credit is not available for students who have a felony drug conviction, and it is phased out for taxpayers with a modified adjusted gross income above $48,000 in 2008. The total amount of all personal tax credits taken by a taxpayer in one year cannot be more than the tax owed plus the tentative alternative minimum tax. See also *Lifetime Learning Credit*.

horizontal analysis. N. A financial analysis tool that uses common size analysis for one company over time. For example, the cost of goods sold as a percentage of sales is compared over several years to see if that relationship is changing or stable.

horizontal combinations. N. A business combination between entities that are in the same business. A horizontal combination allows a corporation to acquire additional customers and additional capacity quickly. If Dell were to acquire Gateway, it would be a horizontal combination because both corporations are involved in the same business function and industry.

host assets. N. Any partnership assets that will produce an ordinary gain or loss if sold.

host contract. N. A term used to identify an aspect of a derivative financial instrument. The derivative is embedded in another nonderivative financial instrument, which is called the host contract. For example, Company A loans Company B $1 million to be repaid in three years. Instead of interest, Company A will receive the difference between the market price of 1,000 shares of Company A stock today, at $40 per share, and the price at the end of each of the next three years. No other interest is paid. The host contract is the $1 million loan. The embedded derivative is the annual payment based on the increase in share price.

hostile takeover. N. A corporate acquisition in which the target does not agree to the takeover and will take expensive actions to avoid it. The costs of avoiding the takeover are not tax deductible.

host instrument. N. A financial instrument that has an embedded derivative. An example is a $1 million loan due in five years that, instead of a stated interest rate and payment, requires the borrower to pay the difference between the current price and the market price on the maturity date of the loan of 10,000 shares of Company X stock. The $1 million is the host instrument and the "interest" payment is the embedded derivative.

housing starts. N. An economic measure of the strength of the economy measured as the number of permits issued to build residential housing during a period of time—usually one month. If the index increases from the previous month, the economy is thought to be getting stronger because those homeowners will be purchasing all the appliances, furniture, etc., necessary to move into the new house.

HR 10 plans. N. See *Keogh plans*.

HSA. ABBRV. Health savings account.

html. ABBRV. Hypertext markup language.

http. ABBRV. Hypertext transfer protocol.

human capital. N. The unrecorded asset made up of a skilled, loyal workforce. Human capital is not on the balance sheet, but may be reflected in increased revenues.

humped yield curve. N. A yield curve that occurs when both short-term and long-term debt have interest rates lower than medium-term debt.

hurdle rate. N. Another name for the minimum return a project or investment must generate to be accepted. The return must exceed the cost of capital—the hurdle—for acting on the project. See also *required rate of return*.

hybrid-costing system. N. A system of allocating costs to products that combines some techniques and aspects of job-order costing and of process costing.

hybrid method. N. A method of accounting used for tax purposes that combines cash-basis with accrual-basis accounting. Usually used by small businesses, the hybrid method accounts for purchases and the cost of goods sold on the accrual basis and uses the cash basis for all other items.

hybrid securities. N. Securities that have characteristics of both debt and equity. Convertible bonds are an example of a hybrid security.

hyperlinks. N. Pictures or words on a website, usually in a different color than the other words, that bring up information associated with the picture or highlighted words when they are clicked on. Hyperlinks eliminate retyping Web addresses to get more information.

hypertext markup language. N. A computer language used for building websites. ABBRV. *html*.

hypertext transfer protocol. N. A method used by a Web browser to translate the programming of a website so that the user can view the website. ABBRV. *http*.

IASB. ABBRV. International Accounting Standards Board.

IASC. ABBRV. International Accounting Standards Committee.

ICFR. ABBRV. Internal control over financial reporting.

IDEA. ABBRV. Interactive Data Extraction and Analysis.

ideal standards. N. A type of standard that assumes perfection. An ideal standard creates the tightest, most difficult standard to achieve.

identity theft. N. Pretending to be someone else when committing a crime. The criminal may use a person's name, address, bank, Social Security number, or credit card information to commit fraud.

IFAC. ABBRV. International Federation of Accountants.

if-converted method of accounting for convertible securities in diluted earnings per share. N. The method that adjusts the numerator of basic earnings per share to reflect what happens if the securities are converted. If convertible bonds are converted into stock, then income would be higher by the amount of interest, minus the taxes. If convertible preferred stock is converted, the numerator of basic earnings per share would not include a deduction for preferred dividends, because if the preferred stock were converted, then no dividends would be paid on it. The denominator would increase by the additional shares issued for the conversion.

IFRS. ABBRV. International Financial Reporting Standards.

IIA. ABBRV. Institute of Internal Auditors.

illegal dividend. N. A declared dividend that is not consistent with the corporate charter or the laws of the state of incorporation. See also *liquidating dividends*.

illegal gratuities. N. A payment or offer of payment of something of value for an official act that favors the entity giving the payment. Distinct from bribery, which tries to influence the official act, illegal gratuities are associated with a completed decision or award.

illiquid. ADJ. An item that does not have a market in which it can easily be sold for cash.

IMA. ABBRV. Institute of Management Accountants.

impaired capital. N. A situation on a balance sheet when the par value of the stock is more than the owners' equity. Impaired capital occurs when the company has experienced losses and the retained-earnings amount is negative, called a retained deficit.

impairment. N. A situation in which the balance sheet value for an asset represents more than the company can recover through continued operation or sale of the asset. First, calculate the net cash flows from the asset. This includes cash flows from the use of the asset and from the sale at the time of disposal. Then, compare the undiscounted net cash flows to the carrying value, or balance sheet value, of the asset. If the net cash flows are less, then the owner of the asset must write down the asset and record a loss on the income statement. The loss is the difference between the balance sheet value and the market value of the asset, or the present value of the net cash flows if no market value is available. Impairment may apply to any asset, and financial institutions must assess the likelihood that debtors will pay interest and principal on their loans. The impairment loss for financial institutions is measured as the difference between the amount of the loan, including any unpaid interest, and the present value of the future payments, discounted using the rate from the original loan. The impairment loss is in the other section of the income statement, with other revenues and gains and other expenses and losses.

implicit rate. N. The rate calculated for a noninterest-bearing note or another set of cash flows with no given discount rate. The implicit rate is the rate that discounts the future cash flows to the present value.

implicit service period. N. A type of service period for stock options that is assumed because it is based on characteristics of the grant. For example, an employee is granted options that can be exercised after the completion of a project and the project is expected to be completed in three years. The implicit service period is three years. See also *derived service period, explicit service period, service period for stock options, requisite service period.*

imprest bank account. N. A special-purpose account that is used for only one type of payment. Only the cash necessary to cover those checks is deposited in the imprest account. Many companies use an imprest bank account for payroll. The exact amount of the total payroll is deposited in the account, and if all employees cash their checks, the balance is zero. The imprest bank account allows the organization to quickly see which checks are still outstanding for certain types of payments.

improvements. N. See *improvements and replacements.*

improvements and replacements. N. A term used in accounting for asset expenditures when an asset takes the place of an existing asset. Expenditures for improvements (or better assets) and replacements (or similar assets) are capitalized, meaning the asset is recorded on the balance sheet rather than as an expense on the income statement. The cost is then allocated to future-use periods through depreciation. This spreads the cost over future accounting periods rather than reducing income in the accounting period by the total amount of the outlay. The actual procedures for recording the asset can vary. One method removes the old asset and puts on the new one, recording a gain or loss in the process if necessary. Another method just adds the new asset to the balance sheet and does not remove the old one, because the book value is nearly zero. A third method, used when a component of an asset is replaced, increases the book value of the old asset by decreasing the accumulated depreciation account.

imputed interest rules. N. Tax regulations that require that a reasonable rate of interest be used in calculating the gain or loss on the sale of an asset. The precise interest rate depends on the value of the property, the type of property, the terms of payment, and the relationship of the buyer to the seller. Section 1274 of the Internal Revenue Service code specifies the amounts. For financial accounting, imputed interest is the interest that is associated with borrowings even if the contract does not specify interest. A logical rate is chosen and the debt's present value is calculated using the discounted-cash-flow approach, with the logical rate as the discount rate.

incentive pay. N. A component of a compensation package based on a company-performance measure. Bonuses and stock options are types of incentive pay.

incentive stock options. N. A type of stock-option plan that allows the employee to pay capital gains tax on the bargain element (the difference between the market price and the strike price) when the stock is sold. There are no tax consequences at the time the taxpayer exercises the option. The corporation granting the option has no compensation expense. Stock-option plans that do not qualify for this classification require the employee to pay regular income tax on the bargain element as soon as the options are exercised, or when the options are granted if the fair market value is known. The corporation must deduct an equal amount as compensation expense. ABBRV. *ISO*.

inchoate interest. N. An ownership interest in real estate that becomes effective at a future date or as the result of a future event.

includible corporations. N. Types of corporations that can be part of an affiliated group, which means that only one tax return must be filed for the entire group. Members of an affiliated group cannot be tax-exempt corporations, foreign corporations, life insurance companies, or S corporations.

income. N. For businesses, the net of revenues, gains, expenses, and losses in an organization. Wages and other earnings are income to individuals.

income bond. N. A bond that only pays interest if the organization has enough earnings to pay the interest.

income from continuing operations. N. An income number that appears on the balance sheet of an organization with nonrecurring items to report. Income from continuing operations includes the ongoing business activities of the organization, but also includes some gains and losses that do not qualify as extraordinary items.

income funds. N. Mutual funds invested in stocks that pay good dividends, to provide investors with income.

income in respect of a decedent. N. Taxable income earned by a deceased person but not received before the time of death. Examples include salaries, dividends, and interest. ABBRV. *IRD*.

income interest. N. The right to receive the income from a property until death, without having actual ownership of the property. Upon death, the property belongs to someone else, who is said to have the remainder interest.

income property. N. An investment in real estate that is supposed to produce returns in the form of income.

income smoothing. N. Taking actions that avoid high variability in income. Income smoothing is accomplished through allocating revenues and expenses to several accounting periods rather than just one, making the income more predictable.

income statement. N. One of the four primary financial statements. The purpose of the income statement is to show the results of operations and to measure the performance of the entity during the accounting period. Synonymous with *profit-and-loss statement*.

income-statement method. N. See *direct method of determining cash from operating activities*.

income stock. N. Companies that pay high dividends. Investors in income stocks are more interested in the current dividends than in the long-term appreciation of stock value.

income stream. N. The cash flows associated with an investment.

income summary. N. A temporary account that may be used to park the debit amount of entries closing the expenses and the credit amount of entries closing the expenses for the period. The net of those two entries is transferred to the retained earnings account.

income tax payable. N. A current liability on the balance sheet that represents the amount of taxes owed to the government. Income taxes payable can be calculated using the Internal Revenue Service regulations, which are not always the same as generally accepted accounting principles.

income-tax-refund receivable. N. An asset account on the balance sheet that represents the refund amount the entity expects. Income-tax-refund receivable arises when an entity makes use of a carryback loss. See also *carryback loss*.

incomplete transfer. N. This situation makes a gift exempt from the gift tax. An incomplete transfer occurs when the giver retains some control of the gift. Examples of incomplete transfers include making a will and naming an heir, in which case no gift has been made. Another example is buying life insurance and naming a beneficiary. Again, no gift has been made because the transfer is incomplete.

incorporated. ADJ. An organization that has filed the necessary papers to become a corporation.

increased limited-expensing election. N. A tax incentive for small businesses in empowerment zones that increases the normal limited-expensing election by $20,000. The increased limited-expensing election allows businesses to deduct amounts rather than capitalize and depreciate those costs. The effect is to reduce taxable income and encourage the purchase of capital assets.

incremental borrowing rate. N. The rate of interest a borrower would have to pay for the next loan received.

incremental budgeting. N. The budgeting process that starts with the previous year's budget amount and adjusts it up or down to reflect anticipated changes in the next year. Synonymous with *baseline budgeting*.

incremental cash flow. N. The additional cash flows that occur because of some action taken. Incremental cash flows are used in evaluating a project or investment. If a corporation estimates it can reduce the cost of a product by 4% if it installs new, more efficient machinery, the incremental cash flow is the difference between the old cost of production and the new cost of production.

incremental cost. N. A cost used in decision making that represents the extra total cost that will result from an alternative. Synonymous with *marginal cost*.

incremental cost-allocation method. N. Allocates support-department costs to different users based on a ranking. The ranking is related to which user is most responsible for the cost. For example, the football coach of Big University is flying to visit an alumni group in Florida on Sunday night, is going to another alumni group in Illinois on Monday, and is flying back to the university on Tuesday. The cost of flying round-trip to Florida is $900, and the cost of flying round-trip to Illinois is $500. A round-trip ticket with an extra stop is only $1,000. The incremental method calls for ranking the users in some way, e.g., since the Florida group is the first meeting and it arranged its meeting before the Illinois group, it should pay the cost of flying round-trip to Florida, or $900. The Illinois group is charged the remainder, or $100. See also *stand-alone cost-allocation method.*

incremental-research-activities credit. N. A tax incentive to encourage businesses to engage in research activities. The incremental-research-activities credit is equal to 20% of the amount of increase in current-year research expenditures. The increase is figured from a historical average level of research spending. This credit combines with the expense deduction in three possible ways. The first method is to take the full credit and then deduct the difference between the increased spending and the amount of the credit. The second method is to take the full deduction for the increased research spending and then reduce the tax credit by the tax rate. The third method is to take the full credit and then capitalize and amortize the increased research spending over five years.

incremental-revenue-allocation method. N. Allocates revenue to different parts of a bundled product based on a ranking. The ranking criteria is determined by the management of the company offering the bundled product. The first item in the bundled product is allocated value equal to its selling price outside the bundled package. The second item in the bundled product is also the allocated value equal to its selling price, and so on. For example, a Las Vegas resort sells a vacation package for $500 consisting of three nights in a hotel, a greens fee for eighteen holes of golf, and a show ticket. Usually, on its own, the price of the hotel room is $200 per night, the greens fee is $100, and the show ticket is $75. If the management of the vacation package ranks the items as (a) hotel, (b) show, and (c) golf, then the revenue allocation using this method would be $500 to the hotel and $0 to both the greens fee and the show.

independence. N. A characteristic of public accountants that is the basis for their credibility in providing attestation and assurance services. Independence means that the public accountant does not have any ties to the client company that would bias the investigation and the final judgment. Independence in fact and in appearance is the professional standard for public accounting.

independent agent. N. A person who sells insurance from several insurance companies rather than just one.

independent checks. N. Part of the internal control system of a company that verifies and monitors other controls in the system.

independent contractor. N. A self-employed person. An independent contractor controls and directs the provision of services and is not an employee. The classification of "employee" versus "independent contractor" is important, because the employer is responsible for matching the Social Security and Medicare taxes of the employee. Independent contractors are responsible for the entire cost of Social Security and Medicare taxes.

independent variable. N. A part of a function or formula that is set to find out what the dependent variable will be. For example, in the cost function, the total cost equals the fixed cost plus the variable cost per unit, times the number of units of activity. The number of units of activity is the independent variable, because it is determined by choice and is not dependent on any part of the function.

indexed bond. N. A bond that calculates interest payments using an inflation adjustment. Indexed bonds protect the investor from purchasing power losses on the interest payments. The maturity value is not adjusted. Indexed bonds were first used in countries with high inflation. In 1997, the U.S. government started selling indexed bonds. Synonymous with *purchasing-power bond*.

index fund. N. A type of mutual fund that tries to replicate the performance of some index, like the Standard & Poor's 500 Index. Index funds usually have lower management fees because they are not actively managed. The decisions are automatic, based on the performance of the index.

indirect costs. N. Costs that are hard to trace to an identifiable product, department, or other cost object. Indirect costs benefit several services or products within the entity. An example of an indirect cost is the electricity used by a factory building that makes several different products. It is impossible to trace the precise amount of utility expense to assign to each product. Instead, managers use a logical allocation method to assign indirect costs to products. See also *common costs*.

indirect labor. N. Labor used in production but not associated with actually making the product. Indirect labor is included in factory overhead. A department supervisor's salary is an example of indirect labor. See also *direct labor*.

indirect materials. N. Materials used for production that only represent a small part of the final product. Indirect materials are included in factory overhead. Examples of indirect materials are glue or staples. See also *direct materials*.

indirect method of determining cash from operating activities. N. One of two acceptable methods of determining cash from operating activities on the statement of cash flows. The indirect method starts with the net income from the income statement and adjusts it for all items included in income that did not affect cash. Synonymous with *reconciliation method*.

individual retirement account. N. A retirement savings device for taxpayers. The individual retirement account allows a taxpayer to make contributions of up to $5,000 or 100% of his or her compensation in 2008, whichever is less, to a savings or investment account. The earnings in the account are not taxed until the taxpayer withdraws them in retirement. The contributions are fully or partially deductible, and the requirements are available in Internal Revenue Service Publication 590. Even if only one spouse is working, both can have individual retirement accounts, as long as the working spouse has enough earned income to cover the contributions. While most devices for tax savings must be established before the end of the tax year, individual retirement account contributions can be made any time before the tax is due. If Taxpayer S makes a deductible contribution to his or her individual retirement account on February 10, 2008, that amount is deductible on the 2007 tax return. See also *Roth IRA, Education IRA.* ABBRV. *IRA.*

industrial value chain. N. The part of the value chain that actually produces the product, starting with raw materials and continuing through all the steps needed before going to the customer. See also *value chain.*

industry ratios. N. The average value for financial ratios, by industry. Industry ratios are used for comparing the firm under analysis to the average firm in the same industry.

industry standards. N. The benchmark for financial ratios. Industry standards are used for comparison in financial analysis to evaluate how well a company is performing compared to companies in the same business. Industry standards are available from many financial services.

inflation. N. An economic condition in which prices are rising for most goods and services. The rate of inflation, rather than its existence, is the key aspect. If prices are rising very rapidly, the rate is high, and it is difficult for consumers to make new purchases.

inflation accounting. N. Financial reporting that adjusts for the changes in price level. Two methods of inflation accounting are constant-dollar accounting and current-cost accounting.

inflation premium. N. A component of the quoted or stated interest rate on a debt security. The inflation premium represents the estimate of inflation over the term of the security. If inflation is expected to be higher in the future, the quoted or stated rate of interest will increase to compensate the lender. The inflation premium is based on expectations of inflation in the future, not necessarily on the current inflation rate.

information and communication. N. One of the five components of an internal control system. This component refers to the accuracy, safety, and completeness of the accounting information and the communication to employees regarding their roles in maintaining the accounting information.

information-content hypothesis. N. A theory for explaining stock-price reaction to management action regarding dividends. The information-content hypothesis maintains that investors interpret management actions as signals of the extra information management possesses. Managers, knowing that future performance will be bad, will cut dividends or announce a smaller-than-expected

increase. Investors interpret the cut as a decreased earnings forecast. The opposite signal is that managers, knowing that future
performance will be good, increase dividends, and investors interpret this as an increase in forecast earnings. Synonymous with
signaling hypothesis.

information return. N. See *Form 1065.*

information system. N. A structure or organized scheme for
collecting, storing, and using data for a purpose. In a business, the
information system organizes data about personnel, finances, operations, and other business activities and then makes it available in
a meaningful form for uses such as budgeting, strategic planning,
and performance evaluation. The information system converts data
into information.

Information Systems Audit and Control Association. N. A professional organization of information technology professionals that
administers the Certified Information Systems Auditor exam and
certification process. ABBRV. *ISACA.*

information systems auditing. N. Audit procedures that include all
parts of the information system: hardware, software, data, procedures, and people. The auditor evaluates the role of the computer
in the internal control of the organization, in the safeguarding of
assets, and in operational effectiveness. See also *audit.*

information-systems risk assessment. N. The process of determining where things can go wrong in the information system and
the probability of those things happening. Information-systems risk
assessment is concerned both with intentional acts and accidents.
The level of risk suggests the type and the amount of audit procedures the auditor needs to perform and affects the cost of the audit.

information technology. N. The combination of hardware, software, data, employees, and procedures involved in computerized data processing. ABBRV. *IT*.

inherent risk. N. A component of audit risk. Inherent risk is the chance that the transaction will be recorded incorrectly through error or fraud. Inherent risk varies with the type of transaction because some transactions are more likely to result in accidental or intentional errors. A credit sale is not likely to be recorded erroneously, but could be recorded early to meet sales forecasts.

initial direct costs. N. Costs associated with setting up, negotiating, and finalizing a specific lease. Initial direct costs do not include marketing or advertising. If the lease is an operating lease, the initial direct costs are deferred and allocated over the term of the lease. If the lease is a capital lease, the initial direct costs become part of the receivable, and a new effective-yield calculation is needed to establish the rate necessary to arrive at the sum of the minimum lease payments and the initial direct costs. The initial direct costs reduce the effective yield.

initial public offering. N. Incorporating an existing unincorporated business and selling stock to the general public for the first time. Synonymous with *going public*. ABBRV. *IPO*.

innocent spouse provision. N. An exception to the rule that if spouses file a joint return, they are both responsible for the entire tax and penalties. The innocent spouse provision applies if items in question belong to the other spouse, if the innocent spouse was unaware of any deception, and if it would be unfair to hold the innocent spouse responsible. The innocent spouse must request this provision within two years of the penalties. If a person meets the qualifications for the innocent spouse provision, then he or she has no liability for penalties or additional taxes.

in-process R&D. N. In-process research and development costs. When one company acquires another, the research and development activities of the target company are allocated a large amount of the purchase price, because that amount is immediately written off. If it was on the balance sheet as an asset at the allocated cost, earnings of future periods are reduced by the amortization of this asset.

input controls. N. The measures a company takes to make certain that correct and accurate data is transferred from source documents into the accounting information system. Input controls can include procedures to ensure that sales are real and that the sales data is correctly entered. See also *application controls*.

input-processing-output cycle. N. The sequence of activities involved in the system that processes accounting transactions.

inputs. N. The components that are required for the production of a product. Inputs include the obvious raw materials and labor, but also include the administrative system that organizes insurance, payroll, and other less visible components.

input trade-off efficiency. N. A component of productive efficiency that focuses on the choice of inputs to the production process and looks at how the inputs combine. Input trade-off efficiency requires that the combination of inputs be the most efficient—in other words, the lowest cost. Companies deal with input trade-off efficiency issues when deciding to replace employees with machines. The mix of labor and machines that maximizes inputs and minimizes cost is the goal of input trade-off efficiency.

in-service distributions. N. Payments of pension benefits while an employee is still working. This usually occurs when the employee is in phased retirement and over 62 years old, making up the reduced wages with pension benefits. New tax laws allow this type of distribution without penalties in certain circumstances.

inside basis. N. A concept used to identify the tax basis of assets received by a business in exchange for an equity interest. The inside basis is equal to the basis of the asset plus any gain recognized by the original owner involved in the exchange. The inside basis may be different than the balance-sheet value.

inside director. N. A member of a board of directors who is not independent of an organization. The inside director may be an employee of the organization or may be associated with another organization that does business with it.

insider. N. Someone who has access to private information about a company and could use that information to achieve trading gains. The Securities Act of 1934 identifies individuals who are directors or officers or who own more than 10% of the common stock as insiders. They are presumed to have enough influence to get that special information.

insider trading. N. Buying or selling stock using private information that is not available to the general public. The trader profits by knowing facts that other investors are not aware of. Insider trading is against the law, and offenders are subject to civil and criminal penalties. An example of insider trading is an executive of a drug company who knows that the government is not going to approve a new drug for sale. Before that announcement, which is sure to lower the price of the drug company's stock, the executive sells many of his or her shares to avoid the loss.

insider trading Forms 3, 4, and 5. N. The Securities and Exchange Commission (SEC) filings required of officers and directors of a company when they buy or sell stock in the company. The forms are publicly available on the SEC's website, www.sec.gov.

insolvency. N. For tax purposes, the amount by which liabilities exceed the fair market value of a business's assets. The amount of the insolvency limits the amount of discharge of debt income that the business can exclude from income.

inspector general. N. The federal office that performs audits of federal agencies.

installment loans. N. See *amortized loan.*

installment-sales method. N. A method of revenue recognition that puts off the recognition of profit to the point of collection. This method records the sales revenue and the cost of goods sold, but then deducts the portion of profit from the installment sales that have not been collected. The company calculates the rate of gross profit on sales annually as gross profit for the year divided by sales revenue for the year. That percentage is then applied to the amount of cash collections for the year's sales to calculate the amount of profit to recognize. If interest is part of the cash collections, and it usually is, that part of the payments has to be accounted for as interest income. One of the keys to using this method is separating the annual sales, cost of goods sold, and collections. This allows for correct calculation of the rate of gross profit and the amount of profit to recognize and defer. The installment-sales method is allowed in situations where the probability of collecting installment sales cannot be estimated.

Institute of Internal Auditors. N. An international professional organization for internal auditors who focus on the efficiency and effectiveness of an organization. The institute awards the certified internal auditor certification through an examination. www.theiia.org. ABBRV. *IIA.*

Institute of Management Accountants. N. A professional organization for accountants working in industry and government. The Institute of Management Accountants publishes the magazine *Strategic Finance* monthly. *Strategic Finance* is read by controllers, chief financial officers, and other accounting professionals. The Institute of Management Accountants was formed in 1919 and originally called the National Association of Cost Accountants. The name was changed to National Association of Accountants in 1939, and the final name change came in 1957 when the organization became the Institute of Management Accountants. www.imanet.org. Synonymous with *National Association of Accountants*. ABBRV. *IMA*.

institutional fund. N. A mutual fund that is low-risk, appeals to large investors, and is usually worth one million dollars or more. Participants in institutional funds are often pension funds or endowments.

institutional investor. N. A large organization that buys and sells huge quantities of stock, usually for a mutual fund or pension fund. Institutional investors can affect stock prices because they have so much money to invest.

institutional shares. N. A class of mutual fund shares that are available only to pension funds, insurance companies, and other institutional investors and that have neither front-end, back-end, or 12b-1 fees. Synonymous with *Y shares*.

in-substance defeasance. N. A situation in which a company with long-term debt buys securities and puts them in a trust designated to pay off the long-term debt.

insured mortgage. N. Loans that are guaranteed against default by the Federal Housing Administration or a private insurance company. In the event of borrower nonpayment, the creditor receives payment from the insuring agency.

intangible assets. N. Noncurrent assets on the balance sheet that have no physical substance but represent a valuable right, such as a patent or a trademark. The cost of intangible assets is allocated through amortization.

integrated accounting software programs. N. Applications that do all types of accounting transactions, including sales, purchases, inventory, payroll, etc. Integrated accounting software programs accomplish this through modules that work off a central database. Some examples of integrated accounting software programs include Peachtree, QuickBooks, Great Plains, Oracle, and SAP.

integrated services digital network. N. A communication channel that allows computers to share information at a high speed. Unlike a telephone line that is used for both voice communication and computer sharing, this type of channel only transmits data between computers. ABBRV. *ISDN*.

integrated test facility. N. A technique used by auditors to verify that computer programs are doing what they are supposed to do. The auditor develops a set of phony transactions and follows them through the input, processing, and output stages of the program. ABBRV. *ITF*.

intellectual property. N. Intangible assets such as copyrights, trademarks, and patents. Intellectual property is usually not capitalized if internally developed. If purchased, then the intangible asset is recorded on the books and amortized over the lesser of the economic life or the useful life.

Interactive Data Extraction and Analysis. N. A software package used by auditors. Interactive Data Extraction and Analysis can access client data and bring it into spreadsheets for the auditor to analyze. It is available for PCs running Windows operating systems. www.audimation.com. ABBRV. *IDEA*.

interbank rate. N. See *London InterBank Offered Rate*.

intercept parameter. N. The point at which the graph of the cost function intercepts the cost axis and the volume is zero. The intercept parameter represents the fixed cost portion of the cost function. The graph of the cost function plots the total cost at various volumes of production.

intercompany dividend. N. A type of intercompany transaction in which one member of a consolidated group (a group of corporations that meet set criteria and file one tax return) pays dividends to another member that is a shareholder in the first member corporation. The dividend must be removed from the recipient's income and from the payer's equity.

intercompany elimination. N. A journal entry made when performing a consolidation that removes the effects of transactions between entities being consolidated.

intercompany profit. N. The difference between the selling price and the cost of the good or service in a sale between entities that present consolidated statements. The intercompany profit is removed through an eliminating entry.

intercompany transactions. N. Business transactions between entities that are part of the same consolidated group. These transactions include, among other things, property rentals by a subsidiary corporation from the parent corporation, loans between member corporations, sales to a corporation that is part of the consolidated group, paying dividends to a member, and providing services to another member. The problem is representing these transactions on the consolidated financial statements.

interest. N. (1) The cost to borrow money. The interest is paid on the amount borrowed and is calculated as a rate, which is usually stated as the rate for a year of borrowing, multiplied by the principal (amount borrowed), adjusted for the time (if less than a year). (2) Having some type of ownership in a business or real estate. If two people each contribute half to buying a house, each has a 50% interest.

interest cost. N. The cost to borrow money. The interest is paid on the amount borrowed and is calculated as a rate, which is usually stated as the rate for a year of borrowing, multiplied by the principal (amount borrowed), and adjusted for the time (if less than a year).

interest coverage. N. See *times-interest-earned ratio.*

interest deduction. N. A tax deduction from adjusted gross income on Schedule A, for certain types of interest that the taxpayer pays. Types of interest that are deductible include interest on borrowings used in the taxpayer's business, mortgage interest, and interest on home equity loans. All interest deductions are subject to limitations based on the total amount, adjusted gross income, and timing of the borrowing. Interest on student loans up to $2,500 may be deductible for adjusted gross income depending on the income level of the taxpayer. Credit card interest, called personal interest, is not deductible.

interest expense. N. An income-statement account that represents the cost of borrowing for the time period covered by the income statement. In a multiple-step income statement, interest expense is not part of operating activities, but is included in other revenues, expenses, gains, and losses. It is not necessarily the amount of cash paid to the lender, though. The cash paid for interest is found on the statement of cash flows. Interest expense is calculated on long-term liabilities such as bonds payable and mortgages. Interest expense is also appropriate for capital leases. See also *interest.*

interest income. N. See *interest revenue.*

interest-only loans. N. A type of borrowing with terms that call for interest payments at regular intervals during the term of the loan and the total principal due at the maturity of the loan. Contrast with amortized loans, in which each loan payment contains some principal along with the interest charged on the unpaid principal.

interest-only strip. N. A financial instrument that provides cash flows to the holder based on the interest paid from a pool of securitized loans. For example, a mortgage lender packages a group of mortgages and sells them. The buyer sells bonds that pay a return to investors based on the interest received from the original borrowers. The returns end when the mortgages are paid off.

interest on the liability (relating to pension plans). N. A component of pension expense. Interest on the liability is the growth in the present value of the benefit obligation because of the passage of time.

interest rate futures. N. A contract in which one entity agrees to deliver a debt instrument with a specified rate and maturity to another entity on a specified date. Treasury bond contracts are interest rate futures that trade on the Chicago Board of Trade.

interest rate parity. N. A concept that states that returns to investors are independent of the country of origin of the investment, and an equal return is achieved at a given level of risk.

interest rate risk. N. The chance that while an investor holds a debt security, the interest rate on similar debt securities will rise, making the investor's security less valuable. Interest rate risk is relevant to long-term debt. If a bank gives a borrower a thirty-year mortgage at 5%, the bank is subject to interest rate risk—the chance that during the next thirty years, interest rates on mortgages will rise above 5%.

interest revenue. N. An income statement account that represents the amount earned on loaned funds for the time period covered by the income statement. On a multiple-step income statement, interest revenue is not included in operating activities, but in the section with other revenues, expenses, gains, and losses. See also *interest*. Synonymous with *interest income*.

interim reporting. N. Financial reports that cover a period of less than a year. Publicly traded companies are required by the Securities and Exchange Commission to file quarterly reports called 10-Qs. Synonymous with *interim statements*.

interim statements. N. See *interim reporting*.

interlocking directorates. N. The boards of directors of two different companies that have directors who are on both boards. This situation is illegal if the companies are in the same industry and are competitors.

intermediary. N. The party that facilitates swaps by bundling swap transactions to construct perfectly offsetting swap positions. The intermediary is compensated through the bundling process by slight differences in interest rates.

intermediate term. N. Bonds that have a maturity in two to ten years. Synonymous with *medium term*.

internal audit. N. A functional area of a large organization that has the responsibility for monitoring the internal controls and evaluating the efficiency and effectiveness of operations. See also *audit*.

internal control. N. A system of practices, measures, and procedures within the operations of an entity that make sure business activities are performed in a manner that is honest and good for the company. In 1992, the Committee of Sponsoring Organizations defined internal control as "a process, effected by an entity's board of directors, management, and other personnel, designed to provide reasonable assurance regarding the achievement of objectives in the following categories—effectiveness and efficiency of operations, reliability of financial reporting, and compliance with applicable laws and regulations." See also *application controls*.

internal control over financial reporting. N. A system of policies and procedures within a company that works to ensure that the accounting records are accurate and that will detect errors, either accidental or intentional. To comply with Section 404 of the Sarbanes-Oxley Act, top management of the company is responsible for reviewing the system for deficiencies. See also *material weakness, control deficiency, significant deficiency.* ABBRV. *ICFR.*

internal linkages. N. The relationships within a company between different functional areas or activities. For example, purchasing and production are key linkages to ensure that adequate inventory is available.

internally developed intangible asset. N. The result of research and development activities or marketing campaigns. Internally developed intangible assets either do not appear on the balance sheet or are on the balance sheet at a value far below the actual value. This occurs because the activities to develop the asset are expensed in the accounting period in which the costs are incurred. A valuable trademark is the result of effective marketing. However, advertising and marketing costs are period expenses, so very little value is allocated to trademarks that are developed by a company. On the other hand, if a trademark is purchased from another company, the entire cost to acquire is reflected on the balance sheet.

internal measures. N. A type of target used to evaluate performance. Internal measures focus on things within the entity such as employee morale.

internal-rate-of-return method. N. A process used in capital budgeting to select the project. The internal-rate-of-return method identifies the discount rate that makes the discounted cash outflows equal to the discounted cash inflows. A computer program or sophisticated calculator usually does the calculation. If the internal rate of return is higher than or equal to the required rate of return, the project is acceptable. ABBRV. *IRR*.

internal reporting. N. Accounting information that is shared within the organization. Internal reporting does not have to conform to generally accepted accounting principles and can be in any form that the entity needs for decision making.

Internal Revenue Code. N. The tax laws of the United States.

Internal Revenue Service. N. A branch of the federal government that collects taxes from individuals, corporations, estates, and other entities. www.irs.gov. ABBRV. *IRS*.

internal-service fund. N. A type of proprietary fund (meaning it performs a business-type function with users paying for the service) used in governmental accounting. Internal-service funds provide those business-type services to other parts of the governmental unit. Contrast with enterprise funds, which provide business-type services to the general public. A printing department is an example of an internal-service fund, because the department provides printing for all the different parts of the government, and the printing charges paid by those other departments cover the costs of the printing department.

internal value chain. N. The activities within a company that work to provide a product. The internal value chain starts with design and development and continues through production, marketing, delivery, and customer service. The focus of management is to identify the key activities in the value chain that are most important to customers. If cost is the key, then all internal value chain activities need to minimize cost. See also *internal linkages*, *external linkages*.

International Accounting Standards Board. N. A group of representatives from various countries working to establish accounting standards that harmonize any one country's accounting requirements with those of other countries. The purpose is to make global investing more efficient. www.iasb.org/Home.htm. ABBRV. *IASB*.

International Accounting Standards Committee. N. See *International Accounting Standards Board*. ABBRV. *IASC*.

International Federation of Accountants. N. A professional organization of the groups participating in the International Accounting Standards Board. The International Federation of Accountants is similar to the American Institute of Certified Public Accountants in the United States, but it is worldwide. The organization issues guidelines, including International Auditing Guidelines, for the practice of accounting in any country. www.ifac.org. ABBRV. *IFAC*.

International Financial Reporting Standards. N. Accounting rules issued by the International Accounting Standards Board. ABBRV. *IFRS*.

International Organization of Securities Commission. N. An international organization that works for better capital markets worldwide through the harmonization of accounting standards between countries with different disclosure requirements. www.iosco.org. ABBRV. *IOSCO*.

Internet. N. The electronic connection of hundreds of thousands of networks around the world. The Internet allows computers to communicate electronically with each other, with or without the help of humans. The communication may be through letters, numbers, or pictures. See also *World Wide Web*.

Internet protocol address. N. The numeric translation of the text universal resource locator (URL). The Internet protocol address is made up of groups of meaningful numbers indicating a geographical area, an organization number, a computer group, and the specific computer's number. ABBRV. *IP address*.

Internet service provider. N. Gives an individual access to the Internet. ABBRV. *ISP*.

interperiod equity. N. A basic objective of fund accounting. Interperiod equity assesses what revenue sources cover the current-year expenditures. The cost of a new school building is an example of an expenditure that must be covered by future revenues.

inter vivos gifts. N. Gifts received by a taxpayer during the giver's lifetime. The gifts are not taxed as income to the recipient if they can be distinguished from compensation or pay for service. If a grandparent gives a 21-year-old grandchild $10,000, the grandchild does not have to include that $10,000 in gross income. If the grandparent owns a business and gives a $10,000 gift to the top salesperson, the salesperson must include the gift in gross income.

inter vivos trust. N. A trust created by a donor during the donor's lifetime. The donor transfers property to the trust and becomes the trustee. Upon the death of the donor/trustee, a successor trustee is named and can distribute the trust assets without going through the probate process. Contrast with a testamentary trust, which is created upon the death of the donor.

in-the-money. ADJ. A term used to describe a situation in an option contract in which it would be advantageous to exercise the contract. A call option that gives an individual the right to buy 100 shares of stock for $14 per share prior to December 31, 2008, would be in-the-money if the market price for the stock was more than $14 per share. The other party to the call option is obligated to sell at $14 no matter what the market price, and the holder could buy at $14 and turn around and sell the stock at the higher market price. A put option that gives an individual the right to sell 100 shares of stock for $14 per share prior to December 31, 2008, would be in-the-money if the market price for the stock was less than $14 per share. The holder of the contract could buy shares in the market at less than $14 per share and then exercise the option to sell at $14.

intranet. N. The electronic connection of computers within an organization that allows the computers to communicate internally. Intranets have many uses within a business, including purchasing, human resource functions, control features, and information sharing. The intranet can keep outsiders from accessing information and usually has security and privacy features.

intraperiod tax allocation. N. Assigning tax expense and benefit to sections of the income statement. Tax expense or benefit is listed on the income statement and is associated with continuing operations. Other individual items, discontinued operations, extraordinary items, cumulative-effect-of-accounting changes, and prior period adjustments are all shown as net of the tax effect, and the amount is disclosed.

intrinsic-value method of accounting for stock options. N. A procedure for calculating and allocating the compensation expense of stock options. The difference between the option price and the market price is equal to the compensation expense. That amount is divided up between the accounting periods in which an employee's service benefits the company (the service period). If the option price and the market price are the same, then no compensation expense is recorded.

intrinsic value of an option. N. The current value of an option that is measured as the difference between the strike price and the spot price. A call option that would give the holder the right to buy 1,000 shares of a stock before December 31, 2008, for $14 per share would have an intrinsic value of $2,000 if the market price, or spot price, was $12 per share.

inventoriable costs. N. See *product costs*.

inventory. N. A current asset on the balance sheet that consists of items that will either be held to sell to customers or be used in the production of goods or services. Different types of inventory exist, and the items in those different types have a similar purpose. See also *finished-goods inventory, raw materials inventory, work-in-process inventory, merchandise inventory*.

inventory control. N. The process of recording increases and decreases of inventory items so that records are accurate and up-to-date. Companies want to maintain adequate inventory to meet sales, but too much or too little inventory can be costly. Another aspect of inventory control is the protection of inventory through security and insurance. See also *inventory turnover*.

inventory conversion period. N. See *average days to sell inventory*.

inventory profits. N. The result of matching current selling prices with inventory costs that are not similar to replacement costs.

inventory turnover. N. A ratio for financial analysis that communicates the efficiency of inventory management. The formula is inventory turnover = cost of goods sold/average inventory held. It is important to match up the time period covered by the cost of goods sold and the time period of the average inventory. If the ratio is high, it means inventory items are not in the warehouse long before sale. If the ratio is low, it means the company has a lot of inventory on hand in relation to the amount it sells. While a high ratio may indicate efficiency, a high ratio may also involve a risk of running out of products and losing sales. A low ratio could mean that the company has obsolete inventory that will never be sold, or that the company has built up inventory in anticipation of higher prices or shortages. Interpretations of the inventory-turnover ratio require comparisons with industry averages. However, some publishers of comparative data use sales in the numerator of the ratio, so the reader has to investigate for comparability.

inverse floaters. N. A financial instrument with an interest rate that is tied to an index or to the prime rate, but that moves in the opposite direction. If an investment's return is tied to the prime rate and moves in the opposite direction, but in an equal amount, the investment paying 4% would move to 3.5% if the prime rate increased by half a percent. Moving in the opposite direction of market rates magnifies the effect of the rate movement.

inverted yield curve. N. A downward sloping yield curve, representing lower interest rates with longer term debt. Synonymous with *abnormal yield curve*.

investing activities. N. A category on the statement of cash flows that includes all cash transactions that involve investing either in the company itself or in another entity. Investing activities usually involve changes in noncurrent assets such as property, plant, and equipment; intangible assets; or, investments. Only the cash amount of the transaction is represented in this category. If some type of financing is involved, it is listed in significant nonactivity. Only the principal portion of loans made to others, or the repayment of the loans, is included in investing activities. Any interest payments from those loans is included in operating activities. See also *financing activities, significant noncash transactions*.

investment. N. The purchase of an asset to earn income or gain.

investment banking house. N. An organization that facilitates the transfer of capital to businesses by designing securities that have the characteristics desired by capital providers. After working with the business to design the security, the investment banking house buys the securities from the borrower and then resells them to the public. Technically, the process involves two sales. The first is from the business to the investment bank, and the second is from the investment bank to the capital provider. The investment banking house acts as a pass-through entity that collects and distributes securities and cash. Contrast with a commercial bank, which works with businesses and individuals and offers more products than securities. The usual investment banking transaction involves a business that wants to sell stock or bonds. Goldman Sachs, Morgan Stanley Dean Witter, Merrill Lynch, and Salomon Smith Barney are examples of investment banking houses.

investment center. N. A responsibility center in which the manager is held accountable for sales, costs, and investments.

Investment Company Institute. N. The national association of mutual funds, unit investment trusts, and closed-end investment funds. www.ici.org.

investment horizon. N. The length of time an investor plans to hold an investment.

invigilation. N. A fraud investigation technique that imposes very strict controls on business processes for a limited period of time so that it is nearly impossible for fraud to take place during the invigilation. Comparisons of receipts or activities during the invigilation with those prior to it can reveal differences that may be attributable to fraud.

invoice. N. A bill that is given to the buyer of goods or services on credit. The invoice pertains to a particular sale. Contrast with a statement, which lists all the activity (sales and payments) from a particular customer over a given period of time.

involuntary conversion. N. The discontinuation of service from an asset through an act outside the owner's control. When accounting for an involuntary conversion, an owner removes the asset (and the accumulated depreciation associated with that asset) from the

balance sheet and records a gain—if the amount of payment
received (e.g., insurance proceeds) is more than the book value of
the asset. The company records a loss if the payment is less than
the book value of the asset. The loss is usually an extraordinary
loss on the income statement. For tax purposes, the taxpayer can
avoid a gain on involuntary conversion if replacement property is
purchased. An example of an involuntary conversion is the loss of
a factory building because of a fire, flood, or earthquake, or
because of expropriation by a government.

IOSCO. ABBRV. International Organization of Securities Commission.

IP address. ABBRV. Internet protocol address.

IPO. ABBRV. Initial public offering.

IRA. ABBRV. Individual retirement account.

IRD. ABBRV. Income in respect of a decedent.

iron curtain approach. N. A technique used to determine the
amount of misstatement in financial statements that calculates the
misstatement based on the amount of error in the current year's
balance sheet. For example, if a company has incorrectly calculated a liability by $100 each of the past three years, the iron curtain
approach would determine the misstatement as $300 in the third
year rather than $100, the amount of the current year expense,
because the $300 is the amount by which the current year's balance
sheet is in error. The weakness of this approach is that the income
statement may not reflect an error correction. See also *rollover
approach.*

IRR. ABBRV. Internal-rate-of-return method.

irregular items. N. See *nonrecurring items.*

irrevocable trust. N. A trust in which the donor cannot regain control of the donated property.

IRS. ABBRV. Internal Revenue Service.

ISACA. ABBRV. Information Systems Audit and Control Association.

ISDN. ABBRV. Integrated services digital network.

ISO. ABBRV. Incentive stock options.

ISO 9000. N. Standards developed by the International Standards Organization recommending certain practices for all world businesses. The focus is on quality management practice in dealing with other businesses and customers.

ISP. ABBRV. Internet service provider.

issued stock. N. The number of shares of stock that have been sold but are not necessarily owned by investors yet. Shares of issued stock may be held by the corporation as treasury stock. The number of shares of issued stock cannot be greater than the number of authorized shares. See also *treasury stock, authorized stock*.

issue price. N. The selling price of a bond or share of stock when originally sold by a company to an investor. The issue price is usually different than the face value of the bond or the par value of the stock.

IT. ABBRV. Information technology.

IT audit. N. Information technology audit. The process that audits the computers, programs, data, and controls that make up the information system of an organization. The IT audit is as concerned with the controls' surrounding programs, data, and processing as it is with the completeness and accuracy of the output. See also *information systems auditing*.

itemized deductions. N. Deductions from adjusted gross income for various personal expenses like medical costs, charitable contributions, and home mortgage interest. Itemized deductions are reported on Schedule A. After completing Schedule A, the taxpayer should compare the amount of itemized deductions to the standard deduction. If the standard deduction is larger, the taxpayer is better off not itemizing. The amount of itemized deduction is limited above certain adjusted gross income levels. See also *standard deduction*.

ITF. ABBRV. Integrated test facility.

January effect. N. The slight rise in the stock market during the first week in January. The rise is thought to be caused by investors reinvesting dollars they got from selling stock prior to December 31, to take advantage of losses for tax purposes.

JIT. ABBRV. Just-in-time inventory system.

job-order costing. N. A method of assigning costs in which costs are collected with each batch, order, or job. Job-order costing is useful if the production deals with distinct orders for customers. Direct materials and direct labor costs are assigned to the job, and overhead is applied at a predetermined rate. The unit cost is calculated by totaling those costs and dividing by the number of units produced. Printers use job-order costing to calculate the cost of wedding invitations. The job-order sheet includes the cost of paper, the type of printing or engraving, the envelopes, and the other charges.

job-order cost sheet. N. A form used by a job-order costing system. The job-order cost sheet collects the costs for a particular contract, customer order, or job. The form may be physical or electronic.

joint and several liability. N. A legal term that places responsibility for an outcome on more than one party.

joint costs. N. Costs of production activities in producing more than one product. For example, the joint costs of raising and transporting turkeys have to be allocated among the various turkey products: whole turkeys, turkey parts, and poultry meal.

joint products. N. Products that undergo the same production processes to a certain point and become identifiable after that point. The point at which joint products are separated into two distinct products is the split-off point. For example, in a refrigerator production plant, two products are made, the "super" and the "super deluxe." These two refrigerators are joint products because they are part of the same production process throughout the construction of the box and the installation of the motor. At that point—the split-off point—the "super" gets plastic shelves, plastic baskets, and a white door, and the "super deluxe" gets glass shelves, heavy-duty baskets, and a wood-paneled door.

joint return. N. A tax return filing status that is applicable to a married couple. The requirements for choosing this status are that the couple are married on the last day of the year, that they have the same tax year-end, and that both are citizens or residents of the United States or that the noncitizen reports all income on the return. A widow or widower who does not remarry before the end of the year can file a joint return in the year the spouse dies if there is a dependent child living at home. Couples in the divorce process can file a joint return if the divorce is not final.

joint tenancy. N. A form of property ownership in which two or more individuals own property together. If one of the owners dies, the ownership remains with the living owner or owners. The ownership cannot be willed to anyone else.

joint venture. N. A business form that is similar to a partnership but involves a single purpose. Joint ventures are often used in areas of the world that require local ownership of business. In that situation, a U.S. company will combine with a local company to do business in that area.

journal. N. The place where business transactions are first recorded. Historically, clerks would write down entries in the order in which they happened. The entry would include the accounts and amounts, which would be debited and credited. While few businesses use the old paper journals, the definition is still accurate and business transactions are still journalized as the first step in accounting. Now most entities use some sort of computerized system. Several different journals accumulate transactions associated with events that occur often (e.g., sales, cash receipts, cash disbursements, and payroll). See also *general journal, sales journal, cash-receipts journal, cash-disbursements journal, payroll journal, purchases journal, special journal entry*.

journal entry. N. The first record of an event in the records of an entity, recording which accounts are increased or decreased for the transaction. See also *journal*.

Journal of Accountancy. N. The monthly publication of the American Institute of Certified Public Accountants. It covers all aspects of accounting from a practitioner's viewpoint and is read by practicing accountants, business professionals, and academics.

Journal of Accounting Research. N. An academic journal published by the Graduate School of Business of the University of Chicago. It focuses on basic scholarship and is read mainly by academics.

jumbo loan. N. A loan of $1 billion or more.

junior debts. N. Borrowings that, in the event of bankruptcy, are paid off after other debts. The hierarchy of payoff puts senior debts ahead of junior debts. That means that if the proceeds are not sufficient to cover all debts, junior debts are less likely to be repaid.

just-in-time inventory system. N. A system for keeping the number of items in inventory at a minimum because of the costs of storing, insuring, and protecting inventory. Ideally, the inventory item would arrive at the business location "just in time" for it to be sold or used in the production process, and therefore, inventory levels would be zero. Practically, this does not work because of unforeseen demand or delivery problems. ABBRV. *JIT*.

just-in-time manufacturing system. N. A structure for organizing manufacturing that focuses on minimizing unused inventory. In just-in-time manufacturing, an item is only produced to satisfy the demand of a customer, whether the customer is internal or external. Ideally, raw-materials inventory is zero, and the materials are delivered just as the production process needs them to meet a documented demand. The key to just-in-time manufacturing is perfect linkages with suppliers. The production process uses a product-focused layout, in which manufacturing cells take a single product from beginning to end. Contrast this with the traditional-process layout, which has all products go through the same process in one location and then move to the next location for the next process.

kaizen costing. N. The process of incrementally reducing costs through eliminating nonvalue-added activities, choosing cost-efficient activities, reducing time or resources used by activities, and sharing existing activities. This system is used in Japan to implement continuous improvement.

kaizen standard. N. The size of the move toward the elimination of all nonvalue-added activities. The kaizen standard is similar to currently attainable standards but is not permanent. Until all nonvalue-added activities are eliminated from a business, the kaizen standards continuously move the required level of performance toward that goal.

Kanban system. N. Originally a Japanese system for accomplishing a just-in-time inventory system. The Kanban system uses cards to indicate units withdrawn from inventory, units in production, and inventory orders to be placed.

keep-or-drop decision. N. The choice of whether to continue producing a product or to eliminate the product. In keep-or-drop decisions, other alternatives may exist, such as to drop the product but replace it with some other product.

keep the quarter open. N. A technique in which sales made after the end of the accounting period are included in the sales for that period. Companies do this to meet earnings or revenue forecasts, under the assumption that the shortfall in the current quarter will be made up in the next quarter.

Keogh plans. N. A type of retirement plan for self-employed taxpayers. If a sole proprietor or partner establishes a Keogh plan, it must cover all employees as well as the owner or partner. The maximum contribution in 2008 is $46,000 or 100% of net income, whichever is less. The contributions for employees is deductible on Schedule C, and the contribution for the owner or partner is deductible for adjusted gross income on Form 1040. Synonymous with *HR 10 plans*.

kickback fraud. N. A type of fraud involving a company employee and an outsider in which the company employee makes it possible for the outsider to receive some extra benefit from transactions with the company, and the outsider then shares that benefit with the employee.

kiddie tax. N. A term used to describe the rule regarding unearned income for children under 14. In a situation where a child under 14 has investment income or some other unearned income, that income is taxed at the parents' highest rate. After the child turns 14, the unearned income is taxed at the child's presumably lower rate. The strategy is to give children under 14 gifts that will appreciate in value without providing any income. If the assets are sold after the child reaches 14, the gain is taxed at either the capital-gains rate or the child's rate, whichever is lower.

kiting. N. A method of double-counting cash. Individuals may use two checking accounts at two different banks, writing a check to deposit in Account B (at Bank B) from Account A (at Bank A). The check writer may have use of the funds in Account B before the check clears Account A, which may not even have the funds to cover the check deposited in Account B. To avoid this practice, many banks restrict the use of newly deposited funds. Large corporations use the kiting technique by transferring dollars from Division A to Division B. If Division A transfers funds to Division B but does not record the transfer right away, and Division B records the transfer of the funds immediately, the transfer amount is double-counted. It is in both Division A's cash and Division B's cash.

knock-in option. N. A type of option that gives one party the right to buy a security only when the security reaches a particular price.

knock-out option. N. A type of option that gives one party the right to buy a security at a specified price during a time period that ends when the price of the security reaches a certain limit. When the price hits that ceiling, the holder of the option must exercise or lose it.

labor efficiency variance. N. A variance indicating how the actual quantity of labor hours used in production compares to the standard quantity. The formula is the difference between actual hours and standard hours for producing one unit, times the actual quantity of units produced. This variance is the responsibility of the production manager, but events such as machine breakdowns are beyond the control of production managers, so the responsibility may rest in another area.

labor-rate variance. N. A variance indicating how the actual cost of labor used in production compares to the standard cost. The formula is the difference between the actual rate per hour and the standard rate, times the actual hours used. This variance is usually small, because wage rates are set by unions and market forces.

ladder. N. Structuring an investment portfolio so that debt securities mature in fairly even amounts annually. A ladder strategy reduces interest rate risk because not all dollars from the portfolio will mature if interest rates are low.

lagging indicator. N. An economic measure that changes in the direction of the economy after the change in the economy is evident. Labor wages are a lagging indicator because a large number of workers are covered by union contracts. After the change in the economy, the next negotiation reflects the change.

lag measure. N. A type of target used to evaluate performance. Lag measures evaluate performance based on the results of past activity and focus on historical operation.

LAN. ABBRV. Local area network.

land. N. An asset account on the balance sheet that represents the historical cost of land plus any special assessments. The land account is not depreciated.

land improvements. N. An asset account on the balance sheet that contains the historical cost of limited-life additions to the land, such as driveways, fences, and parking lots. The land account is not depreciated, but the land improvements are.

lapping of accounts receivable. N. A method of covering up the embezzlement of cash. The employee steals a payment that Customer A sends, and to keep Customer A from receiving a bill for that amount, records a payment from Customer B to Customer A's account. Then, a payment from another customer is recorded to Customer B's account. The result is that only a small number of accounts will show amounts owed that the customer has already paid for. Lapping is difficult for auditors to detect because they sample customer accounts to check for accuracy and the sample may not hit any of the wrong accounts.

large cap. N. A term describing the size of a corporation based on the market value of its stock. If the value (calculated by multiplying the number of shares outstanding by the current market price) is larger than $5 billion, the corporation is described as a large-cap firm. See also *medium cap, micro cap, small cap*.

large stock dividend. N. A dividend in which the company distributes additional shares to existing shareholders at a rate greater than one new share for every four or five shares owned. (If the rate is less than that, it is considered a small or ordinary stock dividend.) For large stock dividends, the retained earnings is decreased by the par value of the new shares, and the stock account is increased by the same amount. See also *stock dividends*.

last in, first out. N. A method of getting the cost of ending inventory by putting the most recent cost of inventory in the cost of goods sold and the oldest costs in the ending inventory. This method results in the value of the cost of goods sold on the income statement representing close to the replacement cost. The choice of costing method is significant only if prices are rising or falling rapidly. See also *LIFO reserve, LIFO effect, dollar-value LIFO*. ABBRV. *LIFO*.

Lazy Susans. N. See *round tripping*.

LBO. ABBRV. Leveraged buyout.

LCM. ABBRV. Lower of cost or market.

leading indicators. N. An economic measure that changes before the entire economy changes. Building permits are a leading indicator, because they increase before the whole economy shows signs of improving.

lead measures. N. A type of target used to evaluate performance. Lead measures evaluate performance based on activities completed at present that are expected to provide improvements or benefits (such as training). Synonymous with *performance measures*.

lead time. N. The time between an inventory order and the order's receipt. Lead time is an important input to calculating the reorder point so that the company does not experience a stock out because inventory has not arrived. Synonymous with *manufacturing cycle time*.

LEAPS. ABBRV. Long-term equity anticipation securities.

learning curve. N. A nonlinear relationship between the number of labor hours per unit and the number of units a worker has produced. The logic is that as the worker is learning the job, it takes more time. As the worker acquires more skill, less time is needed to complete it. Usually, the longer a worker has been doing the job, the more efficiently it is done.

lease. N. A contract between an owner of an asset and a renter of the asset giving the renter the right to use the asset for a specified period of time and a specified set of payments. Two general classifications of leases are operating leases and capital leases. The classification of a lease as either operating or capital is significant because the accounting procedures differ and have substantial effects on income and on financial-analysis ratios. The capital lease is really treated like the purchase of the asset, increasing debt on the balance sheet of the lessee. See also *capital lease, operating lease.* Synonymous with *leasehold.*

leasehold. N. See *lease.*

leasehold improvements. N. A noncurrent asset in the property, plant, and equipment section of a lessee's balance sheet that represents the cost of changes made to leased property that cannot be removed at the end of the lease. The lessee depreciates the cost of leasehold improvements over the life of the lease or the economic life of the asset—whichever is shorter. If Company T signs a ten-year lease for office space and then, to properly configure the space, spends $14,000 to install dividers with a useful life of twenty years, the $14,000 cost is spread out over the ten years of the lease. If the dividers have a seven-year useful life, then the cost is depreciated over seven years.

lease liability. N. The account in the liability section of a lessee's balance sheet that represents the present value of the minimum lease payments on a capital lease.

lease term. N. The period of time covered by a lease. The lease term may be short or may be the entire life of the asset.

least-squares method. N. A statistical method that determines a relationship between two things based on existing data. The least-squares method uses mathematical techniques to calculate the function, similar to the visual fitting of the line in the scatter-plot method. The fitting is done so as to minimize the difference between the existing data and the value predicted by the line. Many spreadsheets have this statistical function built in and call it regression.

ledger. N. An accounting device for collecting all the increases and decreases to accounts. Information from the journal is separated into the effects on specific accounts. See also *general ledger*, *subsidiary ledger*, *journal*.

legacy. N. A distribution of personal property according to the provisions of a will. Legacies are identified by the source of the funds for the distribution and include specific legacies, demonstrative legacies, general legacies, and residuary legacies. See also *abatement*. Synonymous with *bequest*.

legacy system. N. A company's existing computer system, consisting of hardware and software.

legal capital. N. The par value of all stock that a corporation has issued. If the stock has no par value, then the legal capital may be a stated value, declared amount, or total amount paid for the shares. The significance of legal capital is that it represents the minimum amount of stockholders' equity allowed. Dividends cannot be paid if the amount reduces stockholders' equity below the amount of legal capital.

legatee. N. The recipient of a legacy, which is a distribution of personal property according to the provisions of a will.

lender. N. The entity that provides a loan, including money or other assets. The lender charges interest as a fee for the loan.

lessee. N. The participant in a lease contract that is buying the use of an asset owned by the other party to the lease, called the lessor.

lessor. N. The participant in a lease contract that owns the asset and is allowing the other participant, the lessee, to use the asset for a specified period of time and for a specified payment.

letter of audit inquiry. N. An audit technique in which the auditor sends a letter to the client's attorney requesting information on any legal matters affecting the client company. The attorney communicates directly with the auditor on this issue. The purpose is to find any contingent liabilities that the auditor should know about that may require disclosure.

letter of credit. N. A bank letter guaranteeing payments by the customer for a certain period of time or up to a certain amount.

letter ruling. N. See *private letter ruling*.

letters of comment. N. See *comment letters*.

leverage. N. The use of debt to earn a return. For example, assume an investor can borrow $1,000 at 5% and uses the $1,000 to invest, earning 6% on the investment. The 6% investment provides the payment for the original loan plus a return of 1% to the investor.

leveraged buyout. N. A method of eliminating public ownership of a corporation. Management or a group of employees borrows enough capital to buy the stock of the company using the company's assets as collateral for the loan. ABBRV. *LBO*.

leveraged lease. N. A lease arrangement in which the lessor finances the cost of the leased asset, using the asset as collateral. The lessee pays the rent to the lessor, who uses that cash to make payments on the loan. The financing does not depend on the lessee at all and is considered nonrecourse financing. The lessee has no special accounting procedures for a leveraged lease. The lessor accounts for it like a direct financing lease, but some additional details are required. Synonymous with *sandwich lease*.

liability. N. An obligation or debt of an amount that can be measured, belonging to a particular entity. Accounting liabilities are different from legal liabilities in that the accounting liability has to be the result of a past event. If a company signs a contract with labor to increase wages over the next year, the company has an obligation to do that, but no accounting liability exists for those wages until the workers actually work the hours.

LIBOR. ABBRV. London InterBank Offered Rate.

lien. N. A legal claim to an asset in the event of nonpayment. Builders can file a lien against property they are constructing to ensure that if the owner does not pay, they can sell the property for payment.

life-cost management. N. The process of creating long-term advantages through managing the design, development, production, marketing, and servicing of a product. The emphasis is on adding value through cost reduction and through efficiency increases.

life-cycle costs. N. All the costs associated with a product, from planning through abandonment.

Lifetime Learning Credit. N. A type of personal tax credit that reduces the amount of taxes a taxpayer must pay. The Lifetime Learning Credit has a maximum of $2,000 in any one year. It has fewer requirements than the Hope Scholarship Credit because it allows all education expenses, does not require that the student take at least a part-time course load, and is not limited to the first two years of postsecondary work. The total amount of all personal tax credits taken by a taxpayer in one year cannot be more than the tax owed plus the tentative alternative minimum tax.

LIFO. ABBRV. Last in, first out.

LIFO conformity rule. N. Last in, first out conformity rule. The tax law that requires companies that use LIFO (last in, first out) on tax returns to use LIFO for valuing inventories and the cost of goods sold on the balance sheet and income statement. No other inventory-cost-flow assumption has a required conformity rule.

LIFO effect. N. Last in, first out effect. The change from one accounting period to the next in the amount of the allowance to reduce inventory to LIFO (last in, first out). The allowance to reduce inventory to LIFO is the difference between the cost of inventory using the LIFO-cost-flow assumption and the cost of inventory using some other method, like replacement cost or first in, first out (FIFO) that is used for internal reporting purposes.

LIFO layers. N. Last in, first out layers. The increases of inventory that tend to occur yearly when a company uses the LIFO-cost-flow assumption. Companies try to carefully maintain inventory levels because LIFO liquidation can be costly.

LIFO liquidation. N. Last in, first out liquidation. The effect of a reduction in the amount of inventory held by a company using the LIFO-cost-flow assumption. The effect is to match older, presumably lower-than-current inventory costs with current selling prices and to distort income on the high side, resulting in higher tax payments. See also *LIFO layers.*

LIFO reserve. N. Last in, first out reserve. The difference between the cost of inventory using the LIFO-cost-flow assumption and the cost of inventory using some other method, like replacement cost or first in, first out (FIFO) that is used for internal reporting purposes. The LIFO reserve is referred to as the allowance to reduce inventory to LIFO. Companies must disclose either the LIFO-reserve amount or the replacement cost of inventory, if LIFO is used on the financial statements.

LIFO-retail-inventory method. N. Last in, first out–retail-inventory method. A type of retail-inventory method in which the cost-to-retail percentage is calculated without including the beginning inventory. For the basic process, view beginning inventory as a layer of costs that remains unchanged. Add to that layer a new layer for the increase in inventory for the current period, using a cost-to-retail percentage based on current period costs and selling prices. The calculation of the ratio for the current period is simple if prices have been stable during the period. The purchases are divided by the sales adjusted for net markups and net markdowns. That percentage is then applied to the new layer of inventory at retail. That new layer is calculated by subtracting purchases at retail from sales for the period. If prices are not stable, the company has to determine if a real increase in inventory occurred by deflating everything to one price level. Then, any increase is added at the new price level. Under changing prices, the LIFO-retail-inventory method is similar to dollar-value LIFO.

like class. N. Tangible personal property assets that are depreciable and classified within the same general asset class. If assets are like class, then they meet the definition needed for a like-kind exchange.

like-kind exchange. N. A trade or swap of business property that is of the same function and is within the United States. A like-kind exchange has no tax effect because no gain or loss is recognized by either party. The definition of "like-kind" is varied, but strict and spelled out in Internal Revenue Code Section 1031. If property is classified in the same asset class or product class, then the property is like-kind. For non–real estate property, the items need to be nearly identical to qualify as a like-kind exchange.

limit-buy order. N. See *limit order*.

limited-expensing election. N. A tax incentive for small businesses with non–real estate capital-asset purchases of less than $224,000 per year. The limited-expensing election allows the business to deduct amounts rather than to capitalize and depreciate those costs. The effects are to reduce taxable income and to encourage the purchase of capital assets. The business may deduct up to $24,000 of asset purchases.

limited liability company. N. An unincorporated form of business that is considered a legal entity. Limited liability companies (LLCs) provide the same liability protection that corporations provide for shareholders, meaning that members of an LLC are not personally responsible for company debts. For tax purposes, an LLC can be classified as either a corporation or a partnership. Most U.S. LLCs choose to be classified as a partnership and the members pay tax on the income of the LLC. ABBRV. *LLC*.

limited liability partnership. N. A type of partnership in which partners are personally responsible for all debts of the partnership, except those that result from malpractice lawsuits. ABBRV. *LLP*.

limited partnership. N. A type of partnership in which at least one partner does not have personal responsibility for partnership debt. At least one partner, called the general partner, does have personal liability.

limit order. N. An order to buy or sell stock at a better price than the one an investor states. If a stockbroker can buy at a lower price than stated, the broker buys for the investor. If the order is to sell, the broker sells at a higher price than the limit. A limit-sell order locks in gains for the investor because it tells the broker to sell the stock when the price goes above a certain limit. A limit-buy order tells the broker to buy when the price goes below a certain limit. Contrast with a stop order. A stop-loss order saves the investor from bigger losses because the stock is sold when the price goes below a certain level. A stop-buy order helps investors who have a short position because the stock is bought when the price goes above a certain level.

limit-sell order. N. See *limit order*.

linear programming. N. A statistical procedure that finds the best solution to a problem with several unknown aspects. Linear programming requires an objective function that represents the problem. Constraints identify the limits on various aspects of the problem. The procedure uses those inputs to determine the best, or optimal, solution. Computer programs are used to guide users through the inputs.

line of credit. N. The maximum amount of short-term borrowing that a bank preapproves through an informal process. A line of credit allows a customer to automatically borrow, using short-term promissory notes, up to a maximum amount, either in one borrowing or in repeated borrowings. The total outstanding at any one time cannot exceed the maximum. Contrast with a revolving credit agreement, which is a formal contract that requires the bank to provide funds if needed. In addition to interest, the bank receives a fee for agreeing to the contract. A line of credit involves only interest, and the bank is not required to make the loan.

line positions. N. Employees in an organization with a direct connection to the main operating activities. Assembly line workers in an auto factory are line positions. So are the executives and management people directly responsible for the operations. See also *staff positions*.

liquid asset. N. Cash or an item that can be quickly sold for cash without a deep discount to speed the sale. Liquid assets include the most current assets on the balance sheet.

liquidate. v. A way of divesting of a part of a business by selling the assets of that part individually instead of as an operating unit.

liquidating distribution in a partnership. N. Amounts, usually cash, given out by a partnership to a partner, that are equal to or greater than the total amount in the partner's capital account. A liquidating distribution eliminates the partner's ownership interest in the partnership. The partner's capital account cannot be negative.

liquidating dividends. N. Distributions to owners that are more than the retained earnings of the company. The amount of the dividends that exceeds the retained earnings is a return of the owner's investment, not a return on the investment. The additional paid-in-capital account is decreased for the excess amount.

liquidation value. N. The amount received if an asset is sold. This method of valuing assets is useful for those that the company intends to sell soon.

liquidity. N. The ability of an entity to meet current obligations through the use of current assets rather than borrowing.

liquidity premium. N. A component of the quoted or stated rate of interest on a debt security. The liquidity premium represents the difficulty of selling the debt security, should the lender wish to do so. To sell a debt security quickly, the lender would have to reduce the price, and the liquidity premium compensates the lender for that reduction. The liquidity premium is very low for treasury securities because they can easily be sold for cash.

liquidity ratios. N. Financial analysis tools that measure a company's ability to pay bills that are due within a year. Liquidity ratios are calculated using amounts from the financial statements and give information about the relationship between amounts on the financial statements. Analysts then compare the relationships from different companies to evaluate the bill-paying ability. Common liquidity ratios are the current ratio, the quick or acid-test ratio, and the current cash-debt ratio.

listed corporation. N. A business organized as a corporation whose stock is traded on an organized stock exchange.

living trust. N. A way of reducing probate costs by transferring assets to a trust. The disposition of the assets upon the death of the person establishing the trust is determined at the time of establishment. The assets in the trust avoid inclusion in the estate.

LLC. ABBRV. Limited liability company.

LLP. ABBRV. Limited liability partnership.

loan charge-offs. N. The elimination of a loan from the bank's receivables when the bank does not expect the borrower to pay.

loan guarantee. N. A way for the bank to make certain that a loan will be repaid if the original borrower does not pay. A loan guarantee is sought from another party that agrees to pay back the loan if the borrower defaults. Banks often require a loan guarantee for small corporations because owners are not personally liable for the debts of the corporation.

loan-loss provision. N. A bank's estimate of bad debts in relation to the loans it has. The loan-loss provision reduces the book value of the loan receivables on the balance sheet. The loan-loss provision in a bank is similar to the allowance for uncollectible accounts in a business.

loans. N. Contracts in which money is given to a borrower with the stipulation that it be returned with interest. Most loans specify the payment schedule, amount, interest rate, and date of the required payoff. See also *interest-only loans, amortized loan, add-on-basis installment loans, discount-interest loans.*

loan schedule. N. A chart providing information on the repayment of a debt. A loan schedule lists the due date for payments, dollar amount of payments, composition of payments in terms of interest and principal amounts, and principal balance after each payment.

local area network. N. Consists of several computers, terminals, and printers that are connected for the purpose of sharing information, data, software, or printers. Usually local area networks are in one building or on a campus, connecting components that are not scattered over a wide geographical area. See also *wide area network*. ABBRV. *LAN*.

lockboxes. N. Special post office boxes used by companies for receiving customer payments. Customers send the payments to the lockbox address, which is monitored by the company's bank. The bank opens the envelopes, lists the payments, and deposits the checks before notifying the company of the payment details. The company then updates its records to reflect the payments. Lockboxes speed up the deposit process and are useful for a high volume of payments.

locked-in costs. N. Costs associated with the production of goods or services that have not yet been incurred, but unavoidably will be. These costs are associated with design specifications. Synonymous with *designed-in costs*.

London InterBank Offered Rate. N. The rate charged by banks for very large loans to other banks. Similar to the federal funds rate, the London InterBank Offered Rate is applicable when a bank needing cash borrows from another with surplus cash. The rate is set by a small group of big banks in London. Synonymous with *interbank rate*. ABBRV. *LIBOR*.

long bond. N. A bond that matures more than ten years in the future. The thirty-year treasury bond is a long bond.

Long hedge. N. A technique used by an entity anticipating the purchase of an asset in the future to protect against an increase in the price of that asset. The entity buys a call option that gives the right to buy the asset at a specified price during a specified time period. The counterparty agrees to sell the asset under those conditions. The counterparty is willing to do this because cash is received from selling the option.

long-lived asset. N. See *noncurrent asset*.

long position. N. The party to a forward contract that agrees to buy a specified quantity of an asset at a specified price at a specified future date.

long-short fund. N. A type of mutual fund that uses hedge fund trading strategies. Synonymous with *market-neutral fund*.

long-term asset. N. See *noncurrent asset*.

long-term asset turnover. N. A financial analysis ratio that evaluates how efficiently a company uses its property, plant, and equipment. The long-term asset is calculated by the formula average long-term assets held during the period divided by sales for the period.

long-term equity anticipation securities. N. Options that specify a price for an asset that usually have an exercise period of up to three years. ABBRV. *LEAPS*.

long-term liability. N. A liability for which payment is not due within the next year. Contrast with current liabilities, which require payment within the next year. Long-term liabilities on the balance sheet include any borrowing that will not be paid in the next year. Synonymous with *noncurrent liability*.

look-back interest. N. A tax code provision applying to businesses that use the percentage-of-completion method for recognizing income on long-term contracts. For contracts that take more than two years to complete, the taxpayer must compare the tax paid each year based on the estimated total costs to the tax that would have been paid on the actual total costs. If the difference is more than 10%, the taxpayer must pay interest on the difference. That interest is termed "look-back interest."

look-back option. N. An option that is settled as the difference between the high and low of the underlying during the time period covered by the option.

look-back provision. N. A stipulation that allows the determination of a favorable price or value during a time period beginning in the past. This allows employees, for example, to set a price for employee stock purchase plans that may be lower than the current price.

loss. N. The negative difference between the selling price of an asset and the original cost or value recorded in the accounting records, for asset sales that are not part of the normal business operations. A loss results from selling an asset for less than the cost. Contrast with gain, which is the positive difference resulting when the selling price is more than the cost.

loss carryback. N. See *carryback loss*.

loss carryforward. N. See *carryforward loss*.

loss contingency. N. See *contingent loss*.

lowballing. N. The purposeful understatement of earnings forecasts by management. Lowballing is an extremely conservative estimate of earnings used so that the actual earnings will be slightly better, and the stock price of the company will not be negatively affected. The logic of lowballing is that if earnings miss the forecast by a penny, there is a sharp, negative stock-price reaction. If earnings beat the forecast by a penny, no downward price movement occurs. The absolute value of the earnings is not as important as the relationship to expectations.

lower of cost or market. N. The rule for valuing inventory when the replacement cost is less than the original cost. The lower-of-cost-or-market rule is applied after a company determines the balance-sheet value for inventory using a cost flow assumption. That value, which is based on the original or historical cost of the inventory, is then compared to the replacement cost or market value of the inventory. If the replacement cost is less than the historical cost, the inventory is written down to the replacement cost. The inventory account is decreased, and a loss is recorded on the income statement. To avoid overstating or understating losses and inventory, the lower-of-cost-or-market rule limits how low or how high the replacement cost can be. The replacement cost cannot be higher than the selling price less any costs to sell, called net realizable value. The lower limit for the valuation of the inventory is net realizable value less the normal profit margin. The limits, sometimes called the floor and ceiling, restrict companies from manipulating losses to a preferred accounting period. If the inventory is understated, then the loss is increased in the current period. If the inventory is overstated, then the loss is shifted to a future period when the inventory is sold. See also *net realizable value*. ABBRV. *LCM*.

low-income-housing credit. N. A tax incentive for multifamily-housing builders that provides housing for residents who meet income tests. If 20% of the residents earn half or less of the median-area income, or if 40% earn 60% or less of the median-area income, the owner receives a tax credit. The resident profile requirements must exist over fifteen years or the owner must return the credit. Rent increases are limited. This credit can be equal to nearly 70% of the tax basis of new buildings.

low-regular-dividend-plus-extras. N. A dividend policy in which dividends are always at a low, sustainable amount but extra dividends are paid when earnings are much higher.

lump-sum price. N. See *basket purchase*.

M

macros. N. Parts of spreadsheet applications that do several operations with one keystroke. The designer of the spreadsheet puts together several processes in a little program that runs when a key is hit. Macros can make spreadsheets easier to use, but it is also more difficult to find errors in spreadsheets that contain many complicated macros.

MACRS. ABBRV. Modified Accelerated Cost Recovery System.

magnetic disk. N. See *hard disk*.

magnetic-ink character recognition. N. Machine-readable data from magnetically encoded paper. The numbers at the bottom of checks are magnetic-ink characters that machines in any bank in the United States or Canada can read and process. The numbers carry a magnetized charge that the device senses. This is unlike optical character recognition, which uses light sensors. ABBRV. *MICR*.

mag-strip card. N. Plastic cards with magnetic strips holding information that can be read by machines. ATM cards, credit cards, and hotel keys are examples of mag-strip cards.

maintenance. N. An expense on the income statement representing the cost of regular repairs. Maintenance expense is a period cost and decreases income in the period in which it is incurred. Contrast with expenditures, which improve the efficiency or useful life of an asset. Those costs are capitalized and allocated to income over the life of the asset.

majority-interest taxable year. N. The taxable year that applies if a partnership has no business during the year. The majority-interest taxable year is the taxable year of partners owning more than half of the capital in the partnership.

make-or-buy decision. N. The choice of whether to produce a component part for use in a subsequent process or to buy it from an outside supplier. Make-or-buy decisions involve careful analysis of relevant costs to determine the most advantageous action.

making the numbers. N. Meeting earnings or revenue forecasts.

management accounting. N. See *managerial accounting*.

management fraud. N. The perpetration of fraud by executives of a company that usually involves financial statements.

management information systems. N. A functional area of an organization that is responsible for collecting and processing data and for producing reports that present the data in a meaningful way for use in the organization's activities. ABBRV. *MIS*.

management letter. N. A letter from an auditor to a client company's management, listing improvements the company can make. The letter is not a required part of the audit, and management does not have to implement all the suggestions. Contrast with a management representation letter, which is a required part of the audit and is from management to the auditor.

management representation letter. N. A letter from the management of an organization to the auditor of the organization, taking responsibility for the financial statements, formally agreeing to verbal responses made during the audit, and recognizing any other items from the audit that the auditor thinks are important. Usually the letter is actually prepared by the auditor even though it is "from management" and is on the company's stationary. If the management does not agree to the contents of the letter, it serves as a red flag to the auditor and may affect the audit opinion. The management representation letter is a required part of an audit.

management's discussion and analysis. N. A type of disclosure required by the Securities and Exchange Commission that must be included in the annual report and on Form 10-K. Management's discussion and analysis provide their explanations and information on liquidity, capital resources, and operations. Management must inform and explain trends, significant changes, and uncertainties that affect liquidity, capital resources, and operations. ABBRV. *MD&A*.

managerial accounting. N. A type of accounting with the main objective being to provide information that is useful to decision makers within the company. Managerial accounting is not constrained by external requirements; it can be done in any form desired and at any time needed. Synonymous with *management accounting*.

manufacturing cells. N. Used in a just-in-time manufacturing system. Manufacturing cells are a configuration of machines and employees that perform sequential production activities. In a traditional manufacturing setup, the machines performing a single activity on all products would be located together. For example, a traditional wood furniture manufacturing plant would have an assembly process that joined all the parts together for any product. Another area would put on all the hinges or all the closures. A manufacturing cell would perform all the assembly activities in one area. Workers would operate a variety of machines and do several activities.

manufacturing cycle time. N. See *lead time*.

manufacturing overhead. N. See *overhead*.

manufacturing supplies inventory. N. See *factory supplies inventory*.

maquiladora. N. A type of joint venture in Mexico. A maquiladora is a facility in Mexico, established by a U.S. firm, that uses imported materials from the United States, transforms those materials through production, and then exports them back to the United States.

margin account. N. A way for an investor to buy stocks without actually having all the cash necessary to complete the trade. The investor establishes a margin account with a broker by depositing at least a minimum amount of cash or securities. The investor can then buy stock using part cash and part borrowing, paying interest on the borrowing. A margin account can leverage gains. If an investor has a margin account of $3,000 and wants to buy 1,000 shares of a stock costing $5 per share, the purchase price can consist of $2,500 from the margin account, leaving a balance of $500, and a loan from the broker of $2,500. The investor owns all 1,000 shares. If the price goes up to $6 and the shares are sold, the investor receives $6,000, pays the broker $2,500 plus the interest, and keeps approximately $3,500. The return is about 40%. Without the margin account, the return is only 20%. Of course, losses are magnified, too.

marginal cost. N. See *incremental cost*.

marginal investor. N. The term used to identify people who are trading a particular stock at the present time. The marginal investor behaves the way current participants in the trading of the stock behave, and that determines the price of the stock.

marginal revenue. N. The additional revenue a company earns as a result of selling one more item. If the price per unit is constant, then marginal revenue is equal to the selling price. In situations in which businesses give quantity discounts, the marginal revenue will not be equal to the selling price.

marginal tax rate. N. The rate that applies to the next dollar of taxable income. The marginal tax rate changes as taxable income increases. Usually the rate gets higher on incremental income. The concept of marginal tax rate affects tax planning.

margin call. N. A request from a stockbroker for an investor to deposit more money or stock into the margin account. Margin-call requirements are established by the Federal Reserve, but brokers can set theirs higher.

margin of safety. N. The amount above a break-even point, either in number of units sold or in dollars of revenue.

marital deduction for gift tax. N. The maximum gift amount that one spouse can give to the other. The marital deduction is unlimited. No gifts between spouses are subject to gift tax.

markdown. N. A decrease in selling price. A markdown cancellation occurs when a business removes the markdown and the selling price is back to normal. The removal of a markdown up to the point of the original selling price is not a markup. A markup is the amount above the normal selling price. See also *markup*.

market. N. In finance and accounting, this term usually refers to the capital markets, and specifically to the stock market. Different types of capital markets exist, classified by structure, participants, and type.

marketability discount. N. A term used in business valuation for the reduction of the value of closely held businesses because of the costs of selling the ownership interest.

marketable securities. N. Investments by one company in the stock or bonds of another company. The investing company must include the market value of this type of investment in the current asset section of the balance sheet if it intends to sell the investment within a year.

market adjustment account. N. A contra or adjunct account associated with investments. If the investments increase in price, the market adjustment account is increased so that the sum of the investments account and the market adjustment account equals the market value of the investments. If the investments decrease in value, the market adjustment is decreased so that the combination of the investments account and the market adjustment account equals the market value of the investments. See also *valuation account*.

market cap. N. See *market capitalization*.

market capitalization. N. The market value of a corporation's stock. To calculate a corporation's capitalization, multiply the number of shares of stock outstanding by the current market price of one share. The number of shares outstanding is on the balance sheet description of the stock. Synonymous with *market cap*.

marketing costs. N. See *selling costs*.

market multiple analysis. N. A technique for establishing the value of a target company in a merger situation. The market multiple analysis uses the price-earnings ratio for firms similar to the target and multiplies the average income for the target to determine the value.

market-neutral fund. N. See *long-short fund*.

market portfolio. N. A set of investments that contains all the stocks available. The market portfolio is used to represent the basic movements and returns of the stock market.

market-price method. N. See *production-phase revenue recognition*.

market rate (in relation to bonds). N. See *effective yield on a bond.*

market-related value of pension plan assets. N. A technical term that identifies a dollar measure of the assets in a pension plan. The measure can be the fair market value of the assets or a five-year moving average. This value is used in several other calculations related to pension plans. Synonymous with *fair value of plan assets.*

market-research method of estimating the costs of poor quality. N. Using focus groups and surveys of customers and sales staff to estimate the cost of lost sales, customer dissatisfaction, and lost market share.

market risk. N. The part of a stock's risk, the uncertainty of its return, that cannot be removed. Market risk is caused by conditions that affect all firms. Synonymous with *systematic risk.*

market-share variance. N. A tool for evaluating customer profitability that measures the actual market share versus the budgeted market share in terms of dollars. The formula is the difference between the actual market share and the budgeted market share, times the actual market size, times the budgeted contribution margin for the composite unit (a theoretical unit constructed of a mixture of all products with the contribution margin weighted according to the product mix).

market-size variance. N. The difference in the contribution margin due to the change in the size of the total market. The formula for calculating market-size variance starts with determining the difference between the actual market size in units and the budgeted, or estimated, market size. If the actual is bigger than the estimate, the variance is favorable. That difference is then multiplied by the budgeted market share, and that result is multiplied by the budgeted contribution margin for a composite unit at the budgeted sales mix.

market value. N. The selling price of an asset in a market situation. For liabilities, it is the cost to settle the liability in a situation involving nonrelated parties. See also *fair value*.

market value added. N. A financial analysis measure of management's ability since the beginning of the business to maximize shareholder wealth. Market value added is the difference between the value of the company's stock at current prices and the amount of common equity on the balance sheet. The formula is common shares of stock outstanding times the current stock price minus the sum of the amounts in the common stock account added to the additional paid in capital from the sale of common stock and retained earnings.

market-value method of accounting for convertible debt. N. The stock is recorded at the market value of the new shares, and any difference between that amount and the book value of the debt is a gain or loss. Contrast with the book-value method of accounting for convertible debt, in which the convertible debt is removed at its book value, the par value of the number of shares issued is added to the stock account, and the remaining amount is plugged into additional paid in capital.

mark-sense media. N. Forms used with optical character recognition (OCR) devices. The forms usually consist of ovals or rectangles that are blackened and "read" by the OCR device.

mark to market. N. A procedure for valuing investments at the end of the year. The balance sheet value for the investment is equal to the market price on the last day of the year. The unrealized gain or loss may be included in income, depending on the classification of the investment. See *available-for-sale investment, trading securities*.

markup. N. (1) An increase in selling price. (2) The difference between the cost of an item and the selling price of an item. A markup cancellation occurs when a business removes the markup and the selling price returns to normal. The removal of a markup down to the point of the original selling price is not a markdown. A markdown is the amount below the normal selling price.

marriage penalty. N. A consequence of current tax laws that results in married couples paying more taxes on their combined income than the total of the taxes they would pay individually on their own income. The marriage penalty cannot be avoided even if the married couple files separately.

married filing a separate return. N. A tax return filing status that is applicable to married people who want to file separate returns. The rates for this filing status are the highest.

master budget. N. An organization-wide financial plan for operations for the next year. The master budget starts with a sales forecast. The sales forecast determines the inventory needs and progresses through all the steps of the business cycle, to the cash budget. See also *cash budget, sales budget, production budget, overhead budget*. Synonymous with *comprehensive budget*.

matching principle. N. The basis for recognizing when to include expenses on the income statement. The matching principle requires that once the entity has determined which revenues are earned and included in the period's income, then all expenditures on actions to produce those revenues must be included on the period's income statement. That results in "matching" the expenses with the revenues resulting from the expenditures.

materiality. N. The characteristic of accounting information that focuses on how important the information is to making decisions. If the amount of the error or the amount left out of the report is big enough to affect the decision-making process, then that item is considered material.

material participation. N. Determines the character of income and loss from a partnership or S corporation. If the partner is not involved in the day-to-day operations of the entity in a significant, ongoing way, then the income or loss is considered passive.

materials price variance. N. A variance indicating how actual costs for materials compare to standard costs. The formula is the difference between the actual price paid and the standard price for materials (in one unit) times the actual quantity of units produced. The variance is the responsibility of the person in charge of purchasing. It is that person's job to negotiate prices, establish linkages, structure the timing and quantity of purchases in order to receive discounts, and choose suppliers that will meet the standard price.

materials requisition. N. A form used in a job-order costing system to keep track of the costs of raw materials. The quantity and type of materials used are entered on the form, and the cost information is added to the job-order cost sheet. The materials requisition is also an internal control device that monitors inventory use, because it is usually numbered, dated, and signed. Synonymous with *stores requisition*.

materials-usage variance. N. A variance indicating how the actual quantity of materials used in production compares to the standard quantity. The formula is the difference between the actual quantity and the standard quantity for materials in one unit, times the actual quantity of units produced. This variance is the responsibility of the production manager. It is that person's job to monitor waste and scrap in the production process.

material weakness. N. Problems with a company's system of internal control over financial reporting that could allow material errors, either accidental or intentional, to exist in the financial statements. The control techniques and procedures in place that will not allow for detection of the errors because of flaws in operation or design. A material weakness is a very serious condition and will be reported in the financial reports of the company. See also *control deficiency, significant deficiency.*

mature company. N. A company that has been established long enough to finance fixed asset acquisitions from internal sources, such as income or the sales of other assets.

maturity. N. The date on which final payment of a security is paid or received.

maturity matching. N. The practice of financing assets with debt that continues for the approximate life of the asset. Maturity matching allows the asset to generate the cash flows necessary to repay the debt. Financing a factory building with a twenty-year mortgage allows product sales for twenty years to repay the loan. Financing merchandise inventory with a twenty-year note, however, is illogical, because the cash flow from selling the inventory will come in all at once, and the payments will continue for years.

maturity risk premium. N. A component of the quoted or stated rate of interest on a debt security. The maturity premium represents the interest rate risk the lender is exposed to. Interest rate risk is the chance that the interest rate of a debt security will rise while an investor holds it, making the investor's security less valuable.

maturity structure. N. The schedule of when future liabilities are due. The maturity structure of an organization's liabilities is valuable information for assessing future cash flows. If the company has many long-term obligations, the reader of the financial statements knows that the company will have to use cash for those things before paying dividends or internally financing new projects.

maturity value of a bond. N. The last amount the bondholder will receive from the issuer at the date specified in the bond indenture. Synonymous with *par value of a bond, face value of a bond, principal amount of a bond.*

MD&A. ABBRV. Management's discussion and analysis.

mean. N. The average. The formula for the mean is the sum of all values divided by the number of values.

mean-per-unit sampling. N. An audit procedure that is useful when investigating estimated account balances such as warranty liability. Because the targeted account does not have concrete transactions that are summed to get the account balance, the auditor selects a sample of the items on which the estimate is based and develops an estimate for the target account. The auditor compares the newly created estimate with the existing estimate to determine if the existing estimate is fair and reasonable. ABBRV. *MPU.*

measurement date for discontinued operations. N. The date when management formally makes plans to dispose of a segment of an organization. The measurement date is significant because it is the beginning of the phase-out period.

measurement date of a stock option. N. The date the compensation expense of a stock option is calculated, using the intrinsic value method of accounting for stock options.

medical expense deduction. N. A tax deduction from adjusted gross income on Schedule A. The medical expense deduction is limited to the excess of the actual expenses over 7.5% of adjusted gross income. Qualified medical expenses include amounts paid for disease diagnosis, cure, treatment, and prevention plus transportation costs, modifications to buildings or vehicles to accommodate a medical condition, and some insurance costs. The deduction is limited to the amount not reimbursed by insurance.

medium cap. N. A term describing the size of a corporation based on the market value of its stock. If the value, calculated by multiplying the number of shares outstanding by the current market price, is between $1 billion and $5 billion, the firm is a medium-cap firm. See also *large cap, small cap, micro cap*.

medium term. N. See *intermediate term*.

merchandise inventory. N. Items a company buys from a wholesaler to sell to customers, listed on the balance sheet as a current asset. The cost of merchandise inventory sold during a period is transferred to the income statement as the expense, cost of goods sold.

merchant bank. N. Historically, in the United States, banks that provided all banking services, including savings, checking, loans, equity funding, and financial advice. After the Great Depression, regulations prevented banks from offering all of these services. Merchant banks in the United Kingdom offer the same services as investment banking houses in the United States.

merger. N. A business combination in which one company ceases to exist, and the assets and liabilities are brought into the remaining company. One company takes in another, owning all assets and all responsibility for liabilities. Shareholders of the target must approve the merger.

mezzanine section. N. The part of the balance sheet between liabilities and owners' equity. Securities that have characteristics of both debt and equity are disclosed in this section. See also *trust preferred securities*.

MICR. ABBRV. Magnetic-ink character recognition.

micro cap. N. A term describing the size of a corporation based on the market value of its stock. If the value, calculated by multiplying the number of shares outstanding by the current market price, is less than $250 million, then the firm is a micro cap firm. See also *large cap, small cap, medium cap.*

microprocessor. N. The part of a central processing unit that does the calculations, sorting, classifying, and other processes. One part of the microprocessor does the arithmetic and logic, and the other part transfers the data from the RAM to the part that does the calculations. See also *central processing unit, random access memory.*

mid-quarter convention. N. An alternative to the half-year convention that is required for tax purposes if acquisition patterns meet the criteria. If more than 40% of all acquired business property other than real estate is acquired in the last quarter of the year, the business cannot use the half-year convention. Instead, the business must use special tables to compute the depreciation. The mid-quarter convention serves to prevent businesses from taking a half year of depreciation when the majority of newly acquired assets were purchased very close to the end of the tax year.

mileage rate. N. A standard rate for using a personal vehicle for charity or business purposes. As of 2008, the rate for businesses is 50.5 cents per mile, and for charity purposes it is 14 cents per mile.

minimum capital requirements. N. Financial measures that regulators use to ensure that financial institutions have enough capital to meet demands from depositors. Minimum capital requirements are defined in the specific regulations.

minimum lease payments. N. The amounts that the lessee is obligated to pay the lessor in a lease contract. The minimum lease payments include the regular rent payments plus any amount that the lessee guarantees to the lessor at the end of the lease, a guaranteed residual value, any penalty for nonrenewal, and any bargain purchase option amount. The minimum lease payments do not include any repair charges, insurance charges, or maintenance charges.

minimum pension liability. N. The amount of liability that must be on the balance sheet, equal to the excess of the accumulated benefit obligation over the market value of the pension-plan assets. If the value of the plan assets is larger than the accumulated benefit obligation, no pension liability is necessary.

minimum tax credit. N. An amount that mediates the effects of the alternative minimum tax (ATM) that are the result of timing differences. A business can "earn" amounts to be used in the future if the AMT is greater than the regular tax amount. The business can carry that amount to a future year when taxes payable exceed the AMT amount. In that future year, the business reduces the taxes payable down to the level of the AMT amount.

minority interest. N. See *noncontrolling interest*.

minority-interest discount. N. A reduction in the price of an equity interest in a corporation because the interest is not large enough to give the owner control. This is particularly applicable in a small, closely held business. The discount can be used to reduce the valuation of the business for estate purposes.

minority passive investment. N. See *passive ownership*.

minor leaseback. N. A sale leaseback in which the present value of the minimum lease payments is 10% or less of the fair value of the asset. The seller in a minor leaseback treats the transaction like a sale instead of a sale leaseback.

MIRR. ABBRV. Modified internal rate of return.

MIS. ABBRV. Management information systems.

miscellaneous itemized deduction. N. A tax deduction from adjusted gross income on Schedule A that includes things like unreimbursed employee expenses, expenses associated with producing investment income, safe-deposit box rental, and the cost of tax advice and preparation. Miscellaneous itemized deductions appear on Schedule A and are limited to the amount greater than 2% of adjusted gross income.

mixed cost. N. Costs that are not completely fixed or completely variable, but have a fixed portion plus a variable component. In a cabinet-making business, the cost of the telephone is a mixed cost. The fixed component is represented by the line charge, and the variable component is represented by the long-distance charges. Synonymous with *semivariable cost.*

MLM. ABBRV. Most likely misstatement.

MNC. ABBRV. Multinational corporation.

modem. N. Modulator or demodulator. A device that allows two computers to share information through telephone lines.

Modified Accelerated Cost Recovery System. N. A depreciation method used for tax purposes for assets put into service after 1986. The Modified Accelerated Cost Recovery System of depreciation separates depreciable assets into classes that each have a designated life. The actual depreciation calculation is either double declining balance, 150% of declining balance, or straight-line, depending on the class. The Modified Accelerated Cost Recovery System, usually referred to as MACRS, assigns shorter time periods for tax depreciation than the estimated useful life. As a result, companies generally switch to straight-line depreciation. ABBRV. *MACRS.*

modified internal rate of return. N. A decision rule used to choose among investment alternatives that involves calculating the discount rate necessary to have the present value of cash outflows for a project equal to the terminal value. The terminal value is the sum of the future values, using the cost of capital, of each cash inflow from the project, and then that sum is discounted at the cost of capital. The modified internal rate of return adjusts the internal-rate-of-return method in order to use the cost of capital for reinvestment; this is evidenced by calculating the future value of the cash inflows using the cost of capital. ABBRV. *MIRR*.

modified-percentage-of-completion method. N. A method of recording income from a long-term contract, acceptable for tax purposes. The modified-percentage-of-completion method allows the taxpayer to avoid reporting any income in the current tax year on a contract that is less than 10% complete (based on estimated total cost). The first year it is at least 10% complete, the taxpayer can use the percentage-of-completion method. This modified method is useful when contracts are started very close to the end of the tax year and estimates of total cost are rough.

modified perpetual inventory. N. A method of keeping records about the acquisition and sale of inventory. The modified-perpetual-inventory system increases the quantity of inventory at the time of purchase and decreases the quantity of inventory when an item is sold, keeping a running total of inventory on hand. At the end of the accounting period, the company determines the dollar value of ending inventory and the cost of goods sold. See also *periodic-inventory system, perpetual-inventory system.*

monetary item. N. Assets measured in terms of cash that a company has or will have. For example, accounts receivable is a monetary asset. The amount of accounts receivable on the balance sheet represents the cash the company expects to receive when its customers pay.

monetary-unit assumption. N. A basic assumption in accounting for measuring the value or cost of items on the financial statements in terms of dollars.

monetary-unit sampling. N. See *probability-proportional-to-size sampling*.

money laundering. N. The process of disguising the source of cash, usually to avoid taxes or hide illegal activities. Money laundering is a federal crime and banks are required to report any transactions involving large amounts of cash as a deterrent.

money market fund. N. A type of mutual fund for investing in short-term debt securities. Money-market-fund shares are always worth $1, but the interest changes. The mutual fund loans the investment dollars, and shareholders earn interest. Many money market funds allow shareholders to write a limited number of checks against their investment. Although they are not insured by the Federal Deposit Insurance Corporation, money market funds are extremely low-risk.

money markets. N. A physical or virtual location in which borrowing occurs, with the duration of the debt less than one year. Contrast with capital markets, in which the borrowing is for more than one year or is from equity sales.

monitoring. N. One of the five components of an internal control system. This component refers to the evaluation of control performance, one of the theoretical functions of auditing. Managers use auditors to attest to the quality of the accounting information presented, thereby sending a signal to the share-holders that management is doing a good job.

Monte Carlo simulation. N. A complex risk analysis technique using software that picks input values from a probability distribu-tion of variable values and calculates the outcome. The software does this repeatedly and then calculates an average outcome and a standard deviation from that outcome to determine the risk of the project.

months to burnout. N. Measures how long a company can go without debt or equity financing to provide additional cash. The formula is cash plus cash equivalents plus short-term marketable securities divided by the cash burn rate.

mortgage. N. A special type of notes payable that provides the title to property as collateral for the note. Synonymous with *mortgage notes payable*.

mortgage bond. N. A secured bond with real estate or other assets with a ready market as collateral.

mortgage notes payable. N. See *mortgage*.

most likely misstatement. N. A term used in probability-proportional-to-size sampling in the audit process to designate the best estimate of error in a particular account. The most likely misstatement is a component of the upper misstatement limit, which is the highest estimate of error in the account. ABBRV. *MLM*.

moving-average-cost method. N. An inventory cost flow assumption using an average cost of similar items available for sale during an accounting period in a perpetual inventory system. The average cost of an item in inventory is recalculated after every purchase and sale.

moving expense deduction. N. A tax deduction for adjusted gross income requiring a new job to be fifty miles farther from an old residence than the old job was, and the employment to be full-time for thirty-nine weeks or more. Moving expenses only include the cost of moving things, which usually includes the costs of a moving van, travel to the new location, and lodging during travel time. No deduction is allowed for house-hunting trips, temporary housing, meals during travel, or storage charges.

MPU. ABBRV. Mean-per-unit sampling.

multinational corporation. N. A business with activities in more than one country, whose success depends on the economic and political system of more than one country. ABBRV. *MNC*.

multiperiod trend report. N. The overall change in an item of interest over a period of time. The multiperiod trend report shows the value of the item of interest at different points, highlighting the amount and direction of the change.

multiple regression. N. A statistical method that determines the stable relationship between a dependent variable and more than one independent variable.

multiple-step income statement. N. A format for the income statement that classifies revenues, gains, expenses, and losses into operating and nonoperating categories. Multiple-step income statements always start with sales revenue and deduct the cost of goods sold to get gross profit. This relationship is thus highlighted by presentation on the face of the income statement. The single-step format does not do this. The multiple-step format then lists the operating expenses, usually classifying them as selling expenses, general expenses, or administrative expenses. Income from operations, or operating income, is the difference between the gross profit and operating expenses, and is specifically listed. The next section on the multiple-step income statement includes other revenues and gains, expenses, and losses. This section presents items that are not related to the regular business activities, such as interest and gains or losses from selling assets. The multiple-step format then highlights the income before taxes, the net of income from operations, and the "other" section. The next line is tax expense, followed by net income.

multiplier method of estimating failure costs. N. A method of determining total failure costs, including hidden, unmeasured costs. The multiplier method is applied under the belief that total failure costs are a multiple of measurable failure costs. The multiplier is an estimate based on research and experience. For example, if research shows that total costs to find or fix poor quality products is three times the measured cost, then the total failure cost is $2.1 million if the measured cost of finding and fixing poor quality is $700,000. Management can use this information to plan the amount of spending on quality control activities.

Municipal Finance Officers Association. N. A professional association for financial officers who work for municipalities. See also *Government Finance Officers Association*.

mutual fund family. N. See *family of funds*.

mutual funds. N. Another name for open-end funds in which an investment company combines the dollars from many investors to buy assets such as stock, bonds, etc. They are investment structures in which investors buy shares in the fund, which holds a collection of different stocks. Open-end funds allow investors to get out of the investment by selling back to the mutual fund for the net asset value of each share. Mutual fund share purchases are done at the end of a trading day after the net asset value is calculated. A professional manager handles the buying and selling of the stocks for all other investors. A no-load fund does not charge a commission for the purchase of the shares in the fund, while a load fund does charge a commission. All mutual funds charge the fund a management fee. Contrast with exchange traded funds, which can be traded anytime during the trading day, and can be bought on margin or sold short.

mutually exclusive investments. N. Alternatives that require that if one is chosen, the others cannot be undertaken. Choosing one excludes the others from implementation. For examples, a company may have investment alternatives for updating the factory processes through the installation of a conveyor system or through organizing machinery in production cells. If the conveyors are installed, the other arrangement is not possible.

mutually unperformed contract. N. An agreement in which neither party to the agreement has done everything required by the contract. A lease is a mutually unperformed contract at its inception. Synonymous with *executory contract*.

mutual savings banks. N. Entities, mainly located in the northwestern part of the United States, that use money deposited by savers for long-term loans to individuals.

myopic behavior. N. Sacrificing long-term good for meeting short-term budget targets. For example, a manager in charge of delivery can reduce costs by putting off oil changes on the trucks. That will keep costs down in the current accounting period, but it could have serious long-term effects on maintenance costs.

NAA. ABBRV. National Association of Accountants. See *Institute of Management Accountants*.

naked option. N. An option (the right to sell a quantity of an asset at a specified price during a specified time period) in which the seller does not already own the quantity of the asset that must be delivered. If the option is exercised, then the seller has to find and buy the asset to deliver on the contract. Contrast with a covered option, in which the seller does own the asset at the time the contract for the option to sell is made.

NASBA. ABBRV. National Association of State Boards of Accountancy.

NASDAQ. ABBRV. National Association of Securities Dealers Automated Quotations.

NASDAQ composite index. N. National Association of Securities Dealers Automated Quotations composite index. An indicator of trends in the over-the-counter stock market. The NASDAQ composite index is composed of all the stocks listed on the NASDAQ and is weighted for market value. This index is not a particularly good overall indicator of the stock market because the stocks are generally smaller and riskier than those on the New York Stock Exchange (NYSE) or the American Stock Exchange (AMEX).

National Association of Accountants. N. See *Institute of Management Accountants*.

National Association of Securities Dealers Automated Quotations. N. The title of the section in financial newspapers (such as the *Wall Street Journal*) that lists the daily price, volume, and dividend information on over-the-counter stocks. ABBRV. *NASDAQ*.

National Association of State Boards of Accountancy. N. A national organization for all the boards regulating and licensing certified public accountants in all fifty states plus the District of Columbia, Puerto Rico, Guam, the Commonwealth of the Northern Mariana Islands, and the Virgin Islands. www.nasba.org. ABBRV. *NASBA*.

National Society of Accountants. N. A national professional organization for accountants that does not require certified public accountant–certification for membership. The National Society of Accountants does, however, have strict ethical guidelines and continuing education requirements for membership. Members are mainly smaller practitioners. It publishes the *National Public Accountant* nine times per year. www.nsacct.org. Synonymous with *National Society of Public Accountants*. ABBRV. *NSA*.

National Society of Public Accountants. N. See *National Society of Accountants*.

natural business year. N. A continuous twelve-month period that cycles through a buildup for sales, through a period of high sales volume, through a slowdown, to the weakest time. The natural business year is most pronounced in businesses that depend on seasonal influences for operations, such as snowplowing services or retail sales. The natural business year influences the choice of fiscal year for a business, with the year-end being at the slowest time. See also *fiscal year*.

natural termination. N. An end to a partnership that occurs because the partners choose to discontinue it. The partnership ends all business and financial activities, sells the assets, pays the creditors, and distributes the remaining proceeds.

negative balance. N. Describes an account that has a balance that is not typical. For assets and expenses, the normal balance is a debit balance. Assets or expenses with a credit balance have a negative balance. Liabilities, equity accounts, and revenues have a normal credit balance. A debit balance is considered a negative balance. If accounts payable has a debit, or negative balance, it means that more than the actual amount of the bill was paid.

negative confirmation. N. An audit procedure in which the auditor sends a letter to the client's customer requesting that the client review the amount owed and return the letter if the amount is wrong, but do nothing to confirm that the amount is correct. Contrast with a positive confirmation, in which the client is asked to return the letter stating that the amount owed is correct.

negative covenants. N. The restrictions and agreements associated with long-term debt specifying what the borrower must avoid doing. Examples of negative covenants are restrictions on selling or disposing certain assets or on taking on more debt.

negative drift. N. The downward movement of a stock price prior to a quarterly earnings announcement. The downward drift occurs for large corporations providing weekly sales data that is worse than expected. Investors incorporate this information into value estimates of the corporation, which is translated into a lower stock price.

negative equity. N. A situation in which the remaining principal of a loan on an asset is more than the market value of the asset. Negative equity results when the asset's value declines after the purchase. In the 1980s, builders of office buildings encountered negative equity because when construction began, the market for office space was great, but during the time of construction, the market became saturated and owners owed more on the loans than could be generated through rent or sale.

negative goodwill. N. The result of acquiring assets for a price less than the fair value. In a business combination, the acquiring company records priority accounts, those with an easily determinable fair market value, at their fair market value. Items like accounts receivable, inventory, investments, prepaid expenses, accounts payable, and most long-term debt are considered priority accounts. The remaining purchase price is allocated to accounts like land, buildings, equipment, and intangible assets. If the price is less than the total of the priority accounts, the acquiring company records an extraordinary gain for that amount.

negotiable. ADJ. Describes a financial instrument that is accepted as payment because it is easily transferred. Checks are negotiable instruments because creditors will accept them as payment and can easily convert them to cash.

net. ADJ. Describes a gross amount reduced by some corresponding amount. For example, net income is revenues reduced by expenses. See also *net assets*; *net income*; *net purchases*; *net sales*; *net worth*; *accounts receivable, net*; *property, plant, and equipment, net*.

net assets. N. The total dollar value of the assets on the balance sheet reduced by the total dollar value of the liabilities on the balance sheet. See also *net worth*. Synonymous with *equity*.

net-asset value. N. A measure of an investor's ownership share of a mutual fund or other investment company. The net-asset value is calculated as the market value of the assets, less liabilities, divided by the shares outstanding.

net cash flow. N. The difference between the cash coming into a business and the cash going out of a business. This can be for all business activities, for part of business activities, or for a set of transactions associated with one activity. A measure of a company's performance used in financial analysis and management. The net cash flow of a firm is equal to the net income less any noncash revenues plus any noncash expenses. A simplified formula that is often used is net income plus depreciation and amortization expense. All three items in the formula are found on the income statement. A family might look at the net cash flow from buying a new car when the current vehicle needs an expensive repair. The initial outflow to buy the car would be compared to the estimated cost of repairs, lower fuel costs from increased efficiency, lower insurance rates for a car with more safety features, and other cost outflows. The net cash flow is the difference between those estimates.

net earnings. N. See *net income*.

net income. N. Total revenues and gains less total expenses and losses for the accounting period. Synonymous with *net earnings*, *book income*, *bottom line*.

net-income percentage. N. A ratio for financial analysis that indicates the percentage of sales that is income. Calculated as net income divided by net sales.

net long-term capital gain. N. All capital gains on property held longer than one year are reduced by all capital losses from property sales or exchanges held longer than one year. If the gains are greater than the losses, a net long-term capital gain exists.

net loss. N. In a business, the result of expenses and losses exceeding revenues and gains. Contrast with net income, in which the reverse is true, and revenues exceed expenses.

net method for purchase discounts. N. A method of accounting for purchase discounts that highlights the amount of discounts the company did not take advantage of. The company records purchases at the amount on the invoice less the discount it plans to take, the gross amount, increasing accounts payable. Then, when the payment is made within the specified time period, the company reduces cash and accounts payable for that discounted amount. If the company misses the discount period and has to pay the full amount, it reduces cash by the full invoice amount, reduces accounts payable for the discounted amount, and records discounts lost. Then, at the end of the accounting period, the company treats discounts lost just like interest expense. See also *purchase discounts*.

net operating loss. N. A tax concept for the situation in which taxable revenues are less than tax deductions. ABBRV. *NOL*.

net-operating-loss deduction. N. A tax deduction available to sole proprietors. The net operating loss for an individual is calculated starting with taxable income. Then capital losses, net-operating-loss deductions from previous losses, personal exemptions, and other nonbusiness deductions that exceed nonbusiness income are all added back. The result is the net operating loss. The net-operating-loss deduction can then be used to offset income in the two years prior to the year of the loss. Any remaining loss is carried forward to the next three years as a net operating loss in each year.

net operating profit after taxes. N. Represents the amount of income a company would have if it used no debt financing. Net operating profit after taxes is calculated as earnings before interest and taxes times one minus the tax rate. The variables in the calculation are found on the income statement. ABBRV. *NOPAT*.

net operating working capital. N. All current assets used in operations less accounts payable and other current liabilities. Net operating working capital represents the amount of investor-financed working capital.

net periodic pension cost. N. See *pension expense*.

net-present-value method. N. A decision rule for choosing between investments that involves discounting all cash flows from the project using the cost of capital. The net present value is the sum of all the positive discounted cash inflows from things like additional profits, reduced by the discounted cash outflows for things like purchases. The alternative with the highest positive net present value is the best alternative. A process used in capital budgeting to select the project. The net-present-value method discounts all cash inflows and cash outflows to the present using the required rate of return. The present value of the outflows is deducted from the present value of the inflows to get the net present value, which should be positive or zero. ABBRV. *NPV*.

net-present-value profile. N. A graph showing the relationship between the net present value of a project (dollars on the vertical axis), and the cost of capital used to discount the cash flows (plotted on the horizontal axis). The point on the vertical axis where the cost of capital is zero is the difference between the undiscounted inflows and outflows. The point on the horizontal axis where the net present value is zero is the internal rate of return. Plotting the profiles of two investment projects on the same graph illustrates the sensitivity of a project to the cost of capital. The crossover rate is the cost of capital at which both projects produce the same net present value.

net proceeds. N. See *proceeds*.

net purchases. N. The dollar value of a company's inventory purchases during an accounting period reduced by any returns, discounts, or other reductions of the price actually paid for the goods. Net purchases can be used to calculate the cost of goods sold in businesses using periodic inventory systems.

net realizable value. N. The selling price of a product less any costs to complete the product and any costs to sell the product.

net-realizable-value method of allocating joint costs. N. Allocates joint costs to products based on the relative net realizable value, which is the selling price minus costs of processing after split-off. For example, the joint costs of raising and trucking turkeys to a processing center are $250,000. The revenue from selling turkey parts is $420,000, and the revenue from selling whole turkeys is $200,000. The costs to get the whole birds ready for sale are $100,000, and the costs to get the turkey parts ready for sale are $200,000. The net realizable value of the whole birds is the selling price less the separable costs, or $200,000 minus $100,000, which equals $100,000. The net realizable value of the turkey parts is $420,000 minus $200,000, or $220,000. The $250,000 of joint costs is allocated based on the relative amounts of net realizable value. The turkey parts get 220 divided by 320, times $250,000 (or $171,875), and the whole birds are allocated the remainder (or $78,125).

net sales. N. The dollar value of sales made during an accounting period, reduced by any returns made by customers, any discounts given to customers, and any other reductions from the original selling price of the goods. See also *sales discounts, sales returns and allowances.*

net settlement. N. A term used to identify the nature of the settlement of a derivative. A net settlement allows the parties to the contract to settle in cash for the change in value rather than to actually buy or sell the asset or liability.

net short-term capital gain. N. All capital gains on sales or exchanges of property held less than a year are reduced by all capital losses from sales or exchanges of property held less than a year. If the gains are greater than the losses, a net short-term capital gain exists.

net worth. N. The difference between total assets and total liabilities. If the difference is positive, i.e., assets exceed liabilities, then positive net worth exists. If liabilities exceed assets, then negative net worth exists. See also *net assets*.

net worth method. N. A fraud investigation technique that estimates the amount of fraud based on a calculation of an individual's increase in net worth and the amount of funds from known sources, such as wages.

neural networks. N. A type of expert system that is useful for analyzing numerical data because it adjusts the outcomes with each new instance. The neural network finds patterns in data through statistical techniques and develops a model for predicting outcomes. With each new data experience, the model is adjusted.

neutrality. N. An aspect of the primary qualitative characteristic of accounting information—reliability. Accounting information is neutral if it is unbiased and factual.

new markets tax credit. N. A tax incentive available to individuals to encourage investment in community development entities, which are entities that provide financing or assistance for low-income communities or individuals.

New York Stock Exchange. N. The structure for buying and selling shares of stock in New York City. The New York Stock Exchange, which began trading in 1792, is still a face-to-face trading market with floor brokers dealing with specialist firms on the floor. The

New York Stock Exchange visitors' gallery was open until September 11, 2001, when it was closed for security reasons. Only the oldest, largest, and best-known companies can meet the requirements to be listed on the New York Stock Exchange. Synonymous with *big board*. ABBRV. *NYSE*.

nexus. N. A term applied to the relationship between a corporation and a state or other taxing unit. If nexus exists, then the taxing unit can require the corporation to pay the tax. Nexus usually involves somehow doing business in a state or locality.

NFP. ABBRV. Not-for-profit organization.

Nikkei. N. The Japanese stock market index.

ninja loan. N. A risky type of loan, usually made to purchase real estate. "Ninja" stands for "no income, no job or assets." The lender makes a loan like this believing that if the borrower defaults, the value of the mortgaged property will cover the repayment of the debt.

noise. N. Income effects that, while on the income statement in the current period, have no future cash flow benefits and have no effect on the valuation of the company's stock. An example of noise on the income statement is the gain or loss from discontinued operations.

NOL. ABBRV. Net operating loss.

no-load fund. N. A mutual fund investment that does not charge for buying or selling the shares, but does charge fees for managing.

nominal account. N. See *temporary account*.

nominal capital. N. The total par value of all stock a corporation has issued.

nominal rate for a bond. N. See *stated rate for a bond*.

nominal risk-free rate. N. See *risk-free rate*.

nonaccountable plan. N. A method of managing business expenses and reimbursements for employees. An nonaccountable plan does not require the employee to substantiate costs or to return excess reimbursement. If the employee receives reimbursement through a nonaccountable plan, the reimbursement is included in gross wages, and the costs are part of the miscellaneous itemized deduction.

nonbusiness income. N. Usually considered to be interest, dividends, rents, and royalties, but depending on the state, may include gains and losses. Nonbusiness income may be excluded from state taxes if the corporation is not incorporated in the state.

noncancelable lease. N. A lease that does not contain a provision for early termination of the lease by either the lessor or the lessee. A lease may be considered noncancelable if the provisions for cancellation are extremely remote or include penalties and costs that make cancellation unlikely.

noncash expense. N. An expense that is recorded in the business records to accomplish accrual accounting, but for which no cash is used. Depreciation expense is a common noncash expense because it reduces income but does not require any cash payment. It is simply an allocation of the cost of the asset being depreciated.

noncash financing activities. N. Business transactions affecting long-term liabilities or equity accounts that do not involve the use of cash. Paying stock dividends is an example of a noncash financing activity.

noncash investing activities. N. Business transactions affecting long-term assets that do not involve the use of cash. Financing the purchase of equipment with debt is an example of a noncash investing activity.

noncompensatory plans. N. Stock option plans that are available to nearly all employees, have a small discount from the market price, and are not as long-term as stock option plans that are available mainly to executives. Noncompensatory plans are designed to encourage widespread company stock ownership and to raise capital. They are not designed as compensation, and as a result, no compensation expense is recorded.

noncontributory pension plan. N. A pension plan to which only the employer (and not the employee) contributes cash.

noncontrolling interest. N. An account on the consolidated balance sheet when the parent company owns more than half but not all of the subsidiary's stock. The minority interest represents the value of the stock that the parent does not own and appears in the equity section of the balance sheet. Synonymous with *minority interest*.

noncurrent asset. N. A type of asset that does not meet the criteria for classification as a current asset. It will not become cash or be used in the next twelve months. The asset accounts usually included in this designation are property, plant, and equipment; investments; intangibles; and other assets. Synonymous with *long-term asset, long-lived asset*.

noncurrent liability. N. See *long-term liability*.

noncurrent operating assets. N. See *property, plant, and equipment*.

nonfinancial measures. N. A type of target used to evaluate performance. Nonfinancial measures are evaluated by terms other than money, such as by the number of returned checks.

noninterest-bearing note. N. A note that does not specify an interest rate or interest-payment amount, but instead specifies only the payment amount. If the payment is due within a short time, the interest is ignored. However, if it is a long-term note, then interest is determined by an imputed interest rate. The note is recorded at its present value, discounting at the imputed rate, and the interest is spread out over the life of the note. The note-payable liability or note-receivable asset is on the balance sheet at the discounted present value. Synonymous with *zero-interest-bearing note*.

noninventoriable costs. N. See *period costs*.

nonmonetary-asset exchange. N. Trading assets such as inventory items, equipment, buildings, etc. The accounting for nonmonetary-asset exchanges depends on whether the assets are similar or dissimilar. If they are dissimilar, then the asset received is recorded at its value or at the value of what was given up, whichever is more verifiable. Then, the asset given up is removed from the balance sheet, and a gain or loss is recorded if necessary. If the nonmonetary assets are similar, then no gain is recorded unless cash is involved in the exchange. To determine the amount of gain to recognize, the total gain is first calculated as the fair value of assets received less the book value of assets given up. Then, the percent of gain recognized is in proportion of the cash received to the total cash plus the fair value of the assets received. That is the percentage of the gain that should be recognized. If an exchange of similar nonmonetary assets results in a loss, or if the fair value of the asset received is less than the book value given up, then the whole loss is recognized immediately.

nonmonetary items. N. Items on the balance sheet that had their value established a while ago, when dollars had a different purchasing power. Nonmonetary assets include inventories, fixed assets, and intangible assets. Liabilities are usually monetary and require a fixed cash payment. Common stock accounts are nonmonetary.

nonoperating assets. N. Assets not used in producing the operating income of the company. Nonoperating assets include excess cash that is not needed for operations, investments, land held for future use, obsolete inventory, etc. Contrast with operating assets, which usually include cash, marketable securities, accounts receivable, inventories, and fixed assets used to execute the business activities of the company.

nonproduction costs. N. Costs other than direct materials, direct labor, and overhead. Usually the categories used are sales and administrative. Sales expenses include marketing, distribution of products, and customer service costs. Administrative costs usually include product design and development.

nonprofit organization. N. See *not-for-profit organization*.

nonpublic corporation. N. See *closed corporation*.

nonqualified deferred compensation plan. N. A device used by corporations to provide additional incentive to the executives of the corporation that therefore does not meet the requirements to be a qualified plan. This type of plan is usually structured so that the executive does not own the compensation until time passes. That means that the employer does not have a deduction for the amount, and the executive does not have taxable income until the time (or other) restriction is lifted.

nonqualified stock option plans. N. A type of deferred compensation in which the terms do not meet certain Internal Revenue Service criteria. The classification as a nonqualified stock option plan means that an employee must pay tax on an option when it is exercised, or when it is received if the fair market value of the option is known. The corporation granting the option must deduct the same amount as the compensation expense.

nonreciprocal transfers. N. Contributions made by or received by an entity. Usually the contributions involve cash or another asset, but they could also be debt forgiveness. The recipient records the assets at the fair market value and increases the contribution revenue.

nonrecourse liability. N. A personal obligation of a partner that is assumed by the partnership, and none of the partners has any personal liability.

nonrecurring items. N. Events that affect the income for an accounting period but that are separated from the continuing operations of an entity in order to provide better information to the users of the income statement. Nonrecurring items must meet strict guidelines. They include the results of discontinued operations, extraordinary items, and the cumulative effect of change in accounting principle. All other income effects must be included in the main body of the income statement. Because nonrecurring items are listed after tax expense, the amounts of the nonrecurring items are presented net of any tax effects they produce. The separation of nonrecurring items to a special section of the income statement is logical. It helps the reader predict future performance when increases or decreases in income that will probably never happen again are identified as such. See also *discontinued operations, extraordinary items, cumulative effect of change in accounting principle*. Synonymous with *irregular items*.

nonsampling risk. N. The chance that the auditor will not catch material accidental or intentional errors for a reason other than that the item was not included in the sample of items tested. Nonsampling risk is associated with audit personnel or audit program problems. The key to reducing nonsampling risk is good personnel, adequate supervision, and good judgment.

nonshareable problem. N. See *pressure*.

nonstock corporation. N. Not-for-profit organizations (such as colleges, churches, or charities) that use a corporate form of organization.

nonsufficient funds. N. Refers to a situation in which a payee presenting a check for payment does not receive that payment because the account holder does not have enough money on deposit to cover the check. ABBRV. *NSF*.

nontrade receivables. N. Amounts that the entity is owed from sources other than customers. Examples of nontrade receivables include loans to employees and tax refunds that have not been received.

nonunit-level activity drivers. N. Activity drivers that are not related to the number of units produced, but rather to some other aspect of production. Nonunit-level activity drivers include the number of setups of the production machinery and the number of design changes in the product.

nonvalue-added activities. N. Actions or efforts that do not add value for the customer. The three tests for value-added activities are: (a) Does the activity change something, like a product or environment? (b) Is the change one that cannot be done by an earlier action? and (c) Does the change prepare for following activities? If the activity in question does not meet one of these tests, then it is a nonvalue-added activity. Process-value analysis seeks to identify and eliminate nonvalue-added activities. Examples of nonvalue-added activities include scheduling and storing.

nonvalue-added costs. N. Costs that, if removed, would not reduce the usefulness of the product to the customer. Nonvalue-added costs are prime candidates for elimination because customers are not willing to pay for these costs, and they are considered wasteful and unnecessary because they do not add value to the customer. Process-value analysis tries to reduce or eliminate these costs.

no-par stock. N. Equity shares that have no par value associated with each share. When a corporation issues (sells) no-par stock, the entire amount is added to the stock account. Corporations may not set a par value, but instead have a stated value for the equity shares. If that is the case, then the accounting is just like par-value stock. See also *stated-value stock.*

NOPAT. ABBRV. Net operating profit after taxes.

normal absorption costing. N. See *normal costing.*

normal activity capacity. N. The estimate of the quantity of unit-level activity drivers used to apply overhead in a normal costing system. The normal activity capacity is an average quantity that the company expects to produce over the long-term. See also *unit-level activity drivers, predetermined overhead rate, normal costing.*

normal costing. N. A method of measuring and assigning production costs to determine unit cost. Normal costing assigns the real cost of material and labor, but uses an estimate, a predetermined overhead rate, to assign overhead to production costs. Normal costing uses an estimate of overhead because the actual costs are not available in time to do the necessary unit-cost calculations. See also *actual costing, predetermined overhead rate.*

normal cost of goods sold. N. The cost of goods sold amount that includes only applied overhead, with no adjustment if applied overhead differs from actual overhead.

normal pension cost. N. See *service cost.*

normal profits. N. The average profit for all businesses operating within an industry. Earnings that produce a rate of return equal to the cost of capital.

normal spoilage. N. The amount of defective or substandard parts that are produced even if the process is efficient. The process will not operate perfectly, and not all the materials will be perfect. Normal spoilage is calculated as the percentage of good units produced, and management determines the acceptable level of spoilage and calls it normal. The costs of normal spoilage are included in the cost of goods manufactured because the process is unable to produce good products without producing a few bad ones.

normal yield curve. N. An upward sloping yield curve, meaning that if rates are on the vertical axis and time is on the horizontal axis, higher rates are usually expected on longer-term debt.

Norwalk Agreement. N. A memo of understanding between the Financial Accounting Standards Board and the International Accounting Standards Board that articulates the intent of the two boards to issue accounting rules that are compatible. The memo, issued in 2006, signaled the importance of having one set of accounting standards that are used worldwide.

notes payable. N. A formal debt agreement in which the borrower promises to pay certain amounts at specified times. The borrower pays interest on the principal for the period of time the debt is outstanding. If the note does not specify an interest rate, it is necessary to either calculate the rate from the cash flows and the cash value of the item purchased or to use the incremental borrowing rate.

notes receivable. N. A type of trade receivable representing amounts owed by customers for an entity's business activity and involving a written promise to pay the unpaid amount and interest.

notes to the financial statements. N. The structured disclosures placed after the financial statements. The notes to the financial statements consist of additional information, often qualitative as well as quantitative, that is required by generally accepted accounting principles.

not-for-profit organization. N. An organization with a goal of serving society rather than making a profit. Usually not-for-profit organizations have no owners and receive contributions from sources that do not expect anything in return. Churches, museums, and social service agencies are examples of not-for-profit organizations. Unlike for-profit entities that try to maximize revenue and minimize cost, not-for-profits try to maximize revenue so that more expenditures can be made. Synonymous with *nonprofit organization.* ABBRV. *NFP.*

notional amount. N. A term used to identify an aspect of a derivative. The notional amount is the quantity or number of units associated with the derivative. In a stock option allowing the holder to purchase 100 shares at a fixed price of $27 per share, the 100 shares is the notional amount.

NPV. ABBRV. Net-present-value method.

NSA. ABBRV. National Society of Accountants.

NSF. ABBRV. Nonsufficient funds.

NYSE. ABBRV. New York Stock Exchange.

OASDI. ABBRV. Old-age, survivor, and disability insurance.

objective measures. N. A characteristic of targets used to evaluate performance. Objective measures use numerical or quantitative data in the evaluation.

object-oriented programming language. N. A computer programming language that uses components to complete the program. The components are called objects. A programmer may have a component that orders numbers from largest to smallest, and another that does the reverse. Anytime that function is needed in a program, the programmer just uses that module. By reusing modules, the problems in the program are limited to the new code, making debugging much easier.

OCBOA. ABBRV. Other comprehensive basis of accounting.

occupational fraud. N. Perpetrating fraud through one's occupation. Occupational fraud occurs when an employee steals from his or her employer. Inflated expense reimbursements are a form of occupational fraud.

OCR. ABBRV. Optical character recognition.

odd lot. N. A stock trade that involves a number of shares that is not a multiple of 100.

off-balance-sheet financing. N. Structuring loans in a way that avoids recording liabilities on the balance sheet. Funding projects without liabilities can be legal, as in the case of operating leases. The company has the use of the asset and does not record any liability for the lease, resulting in financing that is off the balance sheet.

office audit procedure. N. A type of investigation by the Internal Revenue Service (IRS) in which a taxpayer is asked to bring support for a particular tax item to the IRS office. The IRS will only look at that particular item, not the return as a whole.

Office of Management and Budget. N. A part of the White House with the responsibility of helping the president prepare the country's budget. The Office of Management and Budget also helps the president with research and regulation issues. ABBRV. *OMB*.

offset ratio. N. See *delta ratio*.

offsetting errors. N. See *counterbalancing errors*.

old-age, survivor, and disability insurance. N. See *Federal Insurance Contribution Act*. ABBRV. *OASDI*.

OMB. ABBRV. Office of Management and Budget.

omitted dividend. N. A dividend that investors expected but that was not declared. Analysts view omitted dividends as a signal of future reduced earnings for a corporation. Synonymous with *passed dividend*.

on account. N. A term for credit sales or purchases.

OPEB. ABBRV. Postretirement benefits other than pensions.

open confirmation. N. An audit procedure in which an auditor sends a letter to the client's customers asking them to provide information on the amount the customer owes. Then, the auditor has the responsibility to reconcile the amount in the client's books with the amount provided by the customer.

open-end funds. N. A type of managed investment company that pools investors' money to buy assets for investment purposes. Open-end funds allow investors to get out of the investment by selling back to the investment company for the net asset value of each share.

open-end mutual funds. N. A type of mutual fund that will sell as many shares as needed to meet the investors' demand. Shares in open-end mutual funds cannot be traded on the stock exchange or over-the-counter, but only through the mutual fund company itself. To avoid liquidity problems for investors, mutual fund companies are required to buy back any shares at the request of the investor.

open-market repurchase. N. See *stock repurchase*.

open transactions. N. Changes in assets and liabilities that are not reflected on the income statement, but that do change net assets. These transactions include unrealized gains and losses on investments and on foreign currency translation, and some pension liability recognition. Open transactions are included in comprehensive income.

operating accounts. N. Accounts used in governmental accounting to record the actual amounts, rather than the budgeted amounts.

operating assets. N. The assets used in producing operating income. Operating assets usually include cash, marketable securities, accounts receivable, inventories, and fixed assets used to execute the business activities of the company. Contrast with nonoperating assets, which include assets that are not directly used to generate operating income, such as excess cash and investments.

operating budget. N. Part of the master budget for planning all the activities that go into producing goods or providing services that are the business activities of the entity. The operating budget components are the sales budget, production budget, direct materials purchases budget, direct labor budget, overhead budget, selling and administrative expenses budget, ending finished goods budget, and cost of goods sold budget. Synonymous with *operations budget*.

operating cycle. N. The average time from the acquisition of inventory to the collection of cash from customers. The precise activities in the cycle depend on the type of business. In a manufacturing business, the production phase is included. In a service business, no inventory is involved, just the delivery of service and collection of cash. Businesses with long production phases, like wine or liquor businesses, have long operating cycles.

operating debt. N. Borrowing by a government to cover its day-to-day services, or operating activities. Operating debt may be short-term or long-term, depending on the payment date. An example of short-term operating debt is accounts payable to a vendor. An example of long-term operating debt is unfunded pension liabilities.

operating department. N. A department in a manufacturing company that produces the products for sale. The classification of an operating or production department has ramifications for support-department cost allocation. Synonymous with *production department*.

operating entries. N. Journal entries made during the accounting period for governmental accounting to record actual events. As taxes, fines, and license fees are collected, the amounts are entered in the revenue control account (an operating account) as a credit, and cash is debited. The subsidiary accounts are also credited with the actual amount of collections.

operating expenses. N. Costs associated with the regular business activities of an entity. Operating expenses are listed on a multiple-step income statement after the cost of goods sold.

operating income. N. Sales minus the cost of goods sold minus selling, general, and administrative expenses. On the income statement, operating income is found before the "other revenues, gains, expenses, and losses" section. Operating income can also be calculated by starting with net income and deducting taxes and interest.

operating lease. N. An ordinary lease in which the risks and rewards of owning the property do not pass to the lessee. A classification of a lease transaction that is determined by the transaction not meeting certain criteria. See also *capital lease*. Synonymous with *service lease*.

operating leverage. N. Using fixed costs to increase profits. Operating leverage reduces the variable cost per unit by increasing fixed costs. If the variable cost per unit decreases, then the contribution margin per unit increases, resulting in a bigger increase in profit given an increase in sales volume.

operating loss. N. The result of cost of goods sold and operating expenses exceeding revenues. Contrast with operating income, which is equal to the excess of revenues over the cost of goods sold and operating expenses.

operating performance ratio. N. Various ratios that measure the profitability of a company. The ratios generally compare some measure of revenue or income to something else. See also *asset turnover*.

operating system. N. The set of programs that runs the basic operations of a computer and allows software applications to work.

operating working capital. N. All current assets used in operations. A sharp increase in operating working capital can signal inventory buildup, a slowdown in sales, or a problem with collections.

operational audit. N. A set of procedures to check on the efficiency and effectiveness of a department. The internal audit staff of an organization has responsibility for designing, performing, and reporting on operational audits. Operational audits are an important part of monitoring internal controls and improving the profitability of an organization.

operational productivity measure. N. The ratio of outputs to inputs, measured in terms of quantity or in terms of another physical measure. To determine changes in efficiency, the current year's ratio is compared to a previous year's ratio. If the ratio has increased, efficiency has increased. See also *financial productivity measure*.

operation costing. N. A method of assigning costs that combines job-order costing and process costing. Material costs are applied to products using the job-order method, and conversion costs are applied using the process-costing method.

operations budget. N. See *operating budget*.

OPM. ABBRV. Option pricing model.

opportunity. N. One element of the fraud triangle or fraud diamond. Opportunity is the perception by the fraudster that he or she will be successful at the fraud and will not be discovered.

opportunity cost. N. What was given up to follow one course of action. The wages a student could have earned by not attending school can be considered an opportunity cost of attending college.

opportunity-cost approach to transfer pricing. N. A method of determining a transfer price. The minimum transfer price is the price at which the selling division could sell the object to an outsider. This represents the lowest possible transfer price. The maximum transfer price is the price that the buying division would have to pay if the object was purchased from an outside source. The transfer price should fall in the range that is the difference between the minimum and maximum transfer price.

opportunity cost of capital. N. See *required rate of return.*

optical character recognition. N. A method for inputting data into a computer system. The device "reads" the document using light sensors and lasers. Unlike magnetic-ink character recognition, optical character recognition uses optical—not magnetic—sensors. ABBRV. *OCR.*

optimal capital structure. N. The mix of types of financing, including debt and equity, that maximizes the share price of a firm's stock. Different types of financing have different costs, and the right mix of financing types provides the required return to shareholders. Synonymous with *target capital structure.*

optimal-dividend policy. N. Theoretically, the best amount of dividends a corporation should pay shareholders to maximize the stock price. The amount of current income not paid in dividends is reinvested in the firm and provides growth, resulting in a higher stock price. The optimal-dividend policy finds the point where dividends paid and income retained best reflect investors' desired returns.

opting-out right. N. The legal right of bank customers to prohibit the financial institution from selling or sharing the personal information of a customer. The customer must give written notice to the bank.

option contract. N. Similar to a forward contract, but conveying a right or choice to act, rather than a required act or obligation. An option contract gives the holder the option to buy or sell at a future date, and the writer of the contract must buy or sell the asset. To compensate the writer, the option requires an initial cash payment by the holder.

option premium. N. The cost to buy an option.

option price. N. See *strike price*.

option pricing model. N. A technique for estimating the difference between the price of an asset and the strike price of an option at some point in the future. The option pricing model is a complex formula that uses the following as inputs: the asset's price, the variability of that price, the strike price of the option, the risk-free rate, and the length of time the option is available. ABBRV. *OPM*.

ordering costs. N. An inventory cost when materials are purchased from outside a firm. The ordering costs are all the costs of making and receiving an order, such as clerical costs, document costs, insurance costs, and unloading costs.

ordinary annuity. N. Payments of a fixed amount made or received at the end of regularly spaced time intervals. The interest payments on an interest-only loan are an example of an ordinary annuity.

ordinary expense. N. The terminology used by tax laws to identify business or investment expenses that are deductible. An expenditure meets the definition if it is related to the business or investment activity and if the amount is reasonable. For example, a photographer who shoots pictures at a client's site can deduct a mileage expense to cover the cost of the travel. However, deducting the cost of a luxury sports car to travel to jobs might not be considered an ordinary expense.

ordinary income. N. A tax term used to identify a type of earnings. The most common sources of ordinary income are wages and salaries. Contrast with capital gains, which result from the sale of an asset for more than the cost of the asset.

ordinary-income property. N. A tax term used to describe a type of property donated to a charity. Ordinary-income property is property that, if sold, results in income that is included on the owner/donor's tax return as ordinary income. If ordinary-income property is donated to any type of charity, the deduction is equal to the fair market value of the property less any gain that would have been present if the owner/donor had sold the property. Contrast with capital gain property, which is held by the owner/donor more than a year and, if sold, results in capital gain income.

ordinary loss. N. A tax term that describes a loss other than a capital loss. The test for classification as a capital loss is the sale or exchange of a capital asset at a loss. The two key pieces, the sale or exchange and a transaction involving a capital asset, are necessary for the loss to be considered a capital loss. Otherwise, the loss is an ordinary loss. The classification of the loss as ordinary or capital determines the tax treatment of the loss.

organizational chart. N. See *organizational structure*.

organizational structure. N. The configuration of authority and responsibility in an entity. The characteristics of the organizational structure contribute to the effectiveness of the control environment of the entity. Synonymous with *organizational chart*.

organization costs. N. A noncurrent asset on the balance sheet representing the costs of starting a new corporation, such as state fees, legal fees, initial-public-offering fees, and public-offering marketing fees. The corporation has the choice of expensing these costs immediately or capitalizing them. If they are capitalized, the cost is spread out through amortization over a period of less than forty years. Operating losses are not included in this asset. Federal tax law requires corporations to capitalize organization costs, and they can amortize them over five years for tax purposes.

original-effective-yield rate. N. The rate used to determine the carrying value of bonds payable. The original-effective-yield rate is the interest rate that was in effect at the time the bonds were sold. The carrying value will not be equal to the current market value of the bonds unless the same rate is in effect.

originating temporary difference. N. The first year in which the tax basis of an asset or liability is different than the book value of the asset or liability. For example, a leasing company requires retail customers to pay a lump sum for three years' rent and then to remit a percentage of sales as additional rent every year. The leasing company records that lump sum as a liability—unearned rent revenue. The balance sheet value of that liability is the book value. However, the entire amount is taxed in the year received, resulting in a tax basis of zero. The originating temporary difference is the year the lump sum is received.

OSPR. ABBRV. Other-substantive-procedures risk.

OTC. ABBRV. Over-the-counter market.

other assets. N. A noncurrent asset on the balance sheet that contains several small items with debit balances. Sometimes called deferred charges, the "other assets" section of the balance sheet is somewhat of a catchall account. Examples include deferred tax amounts, prepaid pension costs, and the cash surrender value of life insurance on key employees. See also *deferred charge.*

other comprehensive basis of accounting. N. Refers to an entity that does not use generally accepted accounting principles, but instead uses another type of accounting, such as cash basis or tax basis. ABBRV. *OCBOA.*

other comprehensive income. N. Part of comprehensive income, including those changes in equity, other than investments by owners and dividends, that are not included on the income statement.

other financing uses. N. An account that appears on the statement of revenues, expenditures, and changes in fund balances for a governmental unit. The other-financing-uses account is increased by inflows that are not revenues in the governmental accounting system and decreased by outflows that are not expenditures. An example of an increase to this account is the proceeds from the sale of a used city-maintenance vehicle. An example of a decrease to this account is a transfer to the debt-service fund.

other-substantive-procedures risk. N. The chance that the audit procedures, other than the test of details, will not uncover errors. Included in other substantive procedures are activities like analytical procedures and cutoff tests. ABBRV. *OSPR.*

out-of-the-money. N. A term used to describe a situation in an option contract in which it would not be advantageous to exercise the contract. For example, a call option that gives an individual the right to buy 100 shares of stock for $14 per share prior to December 31, 2007, would be out-of-the-money if the market price for the stock was less than $14 per share. There would be no advantage to paying $14 per share if the stock is available without the option for less than $14. Synonymous with *underwater option.*

output controls. N. The procedures and measures that a company takes to ensure accuracy and to protect the output of the accounting information system. In addition to ensuring that processing is really done, output controls limit access and use of printed reports and computer files. See also *application controls.*

output-level overhead variance. N. See *fixed-overhead volume variance.*

outputs. N. A company's products. Outputs can be any type of product or service.

outside basis. N. A concept used to identify the value of an equity interest, for the owner's tax purposes. The outside basis is equal to the basis of the asset or assets exchanged for the interest.

outside director. N. A member of the board of directors who is independent of the organization. The director is not employed by the organization or associated with it in any way, other than being a shareholder or being on the board of directors. All boards need outside directors.

outsourcing. N. Hiring another company to do a function previously performed by the entity itself. A common outsourcing situation is that of data processing. Outsourcing can be minimal, such as just doing the payroll, or it can be complete, such as when the outside company is the entity's information technology department.

outstanding checks. N. Checks written by an entity that have not yet cleared the bank. The result is a higher balance according to bank records than company records.

outstanding common stock. N. Shares of common stock that are owned by outside investors. It is possible for common stock to have been sold but subsequently bought back by the company and held as treasury stock. Treasury stock is not part of outstanding common stock. The number of shares issued minus the number of shares of treasury stock equals the number of shares of outstanding common stock. Outstanding common stock is used in earnings per share calculations.

overabsorbed indirect costs. N. See *overapplied overhead*.

overapplied overhead. N. The situation that occurs when total applied overhead is more than total actual overhead costs. Overapplied overhead is subtracted from the cost of goods sold at the end of the year. Synonymous with *overabsorbed indirect costs*.

overcosting. N. The result that occurs when the cost per unit is higher than the resource consumption in producing the product.

Overcosting may cause management to set the selling price too high, causing lost sales.

overhead. N. Costs associated with the production of goods or services, but not with direct materials or direct labor. The components of overhead are vital to production, but do not become part of the actual product. The cost of overtime wages is usually considered overhead, even though wages are normally classified as direct labor. The logic is that the overtime exists because of all the jobs in the plant, so the cost should be allocated to all the jobs through overhead. Sandpaper is an example of an overhead cost for a cabinet-making business. Synonymous with *factory burden, manufacturing overhead*.

overhead application. N. See *predetermined overhead rate*.

overhead budget. N. Part of the master budget that identifies all the indirect costs of production and plans the timing of those costs.

overhead control. N. An account used to hold the difference between applied and actual overhead during interim accounting periods. While overhead may fluctuate during the year, these fluctuations are expected to even out. However, for a monthly or quarterly income statement, the company needs to adjust the cost of goods sold, for the variance in overhead. The cost of goods sold can be either increased or decreased as necessary; the other part of the transaction is overhead control.

overpurchasing. N. A way to commit occupational fraud. The fraudster buys two items at different prices, returning the less expensive one but still requesting reimbursement in the more expensive amount. The result is that the fraudster is reimbursed for more than the cost of the item.

overstatement. N. A form of financial statement fraud that states assets or revenues at more than the actual amount with the purpose of reaching some desired financial target.

over-the-counter corporation. N. A business that is organized as a corporation whose stock is not available on the stock exchanges but is traded between dealers and the public. Synonymous with *unlisted corporation*.

over-the-counter market. N. The structure for buying and selling shares of stock that are not listed on either the New York Stock Exchange or the American Stock Exchange. These stocks are traded through a computer network called the National Market System, using members of the network called dealers. The National Association of Securities Dealers regulates the dealers participating in the over-the-counter market. For companies that want to be traded in this market, there are little or no requirements for listing. ABBRV. *OTC*.

owners' equity. N. See *stockholders' equity*.

P

paid in capital. N. See *contributed capital.*

paid in capital in excess of par value. N. See *additional paid in capital.*

P&L. ABBRV. Profit and loss. See also *income statement.*

parallel processing. N. A set of production activities in which two or more steps can be done simultaneously and then combined to finish the product. Products with components are usually produced using parallel processing. Contrast with sequential processing, in which activities must be done in a certain order, one at a time, to complete the product.

parallel simulation. N. An audit procedure in which the auditor uses real data and puts it through a simulated program written specifically for the purpose of testing an aspect of the client's information system.

parent. N. A party to a business combination. The parent is the company that acquires the other party to the combination, the subsidiary.

parent-subsidiary group. N. A type of controlled group in which a set of connected corporations, with a lead corporation, owns 80% of the stock—within the set of connected corporations. The definition of a parent-subsidiary group is used for tax purposes to designate the maximum amount of income in brackets and to limit certain benefits.

Pareto diagram. N. Used to detect quality problems. A Pareto diagram is a bar chart that plots each type of defect against the number of times it happens and identifies the type of quality problem that is occurring.

parking transaction. N. A method of putting inventory on the balance sheet of another entity through a repurchase agreement. See also *repos*.

partial-productivity measurement. N. A statistic based on one input that measures productive efficiency for that particular input. The traditional ratio is the output divided by the input. The input and output may be measured in terms of dollars (a financial productivity measure), amounts, or some other physical measure (an operational productivity measure). The ratio is compared to another point in time to determine if efficiency increases have occurred. If so, the ratio gets larger; if efficiency has declined, the ratio gets smaller.

participating preferred stock. N. Preferred stock that carries the rights to receive the normal dividend, and to receive a return equal to that received by common shareholders if the preferred stock is fully participating. Preferred stock may also be partially participating, meaning that the return is up to a stated percent.

participative budgeting. N. A budgeting process that requires managers' involvement in setting budgets.

partnership. N. An unincorporated business with two or more owners, called partners. All states except Louisiana and the District of Columbia have similar partnership laws. Partnerships are similar to corporations in that they can own property and acquire debt, but different types of partnerships have different characteristics regarding the liability of partners.

par value method. N. A rarely used method of accounting for treasury stock. When the treasury stock is purchased, the acquisition price is compared to the original selling price. If the acquisition price is more than the original selling price, treasury stock is increased for the par value, additional paid in capital is reduced by the remainder of the original selling price, and retained earnings are reduced for the remainder. If the acquisition price is less than the original selling price, additional paid in capital is increased for the difference. If the treasury stock is sold later, the treasury stock account is reduced by the par value of the resold shares, and additional paid in capital is increased or decreased for the difference. If the treasury stock is retired, then both the common stock account and the treasury stock account are reduced by the par value. See also *treasury stock*.

par value of a bond. N. See *maturity value of a bond*.

par value of stock. N. A specified dollar amount associated with each share of stock. It does not represent value, but indicates the maximum amount the owner of the share can lose if the corporation is dissolved. When a corporation sells shares of stock, the par value of the stock is included in the stock account, and the amount above the par value is put in the additional paid-in-capital account. When a corporation issues (sells) par value stock, the cash account is increased and stockholders' equity is increased, splitting the amount between the par value of the shares sold, which is put in the stock account, and the amount above par, which is put in additional paid in capital.

passed dividend. N. See *omitted dividend*.

passive. ADJ. Not active. A descriptor attached to income and losses that determines the tax treatment. See also *passive activity*.

passive activity. N. A tax term that classifies income and losses. To be classified as a passive activity, the taxpayer must not be involved in a significant way in the business operations. Rental activities are considered passive activities, as are many limited partnerships.

passive-activity loss. N. See *passive loss*.

passive income. N. Investment income deriving from businesses and real estate that the entity is not actively involved in via management or sales. Examples include dividends, interest, rent, and capital gains from sales of investments.

passive loss. N. Loss passed from a business to a taxpayer who is not directly involved with the business. Passive loss cannot be deducted by taxpayers when it is passed through a partnership or an S corporation in which the taxpayer does not actively participate in the operations—unless the taxpayer has other passive income to offset it. Any unused amount of passive-activity loss can be carried forward. Most passive losses arise from investments in tax shelters. Prior to 1987, taxpayers could offset ordinary income and other gains with passive losses. After 1987, passive losses could only offset passive income. Synonymous with *passive-activity loss.*

passive ownership. N. An investment in which the investor owns less than 20% of the voting stock of a company and has no influence on the board of directors. Synonymous with *minority passive investment.*

pass-through entities. N. Businesses that are unincorporated or are S corporations and that pay no income taxes because the income is shifted to the owners, who pay the taxes. Pass-through entities "pass the income through" to the owners.

pass-through scheme. N. A type of fraud in which the fraudster sets up a shell company that sells products to a company at inflated prices. Normally, companies buy from approved vendors that have price quotes. In a pass-through scheme, a company employee enables the shell company to become an approved vendor.

pass-through securities. N. A type of investment in which the seller of the security pays the investor's return with payments received from a source other than revenues generated by the seller of the investment. The Government National Mortgage Association (GNMA) buys mortgages from banks and transforms them into an investment opportunity. The investors receive the returns on their investment from the payments on the mortgages. The mortgage payments pass through GNMA to the investors. A similar security exists for car loans.

patent. N. The ownership of a process or product that is protected from use by others through registration with the government. Patents are classified as intangible assets on the balance sheet. Measuring the value of a patent is straightforward if it is purchased. Like any other purchase, the value is the historical cost. If the process or product is developed, only the costs of registration and successful defenses are capitalized. The research costs are expensed as incurred. The cost of a patent is amortized over the economic life of the patent or twenty years, whichever is less. If a defense of a patent is unsuccessful, the owner should take an extraordinary loss for the remaining balance sheet value.

payables. N. Shorthand for all liabilities with "payable" in the title. Usually classified as current liabilities on the balance sheet. See also *accounts payable, notes payable*.

payables deferral period. N. A component of the cash conversion cycle model that measures the time between purchase and payment for materials and labor. The formula is average payables divided by purchases per day, calculated as the cost of goods sold divided by 365.

pay-and-return scheme. N. A type of fraud in which an employee overpays an invoice or pays an invoice twice, and when the excess is returned, steals that amount.

payback method. N. A process used in capital budgeting to select a project. The payback method divides the initial investment by the increase in cash flows per year. The result is the number of years it takes to recover the initial investment.

payback period. N. A decision rule for accepting or rejecting capital budgeting projects. The payback period is the time in years for the project to produce enough profit to cover the original cost of the project. A firm can compare the payback period for two options and choose the one with the shorter payback period.

payment date. N. A significant date for corporations that pay dividends. A payment date is the date when the dividend checks are sent out to the shareholders who owned the shares on the date of record. Because of time lags, the owner on the date of record may not be the owner on the payment date. Market prices are influenced by dividend dates of record and payment.

payment default. N. A situation in which a borrower does not make the required interest or principal payments on time.

payment process. N. Part of the purchasing cycle that involves writing and sending checks to vendors. The payment process must ensure that businesses pay only for goods or services actually received and that the payments are accurate and timely. See also *purchasing cycle*.

payout ratio. N. A measure of profitability used in financial analysis and important to shareholders who value dividends. The formula is cash dividends divided by net income.

payroll costs. N. The total costs to the employer of employing people, including wages, benefits, amounts withheld from employees' checks, matching Federal Insurance Contribution Act tax amounts, and unemployment taxes. The total is an expense on the income statement.

payroll deductions. N. Amounts withheld by the employer from employees' checks. Payroll deductions include taxes, union dues, insurance premiums, and employee savings. The employer incurs a liability to send these amounts to the proper recipients: the government, union, insurance company, and bank. The wage and salary expense on the income statement includes the amounts withheld.

payroll factor. N. A factor used in apportioning business income among states. The payroll factor is equal to payroll within the state divided by total payroll. Payroll includes wages, commissions, and pay for service, but usually not pay to independent contractors. See also *Uniform Division of Income for Tax Purposes Act.*

payroll journal. N. A journal that contains a chronological record of wage and salary payments made to employees. See also *journal.*

payroll process. N. Part of the resource-management cycle that deals with paying employees. The payroll process involves not only preparing accurate and timely paychecks, but also keeping accurate records of earnings and complying with reporting regulations to government entities. See also *resource-management cycle.*

payroll taxes. N. Costs to the employer of having employees. These are amounts that are paid by the employer and not withheld from employees' checks. The most common payroll taxes are federal and state unemployment taxes and Federal Insurance Contribution Act taxes, both Social Security and Medicare. Payroll taxes are included in the wage and salary expense on the income statement. The 2008 rate for employee-paid taxes on Social Security is 6.2% on the first $102,000 of income; the rate for Medicare is 1.45% on all income. For self-employed people, the Social Security rate is 12.4% on the first $102,000, and the Medicare rate is 2.9% on all income. Employers match the Social Security and Medicare amounts and pay a federal unemployment tax of 6.2% on the first $7,000 of income for each employee with a credit for state unemployment taxes paid. Synonymous with *employment taxes*.

PBO. ABBRV. Projected benefit obligation.

PDA. ABBRV. Personal data assistant device.

peak-load pricing. N. Charging a higher price when demand for the product is higher. Airlines use peak-load pricing in setting airfares around holidays.

peanut butter costing. N. The use of an average indirect-cost-application rate that "spreads" the costs smoothly among products or services. Peanut butter costing applies indirect costs as if all products used indirect costs in an identical fashion. The result is undercosting and overcosting of products. Synonymous with *cost smoothing*.

peer review. N. A process that certified public accountant (CPA) firms undergo every three years in compliance with state boards of accountancy or American Institute of Certified Public Accountants (AICPA) requirements. Each CPA firm that audits public companies is investigated by another CPA firm. The investigating firm looks at the quality control features and audit practices of the firm under review and makes the report available to the AICPA and Securities and Exchange Commission.

penny stocks. N. Usually low cost, high-risk stocks that have little value other than speculation.

pension expense. N. The charge against income relating to the pension plan of the company. The pension expense is a combination of five components: service cost, interest cost, expected return on plan assets, amortization of prior-service cost, and amortization of unrecognized net gain or loss. Synonymous with *net periodic pension cost*.

pension fund

412

pension fund. N. The assets that are set aside to pay retirement benefits promised to employees. The pension fund does not appear in the asset section of the employing company, but instead is an entirely separate entity, for both legal and accounting purposes.

pension income. N. An item that appears on the income statement of some companies with extremely overfunded pension plans during a strong bull market. The return on the plan assets exceeds the service cost and interest cost, resulting in an income from the pension expense calculation.

pension plan. N. A type of benefit that an employer provides to an employee in which the employer continues to pay the employee after retirement. The payments can be structured in many different ways, including a lump-sum payment upon retirement or monthly or annual payments. The employer puts cash into a pension fund out of which the payments are made. Pension-plan accounting involves determining the amount of expense on the income statement and recording the cash contributions to the pension fund. The expense is not the amount of benefits paid, but a combination of elements, many of which are determined by actuaries.

P/E ratio. ABBRV. Price-earnings ratio.

percentage analysis. N. See *common-size analysis*.

percentage-of-completion method. N. A method of recognizing revenue on a long-term contract before the contract is complete. To implement the percentage-of-completion method, the organization must be able to estimate how much of the contract is done. The most common method involves two steps. The first step is to compare the costs so far to the total estimated costs and to calculate the percentage of the contract that is complete. In step two, that percentage is applied to the total revenue or total gross profit of the contract to determine how much revenue or profit should be recognized to this point. To get the current period's amount, the previously recognized revenue, or profit, is subtracted from the amount in step two. If the contract is going to result in a loss, the entire loss is included on the income statement as soon as it is known that a loss will occur. The American Institute of Certified Public Accountants Statement of Position 881–1 states that companies should use the completed-contract method only if they are unable to use the percentage-of-completion method. See also *completed-contract method.*

percentage-of-receivables approach to bad-debt expense. N. One method of estimating bad-debt expense. The percentage-of-receivables method relies on analyzing the age of existing receivables to estimate the amount that is uncollectible. The amount is the balance required in the allowance-for-doubtful-accounts contra-asset account. The bad-debt expense is whatever amount is necessary to produce that balance. Usually, the older the receivable, the more likely it is to become a bad debt. So, if the organization has many old receivables, it will need more in the allowance for doubtful accounts, producing a bigger bad-debt expense. This method of estimating bad debts focuses on getting a correct balance sheet value for receivables.

percentage-of-sales approach to bad-debt expense. N. One method of estimating bad-debt expense. The percentage-of-sales approach is useful if historical data shows a steady correlation between the amount of sales in a year and the sales from that year that eventually become bad debts. The relationship of bad debts to sales, a percentage, is multiplied by sales for the current year to estimate bad-debt expense. Bad-debt expense is increased by that amount, and the allowance for doubtful accounts is also increased by that amount. This method of estimating bad debts focuses on matching the expense with the sales that produce it. See also *percentage-of-receivables approach to bad-debt expense, allowance method, allowance for doubtful accounts.*

percent-of-sales method. N. A presentation format for financial statements based on predicted amounts. Each amount is a percent of the forecast-sales amount.

perception of detection. N. A method of deterring employees from committing fraud by giving them the impression that they will be caught if they engage in fraud. A strong system of internal control that is obvious to employees is a key component in establishing a perception of detection.

per diem allowances. N. An alternative method of tracking meals and lodging for employee travel expenses. The Internal Revenue Service supplies tables listing various cities and daily amounts for meals, lodging, and other expenses.

perfect hedge. N. A hedge whose benefits are exactly equal to the losses it was created to cover.

performance audit. N. A type of audit usually associated with government programs. A performance audit involves evaluating the efficiency of meeting the program objectives. Contrast with a program audit, which examines whether the objectives are being achieved.

performance drivers. N. See *lead measures*.

performance measurement. N. Determining how well a company or one of its subdivisions has done during the accounting period. Common measurement methods include profit, revenue growth, cost control, and measures of return. See also *return on assets*.

performance measures. N. See *lead measures*.

performance reports. N. Documents comparing actual outcomes to planned outcomes or to some norm. A manufacturing business may compare costs before and after a new machine design is used.

If the outcome is better, the manager knows that the plan is working. See also *planning*.

performance shares. N. A type of executive compensation in which the number of shares an employee receives depends on the company's success or performance. The success is usually measured in terms of stock price or net income. The awarding of performance shares may also require that the executive remain with the company for a specified period of time. Performance shares are one way of aligning a manager's actions with the best interests of the stockholders, thus reducing agency problems.

period costs. N. A term used to identify costs that are not part of inventory, but that decrease income in the accounting period they are incurred in. Period costs fall into the categories found on the multiple-step income statement: selling expenses, general and administrative expenses, and other expenses and losses. The classification of costs is significant because period costs reduce income immediately, as opposed to product costs, which only reduce income if the product is sold. See also *product costs*. Synonymous with *noninventoriable costs, period expenses*.

period expenses. N. See *period costs*.

periodic-inventory system. N. A way of keeping track of inventory that only adjusts the inventory account balance at the end of the accounting period. Purchases of inventory increase a temporary account called purchases. When inventory items are sold, only accounts receivable or cash is increased and sales revenue is increased. No decrease to inventory is recorded at the time of sale. At the end of the accounting period, the company calculates the cost of goods sold by adding purchases to the inventory amount, which is the value at the beginning of the period. That sum is the cost of goods available for sale. The company does a physical count of the inventory on hand, deducts that amount from the cost of goods available for sale, and the result is the cost of goods sold. The logic is that if a good is no longer on hand, it must have been sold. Periodic-inventory systems are used less often now that computer applications have made perpetual-inventory systems cheaper to use.

periodicity assumption. N. A basic assumption in accounting involving an agreement to evaluate performance at regular time periods. The alternative to the periodicity assumption is to not measure performance except when the company goes out of business. At that time, the initial investment is compared with the proceeds of the liquidation to determine the success or failure of the business. Underlying this assumption is the belief that accounting can provide informative measures of performance for a quarter or a year at a time. Synonymous with *time-period assumption*.

perks. N. See *perquisites*.

permanent account. N. See *balance sheet account*.

permanent difference. N. Differences between pretax financial income and taxable income that will always exist. Some items are included in income on the income statement, such as interest on certain types of municipal bonds, and are never taxed. No deferred tax amounts are associated with permanent differences.

permanent earnings. N. Another term to describe income from continuing operations, i.e., the income that comes from the ongoing business activities of the firm. Contrast with transitory earnings, which are permanent earnings with the addition of discontinued items.

permanent establishment. N. A provision in many tax treaties that allows U.S. corporations to avoid the foreign tax if the corporation uses only mail order or independent sellers in the foreign country.

The U.S. corporation is said to not have a permanent establishment in the foreign country.

permanent fund. N. Part of the governmental funds that account for service activities to citizens. Permanent funds account for assets resulting in earnings that must be used for a specific operating purpose, without touching the principal. A permanent fund works like an endowment, which allows the entity to spend the earnings, but not the principal. An example of a permanent fund is a $2 million donation from which earnings must be used to maintain and enhance a city's botanical gardens.

permanently restricted net assets. N. A classification on the balance sheet of a not-for-profit entity that represents the dollar value of assets that can only be used in a certain way or for a certain purpose. For example, if a church member donates a lake-front property that can only be used for religious retreats, it is a permanently restricted asset of the church. The church cannot rent it out for fishing groups or family reunions, but it can rent it to other church groups.

perpetual-inventory system. N. A way of keeping track of inventory with a running total of the cost of goods sold and the cost of inventory on hand. Any purchases of inventory are recorded with an increase to inventory and either an increase to accounts payable or a decrease to cash. Any sale is recorded with two journal entries. The first increases cash or accounts receivable and increases sales revenue. The second increases the cost of goods sold and decreases inventory. Perpetual-inventory systems have become cheaper and easier to use with the use of point-of-sale scanners and other computerized applications. The alternative to a perpetual system is a periodic system.

perpetuity. N. An annuity that never ends. An annuity is a series of equal payments at equal intervals. To find the present value of a perpetuity, divide the payment amount by the interest rate of the next-best investment opportunity.

perquisites. N. Noncash benefits that employees receive. Some examples of perquisites are nice offices, good parking spots, use of a company car, and club memberships. Synonymous with *perks*.

personal data assistant device. N. A pocket-sized computer device that can store address books, appointment calendars, expense information, and other data. Many have wireless Internet connection capabilities for receiving email. ABBRV. *PDA*.

personal exemptions. N. A deduction from adjusted gross income reducing the amount of taxes a taxpayer will have to pay. This stated amount is changed almost every year. A taxpayer can take exemptions for a spouse and dependents, too.

personal-holding-company tax. N. A tax on corporations that have at least 60% of income from investment income and that consist of five or fewer shareholders owning more than 50% of the stock during the last half of the year. Personal holding companies are useful when personal tax rates are much higher than corporate rates. An individual can become a personal holding company (a corporation) and avoid the high taxes individuals pay. ABBRV. *PHC*.

personal property. N. Any asset that is not real estate or real property.

personal-use property. N. Assets owned by a taxpayer and used outside of business or trade activities. Personal-use property is different than personal property in that personal-use property is anything not used in business activities. Personal property is any property that is not real estate. If a taxpayer is a self-employed photographer, property like a fishing cabin, sports car, and boat are considered personal-use property. If the photographer regularly uses the boat to shoot pictures from the water, then it would be used in the business and would not be personal-use property.

PERT. ABBRV. Program Evaluation and Review Technique.

petty cash fund. N. A supply of cash, usually in a locked box, on hand for small purchases for which use of a business check is inefficient. One employee has responsibility for the petty cash fund. When a small cash purchase is made, the employee puts the receipt in place of the cash used for the purchase. The result is that the box will always have a total of receipts plus cash equal to the cash originally put in the box. When the box is low on cash, the employee records the various expenses and increases the cash in the box.

phantom stock plan. N. A deferred compensation plan in which the amount of the compensation is tied to the company's stock price. The company "pretends" to invest a specified amount in company stock and then sell it at a specified date in the future. The difference is paid to an employee as compensation.

phase-out period for discontinued operations. N. The time period between the measurement date, when management formally commits to the disposal of a segment, and the actual disposal date. The results of operations for the segment are separated from those of continuing operations on the income statement.

PHC. ABBRV. Personal-holding-company tax.

phishing. N. The use of the Internet to persuade victims to disclose private information that the perpetrators can use to commit fraud through identity theft. The scams often involve real-looking bank websites that require divulging passwords or Social Security numbers.

physical evidence. N. One type of evidence gathered in a fraud investigation that is tangible and has a separate existence.

Fingerprints, stolen goods, and forged checks are examples of physical evidence. See also *evidence square*.

physical flow schedule. N. A report prepared in a process-costing system to account for units that were in work-in-process at the beginning of the period, units that were started during the period, and units that remain in work-in-process at the end of the period. The physical flow schedule reconciles the units to account for those in work-in-process (which includes those started during the period) with the units accounted for (those completed plus those still in process).

physical inventory. N. Designates the actual, tangible items that a company is holding to sell to companies. Contrast with the inventory account on the balance sheet, which is the costs associated with the records of inventory items held for resale.

physical-measure method of allocating joint costs. N. Allocates joint costs to products based on weight, number, or some other physical measure. The joint costs of raising and trucking turkeys to a processing center are $250,000. Of 30,000 turkeys, 1,000 will be sold as whole birds, and the remaining 29,000 will be sold as turkey parts. Using the physical-measure method, the turkey parts would be allocated 29 divided by 30 times $250,000 (or $241,667). The remaining $8,333 of joint costs is allocated to the whole birds. The measure could be in pounds instead.

physical-presence nexus. N. A substantial business relationship between residents of a state and a business, not located or incorporated in the state, that allows the state to tax the corporation. The nature of the relationship is through the location of warehouses, retail stores, or some other physical element within the state.

pick-up tax. N. A state tax paid by an estate that is equal to the excess of the federal credit for state death taxes over the actual state death taxes. If the federal credit is larger than the state tax, then the state "picks up" the difference. If the actual state death tax is greater than the credit, the amount is zero.

pink sheets. N. The term used to describe low-priced, thinly traded stocks. Originally the information was sent to dealers on pink sheets of paper.

plain vanilla interest rate swap. N. A contract between two entities to trade future interest payments. Entity A pays interest based on a specified rate and a specified principal amount. Entity B pays interest based on a variable rate and the specified principal amount. This simple type of interest rate swap specifies all the variables and converts variable interest into fixed interest for Entity A and vice versa for Entity B. Synonymous with *generic interest rate swap*.

plan assets. N. Investments set aside by a company in a separate trust to cover the payments to retirees who were part of the company's pension plan. The market value of the plan assets affects the amount of annual pension expense.

planned obsolescence. N. Purchasing machinery and equipment that will wear out at a point in time, even though better, longer lasting assets are available. Planned obsolescence is useful if the purchases are assets for which technology is changing rapidly.

planning. N. A management activity that identifies goals and the specific methods of achieving them. The process of planning usually starts with broad, general outcomes, moves to more specific aspects, and continues until enough details are specified about the work-activity level.

plan sponsor. N. The company that sets up a pension plan for its employees. The plan sponsor gives assets to the plan trustee.

plant assets. N. See *property, plant, and equipment.*

plan trustee. N. A separate legal entity that controls the assets of a pension plan and makes payments to retirees.

PLC. ABBRV. Public limited company.

point-of-sale device. N. A mechanism for collecting and entering information about sales at the cash register. Sales revenue, inventory decrease, and cash or credit information are captured electronically at the time of purchase. Scanners in grocery stores or discount stores are examples of point-of sale devices. ABBRV. *POS.*

points. N. A finance charge associated with a loan, paid at the inception of the loan. One point is equal to 1% of the loan amount. Points increase the effective rate of the loan over the stated rate because more interest is paid to borrow the principal amount. That interest is just charged at the front end of the loan.

poison pill. N. A method of defending against a hostile takeover. The target company issues stock rights that allow shareholders to buy more shares of stock at a very low price with an exercise date triggered by the acquiring company's purchase of stock. That action increases the number of shares necessary for control and therefore increases the price of the acquisition.

pooling method. N. A method of accounting for a business combination that was eliminated in 2001. The pooling method allowed the recording of all the target company's assets and liabilities at the book value when the combination met the strict requirements for pooling. No goodwill was recorded. Pooling allowed subsequent income to be higher because depreciation was determined on old book values, not on the fair market value at the time of combination. Synonymous with *pooling of interests.*

pooling of interests. N. See *pooling method.*

pool rate. N. A method of assigning overhead costs to products in an activity-based cost system, calculated from a homogeneous cost pool and an activity driver. The pool rate simplifies overhead application in activity-based cost systems through the combination of similar overhead costs that are related to production and used in the same proportion by production.

population. N. A term used in audit sampling to identify items with a particular characteristic of interest. A sample chooses some of these items so that the items represent the population's characteristics. The population of purchase orders includes all purchase orders for the accounting period. The auditor chooses a sample of those purchase orders to test.

portfolio income. N. One of three categories of income. Portfolio income consists of the dividends, interest, annuities, and royalties that a taxpayer receives from sources other than his or her business or trade. The other two types of income are active income, which comes from the taxpayer's business or trade, and passive income, which is income other than active or portfolio income. The classification of income is important for the treatment of losses from the various income categories.

POS. ABBRV. Point-of-sale device.

positive confirmation. N. An audit procedure in which the auditor sends a letter to the client's customer requesting that the client review the amount owed and return the letter "confirming" that the amount is correct. Contrast with a negative confirmation, in which the client only has to return the letter if the amount owed is not correct.

positive drift. N. An upward movement of stock price prior to a quarterly earnings announcement. Positive drift occurs for large corporations that provide weekly sales data that is better than expected. Investors incorporate this information into value estimates of the corporation, which translate into a higher stock price.

post–balance sheet event. N. See *subsequent event*.

postclosing trial balance. N. The final trial balance of the accounting period. This trial balance is prepared after the temporary income statement accounts are closed. It only contains balance sheet accounts. See also *trial balance*.

posting. N. The accounting procedure for putting the amounts recorded in the journal into the ledger accounts. Posting can be done manually, or electronically by accounting software.

postretirement benefits other than pensions. N. Health and welfare benefits paid for by the employer after the employee has retired. Health care benefits carry the largest dollar amount of postretirement benefits, but other benefits may include tax services, legal services, and life insurance. The accounting for postretirement benefits other than pensions is similar to that of pension accounting and is specified in Financial Accounting Standards Board Statement 106. ABBRV. *OPEB*.

potential common stock. N. Securities that may be converted into shares of common stock. The potential for additional shares of common stock signals the possible decrease in one of the most important financial statistics—earnings per share. Examples of securities that are considered potential common stock include convertible bonds, convertible preferred stock, stock warrants, and other securities that include the possibility of issuing common stock.

PP&E. ABBRV. Property, plant, and equipment.

PPI. ABBRV. Producer price index.

PPS. ABBRV. Probability-proportional-to-size sampling.

practical activity capacity. N. The estimate of the quantity of the unit-level activity driver used to apply overhead in a normal costing system. The practical activity capacity is the largest quantity that a company expects to produce or use if things operate efficiently and effectively. Practical capacity is the required capacity to determine the fixed manufacturing overhead per unit, and variances are allocated between inventories and the cost of goods sold to determine income. See also *unit-level activity drivers, predetermined overhead rate, normal costing.*

practical capacity. N. A term used to describe a situation in which an entity is producing as much of an activity or product as it can to still be operating efficiently.

practical merger. N. See *type C reorganization.*

predatory pricing. N. An illegal pricing method that sets selling prices below cost with the intention of making it impossible for competitors to continue in business. Then, without competition, the company can increase prices.

predetermined overhead rate. N. A way to assign overhead costs to production costs. A normal costing system uses a predetermined overhead rate, and the rate is calculated using an estimate of overhead cost divided by an estimate of the quantity of an easily measured product cost or driver. A key choice is the driver and the quantity of the driver. Overhead rates can be calculated for the entire manufacturing plant, or for each department in the plant. A traditional predetermined overhead rate estimates the total overhead costs and divides by the number of labor hours. The result is overhead that is applied to production based on how much labor is used by the production process. A predetermined rate only results in a good unit cost if the relationship between the actual overhead costs and labor is strong and positive. Synonymous with *overhead application.*

predication. N. A situation that suggests the occurrence of fraud. The circumstances, as evaluated by professionals, signal that fraud has been occurring, is occurring, or will occur.

predictive value. N. An aspect of the primary qualitative characteristic of accounting information—relevance. Accounting information has predictive value if the decision maker can use the information to forecast, estimate, or guess what will happen in the future.

preemptive right. N. Entitlement to maintain a proportionate share of ownership in a corporation. If a company issues new shares, the current shareholders must be able to buy enough shares to maintain their percentage of ownership. The preemptive right is stated in the corporate charter. The preemptive right prevents the board of directors from neutralizing contrary stockholders by selling shares of stock to agreeing stockholders, thereby reducing the absolute number of votes and the percentage of the votes controlled by the contrary group. Synonymous with *antidilution provision, subscription privilege.*

preferred stock. N. A balance sheet account in the stockholders' equity section representing investment by owners. Preferred stock is a type of equity shares that usually have no vote, but are paid a stated amount of dividends before the owners of common stock. See also *equity shares.*

premium on bonds payable. N. An adjunct liability account that increases the book value of bonds payable. A premium arises when the cash interest is at a higher rate than the rate of return of similar opportunities. The premium on bonds payable is amortized over the life of the bond at every interest payment date, eventually being reduced to zero at maturity. The effective-interest method of amortization is preferred, but straight-line is acceptable if the results are not significantly different. See also *bonds issued at a premium,* *effective-interest method, straight-line depreciation, bonds payable.*

prepaid expense. N. A type of adjusting entry. Recording a prepaid expense decreases the expense for the current accounting period even though the cash has already been paid. This adjustment records an asset for the prepaid expense. Examples include prepaid rent and prepaid insurance.

prepaid interest. N. Interest paid before it has been earned. Prepaid interest is involved in notes in which the borrower does not receive the face value of the note. The lender takes the interest out before distributing the principal amount to the borrower.

prepaid pension asset. N. See *prepaid pension cost.*

prepaid pension cost. N. An asset that may appear on the balance sheet of an employer with a pension plan. Prepaid pension cost is increased by the excess of funding of the pension plan over pension expense. See also *accrued pension cost.* Synonymous with *prepaid pension asset.*

prepayment. N. A category of transactions in which cash is paid before the goods or services are used in the generation of revenue. Rent and insurance are two common examples. The cash for insurance premiums must be paid prior to the start of coverage, resulting in a prepayment.

present interest in a gift. N. The right to use the property or assets of a gift without any limitations. The recipient does not have to wait until a certain age or date to use the gift.

present value. N. The value as of today of a single payment, or a series of payments to be received in the future. The amount (or amounts) is discounted assuming compound interest. The present value is always less than the amount of the single payment or the total of the series of payments.

present value of a bond issue. N. A calculation that determines the cash proceeds from the sale of bonds. First, the maturity value of the bond is discounted using the effective yield on the bond. Then, the interest payments are discounted. The dollar amount of the interest payments per year is the maturity value multiplied by the stated rate. That amount is then divided by the number of payments per year, such as dividing by two for semiannual payments. Then, the interest payment is discounted using the present value of an annuity function, adjusting the number of periods and the effective yield for the number of payments per year. Finally, the present value of the maturity value and the present value of the interest payments are added together, resulting in the present value of the bond issue.

pressure. N. One element of the fraud triangle or fraud diamond. Pressure is the motivation for perpetrating the fraud and is usually related to financial problems that are not easily explainable or sympathetic. Examples include drug use, gambling, and excessive spending. Synonymous with *nonshareable problem*.

pretax adjustment. N. Any accounting entry that affects income before taxes or income from continuing operations. This term signals that the item that produces the entry is not associated with discontinued operations or is not extraordinary.

pretax financial income. N. The income calculated using financial accounting rules—generally accepted accounting principles—but before figuring the income tax expense. See also *book income*.

previous-balance method. N. Procedures for calculating the interest on a debt (usually something like a credit card balance or a bank account) in which the charges are calculated on the balance at the end of the last period. The previous-balance method usually produces the highest amount of finance charges. Contrast with the adjusted-balance method, in which the interest rate is applied to the amount owed after all payments, purchases, and adjustments are made to the balance. Usually this method results in the lowest interest charges. Also contrast with the average-daily-balance method, in which the charges are calculated on a balance that is calculated from a weighted-average calculation of the outstanding amount each day of the period.

previous department costs. N. See *transferred-in costs*.

price-cash-flow ratio. N. A financial analysis tool that measures the amount investors will pay for one dollar of cash flow from a firm, and that indicates what investors think about the past performance of the firm and anticipated earnings. The formula is market price per share divided by cash flow per share. Cash flow per share is equal to net income plus depreciation and amortization expense, divided by the number of common shares outstanding.

price discrimination. N. An illegal act in which the same goods are priced differently for different customers. This does not apply to services.

price-driven costing. N. A procedure for designing and producing a product that starts with market research to determine what the customer wants and is willing to pay. The design and production is then planned to control costs to achieve a profit. Contrast with the method many companies use, in which the selling price is the sum of total cost plus a desired profit. Synonymous with *target costing*.

price-earnings ratio. N. A financial statistic that is calculated by dividing the market price of one share of a stock by the earnings per share number. The price-earnings ratio measures the market's perception of future earnings growth for that corporation. Synonymous with *earnings multiplier*. ABBRV. *P/E ratio*.

price gouging. N. A situation in which powerful companies increase prices unreasonably to take advantage of an event. Many people believe gas stations engage in price gouging when gas prices increase dramatically just before a holiday.

price-recovery component. N. Calculates the part of the change in profit from one period to another that is not attributable to changes in efficiency. The price-recovery component is calculated as the difference between the revenues of the first period and the second period less the difference between the cost of inputs from the first to the second period.

price risk. N. The ambiguity about future asset prices, particularly financial assets. Derivatives can help companies manage price risk.

price standards. N. One element necessary for developing standard costs per unit. Price standards are the amounts that should be paid for normal material, labor, and other resources put into the production process.

price variance. N. One factor in the total budget variance. The price-variance portion is equal to the difference between the actual and standard price per unit multiplied by the actual quantity of units produced. Synonymous with *rate variance*.

pricing model. N. Mathematical techniques used to value derivatives. The Black-Scholes model is one pricing model used to value stock options.

primary beneficiary. N. The investor that absorbs the majority of expected losses or the majority of expected residual returns associated with an investment. The primary beneficiary in a variable-interest entity must consolidate the entity in its financial statements.

primary markets. N. A type of capital market. A primary market is a physical or virtual location where an entity sells its own stock through a new stock issue. Buyers purchase stock from the issuing company in a primary market and the company receives the proceeds from the sale. Contrast with secondary markets, in which owners of financial instruments buy and sell among themselves, rather than from the issuing entity.

primary memory. N. See *random access memory*.

prime cost. N. The cost of direct materials and direct labor. Prime cost is a concept used in manufacturing.

prime rate. N. The rate of interest charged to the best borrowers. The prime rate is the same for all banks and is only available to large, stable corporations or other similar borrowers.

primitive security. N. An investment in which the return is based on the issuer's earnings or financial position. Contrast with a derivative security, in which the return or value of the security is based on situations outside the original issuer.

principal. N. In business, refers to the amount borrowed. The loan payment may include both principal and interest, and in that case principal refers to the amount that reduces the amount owed. The principal at the beginning of a loan is the amount borrowed. The principal balance of a loan is the amount that is still owed.

principal amount of a bond. N. See *maturity value of a bond*.

principal partner. N. Any partner in a partnership who owns 5% or more of the capital and profits.

principal-residence gain exclusion. N. The tax benefit available to homeowners that allows a single taxpayer to exclude from capital gains tax up to $250,000 of gain, and a couple to exclude up to

$500,000 of gain on the sale of a personal residence. The gain is computed as the adjusted basis of the home versus the proceeds of the sale. The adjusted basis is the purchase price plus the costs of major improvements. The proceeds of the sale are the selling price less the costs of selling (such as commissions and attorney's fees). Any amount in excess of the exclusion is treated as a long-term capital gain, for tax purposes. There is no minimum age required to take the exclusion.

prior-period adjustments. N. A correction of an error in any of the financial statements that have already been published by an entity. A prior-period adjustment appears on the statement of retained earnings or the statement of stockholders' equity, whichever one the entity presents. The adjustment amount is net of any tax effect and does not appear on the income statement.

prior-service cost. N. An increase in the pension obligation of an employer, resulting from a change in the pension plan, that gives employees credit for years of employment before the change in the plan. The new benefits are retroactive. For example, if the pension plan originally gave employees a lump-sum retirement payment equal to 10% of the highest salary earned by the employee, times the number of years worked, and the percentage was changed to 11%, that additional 1% on years prior to the year of change is prior-service cost.

private-activity bonds. N. Tax-exempt bonds that are used for the benefit of private businesses. Examples include municipal bonds that finance the construction of a manufacturing facility for private industry or for a sports stadium.

private company. N. A company that has a limited number of share-holders and whose stock is not traded on a public exchange. Private companies can be large or small. Synonymous with *privately held company*.

private enterprise. N. See *closed corporation*.

private letter ruling. N. A decision from the Internal Revenue Service on the tax treatment for a specific situation for a specific individual. The individual pays a fee for this service. Synonymous with *letter ruling*.

privately held company. N. See *private company*.

private markets. N. Physical or virtual locations in which parties to the transaction work out borrowing or equity transactions directly. Contrast with public markets, in which the financial instruments are standardized and the exchanges are structured and organized.

private nonoperating foundation. N. A type of charity that includes foundations, trusts, or similar entities that distribute funds to charitable organizations. The classification of an organization as a public charity is important for determining the deductibility of and the amount of the charitable deduction available to a taxpayer/donor. The Carnegie Foundation is an example of a private nonoperating foundation.

private placement. N. A method of selling securities that is not subject to Securities and Exchange Commission (SEC) public-offering regulations. Private placements can be sold to a limited number of investors having certain characteristics. Private placements are subject to SEC Regulation D. Synonymous with *exempt security*.

private-purpose trust funds. N. A type of fiduciary fund used in governmental accounting. The private-purpose trust fund is used when a government receives or sets aside assets for investment and the earnings from the investment are used for a designated purpose involving other organizations, citizens, or governments.

Private Securities Litigation Reform Act of 1995. N. A significant federal law that requires auditors to report any violation of securities laws to the management and the audit committee. If neither does anything in response, the auditor reports the violation to the board of directors if the violation is material. The board must notify the Securities and Exchange Commission (SEC) within one business day or the auditor is required to report the violation to the SEC.

probability-proportional-to-size sampling. N. A sampling method used in auditing for defining the population as the dollar amount of the account being tested. A sampling interval is calculated based on characteristics of the client, such as expected misstatement. The auditor uses a random start and then advances the amount of the calculated interval to get to a dollar in the account. The invoice, order, or customer associated with that dollar is then included in the sample. The auditor continues on another interval, choosing the item that is associated with that dollar. The larger the item, the more likely it is to be chosen for testing by the auditor, hence the name probability-proportional-to-size sampling. Synonymous with *dollar-unit sampling, cumulative-monetary-amount sampling, monetary-unit sampling, combined attributes–variables sampling.* ABBRV. *PPS.*

probate. N. The cost of managing estate assets and disposing of them. If assets are eliminated from the estate through gifts or trusts, the probate costs are lower.

proceeds. N. The amount equal to the selling price of an asset less any costs to sell. The amount in proceeds from the sale of a home is the sales price minus any commissions, fees, closing costs, repairs to meet local codes, etc. Synonymous with *net proceeds.*

process acceptance. N. Measures taken to prevent poor quality goods from being sent to the customer. Process acceptance involves checking work-in-process to see if it is acceptable.

process costing. N. A method of assigning costs in which costs are collected by process. Process costing is useful if the production involves items that are similar in the amounts of materials, labor, and overhead used.

process creation. N. Establishing a new set of activities that creates a new process for improving efficiency.

process improvement. N. A change in the way an entity operates that starts with an existing set of activities and makes incremental changes in the way things are done, so that the process becomes more efficient. Synonymous with *business reengineering.*

processing controls. N. The measures a company takes to make certain that once data is entered into the accounting information system, no errors are introduced during the processing of that data. Processing controls ensure that all the transactions are processed and that the computer does the processing correctly. Good processing controls play an important role in a good audit trail. See also *application controls.*

process innovation. N. A change in the way an entity operates that completely alters the existing set of activities that make up a process. Process innovation results in significant, rather than gradual, improved efficiency.

process-value analysis. N. A basic activity in activity-based management systems. Process-value analysis investigates sets of actions that form processes within the entity. Specifically, the investigation determines what causes the cost of the activity, exactly what actions or steps are involved in the process, and how well the process is working.

producer price index. N. A statistic published by the U.S. Bureau of Labor Statistics that measures the change in wholesale prices in the economy. ABBRV. *PPI.*

producing departments. N. Subunits of an organization that are directly involved in the production of the product or service. Contrast with support departments, which are not directly involved in the production of the product or service, but are necessary for producing departments to operate.

producing for inventory. N. Manufacturing more items than needed to meet the sales budget. Managers can increase operating income through inventory increases, because more fixed cost is in inventory rather than on the income statement. The cost of a unit does not affect income until it is sold.

product acceptance. N. Measures taken to prevent poor quality goods from being sent to customers. Product-acceptance actions include random testing of finished goods to see if they are acceptable.

product costs. N. The term used to identify costs that are part of inventory. Product costs are all the necessary costs involved in purchasing or making the products the company sells. They include materials, labor, purchase prices, freight charges (to get the materials on site), and other costs to convert the materials or items into products ready to sell. The classification of costs is significant because product costs only reduce income if the item is sold. If the item is not sold, the costs are on the balance sheet as the current asset inventory. See also *period costs*. Synonymous with *inventoriable costs*.

product differentiation. N. A strategy used in business that depends on customer perception of a higher quality product. The quality perception may include aspects beyond durability. It may involve uniqueness or stylishness. A product-differentiation strategy is distinct from a cost-leadership strategy, which focuses on low prices.

product financing arrangement. N. A method of borrowing to cover the cost of inventory without putting the liability for the loan on the books. Company X sells inventory to Company Z, agreeing to buy it back. Company Z borrows, using the inventory as collateral, and gives the proceeds of the borrowing to Company X as "payment" for the inventory. Company X repurchases the inventory, as promised, and the payments meet Company Z's loan payment obligations. The result is that Company X is financing inventory and Company Z has the inventory and liability on its balance sheet. If a time period and an adequate price is specified, Company X cannot avoid reporting the liability. Company Z is willing to do this because it may need more inventory, or because it may want a reciprocal agreement in the future.

production budget. N. Part of the master budget used to plan the timing and the amount of production needed to meet the sales budget and ending-inventory requirements.

production costs. N. Costs directly associated with actually manufacturing items or providing services that are the main operating activity of an entity. Financial reporting standards require that only direct materials, direct labor, and overhead be included in production costs. This classification of cost is used on the income statement in the cost of goods sold, and on the balance sheet in inventory. For internal reports, costs may be assigned differently, depending on the purpose of the report. See also *product costs*.

production department. N. See *operating department*.

production-phase revenue recognition. N. Including amounts in income prior to the sale at the completion of the production of the product. Production-phase revenue recognition occurs when a ready market exists, the goods are interchangeable, and prices are determinable. Companies that produce agricultural products and natural resources can use production-phase revenue recognition. Synonymous with *market-price method*.

production report. N. A document, used in a process-costing system, that identifies the units and costs for a single process. The production report shows the units transferred in and transferred out. The report also shows the costs that were transferred in, the costs that were added, and the costs that were transferred out. From this information, a unit cost is calculated.

production volume variance. N. See *fixed-overhead volume variance*.

productivity. N. (1) The efficient creation of goods or services in an organization. Productivity relates to using a minimum amount of the least-costly inputs for the production of goods or provision of services. Increased productivity means that more output is achieved with the same or lower inputs. (2) A measure of efficiency in business, calculated by dividing the output per period by the total hours worked per period. Productivity increases as a result of advances in technology.

productivity measurement. N. The attempt to estimate the amount of and direction of change in efficiency. Productivity measurement can be actual measurements to evaluate and manage changes for future performance, or it can be what-if analysis used for decision making. See also *partial-productivity measurement, total-productivity measurement*.

product-level activities. N. Actions performed for each product a business has. Product-level activities are distinct from unit-level, batch-level, and facility-level activities. Activity-based costing systems identify the level of an activity to build homogeneous cost pools—because costs in a homogeneous pool must be associated with activities performed at the same level. Activities that use overhead costs in the same proportion can be combined into the pool rate. Examples of product-level activities include marketing a product and developing product-testing procedures.

product life cycle. N. The time between the beginning of a product and its discontinuance. A product life cycle is similar to the lifetime of a person from birth to death.

product stewardship. N. The process of selling products that minimizes environmental damage. Product stewardship may focus on product design, production processes, packaging, and disposal issues.

profile measurement. N. An approach to total-productivity measurement. Profile measurement combines in one organized chart partial-productivity measurements for two time periods. Analysis then shows the trade-offs if ratios move in different directions.

profit. N. A general term that means the amount of earnings or the excess of revenue over expenses.

profitability. N. A business's capacity to earn income. Profitability can relate to performance in the past or to predictions for the future.

profitability ratios. N. Financial analysis tools that measure the success of companies at generating earnings. Profitability ratios are calculated using amounts from the financial statements and give information about the relationship between amounts on the financial statements. Analysts compare the relationships from different companies to evaluate the success or failure of those companies. Common profitability ratios are profit margin on sales, rate of return on assets, rate of return on common stock equity, earnings per share, price earnings, and payout.

profit-and-loss statement. N. See *income statement*.

profit center. N. A responsibility center in which the manager is held accountable for sales and costs.

profit-linked productivity measurement. N. Determining the amount of profit change that is due to changes in productivity. First, determine the input based on the current year's output and the base year's ratio. Dividing the current year's output by the base year's ratio results in the amount of input that would have been used if productivity had not changed. Then, calculate the cost of that supposed input amount. Do that for each input, and the sum is the total cost of inputs that would have been used for the current year's output if no change in productivity had occurred. Then, calculate the actual cost of the same inputs for the current year. The difference is a measure of the increase or decrease in profits from changes in efficiency.

profit margin. N. See *profit-margin-on-sales ratio.*

profit-margin-on-sales ratio. N. A measure of the return, or profit, a company earns on its sales. The formula is net income divided by net sales. If the ratio is 3.8, the interpretation is that every dollar of sales generates 3.8 cents of profit.

profit-sharing plan. N. A type of deferred compensation plan in which the employer contributes amounts to individual employees based on some established formula. For the benefits of the plan to receive favorable tax treatment, the profit-sharing plan must be qualified. See also *401(k), qualified plan.*

profits interest. N. The form of compensation that can be paid by a partnership to a service partner. A profits interest gives a service partner a share of future partnership profits but not of existing capital.

profit-split method. N. A method of determining transfer prices by allocating the profit from intercompany sales among members of the consolidated group in proportion to the value each member adds to the products. This method is rarely used.

profit-volume graph. N. A graph that plots the dependent variable, operating income, on the vertical axis versus the independent variable, number of units sold, on the horizontal axis. The intersection of the graphed line with the horizontal axis is the break-even number of units. The intersection of the graphed line with the vertical axis is the fixed-cost component.

pro forma. N. The presentation of financial statements based on assumptions different than those underlying the published statements. If a company changes from double-declining depreciation to straight-line depreciation, the pro forma amounts for all comparative years would show the income before extraordinary items, net income, and earnings per share as if straight-line depreciation had been used throughout. This allows the users of the financial statements to compare the performance without the confounding factor of a new method of depreciation.

pro forma financial statements. N. The income statement, balance sheet, statement of retained earnings, and statement of cash flows based on a set of events occurring, rather than actual historical data. Pro forma financial statements are often the output of the budgeting and planning process. Managers forecast the amounts on the financial statements to predict the need to raise additional funds or to comply with debt covenants.

program audit. N. A type of audit usually associated with government programs. A program audit involves checking that a program funded with government money is meeting the objectives of the grant. It focuses on effectiveness and compliance with the terms of the grant. Contrast with a performance audit, which examines how efficiently the objects are being achieved.

Program Evaluation and Review Technique. N. A system for efficiently managing a large project with many components. Program Evaluation and Review Technique relies on identifying the sequence of activities necessary for completion and the time needed to perform those activities. The first step is to determine the stages of the project, then order the activities necessary to achieve those stages, including an estimate of the time needed to complete each activity. The project manager can determine which activities can progress simultaneously to speed up the completion. The Program Evaluation and Review Technique method combines the stages, sequence, and activities in a diagram of arrows with time estimates (representing activities) and circles (representing stages). After the diagram is complete, the project manager can estimate the total time necessary to complete the project, taking into account activities that can be done at the same time. Program Evaluation and Review Technique is also useful for monitoring progress, because if an activity is completed later than scheduled, the manager can establish the new completion date. ABBRV. *PERT*.

program trading. N. A method of sending a buy or sell message regarding a stock, using a computer program. Investors—usually institutional investors—can set up a trigger that automatically sells stock when it reaches a certain price. Program trading causes such dramatic moves in the market that when trading reaches a certain volume, the market is closed.

progress billings. N. An account, used in construction accounting, that represents the amount billed to the customer.

progressive tax. N. A tax in which the rate increases as income increases. The federal income tax is progressive because for single taxpayers, the rate on the first $6,000 is 10%, and on the next $22,400 the rate is 15%. As income increases, the rate continues to rise to 27%, 30%, 35%, and 38.6%. Complete information for all income levels and filing statuses is available at www.irs.gov/formspubs.

projected balance sheet. N. See *budgeted balance sheet*.

projected benefit obligation. N. The present value of all pension benefits earned by employees, as calculated by an actuary. This calculation includes all employees and all benefits, even if the employee is not guaranteed those benefits because of vesting. Projected benefit obligation is the largest measure of pension obligation, because for benefits based on years of service and salary level at retirement, the calculation uses estimates of those high, end-of-career salary levels. The only difference between accumulated benefit obligation and projected benefit obligation is the salary level used to calculate the pension benefits. Accumulated benefit obligation uses the current salary, and projected benefit obligation uses the estimated final salary. ABBRV. *PBO*.

project-financing arrangements. N. A type of off-balance-sheet financing in which two or more organizations form a new company to build a project used by all organizations involved. The new company borrows to build the project and repays the debt with the proceeds of the project. The forming organizations guarantee the debt and must disclose that, but the loan for the project is a liability only on the new company's balance sheet—not on the balance sheets of the forming organizations. The effect is that the forming organizations have financed the new project without recording the liability for the borrowing.

promissory note. N. A written promise to pay a certain amount at a certain date. A promissory note is similar to a check, which can be cashed at a future date.

property dividends. N. Distributions to owners that are payable in assets other than cash. First, the assets are adjusted to the fair value, which sometimes involves a gain. Then retained earnings is reduced by the fair value of the property being distributed as the property dividends. Synonymous with *dividends in kind*.

property factor. N. A factor used in apportioning business income among states. The property factor is equal to property within the state divided by total property. The property amount is measured as the average total value for land, buildings, machinery, inventory, and equipment physically located in the state. This factor includes leased property, too. See also *Uniform Division of Income for Tax Purposes Act*.

property, plant, and equipment. N. A noncurrent asset on the balance sheet representing the historical cost of the assets used in the operating activities of the business. Assets in this category usually last a relatively long time and are depreciated over the time of use. Examples include land, buildings, machinery, and furniture. Synonymous with *plant assets, fixed assets, noncurrent operating assets*. ABBRV. *PP&E*.

property, plant, and equipment, net. N. The historical cost of assets used in the operating activities of a business, reduced by the amount of accumulated depreciation associated with those assets.

proportional tax. N. See *flat tax*.

proprietary funds. N. A set of accounts used in governmental accounting to measure the performance of a business-type activity by a government. A city's water treatment facility would be accounted for using a proprietary fund, because the revenue source for the cost of the service comes from charges for water use. The focus of proprietary funds involves measuring the relationship between costs of providing a service and the collections from the users of the service. Unlike a for-profit business, the proprietary fund is supposed to break even, not run a deficit or a surplus.

proprietary view of the firm. N. A perspective that emphasizes the equity of a firm. The defining characteristic of the company is the owners' investment. The accounting equation for the proprietary view is assets minus liabilities equals owners' equity. Contrast with the entity view of the firm, which focuses on assets used to carry out business activities. The accounting equation for the entity view is assets equals liabilities plus owners' equity.

proprietorship. N. See *sole proprietorship*.

pro rata. N. A proportional allocation.

pro rata share for S corporation shareholders. N. Used to determine the pass-through amount for shareholders in an S corporation. This calculation is based on the per share basis, not by the individual shareholder. The income or loss is evenly divided among each day in the year. The number of shares outstanding each day gets an even share of the amount allocated to the day. Each shareholder receives the total of the daily allocations for the time the stock was owned on the Schedule K-1.

prorate. N. To allocate in proportion to something else, such as time. If a cable television charge is $50 per month, and the installation occurred with only five days left in the month, the company should prorate the charge by dividing the $50 by the number of days in the month and then multiplying that amount by five.

prospectus. N. A required document for companies wanting to issue new securities. The prospectus contains information on the company, including the major stockholders, the officers, and the planned use of the proceeds from the sale of the securities. Audited financial statements are also a required part of the prospectus.

proxy. N. A certificate giving someone the power to vote in place of the owner of shares of stock. The vote can be on specified issues or on the membership of the board of directors. A proxy fight happens when a group tries to obtain proxies from many shareholders to push a specific agenda, get rid of current management, or pack the board of directors with like-minded members.

PTP. ABBRV. Publicly traded partnership.

public accountant. N. A general term for noncertified public accountant (CPA) accountants. In some states, a license is available for non-CPA accountants.

public accounting. N. The career in which accountants provide audits and other services for businesses. Contrast with private accounting, in which accountants are employees of a business and provide services only to that business.

public charity. N. A type of charity that includes churches, educational institutions, hospitals, medical schools, governmental units, and organizations supported by the government or the public. The classification of an organization as a public charity is important for determining the deductibility and the amount of the charitable deduction available to a taxpayer/donor.

public company. N. A business that is organized as a corporation, with stock that is owned by many different investors and that can be purchased by anyone.

public limited company. N. The Irish or British equivalent of a public company or corporation in the United States. ABBRV. *PLC*.

publicly traded partnership. N. Any partnership that sells its partnership sales on any organized exchange, either initially or as a secondary market. The Internal Revenue Service made this ruling to stop corporations from masquerading as partnerships in order to preserve the pass-through benefits. ABBRV. *PTP*.

public markets. N. Physical or virtual locations in which standardized financial instruments, such as corporate bonds or common stock, are bought and sold on an organized, structured exchange. Contrast with private markets, in which the parties to the transaction work directly with one another to accomplish the exchange, and the financial instruments take many forms.

public sector corporation. N. An organization that uses a corporate form but is owned by a government. An example of a public sector corporation is the Federal Deposit Insurance Corporation.

purchase commitments. N. A contract in which a buyer agrees to purchase inventory from a seller over a future time period. No accounting entries are made because no goods have been shipped, the price is not predetermined, and the contract can be canceled by either party. The buyer should provide information on the contract in the notes to the financial statements. If more details, such as prices and quantities, are specified in the contract, the buyer only needs to make an entry if the specified price is more than the current market price. Then the buyer recognizes a loss on the income statement. Purchase commitments are a type of executory contract in which neither party has performed, but has only agreed to perform in the future. See also *mutually unperformed contract*.

purchase discounts. N. The dollar amount that a purchaser can deduct from the invoice cost of items bought on credit because of payment within a certain time period.

purchase method of accounting. N. The generally accepted accounting principles requirements for accounting for business combinations.

purchase returns. N. The inventory items that a company returns to the seller. The dollar value of purchase returns reduces the cost of goods sold, either directly (in a perpetual system), or indirectly, through reduced purchases (in a periodic system).

purchases journal. N. A journal that contains a chronological record of all credit purchases made by a company. See also *journal*.

purchasing cycle. N. A cycle that begins with a request by an employee for goods or services and ends with payment of cash to the supplier of the goods or services received. The purchasing cycle tracks purchases of goods and services and amounts owed. It also maintains vendor records and controls inventory levels. The correct amount of payment must be made at the right time to the right vendor.

purchasing power. N. A measure of the value of money based on the amount of goods or services it buys. Synonymous with *buying power*.

purchasing-power bond. N. See *indexed bond*.

purchasing-power gains and losses. N. The change in the amount of goods and services that dollars can buy because of inflation or deflation. For example, if an investor buried $10,000 in his or her backyard in 1970 as a way to save for retirement, the investor would have a significant purchasing-power loss.

pure rate of interest. N. A component of the interest rate charged by a lender that is the actual return a lender expects, assuming no risk of nonpayment and no inflation. The pure rate of interest is usually considered to be 2%–4%.

push-down accounting. N. A method of valuing assets on a subsidiary's separate financial statements. Normally, the subsidiary's separate financial statements are left at book value; when the subsidiary is consolidated with the parent's financial statements, the items are listed at the fair market value for the time of acquisition. Push-down accounting adjusts the subsidiary book values to the fair market value for the time of acquisition, then the separate subsidiary financial statements present those amounts. The Securities and Exchange Commission requires push-down accounting in some instances.

push-through system. N. A term used to describe a traditional manufacturing system that produces goods to meet anticipated customer demand. Contrast with a demand-pull system, which produces goods only when they are needed by customers.

putable bond. N. A financial instrument that allows the buyer of a bond to sell it back to the issuer for a specified price prior to the maturity date.

put option. N. The right, but not the obligation, to sell a specified quantity of an asset at a specified date or during a specified time period, for a specified price. Contrast with a call option, which is the right to buy an asset at a specified price in the future.

puttable swap. N. A swap in which one of the parties can choose to discontinue the arrangement before the initial time period has expired.

QEE. ABBRV. Qualified education expenses.

Q sub. ABBRV. Qualified Subchapter S Subsidiary.

QTPs. ABBRV. Qualified tuition plans. See *529 plan*.

qualified audit report. N. The formal judgment made by a certified public accountant firm after auditing an organization. The qualified audit report is a red flag for readers. It signals that the organization did not follow generally accepted accounting principles in one situation, did not provide adequate disclosure, or did not allow the auditors access to some aspect necessary for the audit. The audit report is included in the required Securities and Exchange Commission filings and in the annual report of the organization. Synonymous with *qualified opinion*.

qualified distribution. N. A pension distribution that is eligible for preferred tax treatment because it meets certain criteria such as time in the retirement account or receipt after age 59½.

qualified education expenses. N. Expenses that include tuition, room and board, fees, tutoring, services for special-needs students, books, supplies, computer hardware, software, Internet access, and transportation. ABBRV. *QEE*.

qualified-family-owned-business exclusion. N. The amount of value, from a closelyheld family business, that can be removed from the estate. This exclusion is supposed to help family businesses avoid having to sell a business to pay estate taxes.

qualified nonrecourse financing. N. Not included in the calculation of the at-risk amount for a partner. Qualified nonrecourse financing is the amount of mortgage liability for which a partner is not liable. The mortgage must be for real estate and from a commercial financial institution. While this amount is included in the outside basis of the partners, it is not part of the at-risk amount.

qualified opinion. N. See *qualified audit report.*

qualified pension plan. N. Pension plans, meeting Internal Revenue Service requirements, that give an employer a tax deduction for cash contributions made to a pension fund and that allow the pension fund earnings to be tax-free.

qualified plan. N. A type of deferred compensation plan in which the investment return qualifies as tax-free. A qualified plan must be managed and controlled by a trustee who is not affiliated with the business. The benefits of the plan have to be available to virtually all full-time employees at a relatively equal level of benefit.

qualified-retirement-savings-contributions credit. N. A type of nonrefundable personal tax credit that reduces the amount of taxes the taxpayer must pay. The credit is equal to a percentage based on adjusted gross income times the amount of retirement savings. The retirement savings equals the amount the taxpayer contributes to an individual retirement account, a 401(k) plan, a 403(b) plan, or another plan. This credit is only available to individual taxpayers filing a joint return with less than $52,000 in adjusted gross income, head-of-household taxpayers with less than $39,000 in adjusted gross income, or any other filing status with less than $26,000 in adjusted gross income. The taxpayer may not be a dependent on another tax return or a full-time student. The total amount of all personal tax credits taken by a taxpayer in one year cannot be more than the tax owed plus the tentative alternative minimum tax.

Qualified Subchapter S Subsidiary. N. A special type of corporation for tax purposes that allows an S corporation to have S corporation status even if it is owned by another S corporation. ABBRV. *Q Sub.*

qualified trust to benefit a minor. N. A method of transferring gifts to children that avoids gift tax and safeguards the assets from childish waste. A qualified trust to benefit a minor must be irrevocable and income or principal may be distributed from the trust assets to a child under 21. The assets left in the trust when the child is 21 become the property of the child, and if the child dies before turning 21, the trust assets remain in the child's estate rather than going back to the originator of the trust. A key part of setting up a trust for the benefit of a child is establishing the child's present interest in the gift if the child's use of the trust assets is limited. The qualified trust to benefit a minor accomplishes this.

qualified tuition plans. N. See *529 plan*. ABBRV. *QTPs*.

quality of conformance. N. A part of customer satisfaction that deals with how well a product compares to the order specifications.

quality of design. N. An aspect of quality that emphasizes how well a product meets customer expectations. Computer makers realized that few new computer buyers wanted or needed a floppy disk drive, and it has become optional equipment. Instead, new computers have combination DVD-CD drives standard. The design changed to meet the needs and wants of the customer.

quality of earnings. N. A characteristic of a company's income with high quality being income that is not managed or manipulated, representing a sustainable, realistic measure of the company's performance for the accounting period.

quality product or service. N. A product or service that meets the customer's expectations. Companies need to produce items or provide services that are in line with what the customer thinks has been purchased in order to achieve customer satisfaction. Customers' expectations are based on performance, aesthetics, serviceability, features, reliability, durability, fitness for use, and how well the product meets specifications. Increases in quality can lead to increases in profitability.

quantity standards. N. One element necessary for developing standard costs per unit. Quantity standards specify the amount of material, labor, or other resource input into the production process that is the normal amount needed for production. The quantity standard serves as a measure of efficiency if the standard quantity of materials is used to produce a product or service.

quantity variance. N. See *usage variance.*

quarterly report. N. See *10-Q.*

quasi reorganization. N. A procedure that eliminates a retained deficit without liquidating the corporation and starting over again. This method is used if a company with a retained deficit has overcome past problems and has a future. Two types of quasi reorganizations exist. Deficit reclassification reduces the retained deficit by reducing additional paid in capital. Accounting reorganization starts with restating assets and liabilities to current values, then adjusts the retained deficit in an equal amount. If a deficit still remains, that is reduced just like deficit reclassification, by reducing additional paid in capital. Companies that use quasi reorganization must disclose that fact for ten years in the notes to the financial statements.

quick asset. N. A subset of current assets including cash, receivables, and marketable securities. Quick assets do not include the current assets of inventory and prepaid items.

quick ratio. N. A measure of liquidity that compares the sum of cash, accounts receivable, and marketable securities to total current liabilities. Synonymous with *acid test ratio.*

quoted risk-free rate. N. See *risk-free rate.*

R

Racketeer Influenced and Corrupt Organizations Act. N. A federal law established in 1970 to enable the prosecution of organized crime even when it is involved in a legitimate business. The Racketeer Influenced and Corrupt Organizations Act prohibits using income from criminal activity to acquire legitimate businesses, and prohibits legitimate businesses from being involved in organized crime. ABBRV. *RICO*.

RAM. ABBRV. Random access memory.

R&D. ABBRV. Research and development costs.

random access memory. N. The part of the central processing unit of a computer that stores data and programs. Random access memory is measured in megabytes (millions of bytes), and each byte holds one letter, number, or punctuation mark in memory. Adequate random access memory is necessary for software to operate efficiently and quickly. Synonymous with *primary memory*. ABBRV. *RAM*.

random-based selection. N. A method of choosing some items from a group or population in which each item has the same chance of being chosen as every other item.

random-walk theory. N. An explanation of the movement of stock prices. Random-walk theory proposes that it is not possible to predict stock price through the analysis of past behavior, because prices move without a pattern, in a random manner.

rate of return on common-stock equity. N. A measure of profitability from the common shareholders' view. The ratio indicates how much income was generated by each dollar of shareholder investment. The formula is net income less preferred dividends divided by average common stockholders' equity. Average common stockholders' equity includes additional paid in capital and common stock accounts. See also *Du Pont equation*.

rate variance. N. See *price variance*.

ratio analysis. N. A method of investigating and assessing the strength of an entity by reviewing relationships among amounts on the financial statements. Ratio analysis involves numerous established ratios that try to measure the liquidity, profitability, efficiency, and long-term solvency of an entity. The ratios are compared to other organizations or to average ratios for organizations in the same type of business to evaluate the entity. Synonymous with *financial-statement analysis*.

rationalization. N. One element of the fraud triangle or fraud diamond. Rationalization is the ability of a fraudster to explain or justify a fraud. Examples include low pay, just borrowing, and saving the jobs of coworkers.

raw materials inventory. N. A type of inventory that consists of the component materials a manufacturer keeps on hand for use in the production of the products the business sells. Raw materials are directly involved in the production process and are usually visible in the product. Synonymous with *direct-materials inventory*.

real account. N. See *balance sheet account*.

real estate investment trusts. N. A type of closed-end fund in which the investment is in real estate if the real estate investment trust (REIT) is an equity trust, or in mortgages or building loans if it is a mortgage trust. If REITs act as pass-through-type entities and distribute 95% of their income, then the REITs themselves are tax-free. ABBRV. *REITs*.

realizable. ADJ. A characteristic of revenue that is required for addition to income. The payment or promise to pay is easily converted to cash.

realized external failure costs. N. The costs of actions or efforts to deal with contaminants already released into the environment and paid for by the organization producing the contaminant.

realized gain or loss for tax purposes. N. The difference between the proceeds of a sale or exchange and the adjusted basis of the asset. The proceeds include not only the cash received, but also the fair market value of property received, and any debt that the buyer takes over.

real property. N. Any asset that consists of land and any buildings on the land. The opposite of real property is personal property, which includes everything that is not land or buildings.

real rate of interest. N. The return earned by lenders after removing the effects of inflation. The real rate of interest is the difference between the stated interest rate and the inflation rate.

recapitalization. N. Changing the capital structure of a company. The most common type of recapitalization is the exchange of debt for equity shares through convertible debt or the payment of debt with shares of stock. Recapitalization reduces the cash outflow for interest payments.

recapture of depreciation. N. A provision that changes the tax treatment of long-term capital gain to ordinary gain. The recapture of depreciation applies when a taxpayer sells an asset, usually real estate that meets certain criteria, and calculates the gain as the difference between the proceeds of the sale and the original cost of the asset. Normally, if the asset was held for more than a year, the gain would be a long-term capital gain, which is taxed at a lower rate than ordinary gains. If, however, the taxpayer has used an accelerated form of depreciation, then the part of the gain from the sale is treated as an ordinary gain. The amount that is ordinary gain is equal to the difference between the accelerated depreciation taken and the amount of depreciation that would have been taken if the taxpayer had used straight-line depreciation. Recapture only applies to individual, not corporate, taxpayers and to property that was put into service before 1986. Since 1986, noncorporate taxpayers have had to use a type of straight-line depreciation specified in the tax code.

receipt. N. Written evidence of payment. The receipt documents that payment was made and received. It indicates the date and amount of the payment.

receivables. N. Shorthand for all assets with "receivable" in the title. Receivables are usually classified as current assets on the balance sheet. See also *accounts receivable, notes receivable*.

receivables collection period. N. See *average days to collect receivables*.

receivable turnover. N. A financial analysis ratio that evaluates liquidity. The formula is net sales divided by average accounts receivable, net. This indicates the number of times receivables are collected in a period. More meaningful is the average days to collect receivables, which divides 365 or 360 by the receivable turnover. The result is the average days it takes to collect a receivable.

recession. N. Economic decline that is measured by a decrease in the value of goods and services produced from one quarter to the next.

reciprocal method of allocation. N. A method of allocating support-department costs to products. The reciprocal method assigns support-department costs to other support departments first. This process recognizes all interactions among support departments and does not use a hierarchy like the sequential method. After the total cost for the support departments is computed, those costs are allocated to producing departments, and finally to products. See also *sequential method of allocation, direct method of allocation.*

reclassification adjustment. N. An adjustment made to unrealized gains or losses on available-for-sale investments, when the investment is sold. The accounting for available-for-sale investments requires that any changes in market value during the year are shown in unrealized gains or losses, in comprehensive income. When an available-for-sale investment is sold, the unrealized gain or loss is reversed and titled a reclassification adjustment.

recognition. N. The recording of an event or transaction in the accounting records. The amounts will affect the financial statements for the accounting period.

recomputation. N. A classification of audit techniques that involves arithmetic procedures performed on data to verify the result obtained originally. While the technique provides factual evidence of accuracy, it supposes that the data involved were correct in the first place.

reconciliation method. N. See *indirect method of determining cash from operating activities.*

recourse. N. A condition of selling receivables to a bank in which the responsibility for customer nonpayment is determined. "With recourse" means the company will buy back any receivables that are uncollectible. "Without recourse" means the bank has to absorb the loss for the uncollectible receivables.

recourse liability. N. A personal obligation of a partner that is assumed by a partnership, but at least one partner still has personal liability for the obligation.

recoverability test. N. The process for determining if an asset is impaired (meaning the owner must reduce the balance sheet value). First, calculate the net cash flows from the asset. This includes cash flows from the use of the asset and from the sale at the time of disposal. Then, compare the undiscounted net cash flows to the carrying value, or balance sheet value, of the asset.

recovery-of-basis doctrine. N. Asserts that taxpayers can recover their investment without paying tax on the amount. If an investor buys $4,000 of a stock and holds on to it for three years and then sells it for $4,000, the investor does not have to include the $4,000 in gross income because it is a recovery of basis. If an investor buys a rental house for $190,000 and takes a depreciation deduction of $9,500 each year for five years until the house is sold, the investor has already recovered $47,500 of the $190,000 basis in the house. The capital gain calculation reduces the basis by the amount of depreciation, thereby increasing the capital gain.

recovery-of-investment test. N. One of the four capitalization criteria for leases. If the present value of the minimum lease payments is equal to or greater than 90% of the fair value of the asset, the lease is a capital lease because it meets the recovery-of-investment test. The choice of discount rate is important in this test because an unusually high rate produces a very low present value, thus avoiding the 90% threshold for capitalizing the lease. Too low a discount rate could produce a present value that is higher than the fair value, and the lessee cannot record an asset at more than fair value. The rule for picking a discount rate requires that the lower of the incremental borrowing rate of the lessee or the rate that is implicit in the lease, if known, is the rate used in discounting the minimum lease payments.

recurring item exception. N. A modification of the all-events test to allow tax deductibility if economic performance will happen within 8.5 months after the end of the taxable year. The liability must still meet the existence test and the measurement test.

redeemable bonds. N. See *callable bonds*.

redeemable preferred stock. N. See *callable preferred stock*.

red herring. N. *(Slang)* A preliminary prospectus that has large red printing on the cover, indicating that the Securities and Exchange Commission is still reviewing the registration materials filed by the company.

red-line method. N. A method of inventory control for indicating when to reorder an inventory item. The red-line method puts an indicator, such as a red line at a certain height, on the container holding the inventory item. When the quantity of inventory reaches the indicator, more of that inventory item is ordered.

reengineering. N. Analyzing and adjusting business processes to improve efficiency, reduce costs, and improve customer satisfaction. Reengineering activities rely on creative thinking involving small changes or complete reorganization to improve quality.

refunding of debt. N. Repaying existing debt and replacing it with new debt. Companies find it advantageous to pay off higher interest debt and replace it with new debt at a lower rate.

registered bonds. N. Bonds issued to a particular person that pay interest to that person. To sell the bond, the registered owner must return the bond certificate to the issuer and have the issuer send a new certificate to the new owner.

registration statement. N. A set of required documents, including a prospectus, that a company files before issuing new stock to the public. Synonymous with *Form S-1, S-1 registration*.

regression. N. A statistical method that determines the stable relationship between independent and dependent variables. Many spreadsheet programs have built-in regression functions.

regressive tax. N. A tax in which the rate decreases as the amount of income increases. The Social Security tax is a regressive tax, because below $87,000 the rate is 7.65%, and above $87,000 the rate is only 1.45%.

Regulation A. N. The Securities and Exchange Commission rules that apply to security offerings of less than $1,500,000.

Regulation D. N. A securities and Exchange Commission regulation that applies to private placement exemptions. See also *private placement*.

Regulation Q. N. A Securities and Exchange Commission regulation that, until 1980, limited the interest rate banks could pay depositors. Regulation Q was initiated in response to the bank failures of the Great Depression. It was repealed in 1980, when it became apparent that innovations like money market funds and gifts for deposits were circumventing the intent of the law.

rehabilitation credit. N. A type of general business tax credit for restoration of older factories and business buildings and for certified historic buildings. The expenditures must be more than the cost of the building or $5,000, whichever is larger, and are calculated as 20% of the costs of restoring the building. The credit offsets tax liability and reduces the depreciable basis of the property. If the property is sold within five years from the time the credit is taken, part of the credit is recaptured. The rehabilitation credit is one of several general business credits, and the total of all these credits cannot be more than an amount based on the net income for the year. The amount of excess can be carried back one year and forward twenty years.

reimbursed employee expense. N. A cost incurred by an employee that is necessary to the performance of the job, for which an employer compensates the employee. The employee can take a deduction for these expenses, but must also include the reimbursement as ordinary income.

reinvestment-rate risk. N. The danger that when a debt security matures, possible investments will be at a lower rate of interest. Short-term debt is subject to reinvestment-rate risk. Contrast with interest-rate risk, which is the chance that while an investor holds a debt security, the interest rate will rise, making the investor's security less valuable. Interest-rate risk is associated with long-term debt.

REITs. ABBRV. Real estate investment trusts.

related party transactions. N. Occur when a company does business with an individual connected to the company. Examples are loans to executives and sales of assets to directors. For tax purposes, a related party is a stockholder who owns more than 50% of the outstanding stock of a corporation. The definition, though, includes not only the individual's stock ownership, but also the family's ownership (including siblings, a spouse, children, grandchildren, and ancestors). Companies must disclose related party transactions because the normal business controls are missing in these situations. Usually, both participants in a business transaction are looking out for their own interests, and that tension results in a fair value. See also *arm's length transactions*.

relevance. N. One of the primary qualitative characteristics of accounting information. Accounting information that will make a difference in a decision is relevant to that decision. See also *conceptual framework*.

relevant cost. N. A type of cost used in decision making. A relevant cost is one that is different for alternative solutions. The decision must take into account the relevant costs to determine the most advantageous decision.

relevant range. N. The range of the level of operating activities within which cost patterns are stable.

reliability. N. A primary qualitative characteristic of accounting information. Accounting information that is reasonably accurate, is unbiased, and that conveys the true meaning of the financial information demonstrates reliability. See also *conceptual framework*.

remainder interest. N. The right to receive ownership of a property after the death of an individual who receives the income from the property. The individual who receives the income has the income interest in the property during his or her lifetime.

renewals. N. Overhauls of existing property, plant, and equipment that are usually expensed.

rent payments. N. The compensation paid to a lessor by a lessee for the use of an asset in a lease agreement. The lease can structure the payments any way acceptable to the parties to the lease. The most common is equal annual or monthly payments.

reorder point. N. The level of inventory that triggers placing an order for inventory. The average units of an item that the company uses per day times the lead time (the number of days it takes to get the ordered items) calculates the reorder point. If demand for the inventory is not predictable, an additional amount is added to the level of inventory triggering the inventory order.

replacement-chain approach. N. A method of evaluating alternative investments for projects that have different project lives. The replacement-chain approach works under the assumption that the project is repeated for another cycle until all projects have the same length. This approach is useful for mutually exclusive projects. Synonymous with *common-life approach*.

replacement cost. N. A measure of an asset's value based on the cost to buy the asset at the time of measurement. Replacement cost is used for asset value under the current-cost method of accounting.

replacements. N. See *improvements and replacements*.

report form of the balance sheet. N. A presentation format of the balance sheet that lists assets, followed by liabilities and equities. See also *account form of the balance sheet*.

reporting currency. N. The currency used for the financial statements and regulatory requirements. The reporting currency in the United States is the dollar.

reporting entity. N. The company or companies for which the financial statements present information. Generally accepted accounting principles require consolidation of subsidiaries with parent companies in some situations, even though the companies are legally separate organizations and operate separately. A change in reporting entity (in other words, a different set of companies is covered by the consolidated financial statements this year from those included in previous years) requires that past years' information presented in the financial statements is restated so that it is comparable.

repos. N. An overnight loan using government securities as collateral. A dealer sells a customer the securities with an agreement to buy them back the next day at a price that is higher (to include the overnight interest). Repos are low-risk because government securities are involved. Synonymous with *repurchase agreements*. ABBRV. *RPs*.

representational faithfulness. N. A subcharacteristic of accounting information that explains reliability. Accounting information that would logically be interpreted by a reader in a way that is consistent with the reality of the business results. Accounting information that does not try to mislead or obscure the true outcomes. See also *reliability, conceptual framework.*

repurchase agreements. N. See *repos.*

required rate of return. N. The lowest satisfactory annual rate of return on an investment. See also *hurdle rate.* Synonymous with *opportunity cost of capital.* ABBRV. *RRR.*

requisite service period. N. The time an employee must work to become eligible to exercise a stock option. See also *derived service period, explicit service period, implicit service period, service period for stock options.*

requisition. N. A formal request for authorization to buy goods or services and to have the organization be responsible for payment. The requisition is an important document in the audit trail because it verifies that the organization needed the purchase for business purposes. The production department sends a requisition for materials to be used for manufacturing products. The purchasing department authorizes and completes the purchase, and eventually the organization pays the invoice after receiving the goods.

resale-price method. N. One of three methods allowed by the Internal Revenue Service of determining transfer prices. The resale-price method backs into the transfer price by starting with the price at which the division receiving the transferred good sells that item and then deducting the normal profit. The normal profit multiplies the gross profit percentage by the selling price.

research and development costs. N. Expenditures made in attempt to discover new knowledge and transform that knowledge into a product or service for sale or use. Any costs during the research and development phase should be expensed immediately, not capitalized. This accounting requirement is based on the problem of determining the value of the asset being created and is consistent with conservatism. ABBRV. *R&D*.

research credit. N. A type of general business credit that allows business credits for increasing research activities and for basic research. The credit for increasing research activities gives businesses a tax credit for 20% of the amount of research costs above the business's average. The calculation of the average is detailed in IRS Section 41. The credit for basic research activities is only available to some corporations that pay organizations, such as universities, to do research for scientific advancement rather than for a specific product or business service.

reseller exemption. N. The code or certificate that excuses a business from paying sales tax on a purchase because the intent is to sell the item to a consumer. Sales tax is usually paid only by the final consumer.

reserve. N. A term that should only be used for appropriation of retained earnings. Historically, companies have set aside amounts as reserves for future use in managing earnings. For that reason, the accounting profession discourages the use of reserves.

reserve borrowing capacity. N. The amount of additional debt that a firm can take on, at a reasonable interest rate, if a good opportunity arises. Firms reserve borrowing capacity so that they do not have to sell stock to finance a new project, which results in sharing the increased profits with more stockholders.

reserved fund balance. N. An account used in governmental accounting to show amounts that must be used to satisfy certain obligations, that are set aside to comply with legal requirements, or that are associated with commitments like outstanding purchase orders or loans to other funds. The reserved fund balance is shown after liabilities on the balance sheet for the governmental unit.

reset date. N. The date on which a variable rate loan or derivative adjusts to a new rate.

residual audit risk. N. Determined after the auditor has analyzed specific account balances for other identifiable risks associated with an account, such as control risk and environment risk. The residual audit risk affects the setting of the level of detection risk. If the residual audit risk is high, the controls may be weak and the account is susceptible to errors. The auditor then sets the detection risk as low, so that more testing of the account balance reduces the risk of errors going undetected.

residual dividend model. N. A method of determining the amount of dividends to be paid. The residual dividend model calculates the amount of retained earnings needed to fund capital projects during the next year. That amount is deducted from the current year's earnings and the remainder, the residual, is paid out in dividends.

residuary legacy. N. A distribution of personal property, according to the provisions of a will, that involves everything left after all other distributions.

resource-management cycle. N. A part of the business process involving human-resource management and fixed-asset management. Human-resource management includes the hiring and training of employees, payroll, and personnel reporting requirements. Fixed-asset management involves keeping the records on fixed-assets purchases, maintenance, valuation, depreciation, and disposal.

responsibility accounting. N. A system that measures performance against some benchmark and rewards the individuals involved. The elements of responsibility accounting involve the following: (a) determining who is accountable for performance; (b) setting up the criteria for measuring performance; (c) comparing actual performance to established criteria; and, (d) rewarding those responsible for meeting or exceeding desired performance levels. Responsibility accounting may be either functional-based or activity-based. See also *functional-based responsibility accounting, activity-based responsibility accounting*.

responsibility center. N. Part of an organization that is under the supervision of a manager who is accountable for that center's performance.

restatement. N. Publishing financial statements with changes to the original amounts. Several large companies issued restatements after the passing of the Sarbanes-Oxley Act, which required company executives to pledge to the accuracy of financial statements.

restoration costs. N. The costs of returning the area from which natural resources were removed back to a useable state. Restoration costs are included in the depletable base of the asset.

restricted cash. N. Amounts of cash that are set aside for a specific purpose, such as minimum balances in checking or savings accounts. If the cash is legally restricted, then the entity should separate it from the cash balance on the balance sheet, indicating that it is restricted.

restricted property plans. N. A device used by corporations to provide additional incentive to executives by granting them shares of stock in the employing company, but not allowing the sale of that stock for a given time period. When the time period expires, the executive is taxed on the market value of the stock and the corporation can deduct an equal amount as compensation expense. Usually, if the executive leaves before the time period is up, the stock is forfeited.

restricted stock. N. Stock given or sold at a discount to employees, whose sale is limited. The limits usually prohibit the sale within a specified period of time and require that the stock be returned if the employee leaves the employer during that time.

restructuring of debt. N. See *troubled-debt restructuring*.

restructuring reserve. N. Amounts set aside in a liability account when the costs of closing plants, consolidating operations, and workforce layoffs are expensed. When the company determines that to be competitive and efficient it must restructure, generally accepted accounting principles require that an estimate of total costs be expensed in the current period. The other half of the entry is to a liability account called restructuring reserve. In the future, as the company experiences the actual costs, the liability is reduced.

retail-inventory method. N. A method of determining inventory in retail operations, without a detailed physical count of the inventory items. The method is based on the relationship between the total cost of goods available for sale at wholesale (or the purchase price) and at retail (or selling price). Start with cost of goods available for sale at the retail value and deduct sales for the period. The result is the retail value of ending inventory. Then, calculate the percentage of sales price that is cost, by dividing the total cost of goods available for sale at the purchase price by the total cost of goods available for sale at retail. Multiply the retail value of ending inventory by that percentage to get an estimate of ending inventory at cost. Businesses can use the retail method for year-end reporting. The physical count of inventory goes faster at the retail price, which is on the item, than at cost, which would require the counter to look up the cost for each item. See also *conventional-retail-inventory method, LIFO-retail-inventory method*.

retained deficit. N. Negative retained earnings as the result of accumulated losses. Companies with a retained deficit may be prevented from paying dividends by the state law governing the corporate charter.

retained earnings. N. An account in the stockholders' equity section of the balance sheet that is the total of all income earned over the life of the organization, minus any distributions to owners made during the same time. Synonymous with *earned capital*.

retained-earnings breakpoint. N. A calculation that finds the maximum amount of capital a corporation can raise before it must sell new common stock. The formula for the retained-earnings breakpoint equals the amount of net income that will be retained in the next year divided by the percent of common equity existing in the firm's capital structure. The percent of common equity in the firm's capital structure, called the equity fraction, equals the sum of retained earnings and common stock, plus additional paid in capital, divided by the total of the capital components of the firm, long-term debt plus preferred stock plus common stock plus additional paid in capital plus retained earnings.

retained life estate. N. See *income interest*.

retention rate. N. The percentage of earnings that a firm does not pay to owners in the form of dividends. The retention rate is equal to one minus the payout ratio. The payout ratio equals cash dividends divided by net income.

retirement of debt. N. See *extinguishment of debt*.

return. N. The additional value received from owning an investment. Return is composed of interest or dividend payments received by the investor, plus any change in the market price of the investment from the original cost. Return is usually expressed as a percentage of the cost of the investment, to facilitate comparison.

returnable deposits. N. A current liability on the balance sheet representing amounts owed to others. If a rental company requires a damage deposit, it incurs a current liability for that amount and it appears on the balance sheet in returnable deposits.

return of capital. N. The result when a corporation pays out dividends in excess of retained earnings. Synonymous with *return of investment*.

return of investment. N. See *return of capital*. ABBRV. *ROI*.

return on assets. N. A measure of profitability that combines the asset turnover ratio and the profit margin on sales ratio. The formula is net income divided by average assets. ABBRV. *ROA*.

return on common equity. N. See *return on equity*. ABBRV. *ROCE*.

return on equity. N. A financial analysis tool that measures how well a company generates earnings compared to the amount of capital shareholders have invested in the firm. The formula is net income divided by average common shareholders' equity. If the company has preferred stock, the preferred stock dividends are subtracted from net income before dividing by equity. Synonymous with *return on common equity*. ABBRV. *ROE*.

return on invested capital. N. A financial ratio used to measure the efficiency with which a company used long-term funds. Calculated as net income divided by the sum of noncurrent liabilities and stockholders' equity. A higher ratio is better. ABBRV. *ROIC*.

return on investment. N. See *return on assets*.

revaluation reserve. N. An owners' equity account on the balance sheet of British companies. The revaluation reserve represents the amount by which the value of the asset exceeds the historical cost. When British companies write up the book value of certain assets, as allowed by the British system of accounting, the company increases the asset account and reduces the associated accumulated depreciation account. Once the accumulated depreciation account is used up, the revaluation reserve is increased.

revenue allocation. N. The assignment of revenue to individual products or activities when the association is not direct. Revenue allocation is most common with bundled products, in which a package of several items is sold together for a discount from the sum of the selling prices for the products individually. The package selling price must be allocated among the different items in the package. Las Vegas resorts sell vacation packages with airfare, hotel, food, show tickets, and a car rental for one price. Then, they must allocate the revenue to the different areas: the airline, lodging department, restaurant, entertainment department, and car rental company.

revenue bonds. N. Bonds that pay interest from a specific source of revenue. Airports, schools, and highways often use revenue bonds.

revenue center. N. A responsibility center in which the manager is only held accountable for the level of sales. The marketing department in an organization is usually a revenue center. The performance of that department is best measured by the amount of sales revenue.

revenue cycle. N. A part of the business process that begins with the customer's order and ends with the collection of cash from that order. The revenue cycle involves tracking sales to customers, filling orders, and sending out accurate and timely bills. The revenue cycle also involves collecting payments and monitoring the timeliness of payments. Identifying the parts of the revenue cycle is important because it can increase the efficiency of operations. The revenue cycle shows the interrelationships between the various departments involved, giving a big-picture viewpoint.

revenue driver. N. The revenue equivalent of a cost driver. A part of business activity that causes revenues to increase.

revenue expenditure. N. Payments made for maintaining the way an asset is currently operating. Examples include maintenance, repairs, and other ordinary service costs. Revenue expenditures reduce income in the period the company makes the expenditure. Many times the determination of capital versus revenue expenditure is not clear-cut and depends on what the asset is. For example, if the heating system needs replacing in a building, and the asset under consideration is the building, the cost is a revenue expenditure and is expensed, because it maintains the building in condition for operation. On the other hand, if the asset under consideration is the furnace, then the cost is a capital expenditure, because it involves the replacement of an asset. See also *capital expenditure.*

revenue growth. N. An increase in sales from one accounting period to the next. Revenue growth does not necessarily mean net income increases. During the 1990s, tech companies were evaluated on revenue growth and many never did realize any net income.

revenue object. N. Similar to a cost object. A revenue object is anything for which a separate revenue amount is needed.

revenue procedures. N. A type of publication from the Internal Revenue Service that provides information on the process, methods, and courses of action for taxpayers. Revenue procedures indicate how to do things. Revenue rulings indicate the correct thing to do.

revenue-recognition principle. N. The rule for identifying when a transaction can be added to income for the accounting period. Under the revenue recognition principle, revenue is included in income when two criteria are met. First, the entity has to have performed nearly all the required activities. Second, the entity has to have received cash, a promise to pay cash, or assets that can be easily converted to cash and can measure the amount of revenue. The first criteria is called the critical event and the second criteria is measurability. The revenue-recognition principle identifies when to include transactions in income. Practice deviates from the rule and is recognized earlier or later, usually determined by the collection certainty or uncertainty.

revenue rulings. N. A type of Internal Revenue Service publication that provides decisions on a certain set of facts. Tax researchers can use these decisions for situations with the same facts. Revenue rulings are published in the *Cumulative Bulletin.* Revenue procedures indicate how to do things, while revenue rulings indicate the correct thing to do.

revenues. N. Increases in income from the main business activities of a company. Revenue is measured as the dollar amount received for activities such as selling products or performing services. Generally accepted accounting principles require that companies can only include revenues that have been earned on the income statement. While most industries have standards, companies can decide just what event signifies that the revenue is earned. Usually, when a sale takes place and the goods are shipped or services are performed, a company earns the revenue. For some natural resources and agricultural products, the company can include the revenue in the period's income as soon as the resource or product is produced and before identifying a buyer. For installment sales where collection is doubtful, sellers can decide to wait until the cash is collected. See also *revenue-recognition principle, gain.* Synonymous with *sales revenue.*

reverse cash merger. N. A business combination in which an acquiring corporation forms a subsidiary and buys all the stock of that subsidiary. Then, the subsidiary uses the cash from the stock sale to merge into the target. The target then is a controlled subsidiary of the acquiring corporation. The only tax result is to the target shareholders. The assets of the target, though, are not at fair market value, reducing the opportunity for the acquirer to recoup through depreciation.

reverse mortgage. N. A mortgage that pays the owner of a home either an annuity or a lump sum because of the equity the owner has in the property. The loan is paid off when the property is sold. One must be at least 62 years old to qualify for a reverse mortgage. Senior citizens use a reverse mortgage to get access to the equity in their homes without having to sell the property, which means they can continue to live in the home.

reverse purchase agreements. N. A way to receive cash for investments without really selling the investments. Reverse purchase agreements are often used by governmental units that have idle cash invested. When the government needs the cash from the investments, it sells them temporarily with the proviso that upon repayment with interest, the exact same investments will be returned.

reverse split. N. Reducing the number of shares of stock outstanding proportionately for all shareholders through a buyback and retirement of the shares.

reversing difference. N. Subsequent years of a temporary difference when the difference between the book value and tax basis of the asset or liability is reduced.

reversing entries. N. Journal entries made after the books are closed on an accounting period, at the beginning of the next one. A reversing entry is exactly the opposite of an adjusting entry, debiting what was credited in the adjustment, and crediting what was debited. The purpose of reversing entries is to make recording transactions easier, and they are optional in the accounting cycle.

reversing transaction. N. A technique to conceal cash larceny in which a fraudster enters a false transaction into the accounting system to make the cash balance with the accounting records. If the fraudster were to steal cash from a cash register, the cash would not reconcile with the sales that were rung up. To remedy this and conceal the fraud, the fraudster could enter a false void to make the amounts balance.

review service. N. A type of accounting service performed by certified public accountant (CPA) firms. A review includes some audit procedures, but not as many as an audit. The CPA firm gives limited assurance that the financial statements are fair to bankers or suppliers that may want some information on the financial condition of the organization. The CPA firm does not issue a formal opinion on reviewed statements.

revocable trust. N. A trust in which the donor can regain control of the donated property.

revolving credit agreement. N. A formal contract between a bank and an entity that requires the bank to loan the entity up to a certain amount at a specified rate. In addition to the interest, the bank receives a fee for agreeing to the contract. Contrast with a line of credit, which is informal, does not involve a fee to guarantee the availability of funds, and does not require the bank to make the loan. The line of credit is only a preapproved amount of borrowing, with no guarantee of the availability of funds.

rework. N. The term used to describe products that are not acceptable quality, but are fixed, meet the quality standard, and are sold at normal prices.

RICO. ABBRV. Racketeer Influenced and Corrupt Organizations Act.

right of return. N. An arrangement between a seller and a buyer that allows the buyer to return unsold products. Sales with a right of return are common for books and magazines. An issue in sales with a right of return is revenue recognition by the seller before the return period has expired.

risk-adjusted cost of capital. N. A modification to the weighted-average cost of capital used to analyze investment opportunities that increases the cost of capital for higher-risk projects and lowers it for lower-risk ones.

risk assessment. N. One of the five components of an internal control system. Risk assessment determines where controls are necessary after analyzing the vulnerable aspects of a business.

risk aversion. N. Investors' preference for less uncertainty about return. For risk-averse investors to purchase securities with higher uncertainty, or higher risk, the possible return must be higher.

risk-based approach. N. A method of organizing an audit by relying on an analysis of various types of risk rather than just on a prescribed set of procedures used across the board. The risk-based approach considers the client characteristics within the context of the client's business to determine what audit procedures to perform, how extensively to perform them, and when to perform them. The risk-based approach to auditing requires that the auditor understand the context in which the organization operates, as well as the way it operates.

risk-free rate. N. The rate of interest associated with U.S. government debt. The risk-free rate is the sum of the real rate plus the expected rate of inflation over the term of the debt. The rate on indexed U.S. treasury securities is the closest approximation to the risk-free rate. Synonymous with *nominal risk-free rate, quoted risk-free rate.*

risk management. N. Using techniques and actions to reduce the effect of future adverse consequences on a business.

risk of incorrect acceptance. N. The chance that an auditor will conclude that the account balance is correct when it is really materially wrong. This type of risk is very serious because the client will not challenge an acceptance of a balance. This is in contrast to the risk of incorrect rejection, which is the chance that the auditor will decide that the account balance is materially wrong when it is, in fact, correct. The audit client will challenge the auditor's declaration that the balance is incorrect and ask the auditor to check it further, probably uncovering the problem. Synonymous with *type 2 error, beta risk, test of details risk.*

risk of incorrect rejection. N. The chance that an auditor will conclude that the account balance is materially incorrect when it is really correct. This risk is not very serious because the audit client will challenge the auditor's declaration that the balance is incorrect and ask the auditor to check it further, probably uncovering the problem. Contrast with risk of incorrect acceptance, which is the chance that the auditor will decide that the account balance is correct when it is really materially wrong. Synonymous with *type 1 error, alpha risk.*

risk premium. N. A component of the quoted or stated interest rate on a debt security. The risk premium represents the chance that the borrower will not pay all or part of the interest or principal. The risk premium increases the quoted interest rate. Lenders assess the likelihood that borrowers will repay and charge higher rates to those with a higher risk of default. The risk premium is also a component of the return an investor may receive. It is equal to the difference between the possible return from the investment and the return from a risk-free investment.

risk/return trade-off. N. The generally accepted idea that an investment with a higher risk of payoff should produce a higher payoff. This implies that if an investor wants a higher return, he or she must be willing to accept a higher risk of that return.

ROA. ABBRV. Return on assets.

robust-quality model. N. A paradigm that views any deviation from the target specifications for a product as unacceptable. While the zero-defects model tolerates small deviation from the target, the robust-quality model assumes that a quality cost is incurred any time a product does not comply with the exact specifications, and that the further the deviation, the greater the loss.

ROCE. ABBRV. Return on common equity. See *return on equity*.

ROE. ABBRV. Return on equity.

ROI. ABBRV. Return of investment.

ROIC. ABBRV. Return on invested capital.

roll-forward period. N. The time period between the confirmation of amounts owed by customers and the end of the year. Usually confirmation of receivables is done prior to the closing of the books for the year, and auditors have to make sure that no problems occurred after the confirmation and the end of the year.

rollover. N. Moving investment dollars from one investment to another. The precise procedures used to roll over an investment are particularly important if the investment has been made from before-tax dollars, such as a 401(k) plan. If the transfer of the asset is not done correctly, the investor must pay taxes on the total amount of the investment. The tax-free rollover involves having the trustee of the original investment transfer it to the trustee of the new investment vehicle. The actual owner of the investment cannot make the transfer, but can only give instructions.

rollover approach. N. A technique used to determine the amount of misstatement in financial statements that calculates the misstatement based on the amount of error in the current year's income statement, ignoring any errors that exist in the balance sheet from previous years. For example, if a company has incorrectly calculated a liability by $100 each of the past three years, the rollover approach would determine the misstatement as $100, the amount of the current year's expense, rather than $300, the amount by which the liability is off, because the $100 is the amount by which the current year's income statement is in error. The weakness of this approach is that the balance sheet error remains. See also *iron curtain approach*.

Roth IRA. N. Roth individual retirement account. A retirement savings device for taxpayers. The Roth IRA does not allow a deduction for contributions, but all withdrawals, both contributions and earnings, are tax-free if the taxpayer is at least 60 years old, if the taxpayer is deceased and the withdrawals are to the beneficiary, or if the withdrawals are used for a first-time home purchase. All contributions must have been in the account for five years to qualify for the tax-free withdrawal. The maximum contribution per year is $5,000 per taxpayer if adjusted gross income is under $114,000, or $166,000 for a couple. The maximum contribution is phased out between $101,000 and $116,000 for single taxpayers and between $159,000 and $169,000 for couples. In contrast to a traditional IRA, there is no required age when withdrawals must begin and there is no deduction for the contributions.

round tripping. N. A scheme to inflate revenues by selling an asset but agreeing to buy it back immediately. The result is an increase in revenue but no increase in net income. Round tripping is used by companies that are evaluated based on revenue increases. Synonymous with *Lazy Susans*.

RPs. ABBRV. Repos.

RRR. ABBRV. Required rate of return.

R-squared. N. A statistical measure of goodness of fit for a regression equation. R-squared is the percent of variation of the dependent variable that the independent variable explains. Values range from zero to one. If the value is very low, then some other variables not included in the data must explain why the dependent variable changes. Synonymous with *coefficient of determination*.

rubber check. N. See *bounced check*.

rubber stamp supervisor. N. A supervisor who does not carefully review documents before signing. The supervisor's signature provides authorization for some activity, often involving money. A fraudster can take advantage of the situation and receive authorization for a criminal act, thus hiding or delaying detection.

S

S-1 registration. N. See *registration statement*.

S-18 registration. N. A form filed with the Securities and Exchange Commission for the purpose of offering shares of stock to the public. It is a simpler version of the S-1 registration because the amount of stock is less than $7.5 million within a year. The form requires audited statements for fewer than three years and less other information than the S-1 registration. It is mainly used by smaller companies.

SAB. ABBRV. Staff Accounting Bulletins.

SAC Report. ABBRV. Systems Auditability and Control Report.

safe harbor rule. N. Protection for companies that make an incorrect forecast if the forecast was prepared carefully and rationally and the company was not trying to mislead users of the forecast. The Securities and Exchange Commission encourages companies to publish forecasts by giving honest mistakes protection from legal action through the safe harbor rule.

safety stock. N. Inventory over the amount needed for production to ensure that the company does not experience a stock out, because demand for the inventory was greater than estimated. The reorder-point calculation may add the safety-stock amount to the lead-time calculation. Synonymous with *buffer stock*.

salary reduction plan. N. See *401(k)*.

sale. N. An exchange transaction between two parties in which each gives up and receives something of value. Sales are the purpose of doing business.

sale leasebacks. N. Transactions in which an owner of a property sells that property to a buyer and agrees to lease the property after the sale. Usually the owner does not move out and then back in again, but just stays in the property. Sale leasebacks are a form of financing, and the gain on the sale is usually spread out over the term of the lease, if the lease qualifies as a capital lease.

sale of receivables. N. See *factoring*.

sales budget. N. The first step in the budgeting process for planning the quantity, timing, and revenues from sales. The sales budget is used to prepare nearly all other budgets.

sales discounts. N. A reduction in the sales-invoice amount that the customer can take if the payment is made within a specified period of time. If the customer pays after the discount period, the entire amount of the invoice is due in a longer period of time. A sales discount is really disguised interest. Synonymous with *cash discounts*.

sales factor. N. A factor used in apportioning business income among states. The sales factor is equal to sales within the state divided by total sales. Sales usually means net sales. See also *Uniform Division of Income for Tax Purposes Act*.

sales journal. N. A journal that contains all the entries for credit sales. See also *journal*.

sales mix. N. The relative proportion of sales each product comprises. Sales mix, in units, is a necessary input to cost-volume-profit analysis in a multiproduct environment. If the sales mix for a company is 5,000 units of product K and 20,000 units of product L, then the sales mix is 1:4. One unit of product K is sold for every 4 units of product L. To use this information in cost-volume-profit analysis, convert the two products into a package containing 1 unit of product K and 4 units of product L. Calculate the costs based on those quantities to get the contribution margin and the contribution-margin ratio for the package.

sales-mix variance. N. A tool for analyzing customer profitability. The sales-mix variance compares the budgeted sales mix to the actual sales mix. The formula used to quantify this variance calculates the variance for each product and sums them. Assume that a company has product A and product B. The first step in the formula is to determine the sales-mix percentage of actual sales of product A and compare it to the budgeted percentage for product A. That difference is then multiplied by the total of all units sold (both A and B) and the budgeted contribution margin for product A. Then, the steps are repeated with product B. The sum of the two is the sales-mix variance. If the difference between the sales mix percentage of actual sales is larger than the budgeted percentage, then the variance is favorable.

sales-quantity variance. N. A tool for analyzing customer profitability. The formula used to quantify this variance calculates the variance for each product and sums them. Assume that a company has product A and product B. The first step is to calculate the actual number of products A and B sold, compared to the budgeted number. If the number is positive, the variance is favorable. Then, that difference is multiplied by the budgeted sales-mix percentage for product A, and that result is multiplied by the budgeted contribution margin per unit of product A to get the sales-quantity variance. The process is repeated for product B. The two variances are summed to get the overall sales-quantity variance.

sales returns and allowances. N. An offset to sales revenue that represents the sales returned. Sales returns and allowances reduce sales revenue.

sales revenue. N. See *revenues*.

sales tax. N. A small percentage of the purchase price of a sale that is added to the final amount charged to the customer. The entity later sends that amount to the state or local government that imposed the tax. The sales tax amount is not included in revenues because the entity is only collecting for the government. Instead, a liability account, sales tax payable, is increased for the tax amount of every sale.

sales type lease. N. A capital lease in which a lessor is carrying a leased asset in inventory and realizes a profit or loss on the lease transaction. The lessor records the initiation of the lease with sales revenue equal to the present value of the lease payments, offset by an asset representing the receivable for the lease payments. The asset is removed from the books of the lessor and moved to the cost of goods sold. Lease payments are a combination of interest and principal amounts, with interest calculated on the receivable balance at the beginning of the period.

sales-value-at-split-off method of allocating joint costs. N. Allocates joint costs to products based on the relative sales value at the split-off point. The joint costs of raising and trucking turkeys to a processing center are $250,000. The revenue from selling the turkey parts is $420,000, and the revenue from selling whole turkeys is $200,000. Using the sales-value-at-split-off method, the turkey parts would be allocated 420 divided by 620 times $250,000 (or $169,355) of the joint costs. The whole turkeys would be allocated the remainder of the $250,000 joint cost (or $80,645).

sales-volume variance. N. One factor causing static budget variance. The sales-volume variance is the difference between the static budget amount of an item and the equivalent item in the flexible budget.

sales with buyback agreements. N. An arrangement between two parties in which Party A sells products to Party B and agrees to buy those same products back in a future accounting period. The effect is to increase revenue in the current period for Party A. The issue in sales with buyback provisions is one of revenue recognition. If the agreement specifies a price that will cover all the costs, Party A will not be allowed to recognize revenue. Instead, Party A must record a liability to repurchase the products. Synonymous with *buy-sell agreements*.

salvage value. N. An estimate of the amount an owner of an asset will receive when the asset is no longer used in the operations of the entity. Usually salvage value is an estimate of what the asset can be sold for when the company disposes of it. Salvage value is used to determine the portion of the asset's cost that the company can depreciate.

sample. N. Part of a larger group, the population, that is used to infer characteristics of the population. For example, if a company sends out five thousand invoices in a year, an auditor might examine fifty invoices for errors to draw conclusions about the number of erroneous invoices a company sends out. The larger the percentage of the population included in the sample, the more certain the inferences are.

sampling risk. N. The chance that an auditor will not catch material accidental or intentional errors because the item was not included in the sample. The audit personnel and program are perfect, but because the error is not among the tested items, it is not discovered. The key to reducing sampling risk is to draw a sample that is representative of the populations.

S&Ls. ABBRV. Savings and loan associations.

S&P 500. ABBRV. Standard & Poor's 500.

sandwich lease. N. See *leveraged lease*.

SAR. ABBRV. Summary annual report.

Sarbanes-Oxley Act. N. Federal legislation enacted in reaction to the bankruptcy of Enron and WorldCom that set up a Public

Company Accounting Oversight Board to set and enforce standards for auditors of publicly traded companies. ABBRV. *SOX*.

SARs. ABBRV. Stock-appreciation rights.

saving. N. Income earned by individuals that is not spent on personal consumption items, but put in savings accounts, used to purchase securities, or contributed to a pension plan.

savings account. N. A method of parking dollars that do not have to be used for living expenses immediately. The owner deposits the dollars with a financial institution and earns interest while the funds remain in the account. Depending on the terms of the account, the owner can withdraw the funds plus the interest.

savings and loan associations. N. Entities that use money, deposited by savers, to finance homes and buildings for borrowers, in addition to loans for other purposes. ABBRV. *S&Ls*.

savings bonds. N. Bonds sold by the federal government that cannot be traded. Savings bonds are structured like zero-interest bonds, in that the purchase price is less than the maturity value.

Savings Incentive Match Plan for Employees. N. A type of retirement savings plan that is easy for small businesses to establish. For a business to be eligible for this type of plan, it must have one hundred or fewer employees who earned at least $5,000 in wages in the current year. The employee contributes up to $10,500 (as of 2008) and the employer matches the contribution and receives a deduction for the amount. ABBRV. *SIMPLE*.

SCARF. ABBRV. Systems-control audit review file.

scatter-plot method. N. A method of determining the cost function of a particular object. The scatter-plot method uses existing data as the basis for predicting the cost function. Several data points are plotted and then a line is fitted to come as close to as many of the data points as possible. The cost function can then be computed using a method similar to the high-low method, using two points on the line.

scenario analysis. N. An analysis technique that focuses on the risk of a project. Scenario analysis starts with a base case, which is the most likely value for all the variables in the project. The outcome of the base case is compared to the best-case and worst-case scenarios. The best-case sets the variables to the most optimistic (but reasonable) forecast values. The worst-case sets the variables to the most pessimistic (but reasonable) values. The comparison among the three outcomes provides insight into the risk of the project, without considering any diversification of risk.

Schedule A and B. N. Part of Form 1040, which is used to file personal income tax. Schedule A reports itemized deductions and Schedule B lists interest and dividends received.

Schedule C. N. A tax form on which individuals report income and expenses from a business. The net income or net loss from this form is transferred to Form 1040.

Schedule M-1. N. A required tax schedule for corporations with assets of more than $25,000 and for partnerships with assets of more than $600,000 and annual receipts of more than $250,000. Schedule M-1 reconciles the entity's financial-statement income with the taxable income. The entity's financial-statement income is increased by nondeductible expenses, losses, revenues, and gains that are not included on the income statement but are taxable. The net income from the financial statements is decreased by income or gain amounts that are not taxable, and by expense and loss amounts that are deductible but are not included on the income statement.

Schedule SE. N. Part of Form 1040, the individual tax form that figures the Social Security and Medicare taxes due on self-employment income.

scope limitation. N. A situation in which the auditors are unable to accomplish all the necessary procedures. The cause may be actions of the client or it may be circumstances out of anyone's control. Some scope limitations make an unqualified auditor's report impossible.

S corporation. N. A special type of corporation that is not a taxable entity. Subchapter S corporations get their name because they are subject to the rules in Subchapter S of the Internal Revenue Code. Regular corporations are taxable entities and are treated just like an individual for tax purposes.

scrap. N. The leftover materials that are not used in the production of an item. If a product requires a component cut from a four-by-eight-foot sheet of plywood, the pieces of plywood that are cut off are the scrap.

scrip dividends. N. Distributions to owners that are really notes payable for the company and notes receivable for the stockholder. Any interest involved is interest expense, but the payable amount is a liability for the company declaring the scrip dividend.

seasonality. N. The clustering of sales revenue in one part of the year. Fuel oil companies have most of their sales in the winter, and beer companies have most of their sales in the summer. Analyzing a company that experiences seasonality in sales requires full-year financial statements to avoid distortion.

seasonal line of credit. N. A type of short-term loan that a company makes use of to finance operating activities when cash is short, due to the cyclical nature of the business. The borrowing takes place as the company gears up for the busy season and is repaid when the sales generate cash.

SEC. ABBRV. Securities and Exchange Commission.

secondary market. N. A type of capital market. A secondary market is a physical or virtual location in which owners of financial instruments buy and sell among themselves. The proceeds from the sale go to the owner, not to the company that originally issued the stock. Contrast with a primary market, in which the transactions are between the issuing company and the buyers.

Section 1231. N. A section of the Internal Revenue Code that specifies the treatment of gains and losses on certain types of assets or property. The types of property included are land or depreciable property used in business activities (if owned for more than one year), timber, coal, iron ore, livestock, and unharvested crops. Inventory is not included. Gains or losses resulting from property that qualifies are calculated separately and then netted. If the gains are greater than the losses, all the gains and losses are treated as long-term capital gains. If the losses are greater than the gains, all the gains and losses are treated as ordinary gains and losses. Losses are limited by the five-year look-back rule. Classification as Section 1231 property is important because it allows for the most favorable tax treatment, capital gains, and ordinary losses.

Section 1245. N. A section of the Internal Revenue Code that specifies the treatment of gains and losses on certain types of assets or property. The types of property included are depreciable personal property and intangible assets that are amortized and used in business. The gain on the sale of this type of asset is an ordinary gain.

Section 1250. N. A section of the Internal Revenue Code that specifies the treatment of gains and losses on depreciable real estate used in business. The gain on the sale of this type of property may be part long-term capital gain and part ordinary gain. The ordinary gain is equal to the difference between the accelerated-depreciation amount, taken over the time the asset has been in service, and the amount that would have been taken if the owner had used the straight-line method of depreciation.

Section 179 expensing election. N. An alternative to depreciation for tax purposes. A taxpayer may choose to expense up to $25,000 (as of 2003) of the cost of any tangible business assets, other than real estate, in the year of acquisition. The property must be used in the business, but must not be held for sale. The expense election is available if the total of all tangible property acquired during the year is $200,000 or less, with a phase out up to $225,000. The expense deduction cannot be more than the taxpayer's taxable income. A carryforward is available for amounts exceeding the taxable income.

Section 404. N. The section of the Sarbanes-Oxley Act that requires a company's management to report on the internal control over financial reporting. The external auditors then issue an opinion on management's assessment. The purpose of Section 404 is to give stockholders more confidence in the published financial reports.

Section 444 election. N. An alternative available to S corporations and partnerships to choose a year-end other than December 31, if the choice does not defer the tax payments more than three months. S corporations and partnerships pass through income and loss to individuals who have a year-end of December 31. The S corporations and partnerships can choose a September 30 year-end and still be in compliance with the payment rule. This allows accounting and tax work to be spread out over a longer period of time, because the entity focuses on getting things done by September 31, and the individual focuses on the first few months of the next year.

Section 704c traditional method. N. Related to allocations in partnerships when a partner has contributed property with a fair market value different from the partner's basis (cost minus tax deductions taken to date). The entire built-in gain or loss is allocated to the contributing partner, but it cannot be larger than the actual gain or loss.

sector spread. N. See *credit spread*.

secured bonds. N. Bonds that are backed by collateral.

Securities Act of 1933. N. Established the Securities and Exchange Commission and required companies selling stock to provide financial information to potential investors.

Securities and Exchange Commission. N. A federal agency that oversees the stock exchanges in the United States and all the companies listed on them. The Securities and Exchange Commission regulates how and when those listed companies present financial information. ABBRV. *SEC*.

Securities Exchange Act of 1934. N. Required companies that wish to sell stock to the public to provide audited financial information to potential investors.

securities-lending transactions. N. A way to receive cash or a higher return on investments without really selling the investments. Securities-lending transactions are used by governmental units that have idle cash invested. When the government needs the cash or wants to earn a higher return, it lends the portfolio to a securities broker for collateral, which can be cash or other securities, with the proviso that when the government returns the collateral it will receive the exact same investment portfolio in exchange.

securitization. N. Selling shares to receive the payments from a pool of assets, usually mortgages, loans, or credit card receivables. Securitization is similar to factoring of receivables, but the assets are usually high-quality receivables, and the seller continues to collect payments and deal with the debtors.

security. N. A financial instrument that represents an ownership interest in property, an entity, or in the debt of an entity.

security market line. N. The graph that results from plotting the required rate of return on the vertical axis and the beta coefficient of stocks on the horizontal axis. The line slopes upward, because as the beta coefficient increases, the stock is riskier than the average stock and the required rate of return to compensate the investor for that increased risk is higher. ABBRV. *SML*.

segment. N. A set of business activities comprising a component of a large company, viewed by management as a distinct part of the company for decision making. For example, a conglomerate may have segments that run franchise restaurants, manufacture clothing, and produce retail grocery products. To meet the management view test, the segment must meet a size or significance threshold. If the segment provides 10% or more of total revenues, produces a profit or loss that is 10% or more of the segments earning a profit or loss, or has 10% or more of the conglomerate's assets, the conglomerate has to provide segment disclosure.

segment disclosure. N. Financial information separated by operating segments within a diversified company. The defining of a segment is based on the way management views the set of business activities. If a set of activities (a segment of the business) meets some thresholds for profit, assets, or revenue, then additional information for each segment is required. Disaggregated, rather than aggregated, financial information is required. For each reportable segment, the company must disclose general information about the segment's products and services, financial information about the segment's profit or loss (including revenue and expense details), information about the segment's assets, the name and percent of revenues provided by large customers, and information about revenues and assets by geographical area. Large companies with several unrelated business activities are required to reveal information by segment so that users can better assess risk and future profitability. Major-customer and geographical-area information is valuable for analyzing the future continuation of profitability. The revenue disclosures help users understand how dependent the company is on the profitability of one segment. See also *segment*. Synonymous with *segment reporting*.

segment margin. N. Similar to contribution margin except it relates to a segment. The segment margin is the amount of profit, after allowing for variable costs and direct fixed expenses, that the segment contributes to covering the common fixed expenses of the organization.

segment reporting. N. See *segment disclosure*.

self-constructed asset. N. An asset built for a company's own use. Railroads and utilities do this regularly. The key issue is how to value a self-constructed asset on the balance sheet, without a purchase invoice. Self-constructed assets include materials, labor, and overhead. According to the Financial Accounting Standards Board rules, the value can also include actual interest or avoidable interest on the construction loan, whichever is less. See also *avoidable interest*.

self-employment income. N. A tax term used to identify a type of earnings that the taxpayer receives from working as a sole proprietor, partnership, or independent contractor. The taxpayer reports this income on Schedule C.

self-employment tax. N. Analogous to the Social Security payroll tax paid by employers and employees. The self-employment tax is paid by individuals who are independent contractors or self-employed, and who therefore have no Social Security or Medicare taxes withheld or paid. Individuals paying this tax may deduct one-half of it as a deduction from adjusted gross income.

self-insurance. N. A situation in which a company assumes the risk of loss, rather than buying insurance to cover the loss. No expense or liability for the self-insurance is allowed, but disclosure is required in the notes to the financial statements.

self-rental rule. N. The rule that turns passive activity into active activity, because rent income is not passive if the rent is from a business that the lessor is involved in.

selling and administrative expenses budget. N. Part of the master budget for planning the outlays for all activities outside of manufacturing. The selling and administrative expenses budget separates fixed and variable components and identifies total costs and the timing of the costs.

selling costs. N. The costs of marketing, sales commissions, product distribution, and customer service are usually considered selling costs. Selling costs appear on the income statement under operating expenses. Synonymous with *marketing costs*.

selling-price variance. N. A flexible-budget variance for revenues. The selling-price variance is equal to the difference between the actual and budgeted selling price per unit times the actual number of units sold. A favorable selling-price variance increases operating income.

selling the crown jewels. N. A method of defending against a hostile takeover in which management sells the most valuable assets of the target company so that the acquisition is less desirable.

sell or process further decisions. N. The choice of whether to sell a joint product at the split-off point, incurring no further costs, or to process it further and presumably receive higher revenues, but also incur additional processing costs.

semiannual compounding. N. See *compounding*.

semivariable cost. N. See *mixed cost*.

senior debt. N. Liabilities of a company that must be satisfied first in the event of liquidation. Holders of senior debt receive proceeds before equity holders.

senior security. N. A security that will be satisfied before others in the case of bankruptcy. Preferred stock is a senior security in relation to common stock, because if the company is liquidated, the preferred stock is redeemed before common stock, and common shareholders only receive something if any proceeds are left.

sensitivity analysis. N. A financial tool for investigating the results of various alternatives. Sensitivity analysis often relies on spreadsheets and computer programs, because assumptions or values involved in a decision are easily altered to see how sensitive the outcome is to input changes. A simple sensitivity analysis could look at the differences in income based on three inputs: selling price, quantity of sales, and inventory purchase price. Synonymous with *what-if analysis*.

SEP. ABBRV. Simplified employee pension plan.

separable costs. N. A term used to describe costs associated with joint products. Separable costs are those that occur after the split-off point and are identified with a separate product.

separately stated items for partnerships, LLCs, and S corporations. N. Income, gains, deductions, losses, and credits that pass through to partners or owners. These items appear on Internal Revenue Service Form Schedule K and are allocated to an individual using Schedule K-1.

separate taxable income. N. The income of an individual member of a consolidated group that has been adjusted for transactions with other members of the consolidated group, or for any items that are adjustments at the group level, such as capital gains and charitable deductions. The sum of all members' separate taxable incomes is adjusted for group-level items to arrive at consolidated taxable income.

separation of duties. N. A basic internal-control measure that safeguards assets by carefully assigning areas of responsibility to employees. The measure separates the duties of authorization, recording, and custody of assets among employees, so that one employee's work verifies and tests another employee's work.

sequential method of allocation. N. A method of allocating support-department costs to products. The sequential method ranks support departments and allocates the support costs down through the order. The collected support costs are then allocated to producing departments and finally to products. See also *reciprocal method of allocation, direct method of allocation.* Synonymous with *step-down allocation method.*

sequential processing. N. A set of manufacturing activities that must be done in a certain order, one at a time, to complete the product. Contrast with parallel processing, which requires that at least two activities be performed at once before the final product emerges.

serial bonds. N. Bonds from a bond issue that mature at different times.

Series EE bonds. N. A type of savings bond. The interest on a Series EE bond is not taxable if it was purchased by an adult after 1989. The bonds must be purchased by the owner, and the proceeds from cashing in the bond must be used for tuition and fees. If tuition is less than the proceeds, only part of the interest is not taxed. Also, the exclusion of the interest is dependent on the level of adjusted gross income, and is phased out over increasing income.

service cost. N. A component of net periodic pension cost. Actuaries calculate it as the present value of pension benefits earned by employees during the current period. Service cost increases the projected benefit obligation for the pension plan and increases net periodic pension cost, an expense on the income statement. Synonymous with *normal pension cost*.

service departments. N. See *support departments*.

service lease. N. See *operating lease*.

service life. N. See *useful life*.

service partner. N. A member of a partnership who acts like an employee of the partnership, performing the services of a normal employee. Compensation payments to a service partner are not salary, but are instead guaranteed payments. See also *guaranteed payment*.

service period for stock options. N. The time over which the compensation expense of stock options is allocated, corresponding to the time periods of operations that benefit from an employee's work. See also *derived service period, explicit service period, implicit service period, requisite service period*.

services. N. A category of product, provided by a business, that involves work for the benefit of the customer. Physicians, attorneys, dry cleaners, and accountants provide services.

service the debt. N. A phrase used to describe activities performed by creditors, such as collecting payments, answering questions from debtors, following up on late payments, and sending payment or notice materials to debtors.

servicing asset. N. Servicing rights for which the estimated cash flows are expected to be more than adequate compensation to the entity providing the service. The entity must recognize a servicing asset or liability whenever it contracts to provide servicing rights. Servicing assets and servicing liabilities are revalued to market value on the balance sheet.

servicing liability. N. Servicing rights for which the estimated cash flows are expected not to be adequate compensation to the entity providing the service. The entity must recognize a servicing asset or liability whenever it contracts to provide servicing rights. Servicing assets and servicing liabilities are revalued to market value on the balance sheet.

servicing right. N. The right to collect payments, handle insurance premiums and taxes, and forward principle and interest to the lender or owner of the mortgage. Servicing rights are usually associated with securitizations of mortgages.

settlement rate. N. The rate used to discount the pension benefit obligations. Actuaries determine the rate based on models and probabilities. The choice of a settlement rate affects the present value of the obligation. A high settlement rate makes the present value smaller than a low rate.

setup costs. N. Inventory costs that occur when materials are produced internally rather than purchased from an outside supplier. Setup costs include organizing and arranging the production facility, paying for idle workers or facilities that are waiting for a product, and the costs associated with calibrating equipment for a different product.

severely underfunded pension plan. N. A pension plan in which the accumulated benefit obligation is more than the fair value of the pension plan assets. The accumulated benefit obligation is the most conservative measure of the pension obligation. If a pension plan is severely underfunded, a minimum balance sheet liability is required with an offset to an intangible asset.

SFAC. ABBRV. Statement of Financial Accounting Concepts.

SFAS. ABBRV. Statement of Financial Accounting Standards.

share-based payment. N. A type of compensation that involves giving employees equity, either directly through shares of stock or through stock options. See also *stock option*.

shared report. N. A standard unqualified audit report that indicates that more than one certified public accountant firm was involved in an audit.

share of stock. N. A representation of a piece of ownership of a corporation. The owner of a share of stock is issued a certificate for each unit; units of the same type of stock are of equal value. Synonymous with *corporate stock*.

shark repellent. N. Any action taken by a target company to fight off a takeover. Poison pills, golden parachutes, and white knights are examples of shark repellent.

shelf registration. N. A way to prepare the registration materials for a new stock offering that will be sold up to two years in the future. This allows the company to issue the securities quickly whenever it needs the cash.

shell company. N. A phony company that is established for the sole purpose of perpetrating fraud. A shell company gives the fraudster a company name to use. Renting a post office box will provide an address. Forming a company in most states only requires a small fee and the filing of some paperwork, making it cheap and easy to set up a shell company. Synonymous with *dummy company*.

shifting income. N. A method of tax planning that reduces taxes by giving children income, usually from an investment. If the child is over 14, the income is taxed at the child's rate. The success is limited, because ownership of the underlying asset usually must be transferred, and the child must be over 14 for it to be beneficial. Shifting income is different than assigning income. Assigning income does not involve a shift in the tax burden. A parent can give a child a bond whose interest is taxed at the child's presumably lower rate. The bond ownership, though, must be transferred to the child, entitling the child to the maturity payout.

short hedge. N. A technique used by the owner of an asset who intends to sell that asset to protect against a decline in the asset's price. The owner buys a put option that gives him or her the right to sell the asset at a specified price during a specified time period. The counterparty agrees to buy the asset under those conditions. The counterparty is willing to do this because cash is received from selling the option.

short position. N. The party to a forward contract who agrees to sell a specified quantity of an asset at a specified price at a specified future date.

short selling. N. A method of making gains on the decrease in the price of a stock. The investor borrows shares from the broker and sells them, then waits for the price to go down and at that time buys the shares to repay the broker. During the waiting time, the investor pays the broker interest on the borrowed shares, betting that the price of the stock will go down. Short selling can result in losses if the investor has to buy back the shares at a price higher than the selling price.

short straddle. N. Selling put options and call options at the same time.

short-term debt. N. Loans for a year or less. Contrast with long-term debt, which involves loans that require payback at a time more than a year in the future.

shrinkage. N. The unexplained difference between the physical count of inventory and the accounting records. Shrinkage is usually caused by employee theft.

SIC code. ABBRV. Standard industrial classification code.

signal. N. Actions by management that are interpreted as representing management information on future performance. Selling new issues of stock is considered a signal of management's belief in poor future performance because losses will be shared with more shareholders.

signaling hypothesis. N. See *information-content hypothesis*.

significant deficiency. N. A control deficiency, or a combination of control deficiencies, that is not as serious as a material weakness, but that requires the attention of a company's management. This means that some internal control technique or procedure, or several of them, exists in a company's system of internal control over financial reporting and the result is the possibility of errors, either intentional or accidental, going undetected. A significant deficiency is not as serious as a material weakness. See also *control deficiency, material weakness*.

significant noncash transactions. N. Transactions that do not involve cash but are material and must be disclosed on the statement of cash flows. Examples include purchasing property, plant, and equipment using debt; refinancing debt; and converting debt or preferred stock into common stock.

similar nonmonetary asset. N. Assets—other than cash, receivables, or investments—that are alike, have the same function, or fulfill the same business purpose. The classification of nonmonetary assets as "similar" is important in an exchange. In an exchange of similar nonmonetary assets, any loss in the amount of the difference between the fair value of assets received and the book value of assets given up is recorded and presented on the income statement. However, a gain is recorded only if cash accompanies the exchange. See also *nonmonetary-asset exchange.*

SIMPLE. ABBRV. Savings Incentive Match Plan for Employees.

simple capital structure. N. A term used to describe the mix of debt and equity of a firm that has no potential common stock, such as convertible securities or warrants.

simple interest. N. A method of calculating interest. The rate is multiplied by the principal times the number of periods the amount is borrowed. In contrast, compound interest for each period is determined by multiplying the rate by the sum of the original amount borrowed plus any unpaid interest. See also *compound interest.*

simple trust. N. An irrevocable trust that holds the donated property and distributes all the income to the beneficiaries. A simple trust does not sell any of the corpus (the donated property) and makes no donations to charities.

simplified employee pension plan. N. A device for establishing an easy-to-administer pension plan for the employees of a small business. The simplified employee pension plan allows the employer a tax deduction for annual contributions to the individual retirement accounts of the employees. The maximum amount depends on the employee's salary or on the defined benefit, if there is one. ABBRV. *SEP.*

single-loop feedback. N. Information about performance that tells managers how well the performance matches the desired level of performance.

single-step income statement. N. A format for the income statement that lists all revenues and gains, and then all expenses and losses (except taxes), without classifying them by source. Taxes are usually separated from the other expenses and losses and are on the last line, right before net income. The single-step income statement is easy to understand.

single taxpayer. N. A tax return filing status that is applicable to an unmarried taxpayer who is not a surviving spouse or a head of household. The requirements for choosing this status are that the person is unmarried. Because the rates are higher for this filing status, it is the least preferred. Unmarried taxpayers would file as a surviving spouse or head of household if they could meet the criteria.

sinking fund. N. A cash or investments set accumulated by a company that has issued bonds. The fund, often a trust, is reserved to buy back the bonds at specified times.

six sigma. N. A management tool developed by Motorola Corporation for improving production processes and quality.

skimming. N. A type of fraud in which funds are taken before being entered into the company accounting system. For example, mailroom employees can take incoming checks, alter them, and deposit them in a bank account for personal use.

slope parameter. N. The steepness of the graph of the cost function. The graph of the cost function plots the total cost at various volumes of production. The slope parameter is the variable cost per unit in the cost function.

slush fund. N. An off-books account that can be used for paying or receiving illegal gratuities or bribes.

small business issuer. N. A category of business for Securities and Exchange Commission purposes. To be classified as a small business issuer, an entity must have had less than $25 million in revenues during the previous year and have less than $25 million in outstanding stock. If classified as a small business issuer, the entity may use Form SB1 or SB2 for registering to issue stock, rather than the more complicated Form A used by large businesses.

small cap. N. A term describing the size of a corporation based on the market value of its stock. If the value of a firm's stock, calculated by multiplying the number of shares outstanding by the current market price, is between $250 million and $1 billion, the corporation is a small cap firm. See also *large cap, medium cap, micro cap.*

small stock dividend. N. A dividend in which the company distributes additional shares to existing shareholders at a rate less than one new share for every four or five owned. (If the rate is greater than that, it is considered a large stock dividend.) For small stock dividends, retained earnings is decreased for the market value of the new shares. The stock account is increased for the par value of the new shares, and additional paid in capital is increased for the difference between the market value and the par value of the shares. See also *stock dividends.*

SML. ABBRV. Security market line.

smoothing. N. A technique used by managers to make earnings less volatile.

snapshot approach. N. See *tagging and tracing approach.*

soft dollars. N. A way that mutual funds pay for some expenses without including them in expenses. Mutual funds acquire "soft dollars" by sending business to a broker. The broker provides the mutual fund with something that the fund would normally have to pay for, such as computer software or hardware. Often, the broker inflates the commissions charged on the trades to cover these costs. Essentially, fund shareholders are paying for the expenses through commissions, which makes the fund's expenses look lower than those of competitors.

sole proprietorship. N. An unincorporated business owned by a single person or by spouses. Sole proprietorships are not legally separate from the owner, even though accounting separates business and personal transactions. The owner has title to the business's assets, is personally responsible for the debts, and may be forced to use personal assets to repay business debts. Synonymous with *proprietorship*.

solvency. N. The ability of an entity to repay long-term debts. A company's solvency depends on earnings and must be sufficient to maintain operations and repay the debts.

solvency ratios. N. See *coverage ratios*.

source document. N. The paper or electronic record of a business transaction. Examples include invoices, checks, and purchase orders. Businesses use source documents to enter data into the accounting system. The source document serves to verify that the transaction really happened and that the amounts entered into the accounting records are correct.

SOX. ABBRV. Sarbanes-Oxley Act.

SPDR. ABBRV. Standard & Poor's Depository Receipt. Synonymous with *Spiders*.

SPE. ABBRV. Special-purpose entity.

special items. N. A term used in governmental accounting to describe items that are either unusual or infrequent and that are under the control of the governmental unit's management. An example of a special item is the sale of city hall at a loss. City management could decide to build a new city hall and sell the old one. Because it is outdated, the sale results in a loss. The event is infrequent, but not unusual.

special journal. N. A journal that only contains the chronological record of a particular type of transaction. A company uses special journals for common transactions like sales. After transactions are journalized, the next step is posting to the ledger. See also *general journal, sales journal, cash-receipts journal, cash-disbursements journal, payroll journal, purchases journal.*

special-order decisions. N. The choice of whether to take on additional production work that is priced differently than normal production work. Special-order decisions require careful analysis to determine if they will be profitable. They are attractive if a business has excess production capacity. Oftentimes fixed costs are not relevant to special-order decisions when excess capacity exists.

special-purpose entity. N. A legally separate trust or corporation that is created by another corporation to accomplish a defined function. The special-purpose entity allows the corporation that created it favorable off–balance sheet treatment for some transactions. ABBRV. *SPE*.

special-revenue funds. N. Part of governmental funds that account for service activities to citizens. A special-revenue fund accounts for revenues that are designated for particular operating activities. The key characteristic is that a particular source of revenue is restricted to a particular use. A special-revenue fund is used if a city has an entrance fee to a park, and the fees are designated for repair and maintenance of the park.

special-use valuation method. N. A way to reduce the value of a family business, usually a farm or ranch, for estate purposes. The fair market value is based on the current use, not on the value to a real estate developer or any other use considered highest and best.

specific identification. N. An inventory cost-flow assumption. Specific identification requires that inventory items be nearly unique, with some way to match a particular cost to a particular item. Specific identification works for products like cars, which have ID numbers; original artwork; or, other distinctive, high-cost products. Specific identification can also be used for special orders in a manufacturing setting.

specific legacy. N. A distribution of personal property, according to the provisions of a will, that involves a distinguishable item, such as a two-carat emerald ring. Other types of legacies or bequests are not so specific. See also *demonstrative legacy, general legacy, residuary legacy*.

specific write-off method. N. See *direct write-off method*.

spider. N. Another name for an Internet search engine that "crawls" through the Web to find something the user has specified.

Spiders. N. See *Standard & Poor's Depository Receipt*.

spin-off of a subsidiary. N. A method of restructuring the ownership of a parent and a subsidiary. The parent corporation owns all the stock of the subsidiary. The value of the parent's stock depends on the performance of the subsidiary, but the parent's stockholders are not owners of the subsidiary. The parent can distribute subsidiary stock on a pro rata basis to its stockholders. Then, the stockholders own both the parent and the subsidiary, but the parent no longer owns the subsidiary.

split-off point. N. The point at which joint products become two separately identifiable products through some action in the production process.

split-up of a subsidiary. N. A method of restructuring the ownership of a parent and its subsidiaries. The parent corporation is just a holding company for the subsidiaries, and the shareholders can eliminate the parent through a split-up. The parent liquidates itself by distributing the shares of the subsidiaries to its shareholders. Since the only assets the holding-company parent had were the shares of the subsidiaries, it ceases to exist, and the shareholders own the subsidiaries directly.

spoilage. N. The term applied to products that are not acceptable quality and that are sold for reduced prices. Many outlet malls sell "seconds" at prices lower than retail. Those seconds, also called irregulars, are not the same quality as the regular product.

spot markets. N. A physical or virtual location in which assets are bought and sold at present, or on the spot. Contrast with a futures market, in which buyers and sellers agree to take part in a transaction at a future date.

spot rate. N. The currency exchange rate that exists if the transaction takes place immediately. A spot rate is used in changing U.S. dollars to Japanese yen at the airport. The spot rate is different than a rate that may be locked in today for a transaction that takes place in the future.

spread. N. The difference between a bid price of a stock and an ask price of a stock. The bid price is the highest price offered (or bid) by a buyer, and the ask price is the lowest price asked by a seller.

springloading. N. The setting of a grant date for a stock option just ahead of a planned announcement of good news. The result is option grants that are more favorable to grantees.

Staff Accounting Bulletins. N. Publications by the Securities and Exchange Commission (SEC) that present how the SEC interprets accounting rules for SEC filing purposes. ABBRV. *SAB*.

staff positions. N. Employees in an organization that have an indirect connection to the main operating activities. They are usually advisors and facilitators, such as accountants and secretaries. Executives and managers in advisory and support roles, such as finance and personnel, are also in staff positions. The other type of position is a line position, which is an employee directly connected to the main operating activities. See also *line positions*.

stand-alone cost-allocation method. N. Allocates costs to different users based on a weighting scheme. The weighting scheme is related to the cost being allocated. For example, the football coach of Big University is flying to visit an alumni group in Florida on Sunday night, is going to another alumni group in Illinois on Monday, and is flying back to the university on Tuesday. The cost of flying round-trip to Florida is $900, and the cost of flying round-trip to Illinois is $500. A round-trip ticket with an extra stop is only $1,000. The stand-alone cost-allocation method calls for allocating the $1,000 based on the relative cost of one ticket to the total cost of two, $1,400. The Florida alumni group would be charged $900 divided by 1,400 times 1,000 (or $642.86). The Illinois group would be charged $357.14. See also *incremental cost-allocation method*.

stand-alone revenue-allocation method. N. Allocates revenue to different items based on a weighting scheme. The weighting scheme may be based on relative selling prices, relative unit costs, the relative number of physical units, or relative stand-alone revenues.

stand-alone risk. N. A type of project risk that looks at the risk of an asset as if it were the only asset held by a firm or the only stock held by an investor. Stand-alone risk is represented by how variable the return from the asset is. Project risk is a consideration in analyzing possible investment opportunities.

Standard & Poor's 500. N. An indicator of stock market trends for large-cap stocks. The Standard & Poor's 500 consists of 500 widely held stocks, most of which are the leading companies in the leading industries. Stocks with more influence on the market (higher market value) are weighted more heavily in the calculation. ABBRV. *S&P 500.*

Standard & Poor's Depository Receipt. N. An exchange-traded fund. Synonymous with *Spiders.* ABBRV. *SPDR.*

standard cost per unit. N. The cost of one unit based on the price standard and quantity standard for materials, labor, and overhead. The standard cost per unit uses standard cost, not actual material and labor cost.

standard-cost sheet. N. A form that specifies all the components of the standard cost per unit. Both quantity and price standards are listed for all direct materials, direct labor, and overhead.

standard-cost system. N. A carefully determined measure of what the cost should be for a product under certain conditions. The system records the actual costs and finds variances. The variances are analyzed to determine efficiency problems.

standard deduction. N. A deduction from adjusted gross income that is a set amount, based on filing status, to cover personal expenses like medical costs, charitable contributions, and home-mortgage interest. Taxpayers calculate which deduction—itemized or standard—gives the greatest tax benefit. If taxpayers use the standard deduction, they do not have to keep records of amounts to justify the deduction.

standard hours allowed. N. A computation based on the quantity of labor hours per unit and the actual units produced.

standard industrial classification code. N. A three- or four-digit number that specifies a company's industry and type of business. A full list of standard industrial classification codes is available from the Securities and Exchange Commission's website, www.sec.gov. ABBRV. *SIC code*.

standard mileage rate method. N. One of two ways of calculating the amount of transportation expense deduction from car expenses. The standard mileage rate method multiplies $0.505 per mile, the 2008 rate, by the number of miles driven for business purposes. The other method of determining this deduction is to take the ratio of business miles driven to the total miles driven and multiply that by the total car expenses for the year.

standard quantity of materials allowed. N. A computation based on the standard quantity of material per unit and actual output in units.

state and local tax deduction. N. A tax deduction from adjusted gross income on Schedule A for the amount of state and local income tax paid by an individual. If the taxpayer receives a refund on state or local taxes, that amount is included in income on the next year's tax return.

stated rate for a bond. N. The interest rate specified in the bond contract that determines the amount of the interest payments. Synonymous with *nominal rate for a bond, coupon rate for a bond, contract rate for a bond*.

stated-value stock. N. Equity shares that have no par value but do have a minimum issue price. When a corporation issues (sells) stated-value stock, the accounting is just like that for par value stock. The cash account is increased for the amount received, the amount of stated value is put in the common stock account, and the amount received above the stated value is added to additional paid in capital.

statement of cash flows. N. One of the four basic financial statements. The statement of cash flows classifies all of a company's cash transactions as operating, financing, or investing activities—the three sections of the statement. The purpose of the statement is to explain the change in cash and cash equivalents from the beginning of the accounting period to the end of the accounting period. Companies must also disclose significant noncash transactions. See also *cash equivalents*. Synonymous with *funds-flow statement, cash-flow statement*.

Statement of Financial Accounting Concepts. N. Official pronouncements of the Financial Accounting Standards Board (FASB) that establish fundamental theoretical underpinnings for future accounting standards. As of the end of 2007, the FASB had issued seven concept statements. They are available at www.fasb.org. ABBRV. *SFAC*.

Statement of Financial Accounting Standards. N. Official pronouncements of the Financial Accounting Standards Board (FASB) that establish correct and legal accounting methods. As of the end of 2007, 160 standards had been issued by the FASB. They are available at www.fasb.org. ABBRV. *SFAS, FAS*.

statement of retained earnings. N. One of the four primary financial statements. The purpose of the statement of retained earnings is to show the changes in the retained-earnings account. The statement of retained earnings is only used if no other changes in stockholders' equity occur during the accounting period. If the entity had any stock transactions, or if any other items change in stockholders' equity, the statement of stockholders' equity is required. See also *statement of stockholders' equity*.

statement of revenues, expenditures, and changes in fund balances. N. A financial report issued by a government that provides information on revenue sources and expenditures by function. The purpose of the statement of revenues, expenditures, and changes in fund balances is to identify the causes of the changes in fund balances.

statement of stockholders' equity. N. One of the four primary financial statements. The purpose of the statement of stockholders' equity is to explain all the changes in all stockholders' equity accounts. If only retained earnings has changed, the entity can present that on a statement of retained earnings. See also *statement of retained earnings*.

static budget. N. A master budget prepared for a given level of production. A static budget is not useful for comparing actual costs to the budget, because the difference between the two may be due to a different volume of produced and/or real cost differences. Contrast with a flexible budget, which can be adjusted for a range of outputs. A static budget is useful for determining if goals are met.

static budget variance. N. The difference between the actual result and the budgeted amount without any adjustment for different volumes of production.

static budget variance for operating income. N. The difference between actual results and the original budget amount.

statistical sampling. N. A method of choosing and investigating some items from a group (or population) to discern a characteristic about the population. Statistical sampling uses probability theory and statistical inference, along with audit experience, to determine the size and method of choosing the sample.

statute of limitations for IRS purposes. N. The period of time after which neither the Internal Revenue Service (IRS) nor the taxpayer can change a return. For most situations, three years is the limit. If the gross income was underreported by 25%, the limit is six years. If fraud was involved, there is no limit.

statutory consolidation. N. A business combination in which at least two independent legal entities become one new legal entity. The two or more original entities no longer exist, and the remaining entity is a new legal entity, usually a corporation.

statutory hybrid plan. N. A type of pension plan that includes cash balance plans and plans that index benefits prior to retirement. This type of plan was designated by the Internal Revenue Service in 2007 and added to the Pension Protection Act.

statutory merger. N. A business combination in which an existing legal entity, a corporation, takes on at least one other existing legal entity. After the combination, only one of the original entities remains.

statutory tax rate. N. The tax rate set by law.

step cost. N. A cost that is fixed over a range of activity, then suddenly increases over another range of activity. An example of a step cost is insurance on delivery vehicles. The costs increase dramatically going from one to two trucks, and incremental partial coverage is not available.

step-down allocation method. N. See *sequential method of allocation*.

stepped-up exercise price. N. An increased purchase price for a warrant that takes effect after a certain date, to encourage warrant owners to exercise prior to that date.

step-transaction doctrine. N. A doctrine stating that the Internal Revenue Service will look at the final outcome in relation to the steps in between, to determine if the steps in between are in place to avoid taxes.

sting taxes. N. Two taxes that are paid by S corporations, even though S corporations are supposedly pass-through entities. Sting taxes are meant to catch C corporations that elect S corporation status intermittently, to achieve tax advantages. The sting taxes are the built-in gains tax and the excess net passive income tax.

stock acquisition. N. A method of performing a business combination in which one company buys 50% or more of another company's voting stock.

stock-appreciation rights. N. A form of stock-based compensation that pays an employee, either in cash or shares of stock, the value of the difference between the market price of the company's stock and a specified price on a designated number of shares. Companies award stock-appreciation rights to motivate employees to work hard and make decisions that will increase the stock price. The higher the stock price, the more compensation employees receive. Unlike stock options, an advantage of stock-appreciation rights is that employees do not need cash available to actually purchase the shares. See also *stock option, stock-based compensation.* ABBRV. *SARs.*

stock-based compensation. N. A reward or payment to employees received in shares of stock determined by the price of the company's stock. See also *stock option, stock-appreciation rights.*

stock bonus plan. N. A type of defined contribution plan that uses employer contributions to invest in the stock of the employing company. The employees receive benefit payments in the form of the employing company's stock.

stock certificate. N. Evidence of part ownership of a corporation. The stock certificate certifies that the individual named owns the share.

stock dividends. N. Additional shares of stock distributed to existing shareholders on a pro rata basis in place of cash or other dividends. Retained earnings is decreased, and contributed capital is increased. Unlike cash, property, or scrip dividends, declaring a stock dividend does not create a liability, and no assets of the company are involved. The accounts involved are all within the equity section of the balance sheet. See also *small stock dividend, large stock dividend, capitalize earnings.*

stockholders' equity. N. A section of the balance sheet that is equal to the difference between total assets and total liabilities. It represents contributions by owners, plus earnings, less any distributions to owners. The stockholders' equity section of the balance sheet also contains the treasury stock account and the unrealized gains or losses that have not appeared on the income statement. Synonymous with *owners' equity.*

stockholder wealth maximization. N. The assumed primary goal of the management of a corporation. Stockholder wealth maximization means that managers will make decisions and take actions that increase the price of the corporation's stock.

stock index. N. A measure of changes in the value of stock prices. The Dow Jones Industrial Average and the S&P 500 are examples of stock indexes.

stock option. N. An arrangement that allows the holder of the stock option to buy or sell a specified number of shares at a specified price during a designated period of time. Stock options are often granted to employees and the specified price is the current market price. The logic is that through hard work and good decision making, the employee can make the company more profitable, increasing the stock price. Then, the employee can buy the specified number of shares at the option price, and turn around and sell them at an increased price, making the difference as compensation. See also *stock-based compensation, incentive stock options, nonqualified stock option plans*.

stock-out costs. N. An inventory cost that occurs when a company does not have the product available when the customer wants to buy it. Stock-out costs involve lost sales and the increased cost of speedy delivery.

stock outstanding. N. The number of shares that a company has sold that are still in the hands of owners outside the company. Stock outstanding is equal to shares issued minus shares of treasury stock.

stock redemption. N. See *treasury stock*.

stock repurchase. N. The action in which a company goes into the stock market and buys some of its own stock from current shareholders. A stock repurchase increases earnings per share because fewer shares are outstanding; it may also increase the stock price. See also *fixed-price tender offer*. Synonymous with *open-market repurchase*.

stock right. N. A type of option given to existing shareholders to purchase additional shares so that they can maintain their percentage of ownership if the corporation is issuing additional stock. The distinguishing features of stock rights include granting to existing shareholders and short time periods.

stocks. N. The term used for inventory on a British company's balance sheet.

stock splits. N. A technique used by corporations to make their stock more accessible. In a stock split, each share of stock is divided into a specified number of new shares, each with a proportionate par value. No account balances change on any of the financial statements when a stock split occurs. The stock account indicates the new number of shares and the reduced par value of each share, but the total remains the same as before the split.

stock subscriptions. N. New companies may sell stock on a subscription basis, which means that the company receives partial payment for the stock, and some other entity handles the sale. The company must create an account to signal that some of the authorized stock will be issued when final payment is received (common or preferred stock subscribed, in the stockholders' equity section). That transaction also increases subscriptions receivable for the amount still owed. The subscriptions-receivable account is not an asset like other receivables, but is rather a contra equity account that is deducted from stockholders' equity.

stock warrant. N. A certificate that gives the owner of the certificate the right to buy a certain number of shares of stock for a specified price within a limited period of time. Stock warrants are different than convertible securities, which are straight exchanges of one security for another, because the warrants require a purchase including the certificate and cash. The accounting for stock warrants depends on whether they are detachable or not. If the warrants are detachable (i.e., they are part of the purchase of another security, like a bond), then the proceeds from the sale of the bond are split up between the bonds and warrants. No allocation is required if the warrants are not detachable.

stop-buy order. N. See *stop order*.

stop-loss order. N. See *stop order*.

stop order. N. An order to buy or sell stock if the price meets a price stated by the investor. A stop-loss order saves the investor from bigger losses, because the stock is sold when the price goes below a certain level. A stop-buy order helps investors who have a short position, because the stock is bought when the price goes above a certain level. Contrast with limit orders. Limit-buy orders tell the broker to buy a stock when the price goes below, rather than above, a certain point. Limit-sell orders tell the broker to sell a stock when the price goes above, rather than below, a certain limit.

stores requisition. N. See *materials requisition*.

straight-line. N. A system of allocating costs, bond premiums, or bond discounts evenly over the life of an asset or liability.

straight-line amortization. N. A method of evenly allocating dollar amounts across time periods. Some assets, mainly intangible assets, are amortized evenly over the economic life of the asset. The discount or premium on a receivable or payable can also be allocated evenly over the time the receivable or payable is outstanding.

straight-line depreciation. N. A method of allocating the cost of a fixed asset to the periods of use. The annual depreciation expense is calculated by first finding the cost to allocate as the historical cost of the asset less the estimated salvage value. Then, that depreciable cost is spread evenly over the estimated useful life of the asset. If the historical cost of a truck was $30,000, and after five years a company estimated it would need a new truck and could sell the old one for $3,500, the depreciable cost would be $30,000 minus $3,500 (or $26,500). The annual depreciation expense would be $26,500 divided by 5 (or $5,300).

strategic cost management. N. A method of management using cost data in planning and controlling the activities of an entity. Information on costs helps management decide whether the business will increase customer value by decreasing what the customer gives up or by increasing what the customer receives—and if the methods to do so are successful.

strategic plan. N. The document that identifies an entity's purpose and activities or accomplishments for the next five or more years. A strategic plan sets priorities for financial resources.

stratification. N. Dividing the population of items into different levels based on a characteristic. In auditing, the characteristic is usually the dollar amount. The top stratum is all items above a certain dollar amount. The population of all the transactions during the year can be stratified into two parts: the top stratum (those above a certain dollar amount) and the lower stratum (those below that amount).

street name. N. A term for the name of a brokerage firm. When a person buys stock, the certificate can be made out in the buyer's name. The stock certificate will be sent to the owner identified on the certificate, and the owner must produce the certificate to sell the share. It is easier to have the certificate made out to the "street name" so that the brokerage firm can keep track of the certificate and can produce it when the buyer wants to sell.

stretching accounts payable. N. Paying later than the required due date. Stretching accounts payable is a conscious business decision, not an accidental late payment, and reduces the cost of missing the discount when paying. If a trade account has terms of 2/10, net 30, meaning that a discount of 2% of the invoice is available if payment is made within ten days, but the entire invoice price is due in thirty days, a business could pay after forty-five days and reduce the cost of missing the discount.

strike price. N. The price at which the holder of a stock option can buy the stock. Synonymous with *exercise price, option price.*

strong dollar. N. The situation that occurs when one U.S. dollar receives more of another currency today than it did in the past. A strong dollar benefits U.S. travelers and reduces the cost of imported goods, because it takes fewer U.S. dollars to buy the same item.

structured note. N. A type of derivative that is a debt security based on another type of debt security. An example of a structured note is a collateralized mortgage obligation.

Subchapter C. N. The portion of the Internal Revenue Code that contains the rules for exchanges between corporations and their shareholders.

Subchapter K. N. The portion of the Internal Revenue Code that contains the rules for exchanges between all types of partnerships, including limited liability companies.

Subchapter S. N. A section of the Internal Revenue Code that governs the operations of nontaxable corporations.

subjective measures. N. A characteristic of targets used to evaluate performance. Subjective measures use qualitative data, opinions, and judgments for evaluation.

subordinated bonds. N. A bond that, in the event of bankruptcy by the issuer, is not paid until other, more senior debt is paid.

subordinated financial support. N. An investment in an entity that, in the event of bankruptcy, is paid off after formal loans.

Investments in equity securities are subordinated financial support because the loans of the corporation are paid before the investors receive their money.

subprime mortgage. N. A mortgage in which the borrower has less than good credit. "Subprime" describes the debtor, not the interest rate.

subscription privilege. N. See *preemptive right.*

subscription warrant. N. A right to buy stock at a specified price during a specified time. Subscription warrants are usually part of a preferred stock or bond purchase, and the amount of stock is proportional to the amount of the original purchase. Subscription warrants usually specify a price higher than the market price of the stock when the subscription is acquired, thereby forcing the owner to hold the warrant until the market of the stock rises.

subsequent event. N. An action or happening that occurs after the date on the balance sheet, but before the financial statements are published. Technically, it should not be reflected on the balance sheet, but because it has a significant effect on the entity, it is disclosed in the notes to the balance sheet. If the subsequent event affects an estimate already on the balance sheet, the entity must adjust the balance sheet to include the effect. Synonymous with *post–balance sheet event, event subsequent to the balance sheet.*

subsidiary. N. A party to a business combination. The subsidiary is the company acquired by the parent, the other party to the combination.

subsidiary ledger. N. A ledger that gives more detail about one ledger account. For example, the accounts receivable subsidiary ledger contains information on each customer's account balance and gives more information than the total in accounts receivable. See also *ledger, general ledger, journal.*

substantial-economic-effect requirement. N. A ruling that applies to partnership allocations. The distributive share amounts on the partnership Schedule K-1s must be similar to the amounts that increase and decrease the capital account for each partner.

substantial equivalency. N. A determination by the state board of accountancy that the education and experience requirements for practice in another jurisdiction are acceptable for purposes of practicing accounting in the state. Substantial equivalency would allow certified public accountants in Chicago to have clients in Gary, Indiana, for example, because states determine the licensing requirements for all accountants practicing in the state.

substantive testing. N. Audit procedures for checking the details of accounting transactions or testing the substance of the transactions. Some substantive testing is always done, but the amount is determined by the strength of the internal control system. If the internal controls are working properly and are strong, less verification of the specific transactions is necessary.

substituted basis. N. In an exchange, the amount at which the asset received is valued. This procedure allows already established businesses to incorporate without huge tax consequences to the entrepreneur. If the participants control 80% of the corporation's stock after the transaction, they can put off a gain until the asset that was received in the transaction, usually stock, is sold. Normally, the basis of the stock would be the market value, which is much higher than the original investment, and the participants would have to pay taxes on the difference at the time the stock is received. However, by substituting the value of the original investment as the tax basis of the stock, the taxes on the gains are not paid until the stock is sold.

successful-efforts accounting for natural resources. N. One of two acceptable methods of calculating the depletable base in the oil and gas industry. This method includes only the exploration costs that result in finding the oil or gas in the depletable base, not the dry wells. The cost of searches that do not produce oil are expensed in the period that the company incurs them.

summary annual report. N. An abridged annual report that provides financial information in a condensed format that is more readable than the full report. While the shorter, more succinct structure may be easier for some users to comprehend, it may give the company an opportunity to mask bad news. ABBRV. *SAR*.

sum-of-the-years'-digits depreciation. N. A method of allocating the cost of an asset to the periods it is used to generate revenue. The book value is multiplied by a fraction in which the numerator is the number of years of useful life remaining at the beginning of the accounting period, and the denominator is the sum of the years of useful life. If, in the first year of an asset with a six-year life (and a $2,000 salvage value) the book value is $8,000, the fraction is 6/(6+5+4+3+2+1), or 6/21. The depreciation expense for the year is $8,000 times 6/21 (or $2,286). In year two, the book value is $5,714, and the fraction is 5/21, resulting in a depreciation expense of $1,360. The sum-of-the-years'-digits depreciation method does not use salvage value in calculating depreciation expense. The asset cannot be depreciated below the salvage value, and that check is performed when calculating the book value. The book value cannot be less than the salvage value.

sunk cost. N. A type of cost used in decision making. A sunk cost is one that has already been incurred; no alternative being considered will affect the amount of cost. For example, the owner of a car replaced the brakes and transmission last year and is faced with another large repair expense this year. The owner is trying to decide whether to do the repair or to sell the car and replace it with a new one. The cost of the brakes and transmission are sunk costs. They should not enter into the decision.

supernormal-growth firm. N. A company that has a dividend growth rate higher than the total economic growth rate. Supernormal-growth firms are usually early in their life cycle and, as time passes, the growth rate slows to that of the average. Examples of supernormal-growth firms are Ford Motor Company in the 1920s, television networks in the 1950s, and software companies in the early 1980s.

supervariable costing. N. See *throughput costing.*

suppliers. N. Business terminology to identify the companies that provide raw materials, inventory items, or other goods used in operating activities.

supply chain. N. The entities involved in providing the services, materials, and information necessary to produce and sell a product or service to customers. An example of a supply chain for a chicken processing plant starts with the farmer who raises the chickens, followed by the trucker who picks up and delivers the chickens to the plant, followed by the processing plant that cleans and packs the chickens, followed by the trucker who takes them to the supermarkets where they are sold to the consumer.

support departments. N. Subunits of an organization that do not directly produce the product or service, but are necessary to do so. Contrast with producing departments, which are directly involved in making the products or supplying the services that are the main operating activities of the entity. Synonymous with *service departments.*

surplus. N. See *earned surplus.*

surviving spouse. N. A tax return filing status that is applicable to a single taxpayer whose spouse died during the year. The requirements for choosing this filing status are that the widow or widower did not remarry before the year-end, is a citizen or resident of the

United States, would have qualified for a joint return if the spouse had not died, and has a dependent child living at home during the whole year. A surviving spouse can take personal exemption for the deceased and use the more favorable joint tax rate and standard deduction.

suspended loss. N. A loss that has been passed through to an owner from a partnership or S corporation that the owner cannot deduct on taxes because of loss deduction rules. Suspended losses are carried forward to use in future years.

sustainable development. N. The concept that current growth, progress, and expansion should be accomplished without negative consequences for future generations.

swaps. N. A type of a derivative financial instrument that is an agreement between two parties to exchange cash at a future date. A swap is like a forward contract, except that both parties deal in cash, and the cash amount is determined by the structure of the swap. If Company A has an obligation to pay variable interest to its creditors, the risk that the rate may go up exists, resulting in higher interest payments for the company. If Company A believes the variable rate will increase, it will arrange a swap to control it. Company A then arranges a swap with Bank B. Company A agrees to pay a fixed rate of interest on a given amount of dollars to the bank, and the bank agrees to pay a variable rate on that same amount. If the variable interest rate goes up, Company A will receive that from Bank B and use it to pay the creditors. The cost of the borrowing is what Company A paid the bank—a fixed rate of interest. If the variable rate goes down, Company A will receive that amount from Bank B and use it to pay the creditors. The cost of borrowing is the same fixed rate of interest, although in this case, that is more than the variable rate. Company A guessed wrong on the rate movement, but it has still reduced the risk and locked in a fixed rate of interest.

swaption. N. A financial instrument that gives the parties the option to enter into a swap.

sweeteners. N. Add-ons or characteristics that make preferred stock or debt securities a more desirable investment. Typical sweeteners include attaching warrants or conversion features to the security. For example, preferred stock that can be converted into common stock in the future would provide the investor with the set return on the preferred stock and the opportunity to get a better return later from common stock.

swing loan. N. See *bridge loan*.

symmetric information. N. Circumstances in which firm outsiders (investors) and firm insiders (managers) have exactly the same information about the firm's future performance.

symmetric-return profile. N. A description of a derivative that can result in either a gain or a loss for the holder and writer.

synchronized cash flows. N. A situation in which cash inflows arrive in time to cover the cash outflows of a business. Synchronized cash flows allow the business to keep a minimum amount of cash idle in a checking account. Some businesses set up billing cycles so that payments from customers are due when the cash outflows are due.

synthetic equity. N. A financial instrument with the essential characteristics of equity, such as stock options. Synthetic equity is important in determining the tax treatment of employee stock option plans in S corporations.

synthetic leases. N. Lease arrangements that result in operating-lease treatment in the financial statements and capital-lease treatment on the tax return.

systematic risk. N. See *market risk.*

Systems Auditability and Control Report. N. A guide used by information systems auditors to identify risks to an information system and the controls that lessen those risks. This report is updated regularly. ABBRV. *SAC Report.*

systems-control audit review file. N. An audit technique used in a computerized information system that flags actual transactions if the transaction meets certain criteria. Program code identifies the transactions for the auditor to review for accuracy and control procedures. Auditors could have checks over a predetermined amount identified by the processing program to check on the large payments. ABBRV. *SCARF.*

SysTrust. N. A type of assurance service, provided by public accountants in the United States and Canada, that evaluates the availability, security, integrity, and maintainability of computer systems. The purpose of the service is to make customers trust the e-commerce systems of companies.

T-account. N. A device for showing the effect of transactions on a particular account. The structure is in the shape of an uppercase letter "T." The name of the account is written across the top, debits are entered on the left side, and credits are entered on the right side.

tagging and tracing approach. N. An audit technique used in a computerized information system that follows actual transactions through the system. Tagging and tracing involves adding an identifying digit to part of the transaction data. A predetermined value in that digit "tags" the transaction, and as the transaction moves through the system, various programs record information about the processing of the transaction, "tracing" its progress. Auditors review the information to determine if the system is properly processing transactions. Synonymous with *snapshot approach*.

Taguchi loss function. N. A method of estimating the hidden costs of poor quality. The Taguchi loss function calculates quality loss as a function of the actual product characteristic's deviation from the target characteristic. Also included in the loss function is an estimate of the amount of loss when the deviation is at its greatest.

take-or-pay contract. N. An off–balance sheet financing method in which an entity agrees to pay for an option to buy a specified amount of goods over a specified period of time. The payments are required even if the goods are not delivered. Take-or-pay contracts usually arise as part of product financing arrangements. The buyer is really financing the project through the required payments, but because of the structure, no liability is recorded. Footnote disclosure is required.

takeover. N. The acquiring of one company by another through stock purchase or exchange. The acquiring company obtains enough of the outstanding stock to control the board of directors.

Takeovers can be friendly or hostile, depending on the reaction of the target.

taking a company public. N. Incorporating an existing unincorporated business and selling stock to the public.

tandem currency. N. Part of a hedging transaction in which a forward contract is based on a different currency than the hedged item.

target capital structure. N. See *optimal capital structure*.

target cost. N. The product cost necessary to produce a specified gross margin on a unit, given the selling price necessary to produce the desired volume of sales. If the target cost is below the current product cost, management needs to find a way to reduce the target cost. Sometimes the target cost is considered to be the cost the consumer is willing to pay.

target costing. N. See *price-driven costing*.

target-payout ratio. N. The percentage of earnings that a firm would like to distribute to shareholders in the form of dividends. The target-payout ratio is influenced strongly by the investors' return preference: dividends or capital gains.

tariff. N. A type of tax imposed by the federal government on foreign goods brought into the United States. Normally, the tariff is paid when the goods enter the country. A tariff is included as part of the cost of the item and becomes an inventoriable cost.

taxable amounts. N. Dollar amounts from transactions or events that increase taxable income.

taxable income. N. A term used to distinguish the income that is determined using tax laws, on which the entity must pay taxes (either from the company's income on the income statement that is measured using generally accepted accounting principles or from the individual's total sources of income). Start with income of all types—not just wages, but also interest, dividends, alimony, and any other type of income. Then deduct adjustments for gross income, which are items designated by tax law including things like individual retirement account deductions, student loan interest, moving expenses, etc. That difference is the adjusted gross income. Then deduct adjustments from gross income, which are the standard deduction or itemized deduction, personal and dependency exemption, and other tax credits. The result is taxable income.

taxable temporary difference. N. Dollar amounts from transactions or events that are not fully taxable in the current period, but will be in the future.

taxable year. N. The time period over which the taxpayer figures taxable income. The taxable year must be the same as the year used for accounting income. For business entities like partnerships and sole proprietorships, the partner or proprietor pays tax on the pass-through income in the year in which the partnership or proprietorship's year ends. Practically, the partnership's or proprietorship's year-end is the same as that of the owners.

tax anticipation notes. N. A type of short-term operating debt used by governments in which the government borrows against the taxes it has or will levy. A tax anticipation note is similar to a note payable or a line of credit that a for-profit business uses to manage cash flow.

tax avoidance. N. The structuring of economic behaviors so that the least amount of tax is paid by the taxpayer. Tax avoidance uses every legal means to reduce tax payments. Contrast with tax evasion, which uses illegal means to avoid paying taxes.

tax benefit. N. See *tax effect of carryback and carryforward losses*.

tax credit. N. An amount that reduces the actual amount of taxes owed. The dollars offset taxes rather than income. Tax credits are distinct from tax deductions in that tax credits offset the amount of taxes that must be paid, and tax deductions reduce the amount on which the taxes owed is figured. Tax credits are more desirable and have a greater beneficial effect for the taxpayer. Some are refundable, meaning that they can reduce the tax liability below zero, so the taxpayer gets a refund. Nonrefundable tax credits can only reduce the tax liability to zero. The excess of the tax credit is not refunded.

tax deduction. N. An amount that reduces taxable income. Tax deductions are limited in amount and nature by tax laws. Tax deductions are distinct from tax credits in that tax credits offset the amount of taxes that must be paid, and tax deductions reduce the amount on which the taxes owed is figured. Tax credits are more desirable and have a greater beneficial effect for the taxpayer.

tax-deferred. ADJ. A description of an activity or transaction that puts off the payment of taxes to the future. Tax-deferred saving for retirement is one example. Tim earns $3,000 every two weeks. He can put a small amount, say $60, into a special kind of plan. Then, his employer calculates the income taxes for withholding on the $2,940. When Tim retires, he withdraws all the $60 deposits, plus the interest, from that plan and pays taxes on it at that time, usually at a lower rate than what he would have had to pay when he was working.

tax-deferred bonds. N. An investment in the form of a bond on which the owner does not pay taxes on the interest until a later time. Series EE bonds are tax-deferred if the owner has an adjusted gross income above a certain amount. The interest accumulates, tax-free, until the bond is cashed in.

tax effect of carryback and carryforward losses. N. A line item on the income statement when an entity has had a net operating loss. Usually just called "tax effect," it represents the amount of refund the entity expects for taxes paid in the past or the amount of taxes it will save in the future, because income in the future can be offset with current-year losses.

tax evasion. N. Illegal methods of circumventing tax payments. Tax evasion is a serious crime with strict penalties. Contrast with tax avoidance, which involves taking all legal deductions and methods to minimize tax payments.

tax-exempt bonds. N. An investment in the form of a bond on which the owner of the bond pays no taxes on the interest. Series EE bonds are tax-exempt if the owner has an adjusted gross income below a threshold amount, and the proceeds from cashing in the bond are used for tuition and fees.

tax form for LLCs. N. Even though LLCs are pass-through entities and do not pay income taxes, they must file Internal Revenue Service Tax Form 1065.

tax form for partnerships. N. Even though partnerships are pass-through entities and do not pay income taxes, they must file Internal Revenue Service Tax Form 1065.

tax form for S corporations. N. Even though S corporations are pass-through entities and do not pay income taxes, they must file Internal Revenue Service Tax Form 1120S.

tax haven. N. Countries with lenient tax laws for foreign companies and individuals. For example, the Cayman Islands, the Bahamas, and Bermuda have no taxes. The purpose of establishing accounts in tax havens is to avoid paying taxes.

tax incentives. N. Rules that promote certain behaviors for saving on taxes. Usually these behaviors have some economic or societal benefit associated with them. Examples include allowing mortgage-interest deductions to promote home ownership and accelerated depreciation to encourage fixed-asset replacement.

tax increment financing. N. A state- or locality-level tax incentive that provides a business an incentive to choose a particular location because the taxing unit (the state or city) agrees to pay the corporation a bonus. The bonus is seen as a portion of the increased tax revenues that will occur when the corporation locates there.

tax-preference items. N. Amounts added to taxable income to arrive at alternative minimum tax. Tax-preference items are usually associated with favorable tax treatment on the tax return, but are reconsidered when figuring the alternative minimum tax. Examples of tax-preference items include the treatment of excess depletion, excess intangible drilling and development costs in the oil and gas industry, excess accelerated depreciation on some real estate, and excluded gain from the sale of a small business's stock.

tax-preference theory. N. A theory that suggests that firms that pay low dividends will have higher stock prices because investors prefer capital gains, which receive favorable tax treatment.

tax return. N. The document filed by individuals, corporations, not-for-profit organizations, partnerships, and other entities that provides the Internal Revenue Service with information for collecting taxes.

tax shelters. N. Investment schemes with the sole purpose of generating losses that the taxpayer can use to offset income from another activity. An abusive tax shelter, a term used by the Internal Revenue Service, denotes a tax shelter that is using illegal deductions.

tax shield. N. A technique used to reduce the tax liability by taking legal deductions. The depreciation tax shield results from deducting depreciation from taxable income. The amount of the depreciation tax shield is equal to the tax rate times the amount of depreciation.

tax treaties. N. Agreements between the United States and foreign countries to eliminate or reduce double taxation of citizens' income earned in the foreign country. The foreign country agrees to eliminate or reduce the tax on its citizens' income earned in the United States.

T-bill. ABBRV. Treasury bill.

T-bond. ABBRV. Treasury bond.

technical bulletins. N. Publications of the Financial Accounting Standards Board that address a particular problem or application of a standard.

technical default. N. A situation in which a borrower has made all required principal and interest payments on time, but has violated at least one debt covenant.

technical efficiency. N. A component of productive efficiency that focuses on the quantity of inputs used. Technical efficiency occurs when the minimum quantity of each input is used in the production process.

technological feasibility. N. A critical point in the development of software after which costs are allowed to be capitalized. Prior to technological feasibility, costs are expensed. Technological feasibility is dependent on the risk of realizing future benefits from the project.

temporary account. N. An account that collects transactions for one accounting period. Temporary accounts begin the period with a zero balance and are closed at the end of the period. Temporary accounts appear on the income statement. See also *closing entry for financial accounting*. Synonymous with *nominal account*.

temporary difference. N. A situation that occurs because the rules for determining the income on the income statement, generally accepted accounting principles (GAAP), are different than the rules for determining the income on which the entity must pay tax. If the difference originates in one year but reverses in another, it is a temporary difference. For example, if the depreciation expense using GAAP is based on a five-year useful life, and the tax laws allow a three-year useful life to calculate the tax deduction for depreciation, then in years one to three, the depreciation expense on the income statement is less than the deduction on the tax return. But in years four and five, the depreciation expense is greater on the income statement than on the tax return. The difference in depreciation originates in years two and three and reverses in years four and five.

tenancy by the entirety. N. A form of property ownership that is like joint tenancy but can only involve a married couple.

tenancy in common. N. A form of property ownership that does not include survivorship benefits. Individuals own the property together, but when one dies, the deceased owner's rights are passed to his or her heirs.

tender offer. N. A way of acquiring another company by publicly offering to buy the stock from the stockholders, usually at a higher price than the market price—in order to offset the resistance by the existing management of the target company. A tender offer can also be used to buy back some of a company's own shares. See also *fixed-price tender offer*.

term bonds. N. Bonds in a bond issue that all mature on the same date.

term structure of interest rates. N. The association between the duration of a debt and the interest rate on the debt. The time to maturity, or duration of the debt, is referred to as the term of the debt.

testamentary transfers. N. Gifts received by a taxpayer upon the death of the giver. These gifts are not taxed as income to the recipient.

testamentary trust. N. A trust created upon the death of the owner of the property. Contrast with an inter vivos trust, which is created during the donor's lifetime.

test data. N. A technique used by auditors to verify that data input is accurate and that computer programs process the data correctly. The auditors create a set of data situations that should cause the program to signal that there is a problem with the data. This might include out-of-range amounts or out-of-sequence document numbers. After creation, the test data are processed and the results are compared to the correct answers. Discrepancies may indicate problems that the auditors need to investigate further.

testimonial evidence. N. One type of evidence gathered in a fraud investigation. Testimonial evidence originates with people and can include interviews, questioning, and lie detector tests. See also *evidence square*.

test of details risk. N. See *risk of incorrect acceptance*.

tests of controls. N. Audit procedures to verify that internal controls are working properly. Tests of controls can be done through observation of employees or documents.

tests of extensions. N. An audit activity in which the auditor remultiplies amounts to check the client's result. For example, the cost per unit is multiplied by the number of units sold to check the extension price on an invoice.

theft act. N. One of the three elements of fraud in which the thievery actually takes place. See also *elements of fraud.*

theoretical activity capacity. N. The estimate of the quantity of the unit-level activity driver used to apply overhead in a normal costing system. The theoretical activity capacity is the largest quantity that the company expects to produce or use when everything works perfectly. See also *unit-level activity drivers, predetermined overhead rate, normal costing.*

theory of constraints. N. A method of achieving better business performance through continuous improvement, reduction of inventories, and reduction of lead times. The theory of constraints involves the following five steps. (a) Determine what the organization's constraints are (in particular, find the binding constraints, which are resources that are at capacity). The constraint that supersedes all others and sets the schedule is called the drummer. (b) Make decisions and plans that make the most of the drummer, through careful scheduling and product mix. (c) Review decisions so that everyone supports the decisions made in the second step. (d) Investigate ways to improve the drummer, and implement them. (e) Repeat the process. ABBRV. *TOC.*

third-party guarantors. N. Entities that act as insurers of residual value for leases. Third-party guarantors allow a lease contract to be classified as an operating lease for the lessee, because without the residual value included in the minimum lease payments, it does not meet the recovery-of-investment test. Third-party guarantors allow a lease contract to be classified as a capital lease for the lessor, because the inclusion of the residual value in the minimum lease payments meets the recovery-of-investment test.

throughput agreement. N. Similar to take-or-pay contracts except that the contract is to buy services from the newly constructed asset. See also *take-or-pay contract*.

throughput contribution. N. A measure in the theory of constraints that is equal to revenues minus the direct materials cost of the cost of goods sold.

throughput costing. N. A method of assigning costs to products by treating only direct materials as an inventoriable cost. All other costs, such as direct labor, indirect costs, and overhead, are considered period costs, reducing income in the period in which they are incurred. The logic for throughput costing is that only direct materials are really variable costs. The cost of labor is relatively fixed for the period because of the difficulty of laying off and calling back several times to meet various production levels. The equipment cost is also nearly fixed, because the organization cannot buy and sell on short notice to meet production demands. Synonymous with *supervariable costing*.

throwback rule. N. A rule that takes effect when a corporation makes a sale to a customer in another state that has no income tax. When the corporation apportions its business income among states, that part of income is not taxed. According to the throwback rule, the state in which the sale originated is allocated that income for tax purposes.

tick. N. The minimum amount of change in the price of a commodity in the futures market. The amount of the tick depends on the commodity. An uptick is a higher price, and a downtick is a lower price.

ticker symbol. N. A unique combination of letters assigned to a company by the Securities and Exchange Commission to identify filings by that company.

TIE. ABBRV. Times-interest-earned ratio.

time deposit. N. An account in which withdrawals of deposits are not allowed without waiting for the maturity date or notifying the financial institution of the intent to withdraw. Contrast with demand deposits (e.g., in checking accounts), from which the account holder can withdraw amounts without waiting for a maturity date or notifying the institution.

time driver. N. An aspect of business activities that, when changed, causes a change in the speed of other activities. The delivery of raw materials is a good example of a time driver. If the delivery is delayed, the production processes are delayed.

time factor depreciation. N. Methods of depreciation based on the duration of the use of an asset. Straight-line depreciation, based on the useful life of an asset, is a common example.

timeliness. N. An aspect of the primary qualitative characteristic of accounting information—relevance. Accounting information is timely if it is available when needed for decision making. See also *conceptual framework*.

time-period assumption. N. See *periodicity assumption*.

time-series analysis. N. A financial analysis tool that focuses on trends over time for a single company. Time-series analysis requires several years of information to determine the rate of change in amounts on the financial statements. Contrast with cross-sectional analysis, which looks at several companies at the same point in time.

times-interest-earned ratio. N. A ratio that measures debt-paying ability. The formula is interest before taxes and interest expense divided by interest expense. The result indicates how many times earnings cover the interest the company must pay. To interpret the adequacy of the ratio, it should be compared to the industry average. Synonymous with *interest coverage.* ABBRV. *TIE.*

time ticket. N. A form used in a job-order costing system to keep track of the direct labor cost used by the job. Employees complete the form by entering hours worked on the time ticket. The cost information is added to the job-order cost sheet.

time value of money. N. A concept in accounting and finance that relates the value of money to the time it is received or paid. The fundamental principle is that dollars received at present are more valuable than dollars promised in the future. The future payment might not be made, and dollars received today can be invested and can be earning interest over time. ABBRV. *TVM.*

timing differences. N. A divergence in the point of recognition of revenues and expenses between financial reporting and the tax return. Timing differences cause deferred tax liabilities and assets.

TIPS. ABBRV. Treasury Inflation-Protected Security.

T-note. ABBRV. Treasury note.

TOC. ABBRV. Theory of constraints.

tolerable misstatement. N. The amount by which an account or group of accounts can be off before the error is considered material. The tolerable misstatement sets the threshold for materiality.

tombstones. N. A slang term for advertisements announcing that a company is going public. The ads usually have a black border and heavy, black print, and look like tombstones.

top-side entry. N. A journal entry done to adjust the books after all normal entries are completed for the accounting period. Top-side entries are usually scrutinized carefully by auditors for signs of financial reporting fraud.

top stratum. N. A term used in auditing to denote the collection of large-dollar items. The top stratum of sales might be all sales over a certain amount. The auditor often looks at all the items in the top stratum.

total budget variance. N. The difference between standard costs and actual costs. Total budget variance involves first finding the standard cost of the output by multiplying the actual number of units produced by the standard cost per unit. This amount is then subtracted from the actual cost incurred to get the total budget variance.

total preventative maintenance. N. Used in a just-in-time manufacturing system to reduce machine failures to zero. In the manufacturing cells used in a just-in-time inventory system, workers are trained to perform maintenance, particularly preventative maintenance. The logic is that if preventive maintenance is adequate, the machines will not break down.

total productive efficiency. N. Consists of two parts. The first is technical efficiency, in which the minimum amount of any one input to the production process is used. The second part is input trade-off efficiency, in which the combination of inputs is the least costly possible combination.

total-productivity measurement. N. Measuring the efficiency of all inputs to the production of goods or services. Total-productivity measurement involves complex and practical approaches to accomplishing this, including profile measurement and profit-linked productivity measurement. See also *profile measurement, profit-linked productivity measurement*.

total-quality management. N. A way of manufacturing products, focusing on perfection. Processes, machines, materials, and workers are assisted in achieving the goal of perfect quality. Companies using total-quality management need good cost information and strong quality measurements. ABBRV. *TQM*.

TPS. ABBRV. Trust preferred securities.

TQM. ABBRV. Total-quality management.

traceable costs. N. Similar to direct costs in that they are assigned to a particular product, territory, or other cost object.

tracing of transactions. N. An audit procedure in which the auditor finds a source document and follows it forward through the processing to the account balance. Contrast with vouching of transactions, in which the auditor chooses a recorded transaction and works backward through the processing to find the source document.

trade accounts payable. N. See *accounts payable*.

trade credit. N. See *accounts payable*.

trade discounts. N. Reductions in the selling prices quoted in marketing materials (such as catalogs) that may be given based on quantity ordered, delivery specifications, or other factors. Trade discounts allow sellers to be more competitive and to avoid printing new marketing materials whenever prices change.

trade loading. N. A method of increasing current period sales by encouraging customers to buy more inventory than they need at the time, making the seller's current period sales look better. The problem is that the customer will buy less inventory in the next period. Trade loading is the term used in the tobacco industry because "trade" is the word used to describe wholesale customers of cigarette producers.

trademark. N. A symbol, icon, word, or slogan that creates the identity for a product or organization. The right to exclusive use of the trademark is achieved by registering it with the U.S. Patent and Trademark Office. The registration covers a twenty-year period and can be renewed an unlimited number of times. Accounting for trademarks is similar to accounting for other intellectual property. The costs of internal research and development are expensed during the process. The costs of registering the trademark, using external experts, and securing a successful defense are all capitalized. If the trademark is purchased, the purchase price is the capitalized cost. The cost is then amortized over the economic life or over any period of time up to forty years.

trade name. N. See *trademark*.

trade-off theory of leverage. N. A theory that describes the balance between the benefit of using debt financing (i.e., the tax deductibility of interest) and the risk of using debt (i.e., the possibility of bankruptcy). The trade-off theory of leverage suggests that the optimal capital structure is at the point that the marginal tax benefits are equal to the marginal bankruptcy-related costs. This theory estimates that some companies, like Microsoft, would be much better off with higher debt levels. However, signaling theory tries to explain through asymmetric information the difference that results in managers, knowing that future performance will be bad, trying to sell more stock to share the losses among more shareholders. The opposite signal is managers, knowing that future performance will be good, trying to finance with debt so that increased income is shared with fewer stockholders than if new stock is sold to accomplish the financing.

trade receivables. N. The combination of accounts receivable and notes receivable that represents amounts owed by customers as a result of business activities. Trade receivables are listed with current assets on the balance sheet. See also *accounts receivable, notes receivable.*

trading on equity. N. Financing through fixed-rate borrowing or preferred stock in anticipation of a higher return than the rate on borrowed funds. If the return on assets is lower than the return on common stock equity, the company is trading on equity at a gain.

trading securities. N. A classification of investments, both debt and equity, that have short holding periods. They appear in the current assets section of the balance sheet. Investments are classified as trading investments based on the intended purpose and the intended holding period. If management intends to earn a return on short-term price changes, and intends to sell the investments within a short time to take advantage of those price changes, the investment is classified as a trading security. Trading securities, which may be either stock or debt, are valued at market value at the end of the accounting period. The change in value is included in income, even though the investment has not yet been sold. Any dividends or interest received are included in income. The unrealized gain or loss is included in income because, since these investments are only held for a short time, the best information includes what would happen if they were sold.

tranch. N. A category or part of a pool of instruments, often mortgages, that provide the payments for collateralized debt obligations. The pool, a large number of mortgages or other loans, is classified by maturity and risk, leaving each tranch containing instruments with a common duration and risk level.

transaction. N. A business event that affects the revenues, expenses, assets, liabilities, and equity accounts of a business.

Companies record transactions as journal entries initially and then post them to the ledger. Eventually the dollar amounts of all the transactions during the accounting period affect the financial statements for the period. Usually transactions involve the business and at least one entity outside the business. See also *journal entry*.

transaction analysis. N. Looking at the beginning and ending balance of an account and determining the transactions that caused the changes. For example, if the beginning balance in notes receivable was $5,400 and the ending balance was $5,700, transaction analysis would investigate whether the change involved an additional loan of $300, or whether a larger loan was made and a repayment of all or part of the original $5,400 caused the change.

transaction processing cycles. N. The collective term for group activities involved with an entity's business activities. See also *revenue cycle, resource-management cycle, purchasing cycle.*

transfer-of-ownership test. N. One of the four capitalization criteria for leases. If the lease specifies that title for the leased asset moves to the lessee at the end of the lease, the lease is a capital lease because it has met the transfer-of-ownership test.

transfer price. N. The price of an item bought or sold between different parts of the same organization. In large businesses, one part of the company makes parts or products used in the operations of another part of the company. The transfer price affects the revenue and expense of the two parts involved.

transferred-in costs. N. Costs in a process-costing system that originated in a previous process. The material, labor, and overhead costs are put into the process, and when the product is sent to the next process, those costs are transferred to that process.

transitory earnings. N. Income effects that, while on the income statement in the current period, are unlikely to continue in the future. The results of discontinued operations and extraordinary items are examples of transitory earnings.

translation adjustment. N. A plug number that forces the total assets to equal liabilities plus equity, when foreign financial statements are translated into another currency. The translation process uses various exchange rates for different types of assets, liabilities, and equities. The result is a balance sheet that does not balance, so the translation adjustment forces that equality. The amount of the adjustment is included in other comprehensive income, but not in current earnings (until the subsidiary using a foreign currency is liquidated).

transportation-expense deduction. N. A tax deduction that is deductible for adjusted gross income if the taxpayer is self-employed, and is deducted from adjusted gross income if the taxpayer is an employee (and the expense is not reimbursed). For the employee, the transportation-expense deduction is part of the miscellaneous itemized deduction. Transportation expense includes taxi fares, car expenses, airfares, tolls, and parking—if the costs are incurred while the taxpayer is working. The taxpayer can either deduct the actual car expenses or take $0.505 per mile (the rate in 2008). The taxpayer must keep mileage records for either method if the vehicle is used for both business and personal activities.

travel-expense deduction. N. A tax deduction that is deductible for adjusted gross income if the taxpayer is self-employed, and is deducted from adjusted gross income if the taxpayer is an employee (and if the expense is not reimbursed). For the employee, the travel-expense deduction is part of the miscellaneous itemized deduction. Travel expense relates to being away from home and includes transportation, meals, lodging, etc. The travel must be related to the business of the self-employed taxpayer or to the employee. Travel-expense deductions are limited if the travel is outside North America. Meals are 50% deductible, and lodging is deductible if the taxpayer is away from home temporarily.

treasurer. N. A staff position that involves managing the finance function. The treasurer raises capital through borrowing and the sale of stock, and manages the cash and investments. The controller has a related position managing all the accounting functions.

treasury bill. N. A short-term debt instrument with the federal government as the borrower. The minimum treasury bill requires a $10,000 investment and has a maturity period of up to one year. Treasury bills are purchased at a Federal Reserve Bank through an auction for new issues, and over-the-counter through securities dealers. Treasury bills are easily sold and have a relatively low rate, but they are nearly risk-free and are exempt from state and local taxes. ABBRV. *T-bill.*

treasury bond. N. A bond that the debtor company purchases in the bond market and holds rather than cancels. The par value of the treasury bond is deducted from the bonds payable liability. A treasury bond is a long-term debt instrument with the federal government as the borrower. These bonds are purchased at a Federal Reserve Bank through an auction for new issues, and over-the-counter through securities dealers. They are easily sold and have a relatively low rate, but they are nearly risk-free. ABBRV. *T-bond.*

treasury certificate. N. A debt security with a maturity of less than one year. A treasury certificate is a low-risk investment because the U.S. government backs the repayment.

Treasury Inflation-Protected Security. N. A type of treasury bond in which the principal and interest are adjusted for inflation. ABBRV. *TIPS*.

treasury note. N. A long-term debt instrument with a maturity period of two to ten years, with the federal government as the borrower. Treasury notes are purchased at a Federal Reserve Bank through an auction for new issues, and over-the-counter through securities dealers. Treasury notes are easily sold and have a relatively low rate, but they are nearly risk-free. ABBRV. *T-note*.

treasury regulations. N. Interpretations of the Internal Revenue Code by the U.S. Department of Treasury. Treasury regulations can be used as a final determination of tax issues.

treasury stock. N. Shares of stock that the issuing company buys back from the public. The company can retire or reissue the treasury stock when it again becomes whatever type of stock it was originally, such as common or preferred. Companies often use treasury stock to meet the need to issue stock when employees exercise their stock options. Treasury stock receives no dividends and has no vote until it is reissued. The treasury-stock account is on the balance sheet as a reduction of stockholders' equity listed after retained earnings. Treasury stock is not an asset. Generally accepted accounting principles allow two methods of accounting for treasury stock. The cost method values the treasury stock at the price paid to reacquire the shares, while the par value method uses the par value of the stock. See also *cost method, par value method*. Synonymous with *stock redemption*.

treasury-stock method of accounting for options and warrants in diluted earnings per share. N. The method that adjusts the denominator of basic earnings per share to reflect the number of shares outstanding after options and warrants are exercised. This method assumes that the company uses the cash from the exercise of the options and warrants to buy back some shares at the market price. This reduces the additional shares outstanding, but because the option price is lower than the market price, an increased number of shares is out; that is the increase in the denominator of basic earnings per share.

trend analysis. N. A technique used in auditing that compares the account balance over time. Auditors investigate any account in which the balance changes by a material amount unexpectedly from one year to the next. The audit program establishes the threshold for materiality.

trend statements. N. A financial analysis tool in which the income statement and balance sheet amounts from several years are stated as a percentage of a base year's amounts. Trend statements show patterns of growth and decline.

trial balance. N. A listing of each account and its balance in the chart of accounts. The dollar amount of accounts with debit balances must be equal to the dollar amount of accounts with credit balances. Inequality of the debits and credits signals a recording error. It may be at the journal stage, when the debits and credits for a particular transaction are not equal, or it may be at the ledger stage, when debits and credits can be posted incorrectly. See also *unadjusted trial balance, adjusted trial balance, postclosing trial balance.*

Trojan horse program. N. A small, disruptive program that exists in a genuine program and acts like a computer virus to destroy data or to slow processing on the host computer.

troubled-debt restructuring. N. Special consideration for the financial problems of a debtor resulting in partial forgiveness, reduced rates, extension of time to pay, or another concession. Troubled-debt restructuring is based on a problem specific to the borrower, not on general economic conditions (such as rate reductions on variable rate debt). Troubled-debt restructuring can either settle the debt for less than the amount owed or adjust the terms of the debt, making it possible for the debtor to pay. When the debt is settled for less than the principal, the debtor often transfers assets other than cash—such as property—to the creditor. In that case, first the asset is adjusted to the fair market value involving an ordinary gain or loss. Then the debt is removed, the asset is removed, and the difference is an extraordinary gain or loss. If the debtor issues stock, the market value of the stock is recorded, the debt is removed, and the difference is an extraordinary gain or loss. Modification of terms is more complicated, and the debtor's gain is calculated using undiscounted cash flows. The creditor's loss is based on cash flows discounted at the rate of the original loan. Synonymous with *restructuring of debt*.

trust. N. Donated property managed by a trustee who is not the donor, for the benefit of beneficiaries who are neither the donor nor the trustee. The purpose of a trust is to distribute the earnings of the trust property or the trust property itself, over time.

trustee. N. The manager of a trust who acts in accordance with the provisions of the trust document. Synonymous with *fiduciary*.

trust indenture. N. The contract specifying the details of a bond issue.

trust preferred securities. N. A type of financing that is called preferred stock, but that has characteristics more like debt. The shares pay regular dividends, just like interest payments, and the issuer can redeem the shares at any time, just like a maturity date. Trust preferred securities are a hybrid security that cannot be included in the owners' equity section of the balance sheet. Companies that issue trust preferred securities put them after liabilities and before owners' equity on the balance sheet in an area called the mezzanine section. ABBRV. *TPS*.

turnaround sales. N. The purchase of an asset by an employee for later resale at an inflated price to his or her employer.

TVM. ABBRV. Time value of money.

two-bin method. N. A method of inventory control that indicates when to reorder an inventory item. The inventory of a particular item is stored in two containers that are usually next to each other. All items taken from inventory are taken from one of the containers. When that container is empty, the item is reordered, and subsequent inventory is taken from the remaining bin. When the order arrives, it is put in the empty container.

type 1 error. N. See *risk of incorrect rejection*.

type 2 error. N. See *risk of incorrect acceptance*.

type I subsequent events. N. Things that happen after the closing of the accounting period that technically do not belong on the statements from that period, for which the financial statements are adjusted. The event is related to something already known during that accounting period. Subsequent events occur after the end of the accounting period, but before the audit report is issued. No adjustment or disclosure is necessary in the previous year's financial statements. If a major customer files for bankruptcy after the end of the accounting period, the allowance for bad debts is adjusted for this event. The customer's account existed prior to the end of the year, so the allowance is adjusted. If a lawsuit, which was ongoing at year-end, is settled after the end of the accounting period for an amount different than expected, the amount is adjusted in the financial statements because the lawsuit was in existence in the prior period.

type II subsequent events. N. Things that happen after the closing of the accounting period that technically do not belong on the statements from that period, which are disclosed because the event is material. If the company was unaware of things surrounding the event before the end of the year, the financial statements are not adjusted, but the information is disclosed. Type I subsequent events do require financial statement adjustments, because they relate to events that were in existence before the year-end. No adjustment or disclosure in the previous year's financial statements is required if the event occurs after the date of the audit report. If a company becomes involved in a lawsuit immediately after the end of the year and settles quickly, the settlement is disclosed but is not reflected on the previous accounting period's income statement.

type A reorganization. N. A type of tax-deferred business combination, either a merger or a consolidation, whose target shareholders receive stock in the continuing corporation for less than half of the purchase price.

type B reorganization. N. A type of tax-deferred business combination in which the stock of the target is purchased with the stock of the acquiring corporation. In a type B reorganization, nothing other than stock can be used in the purchase. After the purchase, the acquirer must control at least 80% of the stock of the target. The 80% can be a combination of previously owned stock and any new purchase.

type C reorganization. N. A type of tax-deferred business combination in which the assets of the target are purchased with the acquiring company's voting stock. The target liquidates after the combination. Synonymous with *practical merger*.

type D reorganization. N. A method of reorganizing a single corporation into independent parts. The originating corporation transfers some of its assets to the new corporation in exchange for stock in the new corporation. Then, the originating corporation distributes the stock to its shareholders.

UAA. ABBRV. Uniform Accountancy Act.

UDITPA. ABBRV. Uniform Division of Income for Tax Purposes Act.

UML. ABBRV. Upper misstatement limit.

unadjusted trial balance. N. The first trial balance at the end of the accounting period. It serves as a check that debits and credits are equal. If they are, the process of recording adjusting entries can begin. See also *trial balance*.

unamortized bond discount. N. The amount of bond discount, which appears on the balance sheet, representing the portion that has not already been used to increase interest expense (on the income statement) above the amount of cash interest paid.

unamortized bond premium. N. The amount of bond premium, which appears on the balance sheet, representing the portion that has not already been used to decrease interest expense (on the income statement) below the amount of cash interest paid.

unappropriated retained earnings. N. The portion of retained earnings that is available for dividends. All retained earnings are assumed to be unappropriated, and the company must partition off part of the retained earnings to be appropriated.

uncollectible account. N. A debt from a customer that the company decides will not be paid. The company removes the account from the total of accounts receivable.

unconditional obligation. N. A requirement for one party to act at a designated date, or when a specified event that is certain to happen occurs. A company may issue redeemable stock that must be repurchased, at a guaranteed price, on July 1, 2010. The obligation to redeem the stock is unconditional. That date is certain to come. Most businesses would classify stock as a stockholders' equity account on the balance sheet. However, even though it is called "stock," it really has the characteristics of debt: a maturity value and a payoff amount. The Financial Accounting Standards Board requires companies issuing this type of stock to include it in liabilities, not in equity.

unconditional pledges. N. Promises made by donors to make a contribution to a not-for-profit organization, which will be fulfilled within the year and require no other event to occur. Unconditional pledges are recorded as a receivable and a revenue in the accounts of the not-for-profit organization.

underabsorbed indirect costs. N. See *underapplied overhead*.

underapplied overhead. N. The situation that occurs when total applied overhead is less than total actual overhead costs. Underapplied overhead is added to the cost of goods sold at the end of the year. Synonymous with *underabsorbed indirect costs*.

undercosting. N. The result when the cost per unit is lower than the resource consumption in producing the product. Undercosting may cause management to set the selling price too low, making sales that do not actually cover costs.

underfunded. N. The situation that occurs when the assets available to a pension plan are not adequate to pay all the benefits earned by employees. If the underfunding meets certain levels, then the company must record an additional pension liability on the balance sheet.

underlying. N. A term used to identify an aspect of a derivative. The underlying is the price or rate associated with the derivative. For a stock option with a strike price of $27 per share, the underlying is the $27. It is important to note that the underlying is not the share of stock, but rather the price of that stock (because the fixed price of $27 determines the value of that stock option).

understatement. N. A form of financial statement fraud that states liabilities or expenses at less than the actual amount with the purpose of reaching some desired financial target.

underwater option. N. See *out-of-the-money*.

underwriting. N. A service provided by investment bankers who sell a new stock issue to the public, guaranteeing the issuer a certain price per share. The underwriter takes the risk that the issue will not sell for the guaranteed price. For that, the investment banker receives a fee.

undesignated fund balance. N. Part of the unreserved fund balance that identifies amounts that have no restrictions on their use. The governmental unit can use those amounts for any purpose. The undesignated fund balance appears after liabilities on the balance sheet of the governmental unit.

unearned income. N. Income that is taxed differently because it is not wages or salary, but is instead from investments or rental property.

unearned interest. N. A liability on the balance sheet of a bank that collects the interest at the time a loan is made.

unearned revenue. N. Revenue for which cash has been received, but the services or goods have not been provided to the customer. Unearned revenue appears on the balance sheet in the liabilities section. Unearned revenue does not increase net income for the period in which the cash was received. Instead, it increases income when the revenue is earned, which is when the services or goods are provided. Synonymous with *deferred revenue on the balance sheet.*

unfavorable M-1 adjustments. N. Items included on Schedule M-1, the reconciliation of net income to taxable income, that are added to net income to get taxable income. These items include nondeductible expenses and losses and revenues and gains that are not included on the income statement but are taxable. The items are unfavorable because they increase net income to get taxable income.

unfavorable variance. N. The difference between the actual cost and the standard cost, when the actual cost is larger. An unfavorable variance happens if the quantity used is more than the standard permits or if the price paid is more than the standard permits.

unfunded deferred-compensation plans. N. A device used in professional sports and in some businesses in which a signing bonus is awarded. It must be only a promise, with no evidence in the contract, no written documentation, and no funds transferred. However, the employer can set up an escrow account to hold the funds. When the executive actually receives the funds, the amount is taxable to the executive, and the employer can deduct the amount.

unguaranteed residual value. N. The estimated asset value at the end of a lease—but not promised or guaranteed by the lessee.

UNICAP. ABBRV. Uniform Capitalization Rules.

unified credit. N. A tax credit used to offset gift and estate taxes. The unified credit is a lifetime maximum tax credit based on the taxable gifts.

Uniform Accountancy Act. N. A model for state legislation regarding the practice of accounting developed by the National

Association of State Boards of Accountancy and the American Institute of Certified Public Accountants. The purpose is to streamline the practice of accounting across state lines by making a license to practice similar to a driver's license. The act is available at www.aicpa.org/Legislative+Activities+and+State+Licensing+Issues/State+News+and+Info/States/uaa. ABBRV. *UAA*.

Uniform Capitalization Rules. N. A list of costs that must be included in either inventory or the cost of goods sold for tax purposes, and is found in Section 263A. In addition to direct materials, direct labor, and manufacturing overhead, factory building costs, factory administration, factory property taxes, quality costs, support services, and pension service costs are all added to the cost of inventory and the cost of goods sold. ABBRV. *UNICAP*.

Uniform Division of Income for Tax Purposes Act. N. Proposes a method of allocating income among states for the purpose of taxing. This act relies on three factors to divide up the income: sales, payroll, and property. The factors are calculated by dividing the dollar amount of sales, payroll, or property by the corporation's total sales, payroll, or property. The factors are then weighted and summed to produce an overall percentage of taxable income reported in the state. That percentage is multiplied by the total income to arrive at the amount for a particular state. See also *sales factor, payroll factor, property factor*. ABBRV. *UDITPA*.

Uniform Principal and Income Act. N. The standard for determining the allocation of income and expenses in trusts. This act is only used if the trust document does not specify the allocation.

unissued stock. N. Stock that a corporation has never sold to the public. The number of shares of unissued stock is equal to the number of authorized shares minus the number issued.

unit cost. N. The result of dividing the total cost of production by the number of units produced. If costs include materials for $1,000, labor for $3,000, and machine rental for $1,500, and a factory produced 500 units, the unit cost would be $5,500 divided by 500 (or $11). The identification of production costs is the key issue and is necessary to get a meaningful unit cost.

unit investment trusts. N. A type of investment in which an entity, usually a broker, buys a portfolio of securities, which is put in trust. The broker then sells "shares" or units in the trust to investors, who receive the payouts from the trust securities in proportion to their ownership. Unit investment trusts are unmanaged investment companies, because the portfolio in trust is not adjusted. Usually it contains securities with a specific maturity, and eventually the trust expires.

unit-level activities. N. Actions that are done for every unit produced. Unit-level activities are distinct from batch-level, product-level, and facility-level activities. Activity-based costing systems identify the level of an activity to build homogeneous cost pools, because costs in a homogeneous pool must be associated with activities performed at the same level. Activities that use overhead costs in the same proportion can be combined into the pool rate. Examples of unit-level activities include assembly or painting.

unit-level activity drivers. N. The basis for applying overhead in a normal-costing system. The item used in the denominator of the predetermined overhead rate is the unit-level activity driver. It represents an educated guess of which activity or thing associated with a product is related to the overhead costs. Common unit-level activity drivers are labor hours, labor dollars, units produced, or machine hours. See also *nonunit-level activity drivers*.

units-of-output depreciation method. N. See *units-of-production depreciation method*.

units-of-production depreciation method. N. A method of allocating the cost of an asset based on output for the accounting period. The total cost is divided by the total estimated number of units that the asset is expected to produce. That result is then used each year as the depreciation per unit. To arrive at the depreciation expense for the accounting period, the number of units produced during the period is multiplied by the depreciation amount per unit. Synonymous with *units-of-output depreciation method*.

universal resource locator. N. See *domain address*. ABBRV. *URL*.

unlevered beta. N. The beta of a firm, if the firm uses no debt financing. Unlevered beta is calculated as beta/[1 + (1–T)(D/E)], where T equals tax rate, D equals debt, and E equals equity. The unlevered beta is used to calculate the effect of a change in the debt-to-equity ratio on the beta of a firm, specifically, how much beta will increase if the debt-to-equity ratio is increased. Managers find this useful for deciding on the source of financing for new projects.

unlisted corporation. N. See *over-the-counter corporation*.

unqualified audit report. N. The opinion of the auditor that expresses no concerns about the financial statements of an entity. The audit opinion is included in the financial statements and is required by the Securities and Exchange Commission if the organization is a corporation listed on a stock exchange. The unqualified audit report does not guarantee that no fraud or errors are present in the financial statements. That level of assurance would be too costly. Rather, the recommended wording is that the statements fairly represent in all material respects the financial position, cash flows, and results of operations, and that the organization uses generally accepted accounting principles. Synonymous with *unqualified opinion*.

unqualified opinion. N. See *unqualified audit report*.

unrealized external-failure costs. N. The costs of actions or efforts to deal with contaminants already released into the environment and paid for by those outside the organization producing the contaminant, i.e., society.

unrealized gain or loss. N. The increase or decrease in the value of an asset owned by an entity. Contrast with a realized gain or loss, which is the difference between the value on the balance sheet (or the original price paid for the asset) and the selling price in a sale that has occurred. If gain or loss is indicated without an adjective, a realized gain or loss is assumed.

unrealized receivables. N. Any partnership receivables that are not included in income because the partnership uses cash-basis accounting.

unrecognized prior service cost. N. The amount of prior service cost that has not yet been included in pension expense. Unrecognized prior service cost is not on any of the employer's financial statements. Changes in pension plans that award retroactive benefits increase the accumulated benefit obligation. If the accumulated benefit obligation is greater than the market value of the pension plan assets, the employer has to record a liability for the difference. The liability is increased and an intangible asset is increased, but it can only be as large as the unrecognized prior service cost. See also *minimum pension liability*.

unrecognized transition asset. N. The unamortized amount of pension plan overfunding that existed at the time a company adopted Statement of Financial Accounting Standards 87, and that remains at the end of the current accounting period. Contrast with an unrecognized transition liability, which occurs if the plan was underfunded at the time of adoption.

unrecognized transition liability. N. The unamortized amount of pension plan underfunding that existed at the time the company adopted Statement of Financial Accounting Standards 87, and that remains at the end of the current accounting period. Contrast with an unrecognized transition asset, which occurs if the plan was overfunded at the time of adoption.

unrecorded assets. N. Amounts that have been earned and are receivable but have not been entered into the accounting records. Unrecorded assets involve adjusting entries at the end of the accounting period.

unrecorded liabilities. N. Amounts that are incurred but not paid and have not been entered into the accounting records. Unrecorded liabilities involve adjusting entries at the end of the accounting period.

unreimbursed employee expense. N. A cost incurred by an employee that is necessary to job performance but that is not repaid. Unreimbursed employee expense is part of the miscellaneous itemized deduction. Examples include uniforms, dues, journal subscriptions, and some travel costs.

unreserved fund balance. N. An account used in governmental accounting to show amounts that are either designated or undesignated for special purposes. The unreserved fund balance is shown after liabilities on the city's or state's balance sheet.

unrestricted net assets. N. A classification of net assets used in accounting for not-for-profit organizations. Unrestricted net assets represent the amounts that are available for current operating activities or any other purpose. The only restrictions on these net assets are from bylaws or articles of incorporation that identify the broad purpose of the organization and from contractual restrictions by creditors or suppliers.

unsecured bond. N. See *debenture bond.*

unsecured loan. N. A loan that requires no collateral.

unsystematic risk. N. See *diversifiable risk.*

unused capacity variance. N. A measure of the unnecessary availability of an activity. The unused capacity variance is measured as the difference between the amount of an activity that is currently available and the amount of the activity that was actually used.

unusual items. N. A category on the income statement for transactions that do not happen often, that are special and are not part of the regular activities of the organization, but that do not qualify for treatment as an extraordinary item. An example of an unusual item is layoff costs associated with general workforce downsizing. The costs are not really normal operating activities, but they do not meet the definition of "unusual and infrequent" necessary for extraordinary losses. The logic is that many businesses conduct layoffs, so it is not that unusual.

unvested pension benefits. N. Pension benefits that the employee does not retain upon resignation or termination. Usually employees earn pension benefits based on contributions by both the employee and the company. If the employee leaves after a short time, he or she gets the dollars he or she contributed, but not the part company put in. Those benefits are not vested.

upper misstatement limit. N. A term used in probability-proportional-to-size-sampling in the audit process to designate the highest estimate of error in a particular account. The upper misstatement limit is a combination of an estimate of the errors that are missed because of sampling, plus the best estimate of the amount of error in the account, plus an adjustment if errors are found in the sampled items. If no errors are found in sampled items, then the upper misstatement limit is equal to the estimate of errors that are missed because of sampling versus looking at every transaction in the account. ABBRV. *UML*.

URL. ABBRV. Universal resource locator. See *domain address*.

usage variance. N. One factor in the total budget variance. The usage-variance portion is equal to the difference between the actual and standard quantity per unit, multiplied by the actual quantity of units produced. Synonymous with *efficiency variance*, *quantity variance*.

use factor depreciation. N. Methods of allocating an asset's cost based on the output obtained from the asset. Units of production is an example of use factor depreciation.

useful life. N. An estimate of the period of time that an asset will contribute to the production of revenues, used to allocate the cost of an asset. The useful life is an estimate and is not always the same as the physical life. A desktop computer will physically last quite a while, but it may not have enough capability to contribute to revenues after a few years because of advances in technology. Synonymous with *service life*.

use tax. N. The tax that states or cities try to collect on items purchased outside the taxing unit that would be subject to a tax if purchased within the unit. This voluntary compliance system tries to catch consumers who attempt to escape paying sales tax.

U.S. General Accounting Office. N. Renamed U.S. Government Accountability Office in 2004. See *U.S. Government Accountability Office.*

U.S. Government Accountability Office. N. The governmental agency that sets the auditing standards for conducting audits of any governmental unit or any organization that receives government contracts, grants, or funds. Previously known as the U.S. General Accounting Office. ABBRV. *GAO.*

vacation-home deduction. N. A tax deduction for the expenses related to renting a vacation home that depends on the number of days the home is rented to outsiders. If the owner does not use the property more than fourteen days or 10% of the days that the property is rented, all the expenses are considered business expenses. If the owner uses it more than the stated maximums, the expenses are prorated between deductible business expenses and nondeductible amounts.

valuation account. N. A contra account that reduces the balance sheet amount of an asset. Valuation accounts are used in conjunction with investments and deferred tax assets. See also *market adjustment account*.

valuation allowance for deferred tax asset. N. A contra account that reduces the deferred tax assets on the balance sheet to an amount that the entity expects to be able to use. The analysis estimates the likelihood that the entity will have enough taxable income to use the deferred tax assets. If the likelihood is less than 50%, the entity has to use a valuation allowance to reduce the balance sheet value of the deferred tax asset.

value-added activities. N. The actions or efforts necessary to operate a business. Value-added activities must change something, like a product or an environment; must not involve a change that could be done at an earlier stage in the process, and, must prepare for other actions.

value-added costs. N. Costs that, if removed, would reduce the usefulness of a product to a customer. Value-added costs are associated with activities that are vital to the success of a product. They include the cost of business activities that are legally required or add value by changing something, like a product or an environment; that do not involve a change that could be done at an earlier stage in the process; and, that prepare for other business actions.

value-added network. N. An intermediary used in computer-to-computer communication, or electronic data interchange, that allows the participants to avoid directly linking the two systems. Instead, both participants connect to the service using a common format to accomplish the electronic data interchange. ABBRV. *VAN*.

value-added standard. N. A condition or level of performance that, ideally, includes no waste in the form of nonvalue-added activities. Value-added standards usually focus on activities or processes, not the performance of individuals. The difference between the actual costs of the activity and the value-added standard is the amount of waste.

value-added tax. N. A consumption tax similar to sales tax. The value-added tax, however, is paid by producers on the difference between the selling price and the cost of materials. ABBRV. *VAT*.

value chain. N. A set of activities for designing, producing, and selling a product or service. Each step or activity in the process adds usefulness or value to the product or service.

value engineering. N. An analysis of value-chain activities to determine improvements in design, materials, or production.

VAN. ABBRV. Value-added network.

variable annuity. N. A type of life insurance that pays the insured an annuity based on the performance of securities in a portfolio established by the insurance company.

variable budget. N. See *flexible budget*.

variable cost. N. A classification of cost defined as one in which the total cost is dependent on some activity, such as miles driven or hours worked, but the cost per unit is constant. In a cabinet-making business, the cost of hardware is a variable cost. The total cost increases as the number of cabinets produced increases.

variable-costing system. N. A system of assigning costs to products that includes only variable costs. The variable-costing system is useful for internal decision making, but is not allowed for tax or financial reporting purposes. One alternative to variable costing is absorption costing. See also *absorption costing*. Synonymous with *direct costing*.

variable-cost ratio. N. An analysis statistic calculated by dividing sales revenue by the total variable cost. The variable-cost ratio represents the part of every dollar of sales that covers the variable cost.

variable interest. N. A type of investment in or relationship with a variable-interest entity. Variable interests change as the value of the variable-interest entity's net assets changes. For example, if Company A guarantees Variable-Interest Entity B's debt, the value, or obligation associated with that guarantee, changes depending on the amount of net assets held by Variable-Interest Entity B. The obligation increases as net assets decline because it becomes more likely that Company A will have to cover the debt. See also *variable-interest entity*.

variable-interest entity. N. An entity that is a candidate for consolidation because, although it is legally a separate entity, another entity controls it. The control is not based on the voting rights associated with stock ownership, but is instead determined by what entity absorbs the majority of the expected losses or expected residual returns. Variable-interest entities are a new term for special purpose entities. See also *special-purpose entity*. ABBRV. *VIE*.

variable-overhead efficiency variance. N. The difference between the actual units of the driver used in production and the standard units multiplied by the standard variable-overhead rate.

Traditionally, direct labor hours or machine hours are used as the driver.

variable-overhead spending variance. N. The difference between the actual variable-overhead rate and the standard variable-overhead rate, multiplied by the actual units of the driver used in production. The actual variable-overhead rate is the total variable-overhead cost divided by the actual units of the driver. Traditionally, direct labor hours or machine hours are used as the driver.

variable rate loan/mortgage. N. See *adjustable rate loan/mortgage.*

varying interest rule. N. Relates to allocations made by partnerships to partners on Schedule K-1. A new partner is allocated separately stated items, income, gains, deductions, losses, and credits, only for the time after admission to the partnership.

VAT. ABBRV. Value-added tax.

vendor fraud. N. A type of fraud perpetrated on a company that involves paying inflated prices for the quality or quantity of goods received.

venture capital. N. A source of funding for new, risky businesses. Dollars come from investors, usually in a limited partnership, and the funds are invested in businesses that are too risky to be able to obtain funds from traditional sources.

verifiability. N. An aspect of the primary qualitative characteristic of accounting information—reliability. Accounting information is verifiable if the measurement can be confirmed by an independent measurer using similar methods of measurement. The cost of an asset is verifiable by using the invoice and other documentation of costs for transportation and installation. See also *reliability, conceptual framework.*

vertical analysis. N. A financial analysis tool that uses common-size analysis for one company within one accounting period to evaluate the relationships among the accounts on the financial statement. For example, for a given year, general and administrative expenses as a percentage of sales are compared to other expenses as a percentage of sales to see if that relationship is reasonable.

vertical combinations. N. Business combinations between entities at different points in the marketing chain. A vertical combination can promote efficiency in one function by being more closely linked to another. If a KFC restaurant acquired Tyson Foods, the combination would be a vertical combination because Tyson prepares chicken for consumption, and the restaurant uses prepared chicken for its menu.

vested pension benefits. N. Pension benefits that are guaranteed to an employee even if that employee resigns and leaves the company. Usually employees earn pension benefits based on contributions from both the employee and the company. If the employee leaves after a short time, he or she receives the dollars he or she contributed, but not the amount the company put in. After working at the company for a designated period of time, the employee will also get to keep the employer contribution amount when he or she leaves. At that point in time, the benefits are vested.

VIE. ABBRV. Variable-interest entity.

virtual private network. N. Software or hardware used to connect a computer user working in a remote location with an entity's local area network. Security of the connection can vary from minimal to very secure, depending on the technology used to establish the connection. Telecommuters use virtual private networks to connect to office networks while working outside the office. ABBRV. *VPN*.

VITA. ABBRV. Volunteer income tax assistance.

volatility. N. In option pricing models, this variable represents the uncertainty of the return of the stock.

voluntary health and welfare organization. N. A not-for-profit organization that meets certain criteria. Voluntary health and welfare organizations derive revenue from contributions from entities, people, or organizations that do not expect or receive any benefits in return. The programs of the organization must be in the area of health and welfare. A charity organization that provides housing for special-needs individuals would qualify as a voluntary health and welfare organization if it is supported mainly by contributions.

volunteer income tax assistance. N. A program of the Internal Revenue Service (IRS) to help low- and moderate-income people prepare their tax returns. The volunteers are trained by the IRS and usually provide service in schools and community centers. Information about the closest site is available by calling the IRS. ABBRV. *VITA*.

voucher system. N. A structured, organized method for controlling the cash and checks in a business by using a form called a voucher, which summarizes and verifies the payment amount and quantities received. A voucher is for a single vendor, but may include several invoices. Prior to payment, the supervisor approves the voucher, and then the check is prepared and sent.

vouching of transactions. N. An audit procedure in which the auditor chooses a recorded transaction and works backward through the processing to find the source document. Contrast with tracing of transactions, in which the auditor finds a source document and follows it forward through the processing to the account balance.

VPN. ABBRV. Virtual private network.

W-2. N. A tax form that indicates the amount of wages, salary, etc., paid to an individual by an employer. The employer must issue the form to the recipient and report the amount to the Internal Revenue Service.

W-9. N. A form used to request a taxpayer identification number from a person to whom an entity paid some form of income, often interest or dividends.

WACC. ABBRV. Weighted-average cost of capital.

WAN. ABBRV. Wide area network.

warranty expense. N. An expense on the income statement representing either actual costs or an estimate of the costs of warranty service. Warranty costs are a type of loss contingency and there are two methods of accounting for them. The first method records the expense for the actual costs of the warranty during the year, and is appropriate if the amount cannot be estimated or the liability is uncertain. Warranty expense is increased, and cash, inventory, or payroll is decreased. The second method accrues an estimate of the amount of warranty costs for the current period's sales based on historical patterns. Warranty expense is increased, and a current liability is increased, matching the warranty expense with the sales revenue. In the future, when the company has to service the warranty, the liability is decreased, and cash, inventory, or payroll is decreased for the actual amounts.

wash sale. N. A technique that contrives a loss to offset an existing gain by selling a devalued investment, recording the loss, and then repurchasing the same or similar stock. The loss is disallowed because the sale was only made to manufacture a loss that could be used to offset a taxable gain on another transaction. The timing of the sale and purchase have to be within a sixty-one-day period, centered on the date of sale.

waste. N. A cost-accounting term representing the cost of inefficiencies in the use of materials or labor. Waste is measured in variances from standard costs.

watered stock. N. An investment in which the market value of the corporation is less than the amount of paid in capital.

weak dollar. N. The situation that occurs when one U.S. dollar receives less of another currency at present than it did in the past. A weak dollar benefits travelers to the United States and reduces the cost of exported goods because it takes less foreign currency to buy the same item.

wealth-transfer taxes. N. A category of taxes that include gift taxes and estate taxes. The taxes are paid by the giver of the gift or by the estate of the deceased, rather than by the recipient of the wealth transfer.

Web browser. N. The software package that allows the user to view graphics on the World Wide Web. Examples of Web browsers are Internet Explorer and Netscape Navigator.

WebTrust. N. An attest service performed by certified public accountants (CPAs) that provides comfort to consumers using e-commerce websites. After investigating the business practices, the CPA awards a WebTrust digital certificate that may be displayed on the website.

weighted-average accumulated expenditures. N. Used to calculate avoidable interest for self-constructed assets. Sum the total expenditures for each month and divide by 12. An entity begins a construction project on January 1 by spending $500. It spends $200 on May 1, $300 on October 1, and $200 on December 1. In February, March, and April, total expenditures in each month were $500; in May, June, July, August, and September, the total each month was $700; in October and November, the total each month was $1,000;

and, in December, the total expenditures were $1,200. The sum is $8,700, and dividing by 12 results in $725 for weighted-average accumulated expenditures.

weighted-average cost method. N. An inventory cost-flow method that calculates the cost of goods available for sale and then divides that cost among the units available for sale. The resulting cost per unit is used to calculate both the ending inventory and cost of goods sold. The weighted-average cost method is used in periodic inventory systems. See also *cost of goods available for sale*.

weighted-average cost of capital. N. A calculation that uses the cost of debt and the cost of equity of a firm, weighted by the proportions of each component. Synonymous with *composite cost of capital*. ABBRV. *WACC*.

welfare-to-work credit. N. A type of general business credit that is an alternative to the work-opportunity credit. The employer can take a credit of up to $3,500 the first year and $5,000 the second year, depending on the amount of wages received for each employee who is considered a long-term family assistance recipient. The employer cannot take both the work-opportunity credit and the welfare-to-work credit for the same employee. The welfare-to-work credit is one of several general business credits, and the total of all these credits cannot be more than an amount based on the net income for the year. The amount of excess can be carried back one year and forward twenty years.

what-if analysis. N. See *sensitivity analysis*.

whistleblower. N. An employee who provides information to management about the illegal acts of another employee.

white-collar crime. N. Criminal acts that usually involve financial or economic transactions perpetrated in a nonviolent way.

Examples include insider trading, embezzlement, bribery, and forgery.

white knight. N. A method of defending against a hostile takeover. A company that is the target of an acquisition finds another company to perform the stock purchase. Usually, the white-knight company that saves the target from takeover is in a different business, so that management is left in place.

white squire. N. A way to avoid a hostile takeover. Another entity that is friendly with the target firm buys just enough of the target company's stock to keep the acquiring company from owning the majority of stock.

whole-life costs. N. All the costs associated with a product for both the seller and the buyer. Whole-life costs include life-cycle costs and the costs a consumer has in owning the product.

wholly owned subsidiary. N. A company that has been acquired by another company. Usually a wholly owned subsidiary is located in a different country than the owner (the parent company).

wide area network. N. Consists of several computers, terminals, and printers that are connected together for the purpose of sharing information, using data, using software, or using printers. Wide area networks usually link widely dispersed parts of an organization and cover large geographical areas like regions, countries, or even the world. See also *local area network*. ABBRV. *WAN*.

window dressing. N. Enhancing financial statements with items that are not substantive, but are perceived to improve the quality of financial statements. Examples include channel stuffing or trade loading, in which sellers encourage customers to buy more inventory than they need at the time, making the seller's current period sales look better.

within-firm risk. N. A type of projected risk that looks at the risk of the investment possibility in relation to the firm only, not to the firm's stockholders. Within-firm risk only considers how the activities within the firm will act to diversify the risk of the project. It is represented by the effect of the investment on future-earnings variability. Synonymous with *corporate risk*.

without recourse. N. A way of selling receivables. The business selling the receivables has no further obligation for payment, even if the customers do not pay the receivables. See also *factoring*.

with recourse. N. A way of selling receivables. The business selling the receivables guarantees that the customers will pay the buyer of the receivables. See also *factoring*.

working capital. N. An analysis tool that measures short-term liquidity. The formula for working capital is current assets minus current liabilities. It represents the excess liquid assets available for operations.

working-capital adjustments. N. Part of the operating activities section on the statement of cash flows. Working-capital adjustments are the changes in current assets and current liabilities that convert net income to cash flow from operating activities. Working-capital adjustments are only used in the indirect method of determining cash from operating activities.

work-in-process file. N. The collection of all job-order cost sheets. The work-in-process file contains all the costs of the accounting period organized by job. The file can be either physical or computer-based.

work-in-process inventory. N. A type of inventory found in the current-asset section of the balance sheet for a company that makes items for sale. Companies that use a constant production process have work-in-process at the end of the accounting period.

Work-in-process inventory contains the costs associated with items that have been started but not finished, raw materials, direct labor, and overhead. Synonymous with *work-in-progress inventory*.

work-in-progress inventory. N. See *work-in-process inventory*.

work-opportunity credit. N. A type of general business credit that a business can elect to use if it employs people who meet certain requirements (e.g., veterans, ex-felons, high-risk youth, food-stamp recipients, etc.). The credit is equal to between 25% and 40% of the first $6,000 of wages paid to the employees. The percentage depends on the duration of the employment and the hours worked during the employment period. The employer must reduce wage expense by the amount of the credit. The work-opportunity credit is one of several general business credits, and the total of all these credits cannot be more than an amount based on the net income for the year. The amount of excess can be carried back one year and forward twenty years.

work papers. N. The documentation associated with an audit. Work papers support the audit report and are owned by the audit firm. Work papers are confidential and are usually kept under lock and key.

worksheet. N. A structured, organized method for accomplishing an accounting task.

World Wide Web. N. Part of the Internet that displays graphics. See also *Internet*.

worm virus. N. A computer virus that does not destroy data but takes up more and more computer memory or disk space until processing stops.

write down. N. The process of reducing the book value of an asset. The amount of reduction is an expense or loss on the income statement for the period. Examples include reducing the value of inventory because part of it is obsolete and unsalable. See also *impairment*.

write off. N. The process of removing an asset from the balance sheet. Most assets are written off by transferring the amount to an expense or loss on the income statement. If an individual customer's account receivable is written off, the dollar amount is removed from the balance sheet, but if the allowance method of bad debts is used, the amount is deducted from the allowance for bad debts, which does not decrease income for the period. The cost of the bad debt was previously captured in income when the item was sold, through an estimate of bad-debt expense. See also *allowance for doubtful accounts, direct write-off method.*

XBRL. ABBRV. eXtensible Business Reporting Language.

year-end adjustment. N. See *adjusting entry*.

years-of-service amortization in pension accounting. N. The method of allocating prior-service cost to pension expense. Years-of-service amortization first calculates service cost per employee year by dividing the prior-service cost by the total number of years that the existing employees are expected to work. Then, each year, the number of employees working is multiplied by the cost per year to calculate the amount of amortization of prior-service cost to include in the pension expense.

Yellow Book. N. A slang term for Government Auditing Standards, which are used to audit government programs, activities, and functions. The Yellow Book contains the Government Auditing Standards.

yield curve. N. A graph of interest rates versus the time to maturity of bonds or debt.

yield to call. N. The rate of return earned by an investor who owns a bond that is redeemed prior to maturity.

yield to maturity. N. The rate of return earned by an investor who receives all required interest payments and holds the bond until the principal is paid at maturity. The yield to maturity is usually very close to the market rate of similar investments available at the time the bond is purchased. When the bond's selling price is more or less than par, the yield to maturity is not the same as the stated rate of interest on the bond.

Y shares. N. See *institutional shares*.

Z

zero-based budgeting. N. The budgeting process that starts at zero and does not factor in last year's budget amount. The zero-based budgeting process requires units to justify expenses and recognize changes in spending.

zero coupon bonds. N. See *deep-discount bonds*.

zero defects. N. A situation in which all products meet specifications, either at the specified value or within a range of the specified value.

zero-interest-bearing note. N. See *noninterest-bearing note*.

zeros. N. See *deep-discount bonds*.

Z shares. N. A class of mutual fund shares that are available only to employees of the mutual fund.

ABBREVIATIONS

AAA. American Accounting Association.

AAER. Accounting and Auditing Enforcement Release.

ABC. Activity-based costing.

ABM. Activity-based management.

ABO. Accumulated benefit obligation.

ACE. Adjusted current earnings.

ACFE. Association of Certified Fraud Examiners.

ACL. Audit command language.

ACRS. Accelerated cost-recovery system.

AcSEC. Accounting Standards Executive Committee.

ADRs. American depository receipts.

AFN. Additional funds needed.

AGA. Association of Government Accountants.

AICPA. American Institute of Certified Public Accountants.

AIS. Accounting information systems.

AMEX. American Stock Exchange.

AMT. Alternative minimum tax.

AMTI. Alternative minimum taxable income.

APA. Advance pricing agreement.

APB. Accounting Principles Board.

APR. Annual percentage rate.

APT. Arbitrage pricing theory.

ARB. Accounting Research Bulletins.

ARM. Adjustable rate mortgage.

ARO. Asset retirement obligation.

ASR. Accelerated share repurchase.

ASWA. American Society of Women Accountants.

ATA. American Taxation Association.

BEP. Basic earning power.

BOM. Bill of material.

C2C. Cash to cash.

CA. Chartered accountant.

CAATs. Computer-assisted audit techniques.

CAO. Chief accounting officer.

CAP. Committee on Accounting Procedure.

CAPM. Capital-asset pricing model.

CBOT. Chicago Board of Trade.

CD. Certificate of deposit.

CDE. Community development entities.

CEO. Chief executive officer.

CESA. Coverdell Education Savings Account.

CFE. Certified fraud examiner.

CFO. Chief financial officer.

CFP. Certified financial planner.

CIA. Certified internal auditor.

CIK. Central Index Key.

CISA. Certified information systems auditor.

CITP. Certified information technology professional.

CMA. Certified management accountant.

CMO. Collateralized mortgage obligations.

COBIT. Control Objectives for Information and Related Technology.

COBRA. Consolidated Omnibus Budget Reconciliation Act.

COD. Cash on delivery.

COMEX. Commodity Exchange in New York.

COO. Chief operating officer.

COSO. Committee of Sponsoring Organizations.

CPA. Certified public accountant.

CPI. Consumer price index.

CPU. Central processing unit.

CTI. Consolidated taxable income.

CVP. Cost-volume-profit analysis.

DJIA. Dow Jones Industrial Average.

DOI. Discharge of indebtedness income.

DRD. Deductions in respect of a decedent.

DRIP. Dividend-reinvestment plan.

E&P. Earnings and profits.

EBIT. Earnings before interest and taxes.

EBITDA. N. Earnings before interest, taxes, depreciation, and amortization.

EDGAR. Electronic Data Gathering, Analysis, and Retrieval system.

EDI. Electronic data interchange.

EFT. Electronic funds transfer.

EIC. Earned income credit.

EIN. Employer identification number.

EITF. Emerging Issues Task Force.

EOQ. Economic-order quantity.

EPS. Earnings per share.

ERISA. Employee Retirement Income Security Act of 1974.

ERP. Enterprise-resource-planning software.

ESOP. Employee-stock-ownership plans.

ESPP. Employee stock purchase plan.

ETF. Exchange-traded fund.

EVA. Economic value added.

FAF. Financial Accounting Foundation.

FAFSA. N. Free Application for Federal Student Aid.

FAS. Statement of Financial Accounting Standards.

FASB. Financial Accounting Standards Board.

FBM. Functional-based management.

FCPA. Foreign Corrupt Practices Act.

FDIC. Federal Deposit Insurance Corporation.

FEI. Financial Executives International.

FFO. Funds from operations.

FHLMC. Federal Home Loan Mortgage Corporation.

FICA. Federal Insurance Contribution Act.

FIFO. First in, first out.

FIN. Federal ID Number.

FNMA. Federal National Mortgage Association.

FOB. Free on board.

FSA. Federation of Schools of Accountancy.

GAAP. Generally accepted accounting principles.

GAAS. Generally accepted auditing standards.

GAO. U.S. Government Accountability Office.

GAS. Generalized audit software.

GASB. Governmental Accounting Standards Board.

GDP. Gross domestic product.

GFOA. Government Finance Officers Association.

GNMA. Government National Mortgage Association.

GUI. Graphical user interface.

HECM. Home equity conversion mortgage.

HIPAA. Health Insurance Portability and Accountability Act.

HSA. Health savings account.

IASB. International Accounting Standards Board.

IASC. International Accounting Standards Committee.

ICFR. Internal control over financial reporting.

IDEA. Interactive Data Extraction and Analysis.

IFAC. International Federation of Accountants.

IFRS. International Financial Reporting Standards.

IIA. Institute of Internal Auditors.

IMA. Institute of Management Accountants.

IOSCO. International Organization of Securities Commission.

IP address. Internet protocol address.

IPO. Initial public offering.

IRA. Individual retirement account.

IRD. Income in respect of a decedent.

IRR. Internal-rate-of-return method.

IRS. Internal Revenue Service.

ISACA. Information Systems Audit and Control Association.

ISDN. Integrated services digital network.

ISO. Incentive stock options.

ISP. Internet service provider.

IT. Information technology.

ITF. Integrated test facility.

JIT. Just-in-time inventory system.

LAN. Local area network.

LBO. Leveraged buyout.

LCM. Lower of cost or market.

LEAPS. Long-term equity anticipation securities.

LIBOR. London InterBank Offered Rate.

LIFO. Last in, first out.

LLC. Limited liability company.

LLP. Limited liability partnership.

MACRS. Modified Accelerated Cost Recovery System.

MD&A. Management's discussion and analysis.

MICR. Magnetic-ink character recognition.

MIRR. Modified internal rate of return.

MIS. Management information systems.

MLM. Most likely misstatement.

MNC. Multinational corporation.

MPU. Mean-per-unit sampling.

NAA. National Association of Accountants.

NASBA. National Association of State Boards of Accountancy.

NASDAQ. National Association of Securities Dealers Automated Quotations.

NFP. Not-for-profit organization.

NOL. Net operating loss.

NOPAT. Net operating profit after taxes.

NPV. Net-present-value method.

NSA. National Society of Accountants.

NSF. Nonsufficient funds.

NYSE. New York Stock Exchange.

OASDI. Old-age, survivor, and disability insurance.

OCBOA. Other comprehensive basis of accounting.

OCR. Optical character recognition.

OMB. Office of Management and Budget.

OPEB. Postretirement benefits other than pensions.

OPM. Option pricing model.

OSPR. Other-substantive-procedures risk.

OTC. Over-the-counter market.

P&L. Profit and loss.

PBO. Projected benefit obligation.

PDA. Personal data assistant device.

P/E ratio. Price-earnings ratio.

PERT. Program Evaluation and Review Technique.

PHC. Personal-holding-company tax.

PLC. Public limited company.

POS. Point-of-sale device.

PP&E. Property, plant, and equipment.

PPI. Producer price index.

PPS. Probability-proportional-to-size sampling.

PTP. Publicly traded partnership.

QEE. Qualified education expenses.

Q sub. Qualified Subchapter S Subsidiary.

QTPs. Qualified tuition plans.

RAM. Random access memory.

R&D. Research and development costs.

REITs. Real estate investment trusts.

RICO. Racketeer Influenced and Corrupt Organizations Act.

ROA. Return on assets.

ROCE. Return on common equity.

ROE. Return on equity.

ROI. Return of investment.

ROIC. Return on invested capital.

RPs. Repos.

RRR. Required rate of return.

SAB. Staff Accounting Bulletins.

SAC Report. Systems Auditability and Control Report.

S&Ls. Savings and loan associations.

S&P 500. Standard & Poor's 500.

SAR. Summary annual report.

SARs. Stock-appreciation rights.

SCARF. Systems-control audit review file.

SEC. Securities and Exchange Commission.

SEP. Simplified employee pension plan.

SFAC. Statement of Financial Accounting Concepts.

SFAS. Statement of Financial Accounting Standards.

SIMPLE. Savings Incentive Match Plan for Employees.

SML. Security market line.

SOX. Sarbanes-Oxley Act.

SPDR. Standard & Poor's Depository Receipt.

SPE. Special-purpose entity.

TIE. Times-interest-earned ratio.

TIPS. Treasury Inflation-Protected Security.

TOC. Theory of constraints.

TPS. Trust preferred securities.

TQM. Total-quality management.

TVM. Time value of money.

UAA. Uniform Accountancy Act.

UDITPA. Uniform Division of Income for Tax Purposes Act.

UML. Upper misstatement limit.

UNICAP. Uniform Capitalization Rules.

URL. Universal resource locator.

VAN. Value-added network.

VAT. Value-added tax.

VIE. Variable-interest entity.

VITA. Volunteer income tax assistance.

VPN. Virtual private network.

WACC. Weighted-average cost of capital.

WAN. Wide area network.

XBRL. eXtensible Business Reporting Language.

WEBSITES

Academy of Accounting Historians
http://accounting.rutgers.edu/raw/aah

Accountants for the Public Interest
www.geocities.com/api_woods/api/apihome.html

Accounting & Tax Database
http://library.dialog.com/bluesheets/html/bl0485.html#top

Accounting Hall of Fame
http://fisher.osu.edu/departments/accounting-and-mis/
the-accounting-hall-of-fame

American Accounting Association
http://aaahq.org

American Institute of Certified Public Accountants
www.aicpa.org

American Society of Women Accountants
www.aswa.org

American Taxation Association
www.atasection.org/ata/index.htm

Association of Certified Fraud Examiners
www.acfe.com

Association of Government Accountants
www.agacgfm.org

Bank for International Settlements
www.bis.org

Beta Alpha Psi
www.bap.org

CPA Journal
www.cpajournal.com

Federation of Schools of Accountancy
www.thefsa.org

Financial Accounting Standards Board
www.fasb.org

Institute of Internal Auditors
www.theiia.org

Institute of Management Accountants
www.imanet.org

Internal Revenue Service
www.irs.gov

International Accounting Standards Board
www.iasb.org/Home.htm

International Federation of Accountants
www.ifac.org

International Organization of Securities Commission
www.iosco.org

Investment Company Institute
www.ici.org

National Association of State Boards of Accountancy
www.nasba.org

National Society of Accountants
www.nsacct.org

ABOUT THE AUTHOR

Kate Mooney is a certified public accountant (inactive) and is the former chair of the Department of Accounting at St. Cloud State University in Minnesota. She teaches financial accounting and was named a 2002 G.R. Herberger Distinguished Professor of Business. She is a member of the Minnesota Society of Certified Public Accountants, and has served on its Board of Directors. She is also a member of the American Institute of Certified Public Accountants and the American Accounting Association.